DICTIONARY

of

GYPSY LIFE AND LORE

DICTIONARY
of
GYPSY LIFE AND LORE

H. E. WEDECK

with the assistance of
WADE BASKIN

C. 1

PHILOSOPHICAL LIBRARY
New York

Copyright, © 1973, by Philosophical Library, Inc.,

15 East 40th Street, New York, N. Y. 10016

Library of Congress Catalog Card No. 72-75317

SBN 8022-2094-0

Printed in the United States of America

INTRODUCTION

The Gypsies have always been regarded as the ultimate nomads, mysterious travelers across the continents, across the centuries. The very term gypsy denotes, in a generic sense, a restless, unsettled, foot-loose person.

They are a strange people, these Gypsies, speaking a hieratic language that, by the force of countless migrations, assimilated the indigenous tongue of each new transient settlement. Hence every language is theirs, in all the countries that have known them; and yet they have retained older idioms, ancient terms and forms that testify to their antique origins.

Without a permanent land, lacking an assured domicile, in the Latin sense, they have rejected city life and have more or less remained dwellers in the open spaces. Some five or six million of them, it is estimated, belong in this category, extended over the continents. They are the last migrants, driven from heath to field to river bank to forest, to valleys and mountain sides, rarely tolerated, repeatedly accused or convicted of sinister activities, of kidnapping and sorcery, of horse-coping and fortune-telling, of thievery, violence, cannibalism.

In the popular mind they are vagrants and poachers horse-traders and craftsmen, dancers, peddlers, fiddlers, tinsmiths and encampments, whirling to the rhythm of the saraband, extracting wild melody from the violin, yet invariably seclusive in their own unassimilating way of life.

Citizens of the world, in a literal sense, a people of tribal clans, they have no well-defined territorial home, no national attachments.

Here, then, is their diversified story, shot through with lamentation and merriment, with catastrophes and resilience.

It is the epic of their wanderings, their beliefs, their characterial peculiarities, their mythological creations, their ceremonials and their loyalties. It is a tale compounded of history spiced with picturesque legend, with colorful sagas and episodes. It is a survey, in short, of the last anomaly in a progressively conventionalized world. Special acknowledgement is made for material from the collection of *The Journal of the Gypsy Lore Society*.

Special thanks are due to Harper & Row, Publishers, Inc., for permission to reproduce some illustrations from *Gypsy Fires in America* by Irving Brown; to J. M. Dent & Sons Ltd. for use of illustrations from *My Gypsy Days* by Dora Yates; and to the New York Public Library for their cooperation in this connection.

H. E. W.

A

ABRAHAM   There is a Gypsy legend that when Abraham
left Ur and traveled into Canaan, the Sintés or Gypsies
accompanied him.
There are many similar legends relating to the origin
and the migrations of the Gypsies from Asia to Europe.

ACADEMIC COURSE   At the Centre Universitaire des Lan-
gues Orientales Vivantes in Paris, a course is given
on the Gypsy language.
There is also a correspondence course for which applica-
tion may be made to Donald Kenwick, Esq. M. A., 61
Blenheim Crescent, London, W. 11.
In adition, there are numerous studies of the various
Gypsy dialects. An important survey of the Welsh Gypsy
dialect was produced by John Sampson. In 1868 J. A.
Vaillant published a Gypsy grammar.

ACCENT   The Hungarian Gypsies have a peculiar accent
when speaking the language of Hungary. Similarly the
Gitános of Spain, when speaking Spanish, are readily
identifiable as Gypsies.

ACCUSED   A poor Gypsy had her donkey taken from her.
A man, with four witnesses, swore that it was his
property. The woman told her tale, and was allowed
two days to bring forward the person who had sold her
the animal. Conscious of her innocence, she was willing

1

to risk prison, if she could not recover the donkey and establish her character. After a great deal of trouble and expense in despatching messengers to bring forward her witnesses, she succeeded in obtaining them. They had no sooner made their appearance than the accuser and his witnesses fled, and left the donkey to the rightful owner, the accused and injured Gypsy.

ADDER'S SLOUGH   A Gypsy superstition credits an adder's slough with bringing good luck. A piece of mountain ash is believed to have the same virtue.

Gypsy folklore, in fact, abounds in superstitions, many of which have been incorporated into actual Gypsy life.

ADHERENCE TO RACE   Gypsy women make their children know their own people. A mother tells her family of the prejudices directed against the Gypsies as such. She relates to them the story of Joseph and Pharaoh in Egypt, and stresses that her people are 'Pharaoh's folk'. She teaches them Romany, but warns them about speaking it in public, among the *busne,* the non-Gypsies. She recounts their lives in tents and caravans, their forced migrations, the banishments suffered by Gypsies, the persecutions and antagonisms: and also she teaches them the way of living among Gypsies.

ADJAMA, TIKNO   This Gypsy philosopher of the Bergsonian school, was also a poet and taught at the University of Louvain in Belgium.

In recent times many Gypsies have risen to professional status, as physicians, lawyers, journalists.

ADMISSION INTO TRIBE   The admission of a non-Gypsy, a *busno* or *gorgio,* into a Gypsy tribe required the entrant to be stained with walnut-juice.

As a rule, however, there is always hesitation and sometimes difficulty in admitting a Gentile, a non-Gypsy into the close-knit, exclusive tribe or clan.

ADORNMENTS Gypsy women and even young Gypsy girls regularly wear ear-rings, very often massive and intricately designed.

Usually, too, the Gypsy women wear strings of beads. These beads are generally black or red — the 'lucky' colors.

Girls and the younger women often have flowers in the hair or small sprays of foliage, like the natives of the South Seas, particularly Tahiti.

AFFECTION Among Gypsies there are strong feelings of family affection. Children in particular are overindulged through an excess of such affection. In the first century B.C. the Roman poets Propertius and Catullus showed the deeply moving humanity and love of Roman parents for their children.

AFFINITIES WITH INDIA The marriage customs of the Gypsies are similar to those of many Hindu castes. A Hungarian Gypsy Society has collected some 1500 folksongs that are closely related in treatment to Indian themes.

AFFINITY WITH RUMANIA The Gypsies who settled in Rumania have linguistic affinities with that country, as is illustrated by the following comparative vocabulary:

English	Gypsy	Rumanian
spring	primivari	primavera
heaven	cherul	cheros
stocking	chorapul	chorab
boots	chisme	chismey

AFRICA There are records extant that indicate the existence of Gypsies in the Sudan, in Mauritania, and in Abyssinia. Throughout their historic wanderings they have appeared in Persia and Turkey, in Greece and the Balkans, in the Scandinavian countries, in Spain and Portugal and the British Isles.

AFRICAN GYPSIES According to one of the earliest gypsiologists, Heinrich Grellman, who belongs in the eighteenth century, Gypsies were to be found in Central Africa. Mollien, a French traveler who reached the sources of the Senegal and Gambia in 1818, said that he found a people, not unlike the Gypsies, and known by the native name of Laaubés. They led a roving life. Their only employment was the manufacture of wooden vessels.

They selected a well-wooded spot, felled some trees, and made huts with the branches. Each family had its chief, and a superior chief headed the whole tribe. They were idolaters and claimed that they could tell fortunes.

AFTERLIFE When a Gypsy dies and all his belongings are burned along with the corpse, the survivor is free from all contact with the dead. There is no urge to 'join' the dead: no impulse, through emotional stress, toward suicide. No regular service is held to commemorate the dead. The survivor belongs to the present. The past is gone. But not entirely: for the *mulos,* the spirits of the dead, are wont to appear and harass the living.

AGRICULTURE In no country are Gypsies found engaged in agricultural pursuits, or in the service of a regular master.

The Empress Maria Theresa attempted to settle them

into sedentary life, without success. So too in Spain they never attached themselves to the soil.

AGRIPPA'S VIEW According to Agrippa, a famous sixteenth century occultist, the Gypsies or Egyptians came from a region lying between Egypt and Ethiopia.
They were, he contended, the descendants of Cush, the son of Ham, Noah's son.

AID FOR BORDER GYPSIES In the nineteenth century on the Scottish borders, there was a very large settlement of Gypsies:

The Gypsies are at present known as a wild and semi-barbarous race, who are feared and dreaded by others, as setting all law, character, religion, and morality at defiance. The original source of all the vicious habits of this tribe lies in their loose, irregular, and wandering mode of life.

There is nothing obviously in the native character, blood, or constitution of the Gypsy to render him more desperate and vicious than others. They are neither better nor worse than other members of society would be if they were placed in similar circumstances. Their wandering for instance exposes them to many peculiar temptations; idleness and rapine lead them frequently into scenes of mischief and wickedness, and necessarily leave them ignorant, uneducated, and uncivilized. Withdraw them therefore from this mode of life, and at as early an age as possible, before they have acquired the bad habits of the tribe, and you save them from innumerable evils, and probably render them valuable members of society. There are cases where Gypsies, separated from their tribe, acquired domestic habits. Let society, therefore, do its duty to these houseless wanderers and regard them

5

not as outcasts, but stretching forth to them the hand of reconciliation let a civilized society grant the Gypsies the privileges of education and the means of improvement.

AIX-LA-CHAPELLE A decree of repression was promulgated in 1728 at Aix-la-chapelle against the Gypsies. At this period, as on many other occasions throughout the centuries, the hostility against the Gypsies was violent and persistent.

ALBAICIN In Granada, the Gypsies live in a kind of series of caves in the district called Albaicin.
In other countries too the Gypsies have at times been compelled to live as troglodytes.

ALL SORTS OF GYPSIES Charles Leland the gypsiologist. while in Russia, was himself surprised at the types of Gypsies that he encountered in Moscow:
There are Gypsies and Gypsies in the world, for there are the wanderers on the roads and the secret dwellers in towns; but even among the *aficionados,* or Romany ryes, by whom I mean those scholars who are fond of studying life and language from the people themselves. very few have dreamed that there exist communities of gentlemanly and lady-like Gypsies of art, like the Bohemians of Murger and George Sand, but differing from them in being real 'Bohemians' by race. I confess that it had never occurred to me that there was anywhere in Europe, at the present day, least of all in the heart of great and wealthy cities, a class or caste devoted entirely to art, well-to-do or even rich, refined in manners, living in comfortable homes, the women dressing elegantly; and yet with all this obliged to live by law, as did the Jews once, in Ghettos or in a certain street, and

regarded as outcasts and *cagots*. I had heard there were Gypsies in Russian cities, and expected to find them like the *kérengni* of England or Germany, — house-dwellers somewhat reformed from vagabondage, but still reckless semi-outlaws, full of tricks and lies; in a word, *Gypsies,* as the world understands the term. And I certainly anticipated in Russia something *queer,* — the gentleman who speaks Romany seldom fails to achieve at least that, whenever he gets into an unbroken haunt, or unhunted forest, where the Romany rye is unknown, — but nothing like what I really found.

ALMS During the Middle Ages, as the Gypsies advanced from the Greek mainland and islands through Central Europe, they were sustained by public and private charity. For ostensibly they were Christian pilgrims, doing seven years' penance for once having rejected Christianity.

ALPHABET Although the Gypsies are predominantly illiterate, it is said that they have a special alphabet of their own, in the form of hieroglyphics or at least conventional symbols and signs that are communicative.

This system is known as *patrin,* or *patteran.* All such hieroglyphics, many of geometrical form, serve to guide successions of migrant Gypsies as they pass along the highways. They furnish information regarding the hostility or friendliness of the native inhabitants, the prospects of securing work or food and other relevant items of interest to all Gypsies.

ALSACE-LORRAINE In the forests of Alsace-Lorraine in the eighteenth century there were large bands of Gypsies who had settled there. Their means of sustenance consisted of constant begging campaigns in the neighboring villages. They claimed alms for their large families and often terrorized the natives into forced acquiescence.

7

AMELIORATION OF GYPSY CONDITIONS Maria Theresa of Austria, interested in bettering the condition of the Gypsies in her realms, issued decrees for their welfare and conduct. They were to be taught the principles of religion. They were to conform, in diet, dress, and language, to the customs of the country.
They were to be required to engage in agricultural occupations.

AMELIORATION OF SPANISH GYPSIES Since the law has ceased to brand them, they have come nearer to the common standard of humanity, and their general condition has been ameliorated. At present, only the very poorest, the pariahs of the race, are to be found wandering about the heaths and mountains, and this only in the summer time, and their principal motive, according to their own confession, is to avoid the expense of house rent. The rest remain at home, following their avocations, unless some immediate prospect of gain, lawful or unlawful, calls them forth; and such is frequently the case. They attend most fairs, women and men, and on the way frequently bivouac in the fields, but this practice must not be confounded with systematic wandering. — *George Borrow*

AMERICAN GYPSIES The American Gypsies do not beg, like their English brothers, and particularly their English sisters. This fact speaks volumes for their greater prosperity and for the influence which association with a proud race has on the poorest people.

A MERRY LIFE After the days of the great persecution in England against the Gypsies, there can be little doubt that they lived a right merry and tranquil life, wandering about and pitching their tents wherever inclination led them. Indeed, any more enviable condition than Gypsy life can hardly be conceived, in England during the latter part of the seventeenth and the whole of the eighteenth century, which were likewise the happy days for Englishmen in general. There was peace and plenty in the land, a contented population, and everything went well. The poor Gypsies were then allowed to sleep abroad, where they wanted: to heat their kettles at the foot of the oaks, and no people grudged cne night's use of a meadow to feed their cattle in.

AMOROUS FORTUNE-TELLING An English young lady who was in love with a certain young man appealed to a Gypsy for help. The latter promised to arouse the young man's feelings for the lady. The latter, as evidence of her confidence, gave the Gypsy the plate that was in the house, together with a gold chain and locket, which the Gypsy promised to return at a given date. The Gypsy went off. She was, however, found, washing her clothes in a Gypsy camp, with the gold round her neck. On returning the articles, she was allowed to escape.

AMULETS As Gypsies were credited with more than ordinary human perception and skill, they were accustomed to sell amulets, charms, periapts of all kinds, apotropaic articles and unguents and potions that were reputed to be effective in warding off misfortune or healing sickness or achieving love, wealth, and happiness.

ANALOGY WITH OTHER RACES Among all the different peoples who have left their mother country and settled in foreign territory, there appears to be no single analogous instance that agrees exactly with that of the Gypsies. Historical records certainly indicate that there have been migrations of people into new lands, where such people remained the same in a strange country.
But then this constancy has been the result of religion, either permitted by the ruler, or maintained by victorious

9

arms on the part of the migrants. Many instances have occurred in which, the people subdued being more enlightened than their conquerors, the latter adopted the customs of the former. On the conquest of Greece the Romans became Greeks. The Franks assumed the mores of the Gauls when they were in possession of Gaul. The Manchus vanquished the Chinese. But Chinese customs prevailed over those of the Manchus. How then did it happen that the Gypsies, who never either established their ways and manners by force, or obtained any tolerance from the governments under which they lived, except for a few and temporary concessions, remained unchanged and virtually resembled each other in every place. in every territory?

ANATORI A Gypsy term applied to Gypsy workers in tin. Among the Gypsies every trade or occupation has a special designation of its own. For instance, the beartrainers who wander around the Balkans are called *oursari*.

ANDALUSIA The Gypsies have in the course of their varied wanderings settled in strange quarters. Among such settlements are the caves in Spain, particularly in Guadix, in Andalusia. Other troglodyte havens are at Benalúa, Puerto Lumbreras, Chinarral, La Chana, and the caves of Almanzora, the Cuevas del Almanzora.

ANCIENT GYPSY CULT The annual Gypsy pilgrimage to Les Saintes Maries de la Mer, in the Camargue, in Provence, held on May 24, is a dedication to the Black Patron of the Gypsies, Sara the Egyptian, the servant of the two Marys. Some gypsiologists, however, regard this ceremonial as a survival, in the traditions and race history of the Gypsies, of an ancient pagan cult.

ANCIENT GYPSY SONGS   In Russia, George Borrow listened to Gypsy songs:

> They commenced singing, and favored me with many songs, both in Russian and Romany. The former were modern popular pieces, such as are accustomed to be sung on the boards of the theatre. But the latter were evidently of great antiquity, exhibiting the strongest marks of originality, the metaphors bold and sublime, and the metre differing from anything of the kind which it has been my fortune to observe in Oriental or European prosody.

ANIMAL MEAT   Although the Gypsies refrained from consuming horse-meat, they were known to eat cats and dogs.

ANIMALS   The Gypsies understand animals and their ailments. Particularly in the case of horses, mules, donkeys, trained bears.

ANIMAL TRAINERS   The Gypsies have long been known for their talent in training animals to perform in villages, in public squares, at fairs and festivals. Principally they were bear-trainers, and belonged to the *oursari,* the occupational designation. Dogs and monkeys were also trained. Molière the French playwright alludes to trained monkeys who could dance.

ANTIPODES   By the second half of the twentieth century the settlements of the Gypsies were virtually world-wide. They appeared in Australia and in Mexico.

APHRODISIAC CAKE   Among Transylvanian Gypsies a magic performance occurs on St. George's Day. Girls bake a cake compounded of certain herbs. The cake is reputed to have the property of reconciling enemies and increasing amorous feelings. It is used regularly as a love

11

charm offered by women to men. Allusion to this practice appears in a Gypsy song:

Kásáve romni ná jidel,
Ke kásávo maro the del;
Sar m're gule lele pekel
Káná Sváto Gordye ável.
Furmuntel bute luludya
Furmuntel yoy bute charna
Andre petrel but kámábe
Ko chal robo avla bake.

No one bakes such cakes as my wife — such bread as she baked for me on St. George's Day. Many flowers and dew were kneaded into the cake with love. Whoever eats of it will be her slave.

APOTHEGM   Gypsy gnomic wisdom is contained in the following stanza:
If foky kek jins bute,
Mà sal at lende;
For sore mush jins chomany
That tute kek jins.
Whatever ignorance men may show,
From none disdainful turn;
For everyone doth something know
Which you have yet to learn.

APPEAL   The nomadic, apparently care-free and unrestrained life of the Gypsies, their unconcern from dwellings and permanent settlements, their disdain for permanent employment in rigidly confined surroundings, has caught the imagination of many men, particularly poets and writers. Among those who have been attracted by the Gypsy way of life and have written of them with sympathy and perception are Cervantes, who of course observed them *in situ* in Spain, Emerson, Victor Hugo, and the American Poet Vachel Lindsay.

ARAB CHRONICLE In an Arabic life of Tamerlane, there is a description of Gypsy life in the East during the fourteenth century. The passage runs as follows:

There were in Samarkand numerous families of Zingari of various descriptions: some were wrestlers, others gladiators, others pugilists. These people were much at variance, so that hostilities and battling were continually arising amongst them. Each band had its chief and subordinate officers: and it came to pass that Timour (that is, Tamerlane) and the power which he possessed filled them with dread, for they knew that he was aware of their crimes and disorderly way of life. Now it was the custom of Timour, on departing upon his expeditions, to leave a viceroy in Samarkand; but no sooner had he left the city, than forth marched these bands, and giving battle to the viceroy, deposed him and took possession of the government, so that on the return of Timour he found order broken, confusion reigning, and his throne overturned, and then he had much to do in restoring things to their former state, and in punishing or pardoning the guilty; but no sooner did he depart again to his wars and to his various other concerns, than they broke out into the same excesses, and this they repeated no less than three times, and he at length laid a plan for their utter extermination, and it was the following: He commenced building a wall, and he summoned the people small and great, and he allotted to everyone his place, and to every workman his duty, and he stationed the Zingari and their chiefs apart; and in one particular spot he placed a band of soldiers, and he commanded them to kill whomever he should send to them; and having done so he called to him the heads of the people, and he filled the cup for them and clothed them in splendid vests; and when the turn came to the Zingari, he likewise pledged one of them, and bestowed a vest upon him, and sent him with a message to the soldiers, who, as soon as he arrived, tore from him his vest and stabbed him, pouring forth the gold of his heart into the pan of destruction, and in this way they continued until the last of them was destroyed. And by that blow he exterminated their race, and their traces, and from that time forward there were no more rebellions in Samarkand.

ARABIA   In his *Travels in Arabia Deserta* Charles Doughty, the nineteenth century English traveler, mentions the existence of Gypsies in Arabia.

ARABIC DICTIONARY   In a well-known Arabic dictionary, under Zott, the comment is: Zott arabicized from Jatt, a people of Indian origin.
Zott is the name by which the Gypsies are known to the Arabs.

ARABS   In Arab records there are traditions that a nomadic tribe dwelling in India was long centuries ago taken captive and brought Westward as far as Baghdad. In later times these people passed under Byzantine control. First defeated by the Arabs and then by the Byzantines, these people are assumed to be the original Gypsies.

ARBOREAL REMEDY   To banish fever, Gypsies go to the forest and shake a young tree. The fever is thus assumed to pass from the victim's body into the tree. This procedure is another form of sympathetic magic.

ARCHDUKE JOSEPH   The Archduke Joseph of Hungary, who belongs in the nineteenth century, could speak

14

Romany and in addition he wrote an important book about the Gypsies and their ways.

He had studied Oriental languages, particularly Hindi, and realized the affinity between Romany and Sanskrit. In introducing his grammar, he wrote:

> At last I succeeded in speaking their language quite fluently. With the aid of the more cultured Gypsies I compiled a vocabulary which shows different dialectal expressions. I have finally written this outline of grammar, also taking into consideration the different rules of the special dialects of Gypsies and their Indian origin. I was considerably helped in this work by the circumstance that I served in Infantry Regiment 60 from 1853-1856, which recruited its personnel from among the Gypsies.

ARGOT Gypsies have a special argot, reserved usually for communication within a Gypsy milieu, among their own people. In the presence of *Gorgios,* non-Gypsies, they prefer not to speak the usual language, Romany.

ARLES In Arles, Provence, there is extant a manuscript entitled *La Légende des Saintes Maries Jacobé et Salomé.* In this sixteenth century manuscript there is reference to Sara, the servant of the two Marys and the patron saint of the Gypsies.

ARMED GYPSIES During the Middle Ages and far into the seventeenth and eighteenth centuries Gypsies, men and even women, carried arms: carbines or daggers, swords, muskets, arquebuses, sabres, javelins, pistols. Records describe such armed bands of nomadic Gypsies in Germany, France, and far North in Finland.

ARMENIAN GYPSIES The Armenian Gypsies, known as Bosha, that is, vagabonds or nomads, speak a language

15

of limited vocabulary but demonstrably connected with the Hindu member of the Aryan family of languages.

ARMS IN FINLAND   At the end of the eighteenth century the Gypsies in Finland had the appearance of pirates. They wore a cutlass in their belt, and a whip studded with iron rings and fortified with an iron buckle.

ARNIM, ACHIM VON   German writer whose novel *Isabella of Egypt* is a romanticized version of the love of an Archduke for an alleged Gypsy girl who turns out to be, on her mother's side, a member of the Dutch nobility.

ARNOLD, MATTHEW (1822-1888) English poet, essayist, and critic. Once he met a Gypsy child by the seashore in the Isle of Man, and asked her:

> Who taught thee pleading to unpracticed eyes?
> Who hid such import in an infant's gloom?
> Who lent thee, child, this meditative gaze?
> Who massed, round that slightbrow, the clouds of doom?

ARRIVAL IN SCOTLAND   Gypsies appeared for the first time in Scotland in 1505. A record is extant declaring that the Lord High Treasurer for Scotland expended seven pounds in behalf of the Gypsies.

ARRIVAL IN SPAIN   When the Gypsies first appeared in Spain early in the fifteenth century, they were divided into numerous bodies, frequently formidable in point of number, while their presence was an evil and a curse in whatever quarter they directed their steps.

ARSON   Often the Gypsies were accused of burning public property. Rejected by some village when they asked for provisions, they could, in retaliation, set fire to a cottage

or a field. Sometimes the fire was due to the mere
into numerous bodies, frequently formidable in point of
negligence of the Gypsies in not putting out a camp fire
of their own. In the sixteenth century they were suspected
of burning public property in Prague.

ARTFUL PRACTICES   The Gypsy fortune-tellers who pretended to a knowledge of future events generally discovered who were in possession of property, and whether
the owners were superstitious or covetous. The Gypsy
then contrived to persuade them that there was a lucky
stone in their house and that if they would entrust all
or part of their money to the Gypsy they would double
and even treble their money.
The Gypsies often gained their point. Tradesmen were
known to have sold their goods at a considerable loss,
hoping to have their money doubled by this means.
If the fortune-teller failed to obtain a large sum at
first, she began with a small amount. Then, pretending
that the sum was too insignificant for the planets to work
on, she got the double amount. Then she decamped with
her booty. In the English counties, in Gloucestershire,
Dorsetshire, and Hampshire, many clients were thus
victimized.

ARYAN RACE   Gypsiologists have asserted that the Gypsies
are categorically of Aryan stock, descended from the
races in Rajputana, the Punjab, and other areas in India.

ASIATIC BUTCHERY   The first Gypsies, it is thought, fled
from Asia when Timur Beg ravaged India: his object
being to convert India to Islam. At this time some
500,000 men, it is estimated, were butchered by Timur
Beg. After this period, it is assumed that whatever
survivors there were came into Europe through Egypt.

A SPANISH GYPSY SONG   A Gypsy song, which George

17

Borrow the gypsiologist rendered into English. It stresses the difficulty of a gorgio or busnó, that is, a Gentile or non-Gypsy, in winning the hand of a Gypsy girl:

Loud sang the Spanish cavalier,
And thus his ditty ran:
God send the Gypsy maiden here,
But not the Gypsy man.'
But high arose the moon so bright.
The Gypsy 'gan to sing,
'I see a Spaniard coming here,
I must be on the wing.'

ASSIMILATION In Eastern and South-Eastern Europe the Gypsies, although always in a minority, seem to feel more at home in a culture that is close to the soil, like their own. But somehow they never assimilate. They retain their ethnic independence and their ethnic identity.

ATLANTIS An imaginative conjective relative to the origin of the Gypsies was the lost continent of Atlantis. Survivors, if any, reached Africa and settled in Egypt. These were the Gypsies, according to the Italian gypsiologist Predari's who published his findings in 1841. A supporter of Predari's view was a Provençal poet, the Marquis Folco de Baroncelli-Javon.

ATTACK ON GYPSY LIFE Early in the seventeenth century a Spanish professor of theology addressed to the consideration of Philip III an attack on the Gypsies. He inveighed against their lack of religious faith, their morality, their barbarous language, and their incapacity to adjust to society. He recommended that all the Gypsies in Spain be exterminated.

ATTAMAN ZIGANSKIE A Russian term applied to the

captain or leader of a tribe of Gypsies. Another designation for a tribal chief, common in the Balkans, is *voivode.*

ATTITUDE OF CHURCH   The Church, whether Catholic, Protestant, or Lutheran, was generally hostile to the Gypsies. In Spain, they were regarded as at least heretical, but usually as pagans. In Holland, baptism of Gypsy children was deprecated. In Sweden the Church was actively antagonistic. In Finland one pastor regarded them as allies of the Archfiend.

In the ninteenth century a change for the better took place. Evangelical missions were instituted for the proselytism of the Gypsies. Such missions included those of the Rev. Crabbe in the New Forest, in England and of the Rev. Baird in Scotland. George Borrow, too, the Romany Rye par excellence, went to Spain in behalf of the Bible Society. He preached to the Gypsies and translated the Gospel into Romany.

ATTITUDE OF SCOTLAND   The Scottish Gypsies had a measure of freedom and tolerance in the sixteenth century in Scotland. They were officially permitted to have control over their own domestic and tribal affairs, and they also had the privilege of trial. With the Scottish monarchs, also they were *personae gratae.* But in the later decades of the century harsh measures were instituted against them. They were accused of being witches, thieves, murderers. In 1573 an Act was passed 'for the staunching of masterful idle beggars, away putting of sorcerers.' Punishment was decreed for Gypsies who read the palm of the hand and told fortunes. They were furthermore enjoined to engage in sedentary occupations and to settle down in specific locations.

But the roving spirit of the Gypsies could not be suppressed.

ATTITUDE TOWARD GYPSIES In contemporary society, the Gypsies in Spain and in Britain live on friendly terms with their neighbors. In Germany the Gypsies suffered deportation, persecution and death at the hands of the Nazis. In Belgium they are generally *personae minime gratae.*

ATZINGANOI A Greek name given to a people who settled among the Greeks. The term Atzinganoi has been equated with the Gypsies.

AUBIGNE, THEODORE D' (1552-1630) French poet, satirist, historian. Author of *Les Aventures du Baron de Faeneste* which presents Gypsy ways in a French setting.

AUSTRIAN GYPSIES Many tabus surround the personal and tribal conduct of the Gypsies, male and female, in the tent and on the road. With regard to food, Austrian Gypsies regard the flesh of cats or dogs as tabu.

AUSTRIAN GYPSY SONG The Austrian Gypsies have many songs which perfectly reflect their character, as the following verses show:

The wind whistles over the heath,
The moonlight fits over the flood;
And the Gypsy lights up his fire,
In the darkness of the wood.
Hurrah!
In the darkness of the wood.
Free is the bird in the air,
And the fish where the river flows;
Free is the deer in the forest,
And the Gypsy wherever he goes.
Hurrah!
And the Gypsy wherever he goes.
(A gorgio rye speaks)

Girl, wilt thou live in my home?
I will give thee a sable gown,
And golden coins for a necklace,
If thou wilt be my own.
(Gypsy girl)
No wild horse will leave the prairie
For a harness with silver stars;
Nor an eagle the crags of the mountain,
For a cage with golden bars;
Nor the Gypsy girl the forest,
Or the meadow, though gray and cold,
For garments made of sable,
Or necklaces of gold.
(The gorgio)
Girl, wilt thou live in my dwelling,
For pearls and diamonds true?
I will give thee a bed of scarlet,
And a royal palace, too.
(Gypsy girl)
My white teeth are my pearlins,
My diamonds my own black eyes;
My bed is the soft green meadow,
My palace the world as it lies.

AUSTRIAN TREATMENT In the eighteenth century the Gypsies in Austria experienced harsh treatment at the hands of the government. They were declared outlaws by the Emperor Leopold. Under Charles VI all male Gypsies were to be put to death. In the case of women and all who were under eighteen years of age, an ear was cut off.

AUTHENTIC ORIGIN OF THE ROMANY The authentic origin of the Romany is lost in ancient Aryan record, and, strictly speaking, his is a prehistoric caste. This was the view of Charles Lee and other gypsiologists.

21

It has now been definitively established that the original home of the Gypsies was Northern India.

AUTHORITY OF CHIEF On occasion, a Gypsy tribal chief or leader might experience resentment or even revolt on the part of his ostensible adherents. Such an instance occurred in Scotland, in the sixteenth century. John Faa or Faw, Count of Little Egypt, appealed to King James V of Scotland for aid in administering justice to the malcontents of the tribe.

AUTO-DE-FE An auto-de-fé was held in 1610 at Logroño in Spain. A group of some fifty Gypsies were put on trial by the Inquisition. They were charged with practicing the occult arts in the cave of Zugarramurdi. They were accused of being sorcerers, vampires, who performed Satanic rites and celebrated the obscene Sabbat in conjunction with their diabolic Master, the Archfiend himself.

AVENTINUS, JOHANNES (1477-1534) Aventinus was a Bavarian historian. He wrote an account of his country entitled *Annales Boiorum,* published in 1554. The work contains references to the Gypsies, in far from complimentary terms with regard to their way of living, their manners, their morality.

AVERSION TO DISSECTION A gypsiologist relates that when a Gypsy died, of consumption, a physician applied to his tribe for the corpse, for the purpose of dissection. But the Gypsies indignantly drove him off with threats.

AVERTING SPELLS To the Gypsies the fields and forests, the streams and hedges are peopled by invisible spirits and demons that must constantly be appeased by spells, charms, incantations. To avert various malefic spells, for instance, inflicted on humans by such spirits, the Gypsies composed salves and potions of which the ingredients were the fat of bears and dogs, together with the oil of rain-worms, spiders, midges — all rubbed into a paste.

B

BABA TSHURKESHTI This Gypsy clan, moving from Central Europe to escape the Nazi onslaught, founded a settlement in the Netherlands.

BABILACH This Gypsy term denotes a tribal chief.
A tribal leader was also known as a Duke, Count, or King. In the Balkans he was called the *voivode,* the leader.

BADAJOZ In Badajoz, the capital of Estremadura, in Spain, George Borrow, the nineteenth century gypsiologist, first encountered the Zincali or Gitános, the Spanish Gypsies.

BAGPIPES Among their musical instruments such as the lute, the xylophone, and the violin, the Gypsies are also skilled in playing on their own type of bagpipes.

BAILES In Spain, late in the sixteenth century and also in the seventeenth, there was violent ecclesiastical opposition to the *bailes,* the dances performed by Gypsy women. They were regarded as lascivious and depraved and tending to corrupt public morals.

BAIRD, REV. JOHN A Scotsman who founded a society in 1838. The object was to reform the Gypsies by giving the children educational opportunities and by settling the adults in permanent homes.

24

BALKAN GYPSIES   In the Balkans, during the Middle Ages and later still, Gypsies were comparatively tolerated because the native population itself was of Asiatic provenance. In Rumania, however, until the nineteenth century, they were brought under the control of the landowners and treated as serfs.

In Sofia, in Budapest, Prague and other Balkan cities there are Gypsies who have risen from their nomadic life and have successfully penetrated into society. Some are university students studying law. Others are physicians, musicians, journalists.

BALKAN HABITATION   In the Balkans and the Carpathians the Gypsies live in sheltered caves, protected by outcroppings of rocks and roofed over with branches.

BALKAN RITES   In the Balkans, when a death occurs, the deceased Gypsy is brought on a bier and displayed to public view at the crossroads.

BALKANS   In the Balkans, Gypsies have always hunted and trained the bear. These trainers are known as Oursari, itinerant bear-leaders. They exhibit the animals at fairs or similar places of popular entertainment.

Other animals, particularly lions and tigers, have been tamed by Gypsies to perform in the circus.

BALKAN SERFDOM   As early as the middle of the sixteenth century there were slaves, Gypsies with their families, attached to the *voivode* or 'lord of the manor' in Rumania. These landowners, throughout the Balkans, had the right of life and death over their Gypsy slaves, as was the case among the Romans.

BALTIC TOWNS   Contemporary records relate that some hundred Gypsies, with women and children, swept through the Baltic towns of Rapstock, Hamburg, Lubeck, in the fifteenth century. They appeared to be, in the popular view, forerunners and spies, examining the circumstances and locations for possibly larger groups of these people who would follow in their wake. It was reported that they had come from Eastern regions. Their leaders rode on horseback and were well-dressed. They called themselves dukes and counts. The rest of them were very shabby. The entire body called themselves Tsigani. According to their own explanation, they were forced to wander from one country to another in expiation, as a penance imposed on them for seven years for having rejected Christianity.

BANISHMENT TO AFRICA　In the eighteenth century Spain deported the nomadic Gypsies to African colonies.
The history of the Gypsies from the Middle Ages onward is a history of exclusion or banishment or deportation from one country to another.

BANJARI　There are also in India the Banjari or wandering merchants, and many other tribes, all spoken of as Gypsies by those who know them. — Charles Leland.

BAPTISMAL CUSTOM　Through expediency, the Gypsies normally had then children baptized in whatever Christian country accepted them. Sometimes the Church enforced baptism on infants. But in Eastern Europe and in Scandinavia the Gypsies met and secretly, in a nocturnal ceremony, unbaptized their children.

BARBARISM　The Scottish gypsiologist Walter Simson wrote: That the Gypsies were a barbarous race when they entered Europe, in the beginning of the fifteenth century, is just what could have been expected of any Asiatic, migratory, tented horde, at a time when the inhabitants of Europe were little better than barbarous themselves, and many of them absolutely so.

BARBARY Although Barbary has long been the home of wild tribes, hostile to newcomers, it is believed that Gypsies appeared in this territory in the nineteenth century. They are called "Those of the Darbushi-fal", that is, Those who are fortune-tellers. They are nomadic. They deal in horses and mules, and have a local reputation for sorcery.

BARBARY PIRATES In the Middle Ages, both as guides and advisers, the Spanish Gypsies helped the Barbary pirates in their plundering forays on the Spanish coast.

BARCELONA Gypsies are said to have reached Barcelona in the middle of the fifteenth century. They appeared in many areas of Spain but are particularly associated with the province of Andalusia.

BARNA, MICHEL He was a noted Gypsy musician of the eighteenth century. His talent secured him the appellation of the Magyar Orpheus. He was court violinist to the Cardinal Count Czaky.

BARON TRENCK AND THE GYPSIES Baron Friedrich von der Trenck (1726-1794) was a military adventurer. He served in the Prussian army and in the Austrian forces. He was executed by Robespierre as a foreign secret agent. One of his adventures he describes as follows:

> Here we fell in with a gang of Gypsies (or rather banditti) amounting to four hundred men, who dragged me to their camp. They were mostly French and Prussian deserters and, thinking me their equal, would force me to become one of their band. But venturing to tell my story to their leader, he presented me with

a crown, gave us a small portion of bread and meat, and suffered us to depart in peace, after having been four-and twenty hours in their company.

BAROSAN When referring to any non-Gypsy who is wealthy, the Gypsies term him *barosan*. Literally, *barosan* signifies: you are great.

BARRIOS In Spain, the Gypsies were confined in various towns to barrios or Gitanerías, that is, quarters exclusively reserved for the Gypsies. Such Gitanerías are to be found in many countries and cities: in Granada, Seville, Budapest, Istanbul.

BASQUE In the seventeenth century the Gypsies had installed themselves in the Basque country. In one of the comedies by Molière, the French dramatist, Gypsy women use Basque drums, which indicates that the Gypsy ways were well known. They were, however, unremittingly harassed. As late as the Napoleonic era the Gypsies in the Basque region were hunted down for deportation to the French colonies. Only Napoleon's war at sea interrupted the banishment.

In the lower Pyrenees the Gypsies who inhabit this region speak both French and Basque in addition to Caló, which is spoken by them largely in Spain.

BASQUE NAMES When the Gypsies settled in the Basque country, they assumed Basque Basque names, just as they assumed Spanish names in Spain and the names of English families in England. Some of these Basque patronymics are: Diharalde, Harosteguy, Iturbide. Some times the birthplace appears as part of the name as: Pierre de Camba, or Jean de Hurt.

BAT A black bag, containing fragments of a bat, worn round the neck by Gypsy children, is believed to ensure good luck.

In Gypsy lore, there are many such charms and amulets intended to bring good fortune to the possessor.

BATAILLARD, PAUL THEODORE (1816-1894)   In the nineteenth century this French gypsiologist considered that the Gypsies had been skilled in metal work, especially bronze, and had introduced these skills into Europe some 3,000 years ago. In 1844 Bataillard published *De l'apparition des Bohémiens en Europe* and in 1849 and 1876 he elaborated on his theories.

BAUDRIMONT, ALEXANDRE EDOUARD French gypsisiologist of the nineteenth century. He reached the conclusion that the Gypsies first inhabited Babylon. The destruction of the city drove them into exile.

BAYURA   All internal affairs among the Gypsies, their tribes and clans and *kumpanías* are decided by the traditional *kris* or law. There is no written code of law among them. But when a case is settled they accept this decision as a precedent. Such decisions, determined in previous cases, constitute a body of legal opinions called *bayura.*

BEAMS, JOHN   A British official who served in India. As a Sanskrit scholar he published *A comparative grammar of the Modern Aryan Languages of India* during the years 1872-1879. He concluded that the Gypsy language belonged in the family of the modern Aryan languages.

BEAR-HUNTS   In the Balkans, especially in Serbia, the Gypsies went bear-hunting. They tamed the bear and trained it to dance, ride a bicycle, and perform similar acts. Now such perfomances with bears are growing rare.

29

BEATRICE OF ARAGON Queen Beatrice of Aragon, wife of Mathias Corvin, King of Hungary toward the end of the fifteenth century, employed Gypsy musicians to entertain her court.

BEGGARS IN SPAIN Winter was the time when the women were generally the most called upon to try their skill in begging. During this season, many of the men remained in their huts, sending the women abroad to forage. They went about in the guise of beggars and commonly exposed to the cold and frost. One child was led by the hand, the other was tied in a cloth to the woman's back, in order to excite compassion in well-disposed people. Whole troops of these Gypsy beggars were common in Spain. They asked for alms with such importunity, as if they thought you could not deny them.

BELGIUM During the years 1420-1422 the Gypsies, under the tribal leadership of Andrew, Duke of Little Egypt, appeared in Brussels and Bruges, where they were received with hospitality.

BELIEFS On account of their migratory habits, Gypsies have adopted, at least nominally, the faith of the country of their sojourn. They are Moslems and Catholics and Protestants. But they also retain their peculiar traditions, mythology, and ancient legends that on occasion coincide with Biblical accounts and again seem akin to the pagan cults of the Middle East.

BELON, PIERRE In the sixteenth century Pierre Belon, a French scholar, proposed Wallachia as the original home of the Gypsies.

BEMISCHE This term is applied to a community of foreigners who appeared in Wurzburg before the fifteenth century.

The Bemische have been identified by gypsiologists as Gypsies.

BENI AROS The Beni Aros, a sect of wanderers in Barbary, have appeared to the cursory observer, said the gypsiologist George Borrow, in the right of legitimate Gypsies: The proper home of these people is in certain high mountains in the neighborhood of Tetuan, but they are to be found roving about the whole kingdom of Fez. Perhaps it would be impossible to find, in the whole of Northern Africa, a more detestable caste. They are beggars by profession, but are exceedingly addicted to robbery and murder. They are notorious drunkards, and are infamous, even in Barbary, for their unnatural lusts. They are, for the most part, well made and of comely feature. They are Moors and speak no language but the Arabic.

BERCOVICI, KANRAD This contemporary Rumanian writer became highly proficient in many European languages. As a youth he spent much time among the Gypsies, listening to their songs and music, and absorbing their distinctive dialects. Many of his novels and short stories deal with Gypsy life in a romanticized style and with a sense of warm sympathy.
In 1928 he published *The Story of the Gypsies,* a study of their life and ways. One collection of his tales is entitled *Ghitza and Other Romances of Gypsy Blood.* These stories range over a wide area, from Rumania to Spain, from Sicily to Carpathia.

BESSARABIA Bessarabia, all Tartary, Bulgaria, Greece, and Rumania, according to a gypsiologist of the nineteenth century, swarmed with Gypsies. In Rumania, a large tract of Mount Haemus, inhabited by the Romanys, acquired from them the name of Tschenghe Valkan, Gypsy

Mountain. This district extended from the city of Aydos to Philipopolis, and contains more Gypsies than any other province in the Turkish Empire.

BETHLEHEM The massacre of the children of Bethlehem, according to an old tradition, was carried out by the ancestors of the Gypsies who settled on the banks of the Danube.

BETROTHAL RITE Among the Gypsies, a betrothed pair threw eggs and apples into the water, to ensure good luck. They also went by night to the river, about a week before the marriage. They lit two candles. If the wind extinguished one of them, it was a bad omen.

BIANCHI, LUCIANA An Italian Gypsy who, exceptionally, headed her tribe in Modena. In many cases the oldest woman in the tribe, on account of age and long experience with her people, had some domestic jurisdiction over a family unit.

BIBLICAL GYPSIES One theory, propounded in the sixteenth century, relating to the origin of the Gypsies, was that they were the true descendants of the patriarch Abraham and his wife Sarah.
Another theory, expounded in the same century, made the Gypsies descendants of an ancient people called the Euxians, neighbors of the Persians. They were known to be skilled in predictions. But many ancient nations were so skilled.

BIBLICAL NAMES About 80% of the Gypsies have Biblical names, such as Delilah, Ezekiel, Bartholomew, Naomi, Elijah, Simeon.

BIBLICAL REFERENCE It was long believed that the original home of the Gypsies was Egypt, because the Gypsies were equated with the Egyptians cited in the Old Testament utterance:
And I will scatter the Egyptians among the nations, and disperse them among the countries; and they shall know that I am the Lord. — *Ezekiel* 30.26.

BIBLIOGRAPHIES The Gypsies have in all countries led such a varied and restless life through the centuries that the references and studies and descriptive works on the Gypsy people reach into the thousands. In the catalogue of the British Museum alone there are some 6,000 items listed, all relating to the Gypsies, their languages and dialects, their dress, their habits.

BIHARI A nineteenth century Gypsy musician. He achieved a notable reputation in Austria, where he played at the royal court.
Many Gypsies have made an international reputation as musicians, particularly as violinists.

BIRDS AND STARS "Tell me this, old friend, if you can tell it, What's the Romany for stars in heaven?" "Yes, master, stars with us are *shirkis*. And from *chiriclos* or birds, I take it, For the birds and stars are like in nature. Stars are only birds of light in heaven, Flying far above our heads forever, Birds of fire which only fly in darkness; And the moon's the lady of the heaven, Coming nightly, certain in her coming, O'er the meadows just to feed her chickens." — *Charles G. Leland*

BIRTH Among the Gypsies there are many strange rituals, chants, symbolisms relating to childbirth. A woman must not give birth in her caravan or tent. When a child is born to a young married couple, the parents are regarded as ritually unclean until the infant receives baptism.

BIVOLARS This Gypsy term denotes buffalo-herders. The bivolars are found along the banks of the Danube. Common among the Gypsies are such descriptive names, for example, as: *oursari,* bear-trainers: *ferari,* shoeing-smiths.

BLACK In the eighteenth century the Gypsies in Brittany were called Blacks, in view of their swarthy complexions. The Gypsies call themselves, in the same sense, *Calo,* Black.

BLACK BROTHERS A term that is sometimes used to denote the Gypsies.
The usual term of greeting is *phral,* brother, used even when speaking to a *gorgio,* a non-Gypsy.

BLACKSMITHS In the Balkans and as far as Greece the trade of blacksmith is in the hands of the Gypsies. The Gypsies have long been known for their craftsmanship in metals: copper, iron, tin: particularly the costorari, tinsmiths, who came from Turkey-Armenia.

BLACKTHORN In Rumania and Hungary the Gypsies often carry a blackthorn stick. It is regarded as a protection against vampires. In Gypsy folklore and mythology, many tales are filled with episodes involving demoniac forces, werewolves, and vampires.

BLOCH, JULES A contemporary French gypsiologist. He has studied the Gypsies particularly in the Middle Ages. Author of *Les Tsiganes,* published in 1953.

BLOOD There was a tradition that the witches in Venice were of Gypsy-Slavic-Greek origin. Such beliefs were part of

34

the Gypsy folklore and sagas. These witches lost all their power, according to Gypsy story, if they were made to shed even one drop of blood.

BLOOD OATH This tribal rite requires that an old leader of a tribe should transfer his status to the new chief by a mingling of drops of blood from each.

BLOOD VENGEANCE As in the case of many Oriental and other peoples, particularly the Afghans who indulge in blood feuds, blood vengeance is a characteristic of Gypsy life. It may be exacted after a long time, but it is not forgotten: usually it involves a woman and her lover. A Gypsy who fears such blood vengance is said to wear 'the dead man's shirt,' and is in constant danger of a violent death.

BOHEMIAN This term was first used in Europe as a synonym for Gypsy toward the close of the sixteenth century.
The term is also used in France to denote the Gypsies.

BOHEMIAN GYPSIES The Archduke Joseph of Austria-Hungary came upon a band of nomadic Gypsies in Bohemia, in the mid-nineteenth century. He discovered that the language they spoke had many Hindu elements in it. As he himself had studied Hindu, he continued his researches into the linguistic composition of the Gypsy language and published a Gypsy grammar.

BOHEMIAN LIFE The Bohemians, that is, the Gypsies, were so called because they were assumed to have originated in Bohemia. Their primary characteristics included nomadic migrations. Hence the term Bohemian acquired the significance of people who prefer to lead a wayward, unconfined, unconventional life, drifting at their own will. Such a life was attributed especially to those of an artistic temperament. The best known example of this Bohemianism is *Scènes de la vie de Bohème,* Henri Murger's depiction of French artistic life in the nineteenth century.

BOLOGNA   In the Middle Ages, in the course of their progress through Europe, the Gypsies reached Italy in the fifteenth century. In 1422 they had established themselves in Bologna.

BOOK OF THE GYPSIES   This expression is at times used with reference to the Tarot. The Tarot cards reputedly first appeared in Europe in the fourteenth century. They have been consistently used by the Gypsies for divinatory purposes.

BOOKS   The first book which ever appeared in Romany was the Gospel of St. Luke — Embéo e Majaro Lucas. The translation, by George Borrow, was published in Madrid in 1838.

BORDE, ANDRE   French scholar who investigated the Gypsy language. In 1542 he published a Gypsy conversational handbook.

BORDER AGILITY   The colony of Gypsies at Kirk Yetholm, on the Scottish borders, was admirably chosen by them. This was their chief settlement in Scotland:

> The secluded situation of the parish, and the immediate vicinity of Kirk Yetholm, more especially to England on one side, and to the wild and pathless range of the Cheviots on the other, may perhaps be given as reasons why the Gypsies originally chose this as their favorite haunt. If at any time pursued by the hand of justice, it was easy, the work of only a few minutes, to cross from the one kingdom to the other, Or if the magistrates on both sides of the border were on the alert,

the nimble-footed Gypsies were soon safe from their pursuit among the wild valleys of the neighboring mountains.

BORI DIKLO A Gypsy term denoting the patterned head scarf usually worn by Gypsy women: also a neckerchief.

BORROW, GEORGE (1803-1881) English writer and linguistic expert. As a boy he frequented the Gypsy camps near Norwich, in Norfolk. He lived with the Gypsies and acquired their Romany tongue.
Although he was remarkably proficient in Arabic, Hebrew, the Scandinavian languages, and Welsh, one of his chief and most enduring passions was Romany. He wandered through England and came in contact with many Gypsies. Later, he became an agent of the Bible Society and traveled for seven years in behalf of this organization in Russia, Morocco, Spain and Portugal. In Spain, which he reached in 1836, he remained for five years, investigating the history, language, and traditions of the Gitanos. He is regarded as one of the most eminent interpreters of Gypsy life. His activity was boundless. He produced a large number of translations from some thirty languages. His works dealing with Gypsies include: *The Bible in Spain, Lavengro, Romany Rye, The Zincali.*
Borrow's reputation in Spain was so widespread that the Gypsies knew him as Don Jorgito El Inglés.

BORROW NOT A GYPSY Charles Leland, the American gypsiologist, met his English counterpart George Borrow in England:
As he was not invariably disposed to like those whom he met, it is a source of great pleasure to me to reflect that I have nothing but pleasant memories of the good old Romany Rye, the Nestor of Gypsy gentlemen. It is commonly reported among Gypsies that Mr. Borrow

was one by blood, and that his real name was Boro, or great. This is not true. He was of pure English extraction.

BOSHA This term, which means *vagabonds,* is applied to the Gypsies of Armenia.
In most European countries, the Gypsies have been termed vagabonds in the native idiom.

BOUGH, SAM (1822-1878) English landscape painter, who was a Romany Rye. A native of Carlisle, he was a shoemaker's son. He entered the town-clerk's office, but while still young he abandoned a law career and wandered about the country, making sketches and associating with Gypsies.

BOUMIANES A French term applied contemptuously to Gypsies. Equally contemptuous have been other terms applied in various countries to the Gypsies: idlers, pagans, vagabonds. Boumianes is a form of *Bohémiens,* Bohemians, as the Gypsies were called in the belief that they stemmed from Bohemia.

BOXERS Boxing is a sport in which the Gypsies have been notable, particularly in England. In the ring they have made pugilistic history. William Cooper, for instance, called the Tinman, was middle-weight champion in 1790. In 1844 Tom Smith became feather-weight champion. At the beginning of the nineteenth century Amos Price, called Posh Price, was middle-weight champion. Later, in, 1857, Tom Sayers was heavy-weight champion.
Others were Jem Driscoll, Digger Stanley, world champion, and, in contemporary times, Théo Médina, Hippolyte Annex.

BRADY, DIAMOND JIM (1856-1917) Financier who amassed a fortune in the diamond mines of South Africa. He died in the United States. Brady was a Gypsy.

BRAILA A town in Rumania where there is one of the oldest Gypsy communities, a district called the Tzigania. There are similar quarters almost exclusively inhabited by the Gypsies in Tangier, Andalusia, and elsewhere.

BRAZIL In the eighteenth century many Gypsies were deported by Portuguese edicts to the colonies in Brazil. The Gypsy colonists were placed under strict supervision and were required to serve in the army to take up some useful trade.

BREACH OF PROMISE In England, the Gypsies never had a breach of promise case. The interested couple did not write letters to each other, because they could not write. When a young man and a woman were able to set up for themselves, they made a pact with each other. Beyond that there was no marriage ceremony, either ecclesiastical or civil.

BREAD The Gypsies are not accustomed to baking bread. They either buy, or beg, or even purloin the loaf. If by chance they do bake, it is done in the eastern method. A wood fire is prepared on the ground; it soon becomes embers. The mother meanwhile kneads the dough, forms it into small cakes, and lays them on the hot ashes.
To the Gypsies, bread has a property far beyond its value as nourishment. It has apotropaic virtues. Gypsies often carried bread or wheat in their pockets, as a defense against ill-luck, ghosts, and witches. For the *beng,* the devil, and the *mulos,* the spirits of the dead, shun bread and its ingredients Bread, in fact, constitutes an amulet or periapt to the Gypsy mind.

BRIDE PURCHASE Among the Gypsies it has long been a custom for a Gypsy to secure a bride at a price suggested by the girl's father. The custom of bride purchase, however, is becoming less prevalent nowadays.

BRITAIN There is a tradition that the Gypsies appeared in Britain in the fifteenth century. Spreading into Wales, Scotland, and Ireland, they were received reluctantly. Under Queen Elizabeth I of England they were ordered to leave the country. They still appeared, nevertheless, in the following century, retaining their tribal ways without resentment on the part of the authorities.

BRONZE AGE The date of the settlement of Gypsies in Europe is so uncertain that there is an anthropological claim that they inhabited Europe in the Bronze Age.

BROOM In Europe peasants often place a broom against a house door, when a Gypsy stands at the entrance. There is a superstition that the Gypsy will flee at the sight of a broom. The superstition is evidently associated with the belief in witches who in the medieval centuries rode to their sinister assignations on broomsticks.

BROTHER The Gypsy term of greeting a stranger is *phral,* which means brother. It is also used in addressing a woman stranger. The term *phral* denotes, in a sense, the attitude of the Gypsies to people in general, who at sight are assumed to be fellow-men.

BROWNE, SIR THOMAS (1605-1682) English physician and writer. In his *Vulgar Errors,* he writes that the Gypsies in Europe were first seen in Germany in the year 1409. In 1418 they were found in Switzerland; and, in 1422, in Italy. In France they appeared on the 17th of August, 1427.

It is remarkable, Sir Thomas Browne adds, that when they first came into Europe, the Gypsies were black, and that the women were still blacker than the men.

BUFFALO BILL Buffalo Bill, who was invited to the Camargue country, in Provence, recognized remarkable resemblances between the Gypsies and the American Indians such as the Sioux and the Iroquois.

BUILDING A HUT An investigator, early in the nineteenth century, thus describes how the Gypsies build:
For their winter huts, they dig holes in the ground, ten or twelve feet deep. The roof is composed of rafters laid across, which are covered with straw and sods. The stable, for the beast which carried the tent in summer, is a shed built at the entrance of the hollow and closed up with dung and straw. This shed, and a little opening rising above the roof of their subterranean dwelling, to let out the smoke, are the only marks by which a traveler could distinguish their habitation. Both in summer and winter they contrive to have their dwelling in the neighborhood of some village or town.

BULGARIA In many countries of their sojourn the Gypsies were reduced often to engage in the lowest menial offices. In Bulgaria the public hangman was invariably a Gypsy. In Bulgaria, about 50% of the Gypsy population has abandoned nomadic habits. The Gypsies are employed in construction works, in factories, and in industrial enterprises. The primary schools are open to the Gypsy children. Promising students proceed to the university. In the professions, there are Gypsy writers, teachers, engineers, physicians.

BULLFIGHTING The Spanish Gypsies have so long been integrated with Spanish ways that many noted bullfighters are of Gypsy blood. Among these is the celebrated Joselito, El Gallo, Chamaco.

BULUBASHA This term denotes the leader of a tribe among the Rumanian Gypsies.

Another term common in the Balkans is *voivode*. Ladislas, in the time of King Sigismund of Hungary, was named by the monarch as Voivode of the Gypsies.

BULWER LYTTON AS A ROMANY RYE The following autobiographical fragment from the unfinished *Life, Letters, and Literary Remains of Lord Lytton* (1883), by his son, the late Earl.

"Pray do!" said I, and I crossed her small palm with silver. "Only, pray, give me a sweetheart half as pretty as yourself".

The girl was, no doubt, used to such compliments, but she blushed as if new to them. She looked me in the face, quickly but searchingly, and then bent her dark eyes over my hand.

"Chut! chut!" she said with a sound of sorrowful pity, "but you have known sorrows already. You lost your father when you were very young. You have brothers, but no sister. Ah! you have had a sweetheart when you were a mere boy. You will never see her again, never. The line is clean broken off. It cut you to the heart. You nearly died of it. You have conquered, but you'll never be as gay again."

I snatched away my hand in amaze.

"You are indeed a witch!" said I, falteringly.

"Did I offend you? I'll not say any more of what has passed; let me look for your good luck in the time to come."

"Do so, and say something pleasant. Conceal the bad fortune as much as you can."

I felt very credulous and superstitious.

"Chut! chut! but that new star thwarts you much."

"What new star?"

"I don't know what they call it. But it makes men fond of strange studies, and brings about crosses and sorrows that you never think to have. Still, you are a prosperous gentleman; you will never come to want; you will be much before the world and raise your head high, but I fear you'll not have the honours you count on now. Chut! chut! — pity! pity! — you'll know scandal and slander; you'll be spoken ill of where you least deserve. That will vex you much, but you are proud, and will not stop to show it. Your best friends and your worst enemies will be women. You'll hunger for love all your life, and you will have much of it; but less satisfaction than sorrow. Chut! chut! how often you will be your own enemy! but don't be down-hearted, there is plenty of good fortune and success in store for you — not like me. Look at my hand. See here, where the cross comes against the line of life!"

"What does that mean?"

"Sorrow — and it is very near!"

"Nay, you don't believe for yourself all that you say to others. Our fortunes are not written in the palm of our hands".

"For those who can read them — yes," said the gipsy. "But very few have the gift. Some can read fortunes by fixing their eyes on anything — the gift comes to them."

I don't pretend to give the exact words of the girl. They were spoken quickly, and often in florid phrases; but, to the best of my recollection, I repeat the substance. We continued to walk on, and talk; we became familiar, and she interested me greatly. I questioned her as to the women of her caste, their mode of life, their religion, their origin, their language. Her replies were evasive, and often enigmatical. I remember that she said there were but two genuine clans of gipsies in England, and that the one bore the generic name of Fahey, the other of Smith, from the names their first dukes or leaders bore. She said that many of their traditions as to their origin and belief were dying out — that some of them had become what she called Christians; though, from her account, it was but a heathen sort of Christianity. She took great pains to convince me that they were not willful impostors in their belief that they could predict the future. I have since learned that though they placed great faith in the starry influences, their ideas were quite distinct from the astrology known to us. Nor was their way of reading the lines in the hand at all like that described in books of chiromancy.

From these subjects we passed on to others more tender and sentimental. The girl seemed to have taken a liking to me, but she was coy and modest.

"I should much like," said I, abruptly, "to pass a few days with you and your tribe. Do you think I might?"

The young gipsy's eyes brightened vividly.

"That I am sure you can, if you can put up with it — the like of you, a real born gentleman. Grandmother does as she will with the men, and I have my own way with her. Oh, do stay! Stop — I don't see that in the lines in my hand — I only see the cross."

I could not help kissing the little hand. She would not let me kiss the lips, which were pursed up in pretty, wistful doubt.

By-and-by, on a broader patch of the common land, and backed by a deeper mass of the woods, I saw before me the gipsy encampment. Just then the sun set. The clouds around it red and purple, the rest of the sky clear and blue, and Venus, the love star, newly risen.

We passed by some ragged, swarthy children lolling on the grass; they rose up and followed us. Three young men, standing round an older gipsy, who was employed in tinkering, stared at me somewhat fiercely. But the girl took me by the hand and led me into the spacious tent. A woman, apparently of great age, sate bending over a wood fire, on which boiled a huge pot. To this woman my young companion spoke low and eagerly, in a language at which I could not guess my way to a word — the old woman looking hard at me all the time, and shaking her at first in dissent; but gradually she seemed talked into acquiescence. The dear little gipsy, indeed, seemed to me irresistible; the tones of her voice were so earnest yet so coaxing. At length she turned round to me and said joyfully —

"You are welcome to stay as long as you like. But stop — what money have you got about you?"

I felt as if an illusion was gone. It went to my heart to hear the girl refer to money. Was her kindness then, all sordid? Was I to buy the hospitable rites proffered to me?

I replied very coldly that I had enough money to pay for any civilities I might receive.

The girl's face flushed, and her eyes sparkled angrily.

"You mistake me. I did not think you could. I spoke for your safety. It may be dangerous to have money. Give it all to grandmother's case. She will return it to you, untouched, when you leave us."

With an inexpressible feeling of relief and trust, I instantly drew forth all the coins about me (about £14) and gave it to the old woman, who took what must have seemed to her a large sum without showing any emotion, and slid it into her pocket.

"You don't think I shall let you lose a sixpence?" said the girl, drawing up her stature proudly.

"Oh, no! I wish it were thousands."

Poor child! At these words the pride vanished; her eyes moistened.

Then the old woman rose and took some embers from the fire, strewed them on the ground, and bade me stand in them. She said something to the girl, who went forth and called in all the other gipsies — men, women, and children. There were about a dozen of them altogether. As soon as they were assembled, the old woman, taking my right hand in hers, and pointing to the embers beneath my feet, began to address them in the gipsy tongue. They all stood listening reverently. When she had finished they bowed their heads, came up to me, and by word and sign made me understand that I was free of the gipsy tent, and welcome to the gipsy cheer.

Resolved to make myself popular, I exerted all my powers to be lively and amusing — hail fellow, well met! The gipsies said little themselves, but they seemed to enjoy my flow of talk and my high spirits. We all sate round the great fire — a primitive Oriental group. By-and-by the pot was taken off, and its contents distributed amongst us; potatoes and bread, fragments of meat stewed to rags, and seasoned with herbs of a taste before unknown to me. Altogether I thought the podrida excellent.

The old crone, who seemed the Queen of the camp, did not, however, partake of this mess. She had a little dish of her own broiled on the embers, of odd, uncouth form. I did not like to be too inquisitive that night, but I learned from my young patroness the next day that her grandmother was faithful to the customs of the primitive gipsies, and would eat nothing in the shape of animal food that had not died a natural death. Her supper had been a broiled hedgehog found in a trap.

I spent with these swarthy wanderers five or six very happy days, only alloyed by the fear that I should be called on to requite the hospitality I received by participating in some theft upon poultryyard or drying-ground, that would subject me to the treadmill. Had I been asked, I very much doubt if I should have had the virtue to refuse. However, the temptation, luckily, was never pressed upon me, nor did I witness anything to justify the general suspicion of gipsy errors as to the *meum* and *tuum*. Once only a fine goose, emerging from the pot, inflamed my appetite and disturbed my conscience. The men generally absented themselves from the camp at morning, together with a donkey and their tinkering apparatus, sometimes returning at noon, sometimes not till night.

The women went about fortune-telling; the children watched on the common for any stray passenger whom they might induce to enter the camp and cross with silver the hand of the oracle; for the old woman sate by the fire all day. My young gipsy went forth by herself — also on pretence of telling fortunes; but we had fixed a spot on the road at which I always joined her; and we used then to wander through the green lanes, or sit on some grassy bank, talking to each other with open hearts.

I think that the poor girl felt for me, not exactly love, but that sort of wild, innocent, fondness a young Indian savage might feel for the first fair face from Europe that had ever excited her wonder. Once the instinctive greed of her caste seized her at the sight of a young horseman, and she sprang from my side to run after him, not resting till he had stopped his horse, crossed her hand, and heard his fortunes.

When she came back to my side she showed me half-a-crown with such glee! I turned away coldly and walked off. She stood rooted to the spot for a moment, and then ran after me and threw her arms round my neck.

"Are you angry?"

"Angry, no; but to run after that young man —— "

"Jealous? oh, I'm so happy! then you do care for me?" As if with a sudden impulse, she raised herself on tiptoe, clung to me, and kissed my forehead. I clasped

47

her in my arms; but she glided from them like a serpent and ran off, back to the encampment, as if afraid of me and of herself.

One morning she was unusually silent and reserved. I asked her, reproachfully, why she was so cold.

"Tell me," she said abruptly, — "tell me truly, do you love me?"

"I do indeed." And so I thought.

"Will you marry me, then?"

"Marry you?" I cried aghast. "Marry? Alas! I would not deceive you — that is impossible."

"I don't mean," cried she impetuously, but not seeming hurt at my refusal, "I don't mean as you mean — marriage according to your fashion. I never thought of that; but marry me as we marry."

"How is that?"

"You will break a piece of burned earth with me — a tile, for instance — into two halves."

"Well?"

"In grandmother's presence. That will be marriage. It lasts only five years. It is not long," she said pleadingly. "And if you want to leave me before, how could I stay you?"

Poor dear child! for child after all she was, in years and in mind; how charming she looked then! Alas! I went further for a wife and fared worse.

Two days after this proposition, I lost sight of her for ever.

That evening and the next day I observed, for the first time, that I had excited the ill-will of two out of the three young gipsy men. They answered me when I spoke to them with rudeness and insolence; gave me broad hints that I had stayed long enough, and was in their way.

They followed me when I went out to join my dear

Mimy (I don't know her true name, or if she had any —
I gave her the name of Mimy), and though I did join
her all the same, they did not speak as they passed me,
but glared angrily, and seated themselves near us.
The girl went up and spoke to them. I saw that the
words on both sides were sharp and high; finally,
they rose and slunk away sullenly. The girl refused to
tell me what had passed between them; but she remained thoughtful and sad all day.
It was night. I lay in my corner of the encampment,
gazing drowsily on the fire. The gipsies had all retired
to their nooks and recesses also, save only the old
woman, who remained on her stool, cowering over the
embers. Presently, I saw Mimy steal across the space,
and come to her grandmother's side, lay her head in
her lap, and weep bitterly. The old woman evidently
tried to console her, not actually speaking, but cooing
low, and stroking her black hair with caressing hands.
At length they both rose, and went very softly out of
the tent. My curiosity was aroused, as well as my compassion. I looked round — all was still. I crept from my
corner, and went gently round the tent: every one
seemed fast asleep; some huddled together, some in
nooks apart. I stepped forth into the open air. I found
Mimy and the old crone seated under the shadow of
the wood, and asked why Mimy wept (she was weeping
still). The old woman put her finger to her lips, and
bade me follow her through a gap in the hedge into
the shelter of the wood itself. Mimy remained still,
her face buried in her hands. When we were in the
wood, the old woman said to me —
"You must leave us. You are in danger!"
"How?"
"The young men are jealous of you and the girl; their
blood is up. I cannot keep it down. I can do what I
like with all — except love and jealousy. You must go."

"Nonsense! I can take care of myself against a whole legion of spindle-shanked gipsies; they'll never dare to attack me; and I don't mind rude words and angry looks. I'll not leave Mimy. I cannot——"

"You must," said Mimy, who had silently followed us; and she put her arms fairly and heartily round me. "You must go. The stars will have it."

" 'Tit not for your sake I speak," said the old woman, passionately; "you had no right to touch her heart. You deserve the gripe and the stab; but if they hurt you, what will the law do to them? I once saw a gipsy hanged — it brought woe on us all! You'll not break her heart, and ruin us all. Go!"

"Mimy! Mimy! will you not come too?"

"She cannot; she is a true-born gipsy. Let her speak for herself."

"No, no, I cannot leave my people!" she whispered. "But I *will* see you again, later. Let me know where to find you. Don't fret. You'll have crosses enough without me. I will come to you later I will indeed!"

She had drawn me away from the old woman while she spoke, and with every word she kissed my hands, leaving there such burning tears.

At length I promised to depart, believing fully in Mimy's promise to return — the promise that we should meet again. I gave her my name and address. She pledged herself to find me out before the winter.

They were both very anxious that I should set off instantly. But my pride revolted at the idea of skulking away from foes that I despised in the dead of night. I promised to go, but openly and boldly, the next day. I was in some hopes that meanwhile the old woman would talk the jealous rivals into good behaviour. She assured me she would try. I told her to give them all my money, if they would but let me stay in peace for a week or two longer. She nodded her head, and went back with Mimy into the tent. I remained without for an hour or so, sad and angry, then I crept back to my corner. The fire was nearly out — all around was dark. I fell into an uneasy, haunted sleep, and did not wake till an hour later than usual. When I did so, all were assembled round the tent, and, as I got up, the three young men came to me and shook hands, their faces very friendly. I thought they had taken the bribe, and were going to bid me stay. No.

"You leave us!" said the tallest of the three. "And we stay at home to accompany you part of the way, and wish you speed and luck."

I turned round. No Mimy was there. Only the old woman, who set before me my breakfast.

I could not touch food. I remained silent a few minutes, then whispered to the crone. "Shall I not even see her again?"

"Hush!" she said, "leave her to take care of that"

I took up my knapsack sulkily enough, and was going forth, when the old woman drew aside and slipped my money into my hand.

"But you must take some."

"Not a penny. Mimy would never forgive it. Off, and away! There will be storm before noon. Go with heart. Success is on your forehead!"

The prediction did not cheer me, nor did the talk of the gipsies who gathered round me, and went with me in grand procession to the end of the common; which, I suppose, they considered their dominion. There they formally took leave of me. I might have gone some three miles, when the boughs of a tree overhanging the neighbouring wood were put aside, and Mimy's dark eyes looked cautiously forth. Presently she was by my side. She only stood a minute, holding me tightly in her arms, and looking me in the eyes, then drawing back her hand and kissing fondly my face and my hands — my very garments. At last she sprang away, and, pointing with her forefinger to her open palm, said, "This is the sorrow foretold to me. See, it begins so soon, and goes on to the end of life!"

"No, no, Mimy! you have promised we shall meet again".

"Ha, ha! a gipsy's promise!" cried Mimy, between a laugh and a screech.

She darted back into the wood. I followed her, but in vain. From that day to this I have never seen, never heard of her. I have sought gipsies, to inquire after her fate; but one told me one thing, one another. I know it not. Probably she was consoled sooner than my vain young heart supposed, and broke the tile with one of her kin. How, even if we met again, should I ever recognise her? Gipsy beauty fades so soon — fades like all illusion, and all romance! — *F. H. Groome*

BUNYAN, JOHN (1628-1688) Noted English preacher and writer. Author of the *Pilgrim's Progress*. In the nineteenth century the gypsiologist Walter Simson declared that John Bunyan was unquestionably a Gypsy.

BURIAL When a member of a Gypsy tribe dies, the relatives usually fast until the deceased is given due burial. In some cases cooked food is taboo. A vigil is also kept during this period by the women in the clan.

Touching the body of the deceased is virtually taboo, and a non-Gypsy, a gorgio or busnó, performs this service. Usually the deceased is buried fully clothed. Money is often placed in the coffin along with other personal belongings of the deceased. A hammer, too, is not infrequently put into the coffin.

Formerly, it was a custom, at the death of a Gypsy, to throw their clothes, their silver or gold ornaments and trinkets, the bedding and utensils belonging to the deceased, even the caravan itself, upon a huge blazing pyre.

The practice has been in vogue within the last half century as well. It must go back to early centuries in Gypsy traditions. The Roman poet Virgil, in Book 4 of the *Aeneid*, describes how Dido, Queen of Carthage, threw all the belongings of her lover Aeneas, even the sword he had left behind, upon a pile that was to be her own funeral pyre. Dido's motive, however, was different from the usual Gypsy ritual.

When a Gypsy dies, he is buried in a remote corner of a village or at the edge of a wood. The site is marked with a wooden post, with the lower end almost touching the head of the corpse. Formerly, the relatives of the deceased took away the head of the corpse and buried it elsewhere, and also drove the post deep into the ground. The belief was that, by thus hastening putrefaction, the soul would all the sooner enter the realm of the dead. In the eighteenth century in Hungary a number of Gypsies were executed on the charge of consuming a corpse. In all likelihood the actions of the burial party were misconstrued by the Hungarians who observed the scene.

BURNING HAIR A Gypsy belief recommends that a hair, hanging on a person's coat, should be burned, in order to avoid injury through witchcraft.

Another belief relating to hair maintains that if witches or the Devil himself can steal a lock of hair, the victim will suffer evil consequences.

BURNS, ROBERT (1759-1796) The famous Scottish poet was familiar with the Gypsies. He knew their ways and character, and his knowledge of them is reflected in the scattered allusions that appear throughout his poetry.

BURNT MEAT The Gypsies are particularly fond of animals that have been destroyed by fire. Whenever a fire has occurred, either in town or country, the next day the Gypsies gather from the neighborhood and draw the suffocated, half consumed beasts out of the ashes. They return to the scene several times, provide themselves with this roast meat, and gluttonize as long as the fire lasts.

BUSNE A word used by the Spanish Gypsies for non-Gypsies.
The singular form is *busnó.*
A synonym of *busnó is gorgio.*
The Gypsies also use the term Gentiles to signify non-Gypsies.

BUSNO This Gypsy term denotes a non-Gypsy. It is probably derived from a Hungarian expression. It corresponds to the Spanish oath *carajo.* The plural form is *busné.*

BUTTER During their wanderings, the Gypsies have imported new words and commodities as well into the countries that have granted them a stay. Butter, for instance, was introduced by them into Spain.

BY THE HAND To the Gypsies, the fields and forests are haunted by spirits and demons that must be constantly appeased or supplicated by means of incantations, spells, and charms. There is a widespread belief that an innocent child is a powerful agent in prophecy and sorcery. Hence in many oaths and spells the expression is used, as follows:

> Tell me, Nivashi,
> By the child's hand,
> Where is my horse?

Nivashi is the powerful water-spirit who is invoked to

reveal the whereabouts of a stolen horse.
Another similar oath runs:
Apo miro dadeskro vast!
By my father's hand!

BYZANTINE CHRONICLES With reference to the intrusion of the Gypsies into Europe early in the fifteenth century, there had previously been occasional and scattered allusions to the wandering Gypsies in the Byzantine chronicles.

BYZANTINE EVIDENCE Byzantine records of the fourteenth century refer to the Gypsies, who were called in Greek territory *Atcingani,* as being settled in the Peloponnesus.

BYZANTINE GYPSIES Gypsiologists have stated that Gypsies appeared in Byzantium as early as the middle of the ninth century.

C

CACHAS This Gypsy term denotes *scissors*. With this instrument the Spanish Gypsy is expert in shearing the backs, ears, and tails of mules. A Gypsy couplet refers to this practice:

I'll rise tomorrow bread to earn,
For hunger's worn me grim;
Of all I meet I'll ask in turn,
If they've no beasts to trim.

CALDEREROS This expression signifies coppersmiths, and is applied to the Spanish Gypsies.
Occupational groups have their distinctive designation: *oursari,* for instance, are the bear-trainers: *costorari* are tinsmiths.

CALES The Gypsies use this term of themselves, particularly in Spain. It is the termination of the compound word Zincalo, which signifies Black Men.

CALLOT, JACQUES (1592-1635) French artist who produced many notable etchings depicting Gypsy life. His interest in this people began when he was young. At the age of twelve, in 1604, he ran away from his home in Lorraine, bound for Rome to study art. On his way he encountered a band of Gypsies and spent several months with them as they advanced as far as Florence. Callot's vivid

56

sketches are comparable, to some extent, to Brueghel's peasant scenes.

CALO This Gypsy term denotes the Romany idiom as spoken in Spain. George Borrow and Walter Starkie were notably proficient in Caló.
They, like several other notable gypsiologists, were excellently versed in Gypsy dialects.

CALO ROM This expression signifies Black Gypsy, a term applied to the Gypsies by themselves, especially in the United States.
The term is also common among the Gypsies of Europe.

CAMENI MICUTI In Gypsy legend, this expression signifies "small men", grey-bearded dwarfs, who work in the mines. They are the Subterraneans.

CAMPING GROUND The usual practice in setting up a Gypsy encampment is to select a site that is as obscured and as remote as possible from public view or main highways. The location is wherever possible near the edge of a forest, or beside a running stream, or at crossroads.

CANADA In Canada, not all the Gypsies who settled there continued their nomadic ways and itinerant occupations. Some rose to professional status, as lawyers, physicians, editors.

CANNIBALISM Gypsies were often held in such fear and horror that in the Middle Ages and even later they were popularly regarded as practicing cannibalism. As late as the eighteenth century, in Austria, forty Gypsies were convicted on this charge and executed. The evidence invariably consisted of neighbors' gossip, folk tales, and hearsay.

CANTE FLAMENCO   This Spanish term refers to a light song of complicated rhythm. The word flamenco denoted the Gypsies who had come from Germany to Spain. The Spaniards called them Germans or Flemings, indifferently. Flamenco itself is a corrupted form of Fleming. There are other explanations and interpretations, however, of this expression.

Flamenco is also applied to the noted Spanish dance.

Flamenco, both song and dance, has Gypsy elements, although it has now acquired a distinctively Spanish identity.

CANTE JONDO   This Spanish term means Deep Song, the ancient characteristic type of song of Andalusia. The Spanish Gypsies have adopted and perpetuated this mode of tragic, haunting chant as a Gypsy expression of their own emotional life.

CANTERBURY   In the early years of their appearance in England, the Gypsies were treated with some consideration and charitableness. But during the sixteenth century under the ascendancy of Thomas Cromwell, Lord Privy Seal, all Gypsies had to be expelled or executed. There is, however, an apocryphal suggestion that at Canterbury Gypsies performed before King Henry VIII.

CARACO, CORAI   These variant names refer to the Gypsies in Provence who are engaged in bull-rearing. Occupational groups have distinctive designations: *costorari,* tinsmiths: *oursari,* bear-trainers.

CAREW, BAMFYLDE MOORE (1693 - c. 1770)   An English adventurer. He ran away from school to join the Gypsies, of whom he ultimately became tribal leader or King. He was transported to Maryland, but escaped and returned to his vagabondage in England and Scotland.

58

CARLYLE, THOMAS (1795-1881) The wife of Thomas Carlyle, the Scottish essayist and historian, was Jane Welsh. Her mother was a Scottish Gypsy, married to a cattle-breeder named Welsh.

CARLYLE ON GYPSIES One morning Charles Leland was walking in London with Thomas Carlyle:
'You have paid some attention to Gypsies,' said Mr. Carlyle. 'They're not altogether so bad a people as many think. In Scotland, we used to see many of them. I'll not say that they were not rovers and reivers, but they could be honest at times. The country folk feared them, but those who made friends wi' them had no cause to complain of their conduct. Once there was a man who was persuaded to lend a Gypsy a large sum of money. My father knew the man. It was to be repaid at a certain time. The day came; the Gypsy did not. And months passed, and still the creditor had nothing of money but the memory of it; and ye remember 'nessun maggior dolore' — that there's na greater grief than to remember the siller ye once had. Weel, one day the man was surprised to hear that his frien' the Gypsy wanted to see him — interview, ye call it in America. And the Gypsy explained that, having been arrested, and unfortunately detained, by some little accident, in preeson, he had na been able to keep his engagement.
'If ye'll just gang wi' me,' said the Gypsy, 'aw'll mak' it all right.'
'Mon, aw wull,' said the creditor, — they were Scotch, ye know, and spoke in deealect. So the Gypsy led the way to the house which he had inhabited, a cottage which belonged to the man himself to whom he owed the money. And there he lifted up the hearthstone; the the hard-stane they call it in Scotland, and it is called so in the prophecy of Thomas of Ercildowne. And

under the hard-stane there was an iron pot. It was full of gold, and out of that gold the Gypsy carle paid his creditor. Ye wonder how 'twas come by? Well, ye'll have heard it's best to let sleeping dogs lie.'

CARRION The Gypsies have no aversion to eating animals that have 'died by the hand of God.' They have often been accused, and known, to have eaten carrion.

In England, farmers seldom refused the Gypsies a sheep that had died in the field. One farmer, however, who had lost a great number of sheep by death, suspected the Gypsies as the cause. He therefore had one of these animals opened, and discovered a piece of wood in its throat, with which it had been suffocated. The Gypsies, who had no objection to creatures that died in their blood, had killed all these sheep in the manner described.

CASIMIR John Casimir, King of Poland and Grand Duke of Lithuania during the sixteenth century, appointed Matthias Korolewicz as voivode or chief leader of all the Gypsies in Poland.

CATALINI AND THE GYPSY Angelica Catalini (1780-1840) was a famous Italian operatic soprano. In his travels in Russia, the gypsiologist George Borrow heard the songs of the Russian Gypsies. He comments:

Perhaps the highest compliment ever paid to a songster was paid by Catalini herself to one of these daughters of Rome. It is well known throughout Russia that the celebrated Italian was so enchanted with the voice of a Moscow Gypsy (who, after the former had displayed her noble talent before a splendid audience in the old Russian capital, stepped forward and poured forth one of her national strains), that she tore from her own shoulders a shawl of cashmere, which had been presented to her by the Pope, and, embracing the Gypsy, insisted on her acceptance of the splendid gift, saying that it had been intended for the matchless songster, which she now perceived she herself was not.

CAVE-DWELLERS In Spain, in the Carpathians and elsewhere, Gypsies have found refuge or shelter in natural caves, which they have converted into temporary homes. At Gaudix, in Spain, there are cave-dwelling Gypsies. At Benalua, near Guadix, there is a similiar cave community.

CAVES Apart from living in tents and later in caravans, Gypsies have shared shelter and domicile in groves, caves, under bridges or aqueducts, in Germany and France and Spain. On occasion, when small bands of Gypsies were on their way and required temporary shelter, the town authorities would provide rooms in an inn or barn provided the tribal leader presented permits or royal or ducal Letters of Safe-Conduct.

CEMETERIES There is no veneration of cemeteries among the Gypsies. After burial the cemetery becomes a matter of little personal concern. One reason for this situation is the fact of the constant change of Gypsy encampments and environment.
Of all the Gypsies, the Sintés visit the graves of the deceased once a year.

CENSUS There is no official census of the population of Gypsies in any one region. But it is estimated that in Russia there are approximately one million. In Rumania, Hungary, and Bulgaria, some 750,000. In Greece and Turkey, conjointly, about 200,000.

CERVANTES The resistance of the Gypsies to the continual calumny and persecution and to the penalties imposed on them by society is expressed by Cervantes. And old Gypsy declares in one of his tales: We sing in gaol but we are silent under torture.

CHAGRIN In Gypsy folklore there is a belief in a demon in the form of a hedgehog. It torments animals, particularly mares.

CHAI This Gypsy term is a modification of *chal,* which means Egypt and, in some Gypsy dialects, heaven. Thus chai may denote: The Men of Egypt or The Sons of Heaven. Most frequently, however, among the Gypsies themselves, *chai* signifies children.

CHAL In their migratory movements toward the West, one tradition brings the Gypsies to Egypt, which is *Chal.* Hence the generic designation of *Romanichals* for the Gypsies identifies them as *Men of Egypt.*

CHALANERIA A Gypsy term that signifies horse-dealing, one of the most popular occupations among the Gypsies. In this respect the Gypsies are so knowledgable that by means of concoctions and other practices they can transform a moribund creature into a horse in temporarily perfect condition.

CHALDEA According to one Gypsy legend, the original home of the Gypsies was Chaldea. It is certain, in any case, that the Gypsies did reach Chaldea in their migration westward from India.

CHANGARS An Oriental people with whom the origin of the Gypsies had been equated.
The Gypsies have at various stages in their history been identified as Egyptians, Bohemians, Ethiopians and various Indian peoples.

CHANGE IN STATUS In the 30's of last century the Gypsy slaves in Moldavia and Wallachia, and subsequently in other Balkan states, began to be liberated and regarded with human indulgence.

Two *voivodes,* landowners named Ghyka, were instrumental in the abolition of slavery in Wallachia and in Rumania. It was only the clergy that resisted the emancipation.

CHANGING THE GYPSY Firdusi, the eleventh century Persian poet, author of the epic *Shah Namah,* wrote of the Gypsies:

For the root that's unclean, hope if you can;
No washing e'er whitens the black Zigan.

CHANTS At the burial of a Gypsy the funeral party will begin lamentation with chants, extemporaneously expressed by relatives and friends.

CHARACTERIAL GYPSY Gypsies, wrote Charles Leland the gypsiologist, are the human types of this vanishing direct love of nature, of this mute sense of rural romance, and of *al fresco* life, and he who does not recognize it in them, despite their rags and dishonesty, need not pretend to appreciate anything more in Callot's etchings than the skillful management of the needle and the acids. Truly they are but rags themselves; the last rags of the old romance which connected them with nature.

CHARACTER OF GYPSIES A gypsiologist described both the English Gypsy Chal, the Romany man, and the Chi, the woman, as follows:

They roamed about in bands, consisting of thirty, sixty, or ninety families, with light, creaking carts, drawn by horses and donkeys, encamping at night in the spots they deemed convenient. The women told fortunes at the castle of the baron and the cottage of the yeoman; filched gold and silver coins from the counters of money-changers; caused the death of hogs in farm-yards, by means of a stuff called drab or drao, which affects the brain, but does not corrupt the blood; and subsequently begged, and generally obtained, the carcasses. The men plied tinkering and brasiery, now and then stole horses, and occasionally ventured upon highway robbery.

The English Gypsies are not drunkards, nor are the women harlots. The crimes of which they were originally accused were principally: theft, sorcery, causing disease among cattle.

Dabbling in sorcery is to some extent the province of the Gypsy woman. She offers to tell the future, and she can prepare love philtres to arouse erotic passions in a particular individual.

Facial and other traits of Gypsies vary with circumstances, with their location, their personal habits. Most are swarthy and in gesture they are quick and restless. They are not noted for cleanliness. They are fond of deceiving and tricking the gullible gorgios. Gypsies are prolific and superstitious. Their outdoor mode of life keeps them, in general, in good health. When sick, they resort to concoctions and incantations and also apply their own traditional herbal and folk remedies. Few even among the most wealthy Gypsies can either read or write. They do not dread an afterlife and, on dying, are anxious about the body, not the soul. They are usually eager to have their children baptized. Their last thoughts are of a handsome coffin and burial in a quiet country churchyard.

CHARACTER OF GYPSY MUSIC Liszt wrote of the music of the Hungarian Gypsies:

Their music is as free as their lives; no intermediate

modulation, no chords, no transition, it goes from one key to another. From ethereal heights they precipitate you into the howling depths of hell; from the plaint, barely heard, they pass brusquely to the warrior's song, which bursts loudly forth, passionate and tender, at once burning and calm. Their melodies plunge you into a melancholy reverie, or carry you away into a stormy whirlwind; they are a faithful expression of the Hungarian character, sometimes quick, brilliant, and lively, sometimes sad and apathetic.

CHARACTER OF HUNGARIAN GYPSIES Grellmann, the noted gypsiologist, described the Hungarian Gypsies as follows:

They are loquacious and quarrelsome in the highest degree. In the public markets, and before ale-houses, where they are surrounded by spectators, they bawl, spit at each other, catch up stocks and cudgels, and brandish them over their heads, throw dust and dirt; now run from each other, then back again, with furious gestures and threats. The women scream, drag their husbands by force from the scene of action. These break from them again, and return to it. The children, too, howl piteously.

CHARACTER OF RUSSIAN GYPSIES I found on inquiry, wrote Charles Leland when he visited Russia in the late 80's:

that the Russian Gypsies profess Christianity; but as the religion of the Greek church, as I saw it, appears to be practically something very little better than fetish-worship, I cannot exalt them as models of evangelical piety. They are, however, according to a popular proverb, not far from godliness in being very clean in persons; and not only did they appear so to me, but

I was assured by several Russians that, as regarded these singing Gypsies, it was invariably the case. As for morality in Gypsy girls, their principles are very peculiar. Not a whisper of scandal attaches to these Russian Romany women as regards transient amours. But if a wealthy Russian gentleman falls in love with one, and will have and hold her permanently, or for a durable connection, he may take her to his home if she likes him, but must pay monthly a sum into the Gypsy treasury; for these people apparently form an *artel,* or society-union, like all other classes of Russians. It may be suggested, as an explanation of this incongruity, that Gypsies all the world over regard steady cohabitation, or agreement, as marriage.

CHARACTER OF WITCH   The Gypsies regard a witch as simply a woman who has gained supernatural power, which she uses for good or misuses for evil according to her disposition. Gypsy folklore is full of tales of witches and their contacts, beneficent or malefic, with human beings. This witch-influence is pervasive in many Gypsy superstitions.

CHARLES III   This Spanish monarch, who ruled from 1759 to 1788, assumed a new attitude toward the Gypsies. In 1783 a law was passed entitled "Rules for Repressing and chastising the vagrant mode of life, and other excesses, of those who are called Gitános.

Instead of encouraging the persecution of the Gypsies, it tried to appeal to them in a more humane sense, to convince them that it would be to their own advantage to renounce their accustomed way of life. The law opened out careers to them, in the arts and sciences. It declared them capable of entering upon any profession, any field of activity that was open to the Spaniards. The only condition would be that of personal capability.

CHARLES VI Again and again the Austrian policy was to repress the Gypsies, under the most extreme penalties. In 1726 Charles VI Emperor of Austria ordered all male Gypsies to be put to death.

CHARM AGAINST FEVER A Gypsy remedy for fever is a concoction of frogs' lungs and livers, powdered and drunk in spirits, to the accompaniment of a magic chant. The chant is a demand for the frogs parts to drive out the victim's sickness.

CHASTITY BELT There was a medieval custom among the Gypsies that involved a chastity belt. Possibly the custom was adopted from the Crusaders. English Gypsy girls used to wear a virginal girdle, symbolically the *zona* of antiquity. It was worn from around the age of twelve until the wedding day. It was attached every morning by the mother and untied in the evening.

CHEN-GUIN An old name of Gypsies. According to legend, through the misrepresentations of a sorcerer, Chen, a Gypsy leader, married his own sister, Guin or Kan. Hence the curse of wandering was brought on the tribe. Chen and Kan symbolize the Moon and the Sun.
Another similar legend relates that the Sun because he seeks continuously to seduce his sister the Moon, everlastingly follows her and is destined to wander forever, like the Gypsies themselves. The Oriental term Chen-Kan became in the course of time Zingan and Zigeuner.

CHILDBIRTH In accordance with a vast corpus of superstitious traditions, a Gypsy woman, to ease her labor, chants the following charm:
Seven Pçuvushe, seven Nivashi
Come into the field,
Burn, burn, oh fire!

They bite the mother's foot.
They destroy the sweet child.
Fire, fire, oh burn!
Protect the child and the mother!

CHILD-STEALING The Gypsies in this country, wrote an English gypsiologist who had worked among them, have for centuries been accused of child-stealing. It is therefore not to be wondered at that, when children have been missing, the Gypsies should be taxed with having stolen them. About thirty years since, some parents who had lost a child applied to a man at Portsmouth, well known in those days by the name of Payne or Pine, as an astrologer. They wished to know from him what was become of their child. The astrologer told them to search the Gypsy tents for twenty miles around. The distressed parents employed constables, who made a diligent search in every direction, but to no purpose. The child was not to be found in their camps. It was, however, soon afterward discovered drowned in one of the father's pits: he had been a tanner. Thus was this pretended astrologer exposed to the ridicule of those who, but a short time before, foolishly looked on him as an oracle.

On another occasion, the same kind of accusation was brought against the Gypsies and proved to be false. The child of a widow at Portsmouth was lost, and after every search had been made on board the ships in the harbor, and at Spithead, and the ponds dragged in the neighborhood, to no effect, it was concluded that the Gypsies had stolen him. The boy was found a few years afterward, at Kingston-upon-Thames, apprenticed to a chimney-sweep. He had been enticed away by a person who had given him sweetmeats; but not by a Gypsy.

CHINGENE OR CHINGHIANE These names refer to the Moslem Gypsies of Asia Minor. As a rule, the migratory

Gypsies adopted the religion and the religious practices of the country of sojourn. But such adoption was usually nominal and temporary, as well as expedient.

CHIROLOGY The study of character by means of an examination of the hand. This practice is a common occupation among Gypsy women.

CHIROMANCY Chiromancy, or palmistry, the art of telling fortunes by reading the lines of the hand, was a Persian practice that was introduced into Andalusia in Spain by the Gypsies. In the family unit, it is the Gypsy woman whose regular occupation is fortune-telling among the gorgios, the non-Gypsies. This occupation of the Gypsy women has a centuries-old tradition throughout all European countries.

CHIVING DRAV A Gypsy expression meaning poisoning: that is, poisoning of cattle. This was a common practice among Gypsies in nineteenth century England.
The poisoning of cattle, however, especially of pigs, does not prevent the Gypsies from begging the farmer for the carcass and making a meal of the animal.

CHORODIES This term applies to wandering outcasts who lead the same type of life as the Gypsies but have no blood or ethnic relationship with Romany people.

CHORROJUMO A Gypsy who had been King of his tribe in Granada, Spain.
At various times in different countries the term King or Queen has been attributed to a tribal leader or to the oldest woman in a clan. There is no sovereignty in the appellation: it is at most an honorific.

CHRISTIAN BURIAL Burial in Christian churchyards was

first conceded to Gypsies of Montenegro under Prince Danilo, who ruled from 1851 to 1860.

Burial ceremonies, however, remain traditionally of Gypsy character.

CHRISTIAN INVOCATION The Gypsies are hardly to be regarded as Christians, but when they wish to contend against the powers of darkness they occasionally invoke Christian influences. If a cow gives bloody milk it is thought to be caused by her eating quail weed, which is a poison. In such a case they sprinkle the milk on a field frequented by quails and repeat: —

> I give to you blood,
> Which is not good!
> The Lord Christ's blood
> Is truly good.
> That is ours!

CHRONICLE OF DALIMIL This Czech document, dating in 1360, refers to the strange idiom of the Gypsies and also to their mendacity.

CHURCH BAPTISM Professing to be church people whenever they speak of religion, the Gypsies generally have their children baptized at the church near which they are born, partly because they think it right, and partly, perhaps chiefly, to attach themselves to the parish. They will sometimes apply to the parish officers for something toward the support of the child. This is called 'settling the baby.' The sponsors at baptism are generally members of the same family.

CHURCH PROHIBITION The Church, both Catholic and Protestant, at all times forbade Christians to consult fortune-telling Gypsies. The practice was denounced in pulpit and synod and text, although an occasional cleric himself was tempted to have his fate read by a Gypsy.

CIBOUR   A fishing village in the lower Pyrenees. It has become a more or less permanent settlement of Gypsies. There are such settlements exclusively inhabited by Gypsies in Andalusia, in Tangier, and in some Balkan countries.

CIGANY   A village in Hungary that, as early as the fourteenth century, was already a Gypsy settlement. Other similar Gypsy encampments existed in Hungary at this period. Similar quarters, reserved exclusively for the Gypsies, exist in Andalusia, in Transylvania and other Balkan regions, in Switzerland, in England and Scotland.

CIRCUMCISION   In the Middle East Gypsy children are circumcized in accordance with Moslem practice.
In their wanderings the Gypsies have frequently adopted the religious practices of the country of sojourn.

CIVILIZED GYPSY   Walter Simson the gypsiolgoist asked: Who ever heard of a civilized Gypsy, before Mr. Borrow mentioned those having attained to such an eminent position in society at Moscow? Are there none such elsewhere than in Moscow? There are many in Scotland. It is this unfortunate prejudice against the name that forces all our Gypsies, the moment they leave the tent, to hide from the public their being Gypsies. For they are morbidly sensitive of the odium which attaches to the name and race being applied to them.

CLASSIFICATION OF EGYPTIAN GYPSIES   There are three kinds of Gypsies in Egypt, — the Rhafarin, the Helebis, and the Nauar. They have secret jargons among themselves; but as I ascertained subsequently from specimens given by Captain Newbold and Sweetzen, as quoted by Pott, their language is made up of Arabic 'back-slang', Turkish and Greek, with a very little Romany, — so little that it is not wonderful that I could not converse with them in it. The Syrian Gypsies, or Nuri, who are seen with bears and monkeys in Cairo, are strangers in the land. With them a conversation is not difficult. It is remarkable that while English, German, and Turkish or Syrian Gypsy look so different and difficult as printed in books, it is on the whole an easy matter to get on with them in conversation. The roots being the same, a little management soon supplies the rest.

CLASSIFICATION OF GYPSIES Ethnically, there are three groups of Gypsies:
  (a) Romanies or full-blooded Gypsies
  (b) half-bloods
  (c) those of mixed blood

CLEANLINESS To counteract the general popular impression that the Gypsies are not a clean people, Gypsy Smith the evangelist declared that a Gypsy who did not keep his person or belongings clean was *chickly,* that is, dirty. The Gypsies, he added, had towels for washing themselves. Before eating any meal, they washed their hands. They were scrupulous about a sick person's spoon or plate or basin. No one in the tent used the utensils except the sick member. When he recovered or died, these utensils were destroyed.

CLIENTS Gypsy fortune-tellers have had as clients many distinguished and notable persons. In Russia, the Empress Ekatarina had her own fortune-telling Gypsy. Christina, the Regent of Spain, was often advised by a Gypsy. George IV, as Regent, consulted the fortune-tellers.

CLOTHING TABUS Many tabus, relating to the person, domestic routine and speech, condition the lives of the Gypsies. In Germany and Hungary in particular there was the prohibition that women's clothing must not be washed together with the men's. In this respect, women's clothing was *mochardi,* that is, defiled, unclean. When a recognized tabu was dishonored, punishment followed.

COBHAM FAIR One of the numerous popular fairs that take place in various parts of England. In the 80's Charles Leland the gypsiologist visited Cobham Fair and wrote a lively description of the scene and its Gypsy participants.

COCONUT In England Gypsies assert that a coconut, given as a gift, brings good luck. In other instance they use charms and amulets for the same purpose.

COHALYI This Gypsy expression, which is used in Hungary, signifies witch-wives or "wise women."
Gypsy mythology is full of legends involving witchcraft and its evil machinations.

COLLEGE OF SORCERY There was a legend regarding a College of Sorcery in Salamanca, according to the Rumanian Gypsies. This college was said to be located far away, deep in the mountains, where the secrets of nature the language of animals, and all magic spells were taught by the devil in person. Only ten scholars were admitted at a time, and when the course had been completed, nine students were dismissed to their homes, but the tenth was detained by the professor in payment. Henceforth, mounted on a dragon, he became the devil's aide-de-camp, and assisted him in preparing thunderbolts and in managing storms and tempests. A small lake, immeasurably deep, high up in the mountains, south of Hermanstadt, was supposed to be the cauldron in which the dragon lay sleeping and where the thunder was brewed.

COLLEGE OF MONS This college, established in 1748 by the Empress Maria Theresa of Austria, granted the Gypsies the privilege of washing for gold in the rivers. This occupation lasted an entire summer.

COLONIES In Germany, as in Spain and Rumania and Transylvania and Portugal, special quarters were established for Gypsies in the eighteenth century. In Spain such exclusively Gypsy quarters were called Gitanerías. In Bulgaria, they are known as Tisanovo. In Hungary, the Gypsy colonies are Cyganyfalva.

COLOR The Gypsies are fond of gaudy, vivid colors. Yellow, red, and green are their favorites. These colors appear on neckerchiefs, on scarves, on the women's voluminous petticoats, on their wide skirts.

COMMENT ON GYPSIES Martín del Río, a Spanish demonographer who belongs in the sixteenth century, regarded the life which the Spanish Gypsies led as one above all others calculated to afford them knowledge of every town in Spain.

They were continually at variance with justice. They were frequently obliged to seek shelter in the inmost recesses of the hills. And when their thievish pursuits led them to the cities, they naturally made themselves acquainted with the names of the principal individuals, in the hope of plundering them.

COMMUNICATION In their movements from one area to another, from one camping site to a more favorable location, the Gypsies are extremely helpful to their tribal members who are expected to advance along the same trail. Hence they are accustomed to leave identifying signs. These signs, in their tangible forms, give tribal and family information, or warnings, or directions. If there has been a wedding, branches of fir are strewn along the roadside. Other Gypsies will readily interpret the symbolic meaning. A birch twig, on the other hand, is a warning to be circumspect. Such signs are in use among all Gypsy tribes, in whatever country they may travel. They constitute, in place of writing, the lingua franca of the Gypsy people. If, in passing a farmhouse, there is a possibility of securing chickens furtively, white feathers lie on the roadside. Bits of rags, pieces of tin, bones, all have their esoteric but readily understood significance, although to the casual passer-by they may appear trivial and meaningless.

COMPARISON OF GYPSIES H. A. Munro Butler Johnstone, author of *A Trip up the Volga to the Fair of Nijni Novgorod,* published in 1875, compares two types of Gypsies: Johnstone speaks with great contempt of these musical Romanys, their girls attired in dresses by Worth, as compared with the free wild outlaws of the steppes, who, with dark, ineffable glances, meaning nothing more than a wild-cat's, steal poultry, and who, wrapped in dirty sheep-skins, proudly call themselves *Mi dvorane polaivii.* Lords of the Waste. The Gypsies of Moscow, to Johnstone, seemed to be a kind of second-rate Romanys or Gypsies, Gypsified for exhibition. — *Charles Leland*

COMPLAINTS In the Middle Ages, when the Gypsies infiltrated into Europe and spread from Hungary to Provence to Spain, the ecclesiastical authorities frequently complained of the heretical views of the roving people, of their allegedly occult practices, and of their dubious personal habits.

COMPLEXION On account of their swarthy skin, the Gypsies in Britain were called Blacks in the eighteenth century.

The Gypsy calls himself *Calo,* which means black in Romany. In Sweden, Gypsies are known as 'Black Tartars.' In Germany they were often termed Negroes.

COMPOSERS The Gypsies have been not only talented musicians, but composers as well, notably in the Balkans. Bihari was one of the most eminent. Along with him may be classed the famous eighteenth century woman, the violinist Czinka Panna, Czermak, Reményi, and Danko.

COMPOSITION OF GYPSY LANGUAGE The Gypsy language may consist of some 3000 words, the greater part of which are decidedly of Indian origin, being connected with the Sanskrit or some other Indian dialect. The rest consist of words picked up by the Gypsies from various languages in their wanderings from the East.

COMPULSORY EDUCATION In Rumania the Gypsies are compelled to send their children to the state schools.
Many European countries are now taking active measures to ensure proper educational facilities for Gypsy children and Gypsy youth as well.

COMPULSORY PROSTITUTION Prostitution among Gypsy girls and women is practically unknown. But during the period of serfdom, which lasted into the nineteenth century, the Gypsies were bound to an overlord, a voivode, in the Balkans. The voivode usually took advantage of the *ius primae noctis.*

CONCEPT OF GYPSY LIFE A historian of the Gypsies analyzed the essential character of Gypsy life:
Take a Gypsy in his original state, and we can find nothing really vulgar about him. What is popularly understood to be Gypsy life may be considered low

life, by people who do not overmuch discriminate in such matters; but view it after its kind, and it is not really low. For a Gypsy is naturally polite and well mannered. He does not consider himself as belonging to the same race as the native, and would rather be judged by a different standard. The life which he leads is not that of the lowest class of the country in which he dwells, but the primitive, original state of a people of great antiquity, proscribed by law and society; himself an enemy of, and an enemy to, all around him; with the population so prejudiced against him, that attempts to change his condition, consistently with his feelings as a man, are frequently rendered in vain.

CONCLUSIONS REGARDING GYPSIES Wherever there are Gypsies, Borrow believed, their manners and customs are virtually the same, though modified by circumstances. The language they speak among themselves is in all countries one and the same, but subjected to modification. Their countenances exhibit a decided family resemblance, but they are darker or fairer according to the temperature of the climate.

CONCUBINAGE A Gypsy view of this custom: Or Persibararse Sin Choro

Gajeres sin corbó soscabar yes manu persibaraó, per sos saro se linbidian odoros y beslli, y per esegritón apucelan on sardañá de saros los Benjes, techescándo grejos y olajais — de sustiri sos lo resaronomó niquilla murmo; y andial lo fendi sos terelamos de querar sin techescarle yes sulibári á or Jeli, y ne panchabar on caute manusardí, persos trutan á yesque lilí.

The Evils of Concubinage.

It is always a strange thing for a man to live in concubinage, because all turns to jealousy and quarreling oaths and curses, so that what is cheap turns out dear. So the best we can do is to cast a bridle on love and trust to no woman, for they make a man mad.

CONDEMNATION In Hungary, according to George Borrow, both sexes among the Gypsies are thieves of the first water. They proceed on foreign excursions with a view to plunder, and continue thus for three or four years. Then they return, rich with spoil, to their previous settlements.

CONDITION OF HUNGARIAN GYPSIES The Gypsy, wherever you find him, is an incomprehensible being, but nowhere more than in Hungary, where, in the midst of slavery, he is free, though apparently one step lower than the lowest slave. The habits of the Hungarian Gypsies are abominable. Their hovels appear sinks of the vilest poverty and filth. Their dress is at best rags, their food frequently the vilest carrion, and, occasionally, if report be true, still worse. Thus they live in filth, in rags, in nakedness, and in merriness of heart, for nowhere is there more of song and dance than in an Hungarian Gypsy village. They are very fond of music, and some of them are heard to touch the violin in a manner wild, but of peculiar excellence. Parties of them have been known to exhibit even at Paris.

CONDITIONS IN GERMANY A traveler and eye-witness described the conditions of the Gypsies in Germany early in the nineteenth century:

I became acquainted with the life and manners of this miserable community of Gypsies when I resolved to visit them and to go first to Friedrichslohra. Grief and horror seized me when I beheld their wretched and neglected condition, of which I heard more in the neighboring villages. They live by begging, stealing, and fortune-telling. The Prussian government has issued very severe edicts against them, but the officers are afraid to put them in force, as the Gypsies are very revengeful. They get their children baptized, hoping to obtain presents: this they do in many parishes. In winter they crowd into small houses. Now and then they sally forth from their dens to procure food by begging, stealing, and poaching. In spring, they spread into the forests, keeping the country in a state of alarm. I found the forest people eating a hog which had died of disease. They devour all the dead cattle they can find. Among themselves they speak a peculiar language. I found only one man who could read.

CONDUCT OF GERMAN GYPSIES Sir Walter Scott, in 1818, published an abridged translation of a German work edited by Dr. John Benjamin Wiessenburch. The title of the book is Circumstantial Account of the Famous Egyptian Band of Thieves, and Robbers, and Murderers, whose leaders were executed at Giessen by Cord, and Sword, and Wheel, on the 14th and 15th November, 1726. Scott describes the general popular view of the Gypsies as disposed to idleness, to theft, to polygamy or rather promiscuous license, and to the practice of child-stealing. Their resources, however, are scanty, and they suffer extremities of hunger and cold.
Scott concludes:

Evidence of the guilt of the other prisoners was also obtained from their confessions, with or without torture, and from the testimony of witnesses examined by the fiscal. Sentence was finally passed on them, condemning four Gypsies to be broken on the wheel, nine others to be hanged, and thirteen, of whom the greater part were women, to be beheaded. They underwent their doom with great firmness.

CONNUBIAL ATTACHMENT The mutual attachment between husband and wife is so deep and sincere that instances of infidelity, on either side, occur very seldom. The Gypsy women, in their encampments, are known to avoid strictly all obscene and lewd conversation.

CONSCRIPTION In the eighteenth century Maria Theresa, Queen of Hungary and Bohemia, ruled that Gypsies must become regular members of society, undergo military service, and send their children to school.

CONTEMPORARY GYPSIES In contemporary Hungary the Gypsies are not considered a national minority nor have they special schools of their own. They are absorbed into the State. Recently there has been formed a Cultural Association of Hungarian Gypsies.

CONTEMPT FOR THE DEAD At a race-course in England an old Gypsy, who had died, lay on the bare ground, with only an old piece of blanket over him. In such detestation were the meanness and wretchedness of his family held that not one of the relatives would attend the funeral. The corpse itself was left in the open air, exposed to swarms of flies until it was interred. A little fence, covered with boughs, was put around the spot where the Gypsy was buried, but the relatives burned the fence as fuel for their fires.

CONTEMPTUOUS NAMES Just as the Gypsies have at various periods in their wanderings been termed vagabonds, idlers, parasites and even more offensively, so they in turn have identifying and uncomplimentary names for the natives of the countries of their sojourn. The Russians are called Big Heads. Rumanians and Bulgarians are designated as *that one.* So the Romans referred to Cleopatra as *illa femina,* that woman.

CONTINENTAL GYPSIES Beginning with the fifteenth century, the history of the Gypsies in Europe follows an abundantly documented sequence of official records and city archives, royal decrees and laws, chronicles of various kind. Such matter is extant in virtually every country where the Gypsies pitched their tents. And that history is highly dramatic, shot through with dolorous episodes, with harsh rejection and banishment, with torture and massacre: pervaded by the constant dread of instant expulsions, of disastrous penalties imposed on them. Yet their resiiience, throughout all these centuries of perplexities and hardships, of poverty and ostracism, survived amazingly. Their ethnic unity, too, remained unimpaired. And at the present time they still persist, retaining the essential characteristics of their ways, making only superficial or necessitated concessions to the advancing changes of society.

The records range over the entire continent, from Germany to Spain, from Sweden to England, from Hungary to Scotland, to Rumania and France, to Italy and Belgium. In a *History of the Gypsies,* by Walter Simson, published in 1865, the author has this to say of the continental Gypsies:

> It appears that none of these wanderers, the Gypsies, had been seen in Christendom before the year 1400 But in the beginning of the fifteenth century this people first attracted notice, and, within a few years after arrival, had spread themselves over the whole continent. The earliest mention which is made of them, was in the years 1414 and 1417, when they were observed in Germany. In 1418 they were found in Switzerland: in 1422, in Italy; in 1427, they are mentioned as being in the neighborhood of Paris; and about the same time in Spain.
>
> They seem to have received various appellatıons. In France, they were called *Bohemians* in Holland,

Heydens — heathens; in some parts of Germany and in Sweden and Denmark they were thought to be Tartars; but over Germany in general, they were called *Zigeuners*, a word which means wanderers up and down. In Portugal they received the name of *Siganos*; in Spain, *Gitanos;* and in Italy, *Cingari.* They were also called in Italy, Hungary, and Germany *Tzinganys;* and in Transylvania, *Cyganis.* Among the Turks and other Eastern nations they were denominated *Tschingenes.* But the Moors and Arabs applied to them perhaps the most just appellation of any — *Charami,* robbers.

CONTRIBUTIONS OF GYPSIES Gypsies, declared Charles G. Leland, the folklorist and gypsiologist, have done more than any race or class on the face of the earth to disseminate among the multitude a belief in fortune-telling, magical or sympathetic cures, amulets and such small sorceries as now find a place in folklore.

CONVEYANCE The wandering Gypsy, in Hungary and Transylvania, endeavored to procure a horse. In Turkey, an ass served to carry his wife, a couple of children, and his tent.

When he reached a place he liked, near a village or city, he unpacked, pitched his tent, tied his animal to a stake to graze, and remained some weeks there. Or if he did not find his station convenient, he broke up in a day or two, loaded his beast, and looked out for a more agreeable situation, near some other town. It was not always in his power to determine the length of his stay in any one place. For the natives were apt to trouble him, on account of his making free with poultry and produce.

CONVERSATION ABOUT A WITCH George Borrow, the

gypsiologist, had a conversation with Antonio, a Spanish Gypsy:

Borrow: That Gypsy grandmother has all the appearance of a sorceress.

Antonio: All the appearance of one! Is she not really one? She knows more crabbed things and crabbed words than all the people betwixt here and Catalonia. She has been amongst all the wild Moors, and can make more drows, poisons, and philtres than any one alive. She once made a kind of paste, and persuaded me to taste, and shortly after I had done so my soul departed from my body, and wandered through horrid forests and mountains, amidst monsters and demons, during one entire night.

COPPERSMITHS Late in the nineteenth century various Gypsy tribal units moved into England, where they have since plied their trade as coppersmiths. Working with metals has for centuries been a Gypsy occupation throughout their European wanderings.

CORFU In medieval records the Gypsies were described as *homines vaginiti,* wanderers. They were received as vassals in Corfu when they came from the Greek mainland, in the later decades of the fourteenth century. These Gypsies, successively under feudal lordship, were in the service of Theodorus Kavasilas, Nicolo di Donato of Altavilla, and Bernard de Saint Maurice. They remained vassals until the beginning of this century, when feudal laws were abolished.

CORONATION In 1937 Marshal Pilsudski of Poland crowned James Kwieck as a Gypsy king. Among the Gypsies, the term King or Queen has frequently been used: but it is merely an honorific.

COSMIC ORDER   Gypsies accept all cosmic phenomena, political upheavals, cataclysms, earthquakes, disease and want as part of the natural order of things, as universal facts that cannot be changed, that are beyond human control, and that therefore are to be regarded as the normal cyclic sequence of human affairs. Relationships with each other, with the society of which they are usually far from being an integral component, and their position and destiny in the world itself are all fixed and determined. Hence the absence among the Gypsies of speculations and probings into the ultimate meaning of life itself. Life is their total absorption in their immediate circumstances.

COSTUME   There is no distinctive Gypsy costume. As a rule the Gypsies use the costumes and dress of their adopted settlement. But their dress is old and worn. It consists of various bits and colorful pieces, all well-worn. Discarded clothes are often presented to them. They may go, in some countries, barefooted, or wear boots or sandals in accordance with native custom. In some countries they adopt the outward appearance of Greeks, or Rumanians, or Spaniards.

COUNTERFEITING   An audacious incident in counterfeiting is recorded by a nineteenth century gypsiologist:

As an honest but simple countryman was journeying along the public road, a traveling Tinkler chanced to come up to him. After conversing for some time, the courteous Gypsy, on arriving at a public-house, invited him to step in. They entered the house, and no sooner had they finished one half mutchken than the Gypsy called for another. But when the reckoning came, the countryman was surprised when the Gypsy declared that he had not a coin in his possession. The countryman also had not a farthing in his pockets. How they were to manage puzzled him not a little. Meanwhile the Gypsy, with his eyes rolling about in every direction, espied a powter basin. This was all he required. Bolting the door of the room, he opened his bag and, taking out a pair of large shears, cut a piece from the side of the basin and, putting it into his crucible on the fire, in no time, with his coining instruments, threw off several half-crowns, resembling good sterling money. The countryman was now terrified of being locked up with a man engaged in coining base money in the very room in which he stood. Every moment he expected someone to burst the door open. His companion, however, was not in the least disturbed, but deliberately finished his coins, and cutting the remainder of the basin to pieces packed it into his wallet. Unlocking the door of the room, he rang the bell, and tendered one of his half-crowns to his host, to pay his score, which was accepted without suspicion.

The Gypsy then offered his companion part of his remaining coins, but the countryman was only too glad to rid himself of so dangerous an acquaintance. The Gypsy, on his part, marched off with his spirits elevated, with liquor, and his pockets replenished with money, smiling at the simplicity and terror of the countryman.

COUNT LADISLAS Sigismund, Emperor of Hungary, gave Count Ladislas, the *voivode* or chief of the Gypsies, jurisdiction over Gypsies' disputes, in the capacity of a judge imposing sentence or granting an acquittal. The royal concession was issued in 1423.

COUPLETS Gitáno couplets resemble metrically the popular songs of the Spaniards. The subjects usually deal with Gypsy life, but occasionally express abuse of the Spaniards or the busné, the non-Gypsies.

COURLAND GYPSY CHIEFS The eighteenth century noted gypsiologist Grellman writes of the Courland Gypsy tribal leaders:

> The Voivode or leader of the Gypsies in Courland is distinguished from the principals of the hordes in other countries, being not only much respected by his own people, but even by the Courland nobility. He is esteemed a man of high rank, and is frequently to be met with at entertainments, and card parties, in the first families, where he is always a welcome guest. His dress is uncommonly rich, in comparison with others of his tribe; generally silk in summer, and constantly velvet in winter.

COURT GYPSIES In Wallachia and Moldavia, in the Balkans when the Gypsies were formerly in servitude, many Gypsies were employed by the owners of vast estates in domestic service, as masons and bakers, carpenters, blacksmiths, coachmen.

COWPER, WILLIAM (1731-1800) Famous English poet whose brother John had a strange experience with a Gypsy:

> In Wright's *Life of William Cowper* will be found the following tale of Cowper's brother John and a Gypsy. When he was a schoolboy, apparently between the years 1741 and 1749, John Cowper and a schoolfellow one day had the curiosity to inquire about their fortunes from a travelling gipsy tinker, or pedlar, who came to beg at the school, in an old soldier's red coat. The gipsy predicted to John Cowper "that he would remain a short time at Felstead, and would, after leaving it, be sent to a larger school; that he would go to the University, and, before he left it, would form an attachment strong enough to give him much disappoint-

ment, as it would not be mutual; that he would not marry before he was thirty; but after that age his fate became obscure, and the lines of his hand showed no more prognostics of futurity." These predictions were fulfilled, as indeed was not very improbable, considering the obviousness of most of them. But John took the prophecy seriously: and, when at Cambridge about 1796, 'The following incident occurred: John Cowper was walking and talking with him (the same friend) in one of the college gardens near a gate, when he suddenly interrupted the conversation and exclaimed, "Did you see that man pass?" The friend, who had observed nothing, asked what man he meant. John Cowper replied, "The very man you and I met at Felstead, and in a soldier's jacket — I saw him pass the gate!" They both ran to it and into the public road, but saw no such person. Cowper said. "It is a warning —you know he could predict nothing of me after my thirtieth year." As the writer who supplied Southey with these facts observes, the dejection at various times of John Cowper, and the fancied apparition of the gipsy pedlar, "were but too surely indications of the same constitutional malady which so often embittered the existence of his brother."

John Cowper was born in 1737 and he died in 1770.

CRAMP According to a Gypsy superstition, if you set your boots crosswise before going to bed, you will ward off cramp in the legs.

There are many such superstitions in Gypsy traditions and folklore.

CREATION OF MANKIND In Gypsy mythology, God baked the first men and women in an oven. Some, however, were kept too long in the oven and they turned out dark:

the black race. The second time God opened the oven door too soon and the baking was not quite ready: the white race. The third time God produced images baked properly to the right color: the Indians, ancestors of the Gypsies.

CREED Or Credo. Translated by the Gypsies of Cordova. Pachabeló en Un-debel batu tosaro-baro, que ha querdi el char y la chiqué, y en Un-debel chinoró su unico chaboró eraño de de amangue, que chaló en el trupo de la Majari por el Duquende Majaró, y abió del veo de la Majari; guilló curádo debájo de la sila de Pontio Piláto el chinobaró; guilló mulo y garabado; se chaló a las jacháris; al trin chibé se ha sicobádo de los mulés al char; sinéla bejádo a las baste de Un-debél barreá; y de oté abiará á juzgar á los mulés y á los que no lo sinélan; pachabélo en el Majaró; la Cangri Majari barreá; el jalar de los Majaries; lo mecó de los grécos; la resureccion de la maas, y la ochi que no maréla.
The Creed

I believe in God the Father all-great, who has made the heaven and the earth; and in the God the young, his only Son, the Lord of us, who went into the body of the blessed maid by the Holy Spirit and came out of the womb of the blessed; he was tormented beneath the power of Pontius Pilate, the great Alguazil; was dead and buried; he went down to the fires; on the third day he raised himself from the dead unto the heaven; he is seated at the major hand of God, and from thence he shall come to judge the dead and those who are not dead. I believe in the blessed one; in the church holy and great; the banquet of the saints; the remission of sins; the resurrection of the flesh, and the life which does not die.

CRETAN GYPSIES It it on record that Gypsies were living in caves as troglodytes in Crete, in the fourteenth century.

CRETE Gypsies appeared on the Greek island of Crete in 1422, according to a historical record. They had advanced eastward from India along the Mediterranean littoral. They were known as Ragari, Muri.

CRIMES It is said that in 1618, more than 800 Gitános scoured the country between Castile and Aragon, committing the most enormous crimes.

CRISTO-DORDI The name of a Spanish Gypsy tribe who have an indurated belief in the actuality of vampire women. Vampires play a dominant part in Gypsy folklore and mythology.

CRUCIFIXION There is a legend that the Gypsies are the descendants of the smiths who made the nails for the Crucifixion. Hence they were condemned to be perpetual wanderers over the face of the earth.

CUBA In Cuba, in the nineteenth century, there were many Gypsies, serving as soldiers, or dealers in mules and red pepper, jobbers, musicians.

CURING CATTLE When the tent-Gypsies, finding that their cattle are sick, do not know the nature of the disease, they take two birds — if possible quails, called by them berecto or füryo — one of which is killed, but the other, sprinkled with its blood, is allowed to fly away.

CURSED Throughout the Middle Ages there was a widespread belief, in every European country, that at the time of the Crucifixion certain smiths supplied the bronze nails for the cross. The descendants of these smiths were the wandering, homeless Gypsies, doomed to roam the earth.

CUZA, ALEXANDER JOHN (1820-1873) Prince Cuza, the first prince of both Moldavia and Wallachia. He himself was of Gypsy origin.

Detail from "Sevilla Gipsy"
painting by Michael Viladnich

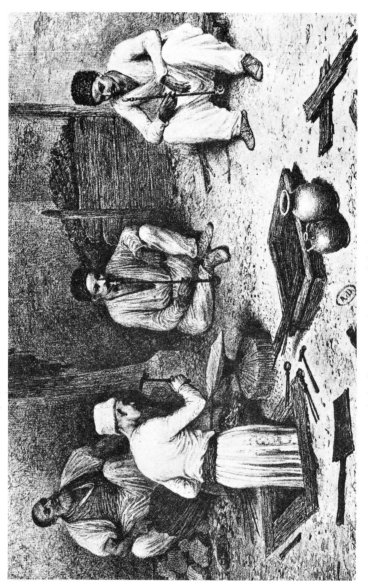

Turkish Gypsies, 19th Century

D

DAMO AND YEHWAH These two names, in Gypsy mythology, correspond to the Biblical Adam and Eve. The stars are their offspring.

Gypsy legends and folklore are full of such fantasies, one of which involves the creation of the world.

DANCE HALLS In Southampton, England, in the mid-nineteenth century, there were numerous dance halls. Those Gypsies who were musicians and played the fiddle or another instrument often appeared in such places. There they 'mingled with the most degraded outcasts of society and with their tambourine and violin excited the unholy dance technically called the two penny hop.'

DANCING One of the most popular activities of the Gypsies, in every period and in most European countries, was the dance. The Gypsies danced in the open, in villages, in public squares, in inns. They danced before royalty at the court of James V of Scotland, in Holyrood Palace, in Edinburgh.

In France, they danced before the court, in the reign of Henry IV and of Louis XIII.

When they danced before the nobility, the latter readily participated. In Molière's play *Le Mariage Forcé,* there is Gypsy dancing: also in *Le Malade Imaginaire.* Royal ballets, in the reign of Louis XIV, included such dances.

In Cervantes' *La Gitanilla*, Preciosa the Gypsy girl is an excellent dancer.

In Turkey, in the seventeenth century, the Gypsies were noted for their dancing ability.

DANES' DIKE   There was a large colony of Gypsies, in the 1860's, encamped in the Danes' Dike, in Yorkshire, along the heights overlooking the North Sea.

A certain Leeds Bookman,' as he got to be known, became familiar with 'these wild dwellers out of doors.' He pitched his tent among them and remained with the Gypsies for some two years. Thus he got a good opportunity of gaining a favorable insight into Gypsy life and character.

DANISH ARMY   When the Danish kings, in the eighteenth century, required men for their armies, they accepted the Gypsies and consequently their families too were accepted in the kingdom.

DANISH CODE   The Gypsies who settled in Denmark were not permitted to remain unmolested. The Danish laws issued in the sixteenth century specified, with regard to the infiltration of the Gypsies into Denmark:

The Tartar Gypsies, who wander about everywhere, doing great damage to the people, by their lies, thefts and witchcraft, shall be taken into custody by every magistrate.

DAR-BUSHI-FAL   This is a Moorish expression signifying *Those who prophecy or tell fortunes.* The term is used by the Moors of Barbary of a sect of men and women who are great wanderers, but have also their fixed dwellings or villages, and such a place is called Char Seharra, or Witch-Hamlet. The manner of life of this people, in every respect, resembles that of the Gypsies of other countries. They are wanderers during the greater part of the year and subsist principally by pilfering and fortune-telling. They deal much in mules and donkeys, and it is believed in Barbary that they can change the color of any animal by means by sorcery and to disguise the creature as to sell it to his very propietor, without fear of recognition. This latter trait is quite characteristic of the Gypsy race, by whom the same thing is practiced in most parts of the world. But the Moors assert that the children of the Dar-bushi-fal can not only change the color of a horse or a mule, but likewise a human being, in one night, transforming a white person into a black, after which they sell him for a slave. On this account the superstitious Moors regard them with the utmost dread, and in general prefer passing the night in the open fields to sleeping in their hamlets. They are said to possess a particular language which is neither Shilhah nor Arabic, and which none but themselves understand. It would appear that the children of the Dar-bushi-fal are legitimate Gypsies, descendants of those who passed over to Barbary from Spain.

If the legitimate Gypsies really exist in Barbary, they are the men and women of the Dar-bushi-fal.

DARDISTAN This territory, in Western India, is by some gypsiologists assumed to be the original home of the Gypsies.

DAUGHTER OF THE REGIMENT In the seventeenth and eighteenth centuries, when Gypsies were given the offer of enlistment in the national forces of France, Spain, Portugal, and other countries, the women folk, wives or daughters, followed the regiment, on the march or in quarters.

DAY OF THE SERPENT Among the Gypsies there is an annual Day of the Serpent. The serpent is a diabolic creature, and on this Day an attempt is made to kill serpents in order to ensure good luck for the coming year.

DEATH On the approaching death of a Gypsy, the dying person is taken outside into the open, as it is a tradition to avoid death within the enclosed space of a caravan or tent.

DEBAUCHERY OF WITCHES In Gypsy folklore the witches meet in riotous dancing and debauchery. Their type of erotic dancing, according to the gypsiologist Leland, stems from the Orient, and even from antiquity.
Among the English Gypsies, there is a deep belief that witches are some kind of specially gifted sorceresses or magicians. In a general sense, the witch, in Gypsy tradition, is a haunting terror of the night.

DEBRECEN Although this Hungarian town is almost exclusively Magyar in composition and inhabitants, the Hungarian Gypsies have a special quarter for themselves. This has been the case particularly in Spain, where several cities, Seville and Granada among them, have assigned areas exclusively for Gypsy settlements.

DEBTS The Gypsies are extremely scrupulous and punctual in paying debts. If a debt is owed to a Gypsy, a time and place are arranged by the Gypsy. If the debtor disappoints him, he is by Gypsy law or *kriss* required to pay double the amount, or to give some personal service.

DECLINE OF GYPSIES George Borrow who lived among the Gypsies and wrote about them with such knowledge and affection, declared that the Gypsies were, as a people, dying out.

DE DEVELESKI A Gypsy expression meaning The Divine Mother. The Divine Mother signifies the earth, or the universe.
Gypsy mythology includes many imaginative concepts relating to cosmic phenomena and their associations with mankind.

DEFAMATION In a book entitled *Gypsy Life,* published in London in 1880, the Gypsies are represented, falsely, according to the gypsiologist Francis Hindes Groome, as 'firing ricks, farming gorgios' babies, and kicking their own babies to death; in which 'gutter-scum Gypsies, ditchbank sculks, agents of hell' are among the most kindly epithets.

DEFENSE OF FORTUNE-TELLING The Gypsy women who make an occupational practice of telling the fortune of a gorgio, a non-Gypsy, do not conceive their performance as harmful or deceitful or essentially unlawful. Their predictions are generally favorable: long life, a happy marriage, misadventures and disappointments, that would however be overcome. The predictions, in a wide sense, range over the human experience in which good and evil, malefic conditions and auspicious occasions alternate through the course of a person's life. What the Gypsy fortune-teller actually forecasts, then, is a blueprint of any human life, to be filled in specifically by the person himself.

DEFIANT GYPSIES The Gitános in Spain not infrequently made their appearance in considerable numbers, so as to be able to bid defiance to any force which could be assembled against them on a sudden. Whole districts thus became a prey to them, and were plundered and devastated.

It is said that, in the year 1618, more than eight hundred of these wretches scoured the country between Castile and Aragon, committing the most enormous crimes. The royal council despatched regular troops against them, who experienced some difficulty in dispersing them.

DEGRADATION   The craft of the smith, which was practiced for centuries by the Gypsies, was held degrading for the inhabitants among whom they settled. In Montenegro, the government established in 1872 an arsenal at Reika, but no native Montenegran could be found to fill the posts, although these were well-paid. Gypsies had to be accepted.

DEKKER, THOMAS (c.1572-c.1632)   In his Miscellany entitled *Lanthorne and Candlelight,* the English dramatist wrote of the Gypsies in a violently condemnatory tone. He excoriated their vices, calling them, as the Elizabethan expression ran, 'Moon Men'. He gave, however, precise details about their *patteran,* their clothes, and their migratory ways.

DEL RIO, MARTIN   A sixteenth century Spanish demonographer. He considered that the Spanish Gypsies had during their migrations forgotten their original language and had a language of their own, called *Zirigenca* or *Gigonza.*

DEMITRI-TAIKON, JOHAN (1879-1950)   A noted Swedish Gypsy. He created poetic themes in a Gypsy background.

DEMONIAC WORLD   To the Gypsies, the invisible world is full of agents, forces, demons, elementals whose purpose is to harass human beings. They haunt the winds and storms, the rocks and the lonely caverns.

DEMONS AND REMEDIES To the Gypsy mind, it is the demons, the *mulos,* the malefic spirits of the dead, that bring trouble and ill-health and sickness upon the living survivors. When sickness does occur, the treatment is generally confined within the family or tribe. Doctors are rarely summoned. Old traditional remedies are used by the wise old women of the tribe, the repositories of Gypsy healing lore. The remedies include herbal concoctions, old family recipes that involve unpleasant and repulsive ingredients such as snake fat, intestines of animals, pulverized insects. In addition, spells and incantations are in common use, together with charms and periapts and fantastic amulets.

DEPORTATION In the seventeenth century, in Edinburgh, Scotland, a number of Gypsies were deported to Barbados and Jamaica. Early in the eighteenth century, again, several Gypsies were banished to Virginia. From the Iberian peninsula Gypsies were sent to Africa and South America. England sent them to Australia.

DESCENT FROM ADAM According to a Gypsy legend, the Gypsies were regarded by themselves as descendants of Adam and a wife that he had before Eve.
Gypsy folklore comprises many similar imaginative beliefs and theories and fancies.

DESCRIPTIVE TOWNS In their wandering up and down the British Isles, the Gypsies devised descriptive and readily identifiable names for many countries and towns. These names stressed the characteristic features of places, from a Romany viewpoint. Thus Birmingham

was The Black Town, on account of its smoky atmosphere. Yarmouth of course was the Fishy Town. Nottingham was known as Boxers' Town. Lancashire was appropriately termed The Witches' County. Ely, with its cathedral, was designed as The Clergyman's Town, and similarly Canterbury became My God's Town. Newcastle was neatly termed Coal Town, while the ominous Botany Bay was The Transported Fellow's Country.
York is characteristically The Great Church Town.
London is merely Bori Gave, The Big Accumulation.
Kent is picturesquely Apple-tree Country.
Wales is Porrum - engresky tem, The Leak-eaters' Country. Porrum, it may be noted, is the Latin for leak.
Scotland, however, was known as the Lousy Fellows' Country: Juvlo-mengreskey ten.

DESIGNATION OF TRIBAL LEADERS Corresponding to the country of their sojourn, the names of the Gypsy tribal leaders often assumed the native designation. In most countries, they retained the honorific self-imposed titles of lord, knight, prince, count, duke, marquis, king. In the Balkans, they were usually termed *voivodes,* chiefs. In Wallachia, they were *cnez.* In the Ukraine, the term was ataman. In France they were frequently called captain.

DESIGNATIONS Wherever they put up their tents in their restless wanderings, the Gypsies were designed by the natives of each respective region. Thus in Iraq they are known as Luli. In Persia, they were termed Zangi. In Afghanistan, Kauli. The Greeks knew them as Katsiveloi, while Turks and Syrians called them Tzinganés. In Rumania their designation is Tigani: Zingari in Italy. In Greece they are also called Egiftos, and in Holland

Gyptenaers: the two latter terms being associated with their putative association with Egypt.

The terms Saracens and Moors have been applied indifferently to them. In English-speaking countries the common term is Gypsy. In Germany the Gypsies become Zigeuner: In French territory, Tziganes. In Portugal, Ciganos. In Spanish, Gitanos. In a generic sense, Gypsies are often designated as Bohemians. To a Gypsy, on the other hand, a non-Gpsy is a gorgio, or a gadjo, which means a boor or peasant.

DEXTERITY The Gypsies were generally praised for their dexterity and quickness in working with metals, despite the wretched tools they had to operate with. When any piece of work required much time to finish, they were apt to lose their patience, and in that case became indifferent whether it was well executed or not. They never submitted to labor so long as they had a dry crust or anything else to satisfy their hunger. They frequently received orders to fabricate different articles. But if not, no sooner were a few nails or some other trifles manufactured than man, woman, and children dislodged, to convey their merchandise from house to house for sale, in the neighboring villages. Their trade was carried on sometimes for ready money, sometimes by barter for eatables or other necessities.

DIALECTS In the eighteenth century H.M.G. Grellman, Charles Richardson and Marsden, philologists, made a collection of Romany words as spoken in Hungary, Germany, and England. From an examination of this comprehensive vocabulary they concluded that in general this vocabulary stemmed from Sanskrit or Hindustani.

DIASPORA The diaspora or dispersal of the Gypsies has been far-flung. They have touched all regions of the world, every continent: from Wales to the Argentine, from Sweden to Australia, from South Africa to Spain. They have no national land of their own, no homeland, but they make every country their own.

DICTIONARY DEFINITION An eighteenth century French dictionary defined the Bohemians, that is, the Gypsies, as itinerant vagabonds who live by theft and cunning and particularly by fortune-telling.

DIDDIKAI A Gypsy term that denotes a half-caste. F. E. Smith, the Earl of Birkenhead (1873-1930), the eminent English Lord Chancellor, was of Gypsy blood in respect of one parent.

DIFFERENCE OF HUNGARIAN GYPSY The Hungarian Gypsy differs from all his brethren in being more intensely Gypsy. He has deeper, wilder, and more original feeling in music, and he is more inspired with a love of travel. Numbers of Hungarian Romany chals — in which all Austrian Gypsies are included — travel annually all over Europe, but return as regularly to their own country. I have met with them exhibiting bears in Baden-Baden. These Ricinari, or bear-leaders, form, however a set within a set, and are in fact more nearly allied to the Gypsy bear-leaders of Turkey and Syria than to any other of their own people. They are wild and rude to a proverb, and generally speak a peculiar dialect of Romany, which is called the Bear-leaders' by philologists. I have also seen Syrian-Gypsy Ricinari in Cairo. — *Charles Leland*

DIFFERENCE IN FOOD HABITS Gypsies who are more associated with city people are remarkable in their diet.

Others, on the contrary, whose lives are spent in migration or in remote areas have their table furnished in a very irregular way. Sometimes they fast. The greatest luxury to them is a roast of cattle that have died of any distemper. It is immaterial whether it is the carrion of a sheep, hog, cow, or other beast, horse-flesh only excepted. They are so far from being disgusted with this kind of food that to eat their fill of such a meal is to them the height of the picture. When they are censured for their taste, they reply: The flesh of a beast which God kills must be better than that of one killed by the hand of man.

DIKLO A Gypsy term meaning a crimson kerchief. This is the identifying headgear of a married Gypsy woman.

DISEASE Infectious diseases are rare among the Gypsies, while their outdoor life immunizes them from many common complaints such as colds and influenza.
For other ailments, the Gypsies use a corpus of traditional remedies involving plants, roots, and various herbs.

DISEASE AMONG CATTLE Wherever they pitched their caravans or tents, the Gypsies were accused of being able to bring disease and death upon cattle by occult means. This practice was not unknown in England during the nineteenth century. The Gypsies poisoned cattle and pigs, and then, at their request, were given the dead animals gratuitously by the farmers. The poison, it was said, affected only one part of the animal, and the rest was used by the Gypsics for their food.

DISPERSAL OF GYPSIES Early in the nineteenth century a noted gypsiologist commented on the numerous hordes of Gypsies, widely dispersed over the face of the earth.

They wander about in Asia, he asserts: in the interior
of Africa they plunder the caravans of traders. They
have overrun most of the countries of Europe. America
seems to be the only part of the world where they are
not known.

DISRUPTION IN EUROPE   When the Gypsies first appeared
in Europe early in the fifteenth century, Europe itself
was in such a turmoil for almost a century that conditions
prevented any determined attention from being paid to
the inroads of the Gypsies. England was waging desperate wars against France. England itself was in the throes
cf a long and bloody civil conflict. There was a religious
and racial struggle between the Spaniards and their invaders. Eastern Europe was struggling with the Turks.
The Swiss were fighting for independence. In Central
Europe the religious wars of the Hussites created turbul-
ence and strife. The Byzantine Empire was approaching dis-
solution. Asiatic power was menacing the European continent. All these factors contributed to the almost unob-
served infiltration of the Gypsies into Europe.

DISTINCTIONS   There is a distinct difference between the
Spanish Gypsy and the other Gypsies of the European
continent. The Spanish Gypsies are *Gitanos*: the others
are the *Hungaros* the foreign Gypsies.

DISTRIBUTION OF GYPSIES   There are settlements of Gypsies in almost every country, but numerically there has
always been a difficulty in estimating the Gypsy population
in any specific area. However, it is largely accepted that
the greatest Gypsy population is to be found in the
Balkans. With respect to the northern countries of Europe,
England has the largest number of Gypsies.

102

DIVERSITY OF OCCUPATION Since Gypsies appeared on the European scene, their trades and occupations have increased in relation to the type of work required of them in each country. There are on record more than one hundred such occupations in which Gypsies now engage: from harpers to snake-charmers, from monkey-trainers to acrobats, from jockey to mole-catcher.

DIVINATION The Gypsies of Eastern Europe often tell fortunes or answer questions by taking a goblet or glass, tapping it, and pretending to hear a voice in the ring which speaks to them.
Divining by goblet is still a common Gypsy practice.

DIVINATORY APPARATUS In making predictions, the Gypsy fortune-tellers use, in addition to sets of cards called the Tarot, shells, bones, beans, a divining-drum, tea or coffee grounds.

DIVINING PRACTICES Through the ages there have been various methods of divination, of revealing the future, among the Persians, Babylonians, the Egyptians and the Romans. These methods have included star-gazing and augury, necromancy, oracular utterances and Sibylline prophecies. In modern divination, however, the techniques of the Gypsies have been the most popular and most regular practices. The Gypsies have for centuries preserved a unique reputation for prognostication, for reading both the past and the future, by means of dice and dominoes, by dreams and phrenological study, by tea leaves and crystal balls, all for the purpose of wresting the secret and traditional lore that has been transmitted to the Gypsies through countless generations.
And the practitioners *par excellence* have been the Gypsy women, the repositories of the ways of the seer, of the

103

mystic entrance into secretive arcana. Their primary technique is the use of cartomancy, reading the cards, in particular the pack of seventy-eight Tarot cards, the Major Arcana and the Minor Arcana.

DIVISIONS Largely, Gypsies may be classified into two major groups. One group consists of those who have ceased to wander and have settled into some form of permanence in a country. The other group is composed of those who, moving from one territory to another, never become integrated with the native population.

DIVORCE If a Gypsy woman is found to be unfaithful to her husband, a divorce takes this peculiar form. The Gypsies lay upon the head of a horse the sins of the offending woman and generally let her go free. The horse is the scapegoat. The horse is sacrificed in expiation of the woman's misdeeds. A chronicler relates:

> I have been informed of an instance of a Gypsy falling out with his wife, and, in the heat of his passion, shooting his own horse dead on the spot with his pistol, and forthwith performing the ceremony of divorce over the animal without allowing himself a moment's time for reflection. Some of the country people observed the scene and were horrified. It was considered by them as merely a mad frolic of an enraged Tinkler.
> This sacrifice of the horse is also observed by the Gypsies of the Russian Empire. In the year 1830 a Russian landowner stated to me that the Gypsies in the neighborhood of Moscow and on the Don sacrificed horses, and ate part of their flesh, in the performance of some very ancient ceremony of idolatry.

DOBRUJA This region of Dobruja, in Rumania, has Gypsy settlements. The Gypsies have traits that suggest remote

Tartar ancestors. Some of these Gypsies profess Islam, but without conviction. They assume the official religion of the country where they encamp.

DOGS' COLLOQUY This is the title of a story by Cervantes, The dog is the spokesman and interpreter in depicting the actual life of the Gypsies in Spain.

DOMESTIC ANIMALS To prevent domestic animals from straying or being stolen, Gypsies drive them in front of a fire. The animals are then struck with a blackened switch, while an apotropaic incantation is chanted.

DOMESTICATED GYPSIES With respect to the domesticated Gypsies who had a settled habitation and a regular trade of some sort, such as that of a smith, an early nineteenth century description is illuminating:

> Their habitations are conveniently divided into chambers, and are furnished with tables, benches, decent kitchen furniture, and other necessities. The few who farm, or breed cattle, have a plough and other implements of husbandry. The others have what is necessary for carrying on their trade, though even here you are not to expect superfluity. Habitation, clothes, everything indicate that their owners belong to the poor class. They are very partial to gold and silver plate, particularly silver cups. They lose no opportunity of acquiring something of the kind, and will even starve themselves to procure it. Though they seem far from anxious to heap up riches for their children, yet these frequently inherit a treasure of this sort and are obliged in their turn to preserve it as a sacred inheritance. The ordinary traveling Gypsies, when in possession of such a piece of plate, commonly bury it under

the hearth of their dwelling. This inclination to deprive themselves of necessities in order to possess a super-fluity is a curious custom, yet it appears to be ancient.

DOOM OF SERBIAN GYPSIES According to a legend prevalent among Serbian Gypsies, there is a belief that their ancestors stole the fourth nail of the Cross and as a punishment the Gypsies were doomed to wander for seven years, or seven centuries.

DOWRY Among Gypsies it is the custom for a payment for the bride to be made by the prospective groom. The greater the payment, the greater the prestige and value of the bride in the eyes of the groom. In France, la dot operates in the opposite sense.

DREAM BOOK The popular notion that the Gypsies were remarkably skilled in foretelling the future was so wide-spread that in the 80's many booklets and manuals were on the market, all dealing with the reputed Gypsy occult skills. One such manual was entitled The Gypsy Witches' Dream Book and Fortune Teller. The front cover, in red and black, depicted a traditional witch, wearing a high conical hat, crouching over a cauldron in front of her tent.

The contents included a list of dreams with their signi-fication: lucky numbers: the art of foretelling future events by cards, dice, dominoes, tea and coffee grounds. Also the art of portraying character through the phy-siognomy and the signification of moles. Prognostication of birth for each day in the week. An explanation of signs and auguries: and a list of lucky days, weeks, and months. The interpretation of dreams, according to the putative Gypsy tradition, absorbs a major part of the booklet. To dream of an accident portends great success. To dream of apes signifies that you have secret enemies. For a man to dream that he has a long beard denotes good fortune and a happy marriage. To dream of carpets denotes success in love. To dream that you are drinking coffee denotes want and disappointment in love. To dream that you are eating eggs is a good omen. To dream of Gypsies forbodes a short life. It is very fortunate to dream of milk. To dream of a polecat denotes an ill-natured wife or a brutal husband.

The child born on Sunday will obtain great riches. Those who are born on a Friday will die rich.

There are hints on reading your fate by cards. How to tell your fortune in the coffee grounds. How to analyze character from the moles on the face.

Many of the items in these books belong in the traditional body of Gypsy lore and mythology.

DREI ZIGEUNER *The Three Gypsies.* This is a poem by Nikolaus Lenau (1802-1850), Hungarian epic and lyric poet.

DRESS It is not often that one sees a Gypsy well dressed, even when he possesses expensive clothing. But their women are fond of finery. They like broad lace, with which they decorate their bonnets. They also appreciate large earrings, a variety of rings, and glaring colors.

A Gypsiologist relates an incident that illustrates the Gypsy love of finery. The time is the early nineteenth century, in England; a Gypsy woman obtained a large sum of money from three maiden ladies by pledging that the amount would be doubled by her secret art of conjuration. She then decamped to another district, where she bought a blood-horse, a black beaver hat, a new side-saddle and bridle, a silver-mounted whip, and then vanished in her finery to the fairs.

The dress of the Gypsies is highly distinctive, particularly in the case of the Spanish Gitános:

> The dress of the Gitáno varies with the country which he inhabits. Both in Rousillon and Catalonia his habiliments generally consist of jacket, waistcoat, pantaloons, and a red faja, which covers part of his waistcoat. On his feet he wears hempen sandals, with much ribbon tied round the leg as high as the calf. He has, moreover, either woolen or cotton stockings. Round his neck he wears a handkerchief, carelessly tied; and in the winter he uses a blanket or mantle, with sleeves, cast over the shoulder. His head is covered with the indispensable red cap, which appears to be the favorite ornament of many nations in the vicinity of the Mediterranean and Caspian Sea.
>
> The neck and the elbows of the jacket are adorned with pieces of blue and yellow cloth embroidered with silk, as well as the seams of the pantaloons. He wears, moreover, on the jacket or the waiscoat, various rows of silver buttons, small and round, sustained by rings or chains of the same metal. The old people, and those who by fortune or some other cause exercise, in appearance, a kind of authority over the rest, are almost always dressed in black or dark-blue velvet. Some of those who affect elegance amongst them keep for holidays a complete dress of sky-blue velvet, with embroidery at the neck, pocket-holes, armpits, and in all the seams. In a word, with the exception of the turban, this was the fashion of dress of the ancient Moors of Granada.
>
> During the Renaissance the dress of the Gypsy women often followed the dress of the country in which they

were settled, particularly in Italy and France. Women wore headgear like turbans and gaily-hued copes. Until late in the eighteenth century they wore the hair long, down to the shoulders, or tucked into a turban or plumed hat. Sometimes, as in Spain and Portugal, the Gypsies were required to wear distinctive dress in contrast with the native population.

DRUIDS The origin of the Gypsies, through the centuries, was the subject of the most fantastic speculations and conjectures. Early in the eighteenth century a German scholar, Kleistern, equated the Gypsies with the ancient Druids, the Celtic people of Gaul.

DSCHUMA In Gypsy legend, a dschuma is a fierce maiden, or sometimes an old witch, who represents disease incarnate.

Gypsy folklore is packed with imaginative tales of monstrous creatures, demons, woodland spirits who exert influence, sometimes benign and more often malefic, on human beings.

DUAL FUNCTION The Gypsy women were traditionally fortune-tellers. But while so doing they have been described as adroit pickpockets. Sebastian Münster (1489-1552), author of *Cosmographia Universa,* described them thus:

The old women read fortunes from the hand and while they predict the number of future husbands or children or wives, they cunningly rummage in the purses of their clients and pilfer without a smile.

DUAL PURPOSE There is a tradition that formerly the Gypsies used poison against enemies and cattle. The term for poison, *drab,* is also the same for medicine. The concoction could therefore serve the double purpose of a fatal application.

DUAL RELIGION   Ostensibly the Gypsies have at times professed the Christian faith. For centuries, and continuing into the present time, services have been held annually in May in the crypt of Les Saintes-Maries de la Mer, in the Camargue country, in Provence. The Gypsies make their annual pilgrimages, from many distant countries, to this church, to worship Saint Sara of Egypt, their Black Patron Saint.

On the other hand, a pagan element enters at this point. Sara's shrine is believed to be founded on an ancient Mithraic altar, and Mithra was the Sun-god, the cult deity of ancient Persia, the divinity of Fire.

DUKES   When the Gypsies first reached England, they were reputed to have come from Egypt. Hence they were called "the Lords and Earls of Little Egypt."

In the course of their wanderings they have also at various times assumed for themselves the honorifics of Count, Marquis, King, Queen, Duke.

DUNCAN, ISADORA (1878-1927)   The famed American dancer, during her tours in Vienna, Budapest, Moscow, evidently came in contact with Gypsy dances and Gypsy music, for she acknowledged her passionate appreciation of Gypsy music.

E

EARLIER ESTIMATE According to the accounts and descriptions of travels, historical records, chroniclers, municipal and governmental decrees, with regard to Gypsies and their ways, the Romanys were frequently looked upon as a savage people, black roving migrants, unsettled, untrained, unsocial.

EARLY GYPSIOLOGIST Among early scholars who wrote on the Gypsies and investigated their origin were Andrew Boorde, in the sixteenth century, Bonaventura Vulcanious, a Dutch Hellenist of the sixteenth century, and Job Ludolf, who belongs in the late seventeenth century.

EARLY STUDIES M. Pau Szathmari was a Hungarian professor of theology at Kolozsvar. He prepared the first Gypsy-Latin-Hungarian Dictionary: *Vocabularium* Zingarico-Latinum et Hungaricum. It was published by the Hungarian Society of Linguistics in 1796.
Early in the nineteenth century a monk named J. Koritschnyak published a Gypsy grammar. Other philological studies of the Gypsy language were subsequently produced by J. Szmodich and J. Bornemissza.

EARTH-SPIRITS In Gypsy mythology, these earth-spirits are called Pçuvushi. The members of one of the Hungarian Gypsy tribes trace their genealogy to these earth-spirits. The earth-spirits are beings in human form who dwell under the earth. There they have cities, but they very often come to the world above. They are ugly, and the men are covered with hair. They carry off mortal girls for wives. Their life is hidden in the egg of a black hen.

The Gypsies also believe that the Earth-spirits, the Pçuvushi, are specially interested in animals. These spirits also teach women the secrets of medicine and sorcery.

EASTWARD MARCH In the sixteenth century the Gypsies arrived in Estonia, in Southern Russia, and in the Ukraine. Other Gypsies moved on to Moscow, two centuries later, having made a trek from Moldavia.

ECONOMY In the Gypsy tribe the economy of the family unit rests with the women folk, who invariably perform all the laborious tasks involving the daily routine.

EDICTS Within a period of half a century, from 1701 to 1750, some eighty edicts were promulgated in Austria and Germany against the Gypsies. Repeatedly, through the centuries, the Gypsies were expelled by edicts and decrees from one country after another.

EDUCATION In the eighteenth century the laws of Transylvania decreed that the children of Gypsies be taken from their parents to be educated by the state. A Platonic concept.

In England, since 1908, Gypsies have been absorbed into state and Church primary schools. In France, there are no formal state educational facilities.

In the USSR, in large urban areas, there are special Gypsy schools. Elementary teaching is conducted in Romany and Russia. There are also technical schools adapted to their needs.

In Morocco, there are nomad mobile schools, with headquarters in Casablanca.

In Germany, attempts are made to absorb the Gypsies into state schools.

In Sweden, a government Gypsy Commission was appointed in 1954. Mobile schools are proposed for the summer months, and state schools in winter.

A further step is the proposal to establish a Permanent Consultant on Gypsy Affairs under the Social Welfare Board.

In Finland, research was made into the illiteracy of the Gypsies. One third of the adult population was found to be illiterate. Of the others, 50% were unable to write.

EFFECTIVE DISGUISE Alexander Brown, a Scottish Gypsy, was in need of meat for his tribe. He had observed, grazing in a field, a bullock that had, by some accident, lost about three-fourths of its tail. He procured a tail of a skin of the same color as that of the animal and ingeniously tied it to the remaining part of its tail. Disguised in this way, the animal was driven off by the Gypsy. But after shipping the beast at the ferry, a servant, who had been sent in search of the Gypsy, overtook him as he was stepping into the boat. An altercation about the bullock immediately began. The countryman said he could swear to the identity of the animal in Brown's possession, except for its long tail. He started to examine it closely when the ready-witted Gypsy took his knife out of his pocket and, in view of all present, cut off the tail above the juncture, drawing blood instantly. Throwing the piece into the sea, he called out to his pursuer, angrily, "Swear to the ox now, and be damned to you." The countryman said not another word but returned home, while the Gypsy proceeded on his way with his prize.

EGIPCIOAC In the Basque province the Gypsies are called Egipcioac, that is, Egyptians. There was a belief, especially in the Middle Ages, that the Gypsies originated in Egypt. A tribal leader thus called himself frequently Duke of Little Egypt.

EGYPTIAN EXILE A Gypsy lament for their presumed lost homeland in Egypt. Their horses now drink the waters of the Spanish Guadiana:

> The region of Chal was our dear native soil,
> Where in fulness of pleasure we lived without toil;
> Till dispersed through all lands, 'twas our fortune to be
> Out steeds, Guadiana, must now drink of thee.
> Once kings came from far to kneel down at our gate,
> And princes rejoic'd on our meanest to wait;
> But now who so mean but would scorn our degree —
> Our steeds, Guadiana, must now drink of thee.
> For the Undebel saw, from his throne in the cloud,
> That our deeds they were foolish, our hearts they were proud;
> And in anger he bade us his presence to flee —
> Our steeds, Guadiana, must now drink of thee.
> Our horses should drink of no river but one;
> It sparkles through Chal, 'neath the smile of the sun,
> But they taste of all streams save that only, and see —
> Apilyela gras Chai la pani Lucalee.

EGYPTIAN ORIGIN According to one legend, when the Egyptians tried to cross the Red Sea, only two persons escaped: a man and a woman. They were the traditional founders of the Gypsy people.

EGYPTIAN PROVENANCE Despite the unassailable view now current that the Gypsies are of Indian origin, there are Gypsy songs that suggest an Egyptian background. One such song runs:

I come from Egypt, and,
wandering over the whole world,
I sustain myself.
I was born in Egypt
and the entire world
is my homeland
because I come from there.

EGYPTIAN SCENE   Noon in Cairo. Just within the archway, in its duskiest corner, there sat all day a living picture, a dark and handsome woman, apparently thirty years old, who was unveiled. She had before her a cloth and a few shells. Sometimes an Egyptian of the lower class stopped, and there would be a grave consultation, and the shells would be thrown, and then further solemn conference and a payment of money and a depature. And it was world-old Egyptian, or Chaldean, as to custom, for the woman was a Rhagarin, or Gypsy, and she was one of the diviners who sit by the wayside, casting shells for auspices, even as shells and arrows were cast of old, to be cursed by Israel.

EJIFTOS   In Greece, where there is a comparatively large Gypsy population, the Gypsies are known as Ejiftos or Giftoi. Etymologically, these two terms are related to the Egyptians, as the Gypsies were called in former times.

ELIOT, GEORGE   The English nineteenth century novelist and poet was the author of the poetic *Spanish Gypsy,* a theme that was having literary popularity at the time.

ELIZABETHAN REIGN   In the reign of Queen Elizabeth the number of Gypsies in England was estimated at 10,000. All such estimates are scarcely even approximations, on account of the wandering habits of the Gypsies.

EL MURCIANO The nickname of Francisco Rodríguez, a Spanish Gypsy who belongs in the nineteenth century and who was famous for his musical talent.

EMERSON, RALPH WALDO (1803-1862) The famous American essayist and poet was deeply interested in Gypsy life, as is evidenced by his poem *The Romany Girl.*

ENCAMPMENTS In England there are encampments of Gypsies in the New Forest, in Blackpool in the North, and near the Malvern Hills.

ENCYCLOPEDIE In eighteenth century France the *Encyclopédie,* in which Denis Diderot was a prominent collaborator, defines the Bohemians, that is, the Gypsies, as vagabonds who tell fortunes, dance, sing, and steal: this was the contemporary view.

ENDURANCE The Russian Gypsies' power of resisting cold is wonderful, wrote George Borrow the English gypsiologist on a visit to that country in the nineteenth century. It is not uncommon to find the Gypsies encamped in the midst of the snow, in slight canvas tents, when the temperature is twenty-five or thirty degrees below the freezing-point. But in the winter they generally seek the shelter of the forests, which afford fuel for their fires and abound in game.

ENGLAND Some hundred Gypsies were condemned to death in Yorkshire, in 1596. They were reprieved, however, on account of the heart-breaking lamentations of the Gypsy children.

ENGLAND FOR THE GYPSIES George Borrow, who was a Romany Rye and knew the English Gypsies, wrote of them in their English evironment:

No country appears less adapted for that wandering life, which seems so natural to these people, than England. Those wildernesses and forests, which they are so attached to, are not to be found there. Every inch of land is cultivated, and its produce watched with a jealous eye. And as the laws against trampers, without the visible means of supporting themselves, are exceedingly severe, the possibility of the Gypsies existing as a distinct race, and retaining their original free and independent habits, might naturally be called in question by those who had not satisfactorily verified the fact. Yet it is a truth that, amidst all these seeming disadvantages, they not only exist there, but in no part of the world is their life more in accordance with the general idea that the Gypsy is like Cain, a wanderer of the earth. For in England the covered cart and the little tent are the houses of the Gypsy, and he seldom remains more than three days in the same place.

ENGLISH DIALECT The dialect of the English Gypsies, though mixed with English words, may be considered as tolerably pure, from the fact that it is intelligible to the Gypsy race in the heart of Russia.

ENGLISH GYPSIES The first arrival of the Gypsies in England appears to have been about the year 1512, according to John Hoyland, a gypsiologist of the early nineteenth century. Violent persecution arose with the intent of complete extermination of the newcomers. There were constant hangings, and terror spread and remained with the unwelcome migrants. The persecution eased in the course of time until it was possible for each Gypsy tribe to select a particular circuit as the focal point of their settlements. Is it probable, as some contend, that the Gypsies may have arrived in England at an earlier period. It is recorded that certain Egyptians, banished from their country, reached England. The speech that they used was the 'Egyptian' language. These people, traveling about the country and practicing their wily arts, were welcomed among the country people, and profited by palmistry and telling fortunes. So much so that they outwitted poor country girls, relieving them both of money, silver spoons, and their best clothing. They had a leader of the name of Giles Hather, who was termed their king: and a woman of the name of Calot was called queen. They rode through the country on horseback, in strange attire.

In appearance their complexion was dark, their forehead rather low, and their hands and feet small. The men were taller than the English peasantry, and far more active. They spoke the English language with fluency.

ENGLISH GYPSY QUARTERS A description of English Gypsies in the Potteries, London, in 1864:

It is not far distant from the most fashionable part of London, from the beautiful squares, noble streets, and thousand palaces of Tyburnia, a region which, although only a small part of the enormous metropolis, can show more beautiful edifices, wealth, elegance, and luxury, than all foreign capitals put together. After passing Tyburnia, and going more than halfway down Notting Hill, you turn to the right and proceed along a tolerably genteel street till it divides into two, one of which looks more like a lane than a street, and which is on the left hand, and bears the name of Pottery Lane. Go along this lane, and you will presently find yourself amongst a number of low, uncouth-looking sheds, open at the sides, and containing an immense quantity of earthen chimney-pots, pantiles, fancy-bricks, and similar articles. This place is called the Potteries, and gives the name of Pottery Lane to the lane through which you have just passed. A dirty little road goes through it, which you must follow, and presently turning to your left, you will enter a little, filthy street, and going some way down it, you will see, on your right hand, a little, open bit of ground, chock-full of crazy, battered caravans of all colors — some yellow, some green, some red. Dark men, wild-looking, witch-like women, and yellow-faced children are at the doors of the caravans, or wending their way through the narrow spaces left for transit between the vehicles. You have now arrived at the second grand Gypsyry of London — you are amongst the Romany Chals of the Potteries, called in Gypsy the *Koromengreskoe Tan,* or the place of the fellows who make pots; in which place certain Gypsies have settled, not with the view of making pots, an employment which they utterly eschew, but simply because it is convenient to them, and suits their fancy.

A goodly collection of Gypsies you will find in that little nook, crowded with caravans. Most of them are Thatchey Romany, real Gypsies, 'long-established people of the old order.' Amongst them are Ratzie-merscroes, Hearnes, Herons, or duck-people; Chumo-mescroes or Bosvils; a Kaulo Camlo (A Black Lovel) or two, and a Beshaley or Stanley.

Though the spot may be considered as the headquarters of the London Gypsies, the whole neighborhood, for a mile to the north of it, may to a certain extent be regarded as a Gypsy region. Here their tents, cars, and caravans may be seen amidst ruins, half-raised walls, and on patches of unenclosed ground. Here at night the different families, men, women, and children, may be seen seated around their fires and their kettles at their evening meal.

The arches of the railroad which bounds this region on the west and north serve as a resort for the Gypsies, who erect within them their tents, which are thus sheltered in summer from the scorching sun, and in winter from the drenching rain.

ENGLISH GYPSY SONGS

Our blessed Queen
Coaches fine in London,
Coaches good in London,
Coaches fine and coaches good
I did see in London.
Run for it!
Up, up, brothers.'
Cease your revels!
The Gentile's coming —
Run like devils!

ENGLISH GYPSY SPEECH The English Gypsy speech is very scanty, amounting probably to not more than 1400 words, the greater part of which seem to be of Indian origin. The rest form a strange medley taken by the Gypsies from various Eastern and Western languages. Some few are Arabic; many are Persian; some are Slavic-Wallachian; others genuine Slavic. Here and there a modern Greek or Hungarian word is discoverable. But in the English Gypsy tongue only one French word has been noted — namely, *tass or dass,* by which some of the very old Gypsies occasionally call a cup.

ENGLISH LOVE CHARM An English Gypsy prescribed the following recipe as a love charm:

Take an onion, a tulip, or any root of the kind; plant it in a clean pot never before used. While you plant it repeat the name of the one whom you love, and every morning and evening say over it:
As this root grows,
And as this blossom blows,

May her heart be
Turned unto me!

ENGLISH PERSECUTION Shortly after their first arrival in England, which is upward of four centuries ago, a dreadful persecution was raised against the Gypsies, the aim of which was their utter extermination. Being a Gypsy was regarded as a crime worthy of death, and the gibbets of England groaned and creaked beneath the weight of Gypsy carcasses, and the miserable survivors were literally obliged to creep into the earth in order to preserve their lives.

But these days passed by. Their persecutors became weary of pursuing them. The Gypsies showed their heads from the holes and caves where they had hidden themselves. They ventured forth, increased in numbers, and, each tribe or family choosing a particular circuit, they fairly divided the land amongst them.

ENGLISH ROMANY The dialect of Romany, spoken by the English Gypsies, is mixed with English words. But it is reasonably pure, and it is intelligible to the Gypsy people in the heart of Russia.

ENGLISH TRADES In the nineteenth century the English Gypsies generally were engaged in chair-mending, knife-grinding, tinkering, and basket-making. Some Gypsies sold hardware, brushes, corks, while many practiced rat-catching.

ENGRO On account of the comparative poverty of Romany, the terminations *-engro,* fellow and *-engri,* thing are in frenquent use. Affixed to a noun or verb the complete word designates, descriptively, some object or type of person for which there is no specific Romany name. In Hindustani, wallah serves somewhat the same purpose. A punkah is a fan: a punkah-wallah is a fan-fellow, that is, the operator of the fan.

Pov, in Romany, means the earth. *Povengri* therefore signifies an earth-thing, that is, a potato. So *poggramengri* is a breaking-thing, that is, a mill. So *peamengri* denotes a drinking-thing, a teapot. Neologisms are made by a combination of already existing words and the termination -engro. For instance, a slack-ropedancer might be denoted by the compound word *bittitardranosh hellokellimengro*: a slightly-drawn-rope-dancing fellow. *Duicoshtcurenomengri* signifies a thing beaten with the fingers: that is, a tambourine.

ESCAPE In earlier times in Spain, when incoming Gypsies were subject to the possibilities of sudden assaults, seizures, or even extermination, they were always prepared to make for the sierra, the winding paths, the caves, the thickets, where they could find a secure, well-hidden refuge.

ESCHATOLOGY It is a Gypsy tradition to burn the corpse of a deceased person after the body has been dug out of the grave. The belief is that the soul cannot leave the earth until this act is performed.

ESMERALDA A Gypsy girl who is a prominent character in Victor Hugo's novel *Notre Dame de Paris.*

ESTIMATED CENSUS Heinrich Grellmann the noted eighteenth century gypsiologist, estimated that in his day there were some 700,000 Gypsies in the world, and that the greatest number were to be found in Europe. In Spain,

Balkan Gypsies, 19th Century

Gypsies (Ulm, about 1872)

he considered, there were around 60,000: in Hungary, some 500,000. In Constantinople they were numberless.

ESTRAMADURA   In Badajoz, the capital of Estramadura in Spain, George Borrow, who spent several years in Spain circulating the Scriptures, first fell in with those singular people, the Zincali, Gitános, or Spanish Gypsies.
It was here I met with the wild Paco, the man with the withered arm who wielded the shearing scissors with his left hand: his shrewd wife, Antonia, skilled in hokkano baro, the Great Trick for outwitting the gullible gorgio: the fierce Gypsy, Antonio Lopez, their father-in-law: and many other almost equally singular individuals of the Errate or Gypsy blood.
The Gitános of Estramadura call themselves Chai or Chabos, and they say that their country of origin was Chal, that is, Egypt.

ETHNIC UNITY   One the notable features of the Gypsies is their determined sense of exclusive and seclusive tribal unity. Equally remarkable is the fact that, despite the exclusiveness of the tribal group, there is a strong and persistent sense of the fundamentally homogeneous unity of the Gypsies as a people, in respect of certain traditions and despite distinctions of dialect and similar disparities.

ETYMOLOGY OF DIDDIKAI   The Gypsy term *diddikai*, which denotes a person who is only half-Gypsy, is actually a slang expression formed from two words: *dik* and *akai*: Look here!

EVIL EYE   One of the crimes of which the Gypsies have been accused is casting the Evil Eye. The Gypsy expression is Querelar nasula, which signifies *causing sickness*. Some Gypsy women sell remedies, compounded of various drugs, for curing the condition. In the Orient, the common remedy is spittle.

As an apotropaic means of protecting a child from the Evil Eye, a Gypsy mother made a brew of coals, garlic, and meal, boiled down to a dry residium. This mass was then put into a small three-cornered bag and hung about the child's neck, while an incantation was recited nine times. In Turkey, where there are Gypsy colonies, Turkish shepherds wear cloaks adorned with charms of various kinds intended to avert the Evil Eye.

EXCLUSION Gypsies were excluded from the Netherlands under pain of death, by Charles V and afterward by the United Provinces in 1582. Banishment from one country after another was the lot of the Gypsies throughout the Middle Ages and later.

EXCLUSION FROM SWEDEN Sweden expelled the Gypsies on three separate occasions. An order for their expulsion appeared in 1662. The Diet of 1723 promulgated a second decree. In 1727 this decree was re-affirmed, with additional severe penalties.

EXCOMMUNICATION The reputation of Gypsies in medieval Europe was so sinister that in the fifteenth century they were driven out of Paris and excommunicated.

EXECUTIONERS In the Balkans, particularly in Rumania, the Gypsies were employed as executioners in the nineteenth century. Bernard Gilliat-Smith, the noted gypsiologist mentions a notice that appeared in an Armenian paper in 1909. The reference was to three Gypsies who were employed at a Turkish execution.

EXODUS It is thought that the Gypsies left their original home in India between the ninth and the eleventh centuries

A.D. There are, however, strong presumptive evidences that Gypsies had already appeared in Persia in the fifth century A.D.

EXPEDITIONS Expeditions to Karakorum, an area south of the western Himalayas, have established the existence of the tented empire of Karak Khitan in India. Scattered Indian tribes still speak a language almost identical to the purest dialect of the Gypsies. This is the Prakrit dialect of Sanskrit. At the beginning of the first century A.D. the Sanskrit language was completely reformed. The Gypsy speech, however, has no trace of this reform and ante-dates the Sanskrit linguistic changes.

EXPERIENCES IN ENGLAND In the earlier centuries the Gypsies wandered over England, encamping in uninhabited spots. They were feared by the people and looked upon as thieves and foreign sorcerers.

Each tribe or clan bore a particular name, and each tribe had its own special location, its own area of settlement or encampment.

EXPOSITION OF PARIS At the Paris Exhibition of 1878 Charles Leland the gypsiologist saw Les Bohémiennes de Moscow, a band of Russian Gypsies, singers and musicians who performed before the French public. Leland quotes a review of the performance:

> The Hungarian Tziganos (Zigeuner) are the rage just now in Paris. The story is that Liszt picked out the individuals composing the band one by one from among the Gypsy performers in Hungary and Bohemia. Half-civilized in appearance, dressed in an unbecoming half-military costume, they are nothing while playing Strauss' waltzes or their own; but when they play the Radetsky Defile, the Racoksky March, or their marvelous czardas, one sees and hears the battle, and

it is easy to understand the influence of their music in fomenting Hungarian revolutions; why for so long it was made reasonable to play or listen to these czardas; and why, as they heard them, men rose to their feet, gathered together, and with tears rolling down their faces, and throats swelling with emotion, departed to do or die.

EXPULSION   The history of the Gypsies has for centuries been a sequence of sporadic banishment, legal and social restrictions, public hostilities, and repeated expulsions from one territory to another. Across the continent of Europe they have been the eternal outcasts. One reason for the hostile attitude toward the Gypsies is that they have persistently retained the identifiable exclusiveness of a people who never settled into the social frame. They have thus unceasingly encountered rejection, as they have never been an integrated element in society. They have never shed their traditions, their beliefs, their passion for the open spaces, their hatred of regimentation. In short, they have never adjusted to conventional civic life. They always yearned, as Borrow knew, for the wind on the heath.

Thus, throughout Europe, banishment has been the badge of their tribes. A sixteenth century law, for example, forbade their entry into England. Early in the eighteenth century, again, they were driven out of Austria. In Switzerland they had already experienced the same fate at the beginning of the sixteenth century.

In the sixteenth century, too, the Gypsies, regarded as vagabonds and scoundrels under the designation of Egyptians or Bohemians, were banished from France under penalty of the pillory or even hanging.

EXPULSION FROM PORTUGAL   Philip III, at Belem in Portugal, issued a decree in 1619, commanding all the

Gypsies in the kingdom to leave the country within the term of six months, and never to return under pain of death. Those who should wish to remain were to establish themselves in cities, towns, and villages, of one thousand families and upward, and were not to be allowed the use of the dress, name, and language of Gypsies, in order that, *for as much as they are not such by nation, this name and manner of life may be forever confounded and forgotten.* They were moreover forbidden under the same penalty to have anything to do with the buying or selling of cattle, whether great or small.

This was the usual type of interdiction imposed on the Gypsies in virtually every country in Europe where they settled or attempted to do so.

EXTINCTION OF THE GYPSIES In the mid-nineteenth century George Borrow, the famous gypsiologist, predicted the extinction of the Gypsies. He declared that within fifty years they would disappear entirely. This was also the view of Charles G. Leland, another eminent gypsiologist. The contrary opinion, according to other investigators, seems to be the case. Despite inevitable changes in dress and occupation and older Gypsy customs the Gypsy still persists. The argument used is that for a'l the changes in English customs, or in French ways, or in Italian mores, the English nation, the French nation, and the Italian nation all persist. The logic of course is faulty. For in each case mentioned the English, the French, and the Italians have been for hundreds of years a territorial unit, knit together ethnically, and they have been preserved to that extent in that they had a permanent homeland.

The Gypsies, on the other hand, have been everlasting wanderers. They have no national homeland. They have no political unity. They persist, however, as an ethnic entity, as the embodiment of a certain unchanging way of life, of a certain identifiable concept of Gypsy.

EYE LOTIONS Gypsies have traditionally concocted their own remedies for various ailments. Most of the ingredients consisted of roots, plant juices, herbs of various kinds. Eyebright, for example, was regarded as a specific for inflamed eyes. For a similar purpose ground ivy was prescribed.

EYES It is generally accepted that a Gypsy may, apart from other characteristics, be readily recognized by his piercing, magnetic gaze. The eyes, it is admitted by investigators who have lived among the Gypsies for any length of time, have a glinting, highly developed sharpness.

F

FAA A common name among many Gypsies who settled in Scotland was Faa or Faw.
The Gypsies who settled in England adopted the names of English families: Stanley, Lee, Herne, Burton, Boswell, Lovell, Cooper, Smith.

FAIR AT VERDU This Spanish fair in Catalonia, celebrated annually around mid-April, dates back to the fourteenth century. At this fair Gypsies predominate in large numbers. Verdú is the place of birth, in 1580, of St. Peter Claver, the patron of the negroes in the USA.

FAIRIES In Gypsy mythology, at a childbirth, food is set out for the fairies who visit the new-born infant and, like the Fateful Sisters of antiquity, determine the child's destiny.

FAIRY FOOT A Gypsy superstition. A fairy foot is the skeleton foot of a mole. Its possession is believed to be a remedy for rheumatism. Gypsy lore abounds in such superstitions, many of them associated with remedies for a host of illnesses, both human and animal.

FAIRY RING In Gypsy mythology witches and fairies perform their mysterious dances under the light of the moon. Anyone who interrupts them or observes them is bound to fall sick. The Gypsy expression runs:
naiso ie na vilnisko Kolo — he stepped on a fairy ring.

FALSE ACCUSATION The following anecdote, according to a nineteenth century English gypsiologist, will prove the frequent oppression experienced by the Gypsies. Not many years since, a collector of taxes in a country town said he had been robbed of fifty pounds by a Gypsy. Shortly afterward, being at Blandford in Dorsetshire, he fixed on a female Gypsy as the person who robbed him in company with two others, and said she was in man's clothes at the time. The Gypsies were taken and kept in custody for some days. Had not a farmer voluntarily come forward and proved that they were many miles distant when the robbery was said to have been perpetrated, they would have been tried for their lives and probably hanged. Their accuser was afterward convicted of a crime for which he was condemned to die, when he confessed that he had not been robbed but had himself spent the whole of the sum in question.

FAMILY AFFECTION "If we suppose," wrote a gypsiologist last century, "the Gypsies to have been heathens before they came to England, then their separation from paganism and cruelty brought them many advantages, some of which were inherent in their character and way of life. They had warm, conjugal, parental and filial sensibilities. They took great care of those who were aged, infirm, sick and blind among them. The gypsiologist, who was particularly interested in their spiritual life, added that he was aware of the general popular opinion that the Gypsies were cruel to their children. But their fits of angry passion were probably not more frequent than among other classes of society. When the angry outbursts subsided, their conduct toward their children was very affectionate. The attachment of Gypsy children to their parents was equally admirable. The affection among sisters and brothers, moreover, was very deep.

FAMILY GOLDWASHERS   In the year 1770 there were, in the districts of Uj-Palanka, Orsova, and Caransebes, upward of eighty goldwashers, all of whom had families, and followed their business, with their wives and children. Yet this number of hands delivered only six or seven hundred ducats worth of gold.

FAMILY MATTERS   Domestic affairs, divorce and similar occasions are usually settled by Gypsies within the tribal group, without recourse to a civil court.

FAMILY NAMES   Among the Gypsies, these names include: Santiago, Amaya, Flores, Buglione, Doerr, Papineschti, Ivanoff, Mineschti, Heredia, Gordon, Herns, Lee, Lovall.

FARANDANGOS   A Spanish Gypsy tribe that in the late eighteenth century was notorious for the truculent and arrogant ways of its members. Throughout their sojournings in Europe, some tribal groups acquired similar reputations.

FARAONI   During the Middle Ages the Gypsies were thought to have come originally from Egypt: hence their general designation as Egyptian. In Hungary they are known as Faraoni, the people of Pharaoh. In Portugal they were called Gregos, Greeks, because they had long been settled in Greece and their language was largely interlarded with Greek words.

FARKAS   Ferdinand Farkas, a Hungarian priest, was so sympathetic to the condition of the Hungarian Gypsies that he established an educational institute at Neuhausel: but it was of brief duration.

FASTING   Many Gypsies are accustomed to fast on Friday, But there is, to them, no religious significance in this practice.

In the course of their migrations the Gypsies regularly assumed the external or ceremonial characteristics of the religion of the country where they settled.

FATE   Across Europe, from the Baltic States to the Iberian Peninsula, from Russia to Germany, the fate of the Gypsies, through the centuries, has been lifelong persecution, interspersed with slavery and massacre.

FEAR OF GYPSIES   In nineteenth century Scotland a mother would quieten a terrified child by crooning:

Hush nae, hush nae, dinna fret ye;

The black Tinkler winna get ye.

They frightened their own children by saying that they would be given to the *gorgio,* the non-Gypsy.

FEAR OF PUBLICATION   The American gypsiologist Charles Leland declared that the Gypsies disliked a gorgio, a non-Gypsy, to question them about Romany for the purpose of publication in book form:

The silly dread, the hatred, the childish antipathy, real or affected, but always ridiculous, which is felt in England, not only among Gypsies, but even by many gentlemen scholars, to having the Romany language published is indescribable.

FEMININE NAMES   Among the Gypsies, the following feminine names are to be found, many of them exotic and picturesque:

Pendivella, Virginta, Kisaiya, Ocean Solis, Zuba, Vashti, Bazena, Truffeni, Perpinia, Starlina.

132

FERDINAND AND ISABELLA Ferdinand and Isabella of Spain, in the edict of 1492, expelled the Jews from the country. Under the same decree the Gypsies too were banished. For the Gypsies, this was the first decree issued against them.

FERTILITY DANCE There are certain ritualistic dances performed by the Gypsies that have a special purpose. The rain dance, for instance, the *Paparuda.* Also the *dodolé* which is directed toward cattle to preserve them from sterility. Such dances are common practices in many races, both in antiquity and among primitive tribes in Africa and in Pacific Islands.

FESTIVALS Among the Gypsies the Spring Feast, celebrated in secret, without publicity, is the forerunner of the Gypsy annual migration, the separation of families and clans, and the start of the roaming period. The Feast of Kettles, celebrated in autumn within the tribal community, symbolizes the returns from the nomadic period, the Gathering of the Clans once more.

FEVER REMEDY A Gypsy remedy for a fever consists of a concoction of the lungs and livers of three frogs, powdered and drunk while the following chant is recited:
Cuckerdya pal m're per
Cáven save misece!
Cuckerdya pal m're per
Den miseçeske drom odry prejiál
Frogs in my belly
Devour what is bad!
Frogs in my belly
Show the evil the way out!

FICTIONAL ROMANTIC GYPSY The vagaries of Gypsy life, the conditions in which the Gypsies live in tent or caravan, and their sense of isolation and exclusiveness from the rest of the inhabitants in whose country they find a home — all these factors have obscured the romantic features of Gypsy life.

Their passion for music, their love of dancing, even the practice of fortune-telling, their strange legends and still stranger history — all these strands, woven together with other elements, have at times given the Gypsies a romantic, unrealistic character. As, for instance, when they are presented in musical comedy and opera, merry making and care free, dressed in colorful costumes, performing quaint ceremonials.

So Konrad Bercovici, who himself is a Rumanian Gypsy and who has both fictionally and historically been the champion and the spokesman of Gypsydom, has produced, in the course of his writing career, a series of tales that have deliberately glamorized and romanticized Gypsy life. He has depicted the Gypsy in the New World, in the Balkans, in tent and on the moor. And, for all the romantic tone, Bercovici has expressed the fundamental way of Gypsy life.

He tells of the old chants and songs, of 'old, unhappy, far-off things and battles long ago.' He tells of wolves and vampires, of witches and sorcery, of mysterious philtres, of miraculous disappearances. He tells of conflicts of the Russians and the Turks and the Hungarians. He tells of men who returned to life after death. He presents all the rich drama of this people, its loves and violence, its smugglers and fiddlers, its secret hiding-places in the Carpathian Mountains. And all this with a cavalier gesture, a defiance of fate, a relish of life itself.

A characteristic collection of Bercovici's short stories about the Gypsies is *Singing Winds*: how a vineyard was saved: the love story of Petra and Nica: Sava's Gypsy band. These tales, like all his tales, are seen through eyes misty with unreality, fortified with truth.

The Gypsy term for a fiddler is *Prastermengro.*
The fiddle is a primary musical instrument in the encampments of Gypsies throughout Europe.

FIDDLING SONG A Romany scene, with Gypsies fiddling:
Romany chalor
Anglo the wudder
Mistos are boshing:
Mande beshello
Innar the wudder
Shooning the boshipen.
Roman lads
Before the door
Bravely fiddle:
Here I sit
Within the door
And hear them fiddle.

FIELDING, HENRY 1707-1754) English novelist and dramatist. In his novel entitled *Tom Jones* he introduces a
Gypsy community and depicts their manners and their
mode of speech.

FIGURATIVE LANGUAGE Some Romany poems have, apart
from their literal meaning, a more subtle significance, as
in the following short piece:
Can you rokkra Romany?
Can you play the bosh?
Can you jal adrey the steripen?
Can you chin the cost?
Literally:
Can you speak the Romany tongue?
(well enough in an argument?)
Can you play the fiddle?
(in a masterly way?)
Can you eat the prison-loaf?

(Can you accept a prison sentence?)
Can you cut and whittle?
(Can you earn a living?)

FINDING A HUSBAND The Gypsy girls of Transylvania believe that spells to 'know your future husband' can be best carried out on the eve of certain days, such as New Year, Easter, and Saint George. On New Year's Day they throw shoes or boots on a willow tree, but are only allowed to throw them nine times. If the shoe catches in the branches the girl who threw it will be married within a year.

On the same eve they go to a tree and shake it by turns, singing: —

Scattered leaves around I see,
Where can my true lover be?
Ah, the white dog barks at last!
And my love comes running fast!

If during the singing the bark of a dog should be heard, the damsel will be married before New Year comes again. Again: To see the form of a future husband a Gypsy girl must go on the night of Saint George to a crossroad. Her hair is combed back, and, pricking the little finger of the left hand, she must let three drops of blood fall on the ground while saying:

I give my blood to my loved one,
Whom I shall see shall be mine own.

Then the form of her future husband will rise slowly out of the blood and fade as slowly away. She must then gather up the dust or mud-blood, and throw it into a river. Otherwise the Nivashi or Water-spirits will lick up the blood and the girl be drowned within the year.

FINLAND In Finland, and also in Lapland, many Gypsies have become reindeer herdsmen. In other countries they have usually adhered to old traditional occupations: horse-dealing, tinsmiths, coppersmiths, basket-weaving.

FIRDUSI   In his epic poem, the *Shah Nomah,* The Book of Kings, Firdusi, the Persian poet who flourished in the eleventh century, writes of the Gypsies:
No washing e'er whitens the black Zigan.

FIRE-ARMS   In Brazil the Gypsies had the use of fire-arms. This custom continued into the beginning of the nineteenth century. In the Middle Ages, in Europe, carrying arms was not unknown, especially among the tribal leaders.

FIRE WORSHIP   Along with Christian rites the Gypsies are believed to have retained some elements of the ancient pagan cult of Mithra, the Persian divinity of Fire and Water. In Hungary, the Gypsies performed a ceremony associated with the fire cult. For apotropaic purposes, before the birth of a Gypsy child, a fire was lighted and kept burning until the child was baptized. As the flames soared, a Gypsy woman recited a chant beseeching protection, by means of the fire, against the malefic spirits of the Earth and of Water.

FIRST APPEARANCE   The term Gypsy first appeared in English in the sixteenth century. It was associated with Egypt, the presumed original home of the Gypsies.

FIRST BOOK   Among the Gypsies there is a belief that the Tarot cards, used by the Gypsies in fortune-telling, constitute the first written book, and that these cards contain the theory of the entire universe as conceived by the Chaldean priests and astrologers.

FIRST GYPSIES IN AMERICA   The *Family Herald,* an English journal published in London, in an item dated woods of Hoboken, facing New York. They aroused great interest and curiosity because they were the first of such nomads ever seen in America.

of Rouen. But there was general public hostility to these nomadic strangers.

FLAUBERT, GUSTAVE (1821-1880)   Famous French novelist. He made contacts with Gypsy camps near his home town

FLEMINGS   The name Flemings, by which a century ago the Gypsies were known in various parts of Spain, would probably never have been bestowed on them but from

FOLK POETRY   The Hungarian Gypsies possess a large body the circumstances of their having been designated or believed to be Germans, as German and Fleming were considered by the ignorant as synonymous terms.

of traditional folk poetry, songs, and tales. Permeating 1851, referred to a tribe of Gypsies encamped in the this popular literature are the superstitions and mythological concepts that include the *Nivashi,* the water fairies, the *Urme* who determine human destiny, the *kesali,* the fairies who dwell in the forests, the *phuuus* who are subterranean ghosts, and the strange bird the *Carana.*

FOLLOWING THE GYPSY TRAIL   Numerous groups and individuals of various types, both culturally and socially, have felt the lure of the road, the wind on the heath, the pull of the Gypsy trail. These people have attached themselves, sometimes for a brief spell, at times for long years on end, to the nomadic race of Gypsies. These gorgios, these non-Gypsies, men and women, sometimes young lads, like the painter Jacques Callot, have hankered after the apparent freedom of movement enjoyed by the Tziganes. Some have absorbed the Gypsy way of life. Some wished to learn their customs and traditions and their languages or dialects. Some have been inspired by the endless more or less voluntary migrations of the Gypsies. They have rejected the confinements and the restrictions of city life, of organized society, of sedentary settled occupations, of the repetitiousness of the daily routine. Some of those who have assimilated the Gypsy life have been scholarly researchers. Walter Starkie and Irving Brown, for instance, were interested primarily but far from exclusively in Gypsy music. Charles Leland the American gypsiologist investigated Gypsy folklore and legend. George Borrow liked the race and at the same time was fascinated by their language. John Sampson spent years with the Welsh Gypsies, gathering material for his vast philological survey of the Welsh Gypsy dialect. Some felt the spirit of adventure itself, and realized that the Gypsies alone symbolized the spirit of the earth-wanderer, of the medieval troubadour, of the citizen of the world who had no permanent home and who made every country his home.

In some instances the urge to join with the Gypsies was the result of family conflict, the desire to escape from a harsh reality. Or a gorgio, impassioned for a Gypsy girl, must follow her until by marriage he can be accepted into her tribe as frequently happened in the Balkan countries. Some, finally, have been army deserters or criminals who have wanted to lose their identity among the migratory Gypsies.

FONTANA, GIAN (1897-1935) Teacher, poet, and writer in the Surselvan dialect of the Swiss-Romansch language. In his tale *The Gypsies* he depicts a rustic scene in the Valdei lands, with Gypsies encamped in the fields, mending pots and pans, collecting the leftover grain in the harvested fields. The Gypsies are accused of stealing bread and making off with goats. There is ever present the sense of fear and hostility with regard to the Gypsies, as there always was for centuries throughout Europe.

FOOD Gypsies are especially fond of berries, vegetables, mushrooms, hedgehog, game and fowl wherever these are available. Gypsies are inveterate smokers. Even children as well as women are addicted to cigarettes. The older Gypsy women prefer to smoke a pipe.

FOOD HABITS It has been asserted that the Gypsies, in all parts of the world, are indifferent to the type of food they eat, provided that they can appease their hunger; and that they have have no objection to partake of the carcasses of animals which have died a natural death and have been left to putrefy by the roadside: moreover, that they use for food all kinds of reptiles and vermin.

In this there is a great deal of exaggeration, but it must be confessed that, in some instances, the habits of the Gypsies in regard to food would seem at the first glance to favor the supposition. This holds true chiefly of the Gypsy race who still continue in a wandering state, and who doubtless retain more of the ways and customs of their forefathers than those who have adopted a sedentary life. There can be no doubt that the wanderers among the Gypsy race are occasionally seen to feast upon carcasses of cattle which have been abandoned to the birds of the air. Yet it would be wrong to conclude that the Gypsies were habitual devourers of carrion. Carrion it is true they may occasionally devour from want of better food, but many of these carcasses are not in reality the carrion which they appear, but are the bodies of animals which the Gypsies have themselves killed by the poison called *drao* or *drab,* in the hope that the flesh may eventually be abandoned to them.

FOOD TABUS George Borrow explains some flood habits of the Gypsies:

Know, then, O Gentile, whether thou be from the land of the Gorgios or the Busne, that the very Gypsies who consider a ragout of snails a delicious dish will not touch an eel, because it bears resemblance to a snake; and that those who will feast on a roasted hedgehog could be induced by no money to taste a squirrel, a delicious and wholesome species of game, living on the purest and most nutritious food which the fields and forests can supply. I myself, while living among the Roms of England, have been regarded almost in the light of a cannibal for cooking the latter animal and preferring it to hotchi witchi barbecued or ragout of boror. "You are but half Romany, brother," they would say, "and you feed like a Gentile, even as you talk. If we did not know you to be of the royal blood of Pharaoh, we should be justified in driving you forth as a dog man, one more fitted to keep company with wild beasts and Gorgios than gentle Romanys."

FORBIDDEN LANGUAGE In the early nineteenth century, the Gypsy language, Calo, was forbidden to the Spanish Gypsies. On one occasion, in an inn, George Borrow the gypsiologist, spoke in Calo to a Gypsy:
"Brother," said Antonio, "you did wrong to speak to me in Calo, in a posada like this. It is a forbidden language. For, as I have often told you, the king has destroyed the law of the Calés"

FORGIVENESS Fear of harm from the spirits of the dead is so great among the Gypsies that if a person has not been on friendly terms with the deceased, he goes to the grave and, sprinkling some drops of water on it, repeats:
T'avel jerto mandar. Na ker mango baja. Delo simas tu sa — I forgive you. Do not harm me. I behaved badly toward you.

FORMULAIC GREETING   It is not of course the case, as is popularly supposed, that illiteracy is totally pandemic among the Gypsies. When a Gypsy did write a letter, he began with a customary introduction: I shall be glad if you are in good health. Mine is good.

This formulaic greeting corresponds to the Roman way of beginning a letter with the abbreviations: S. V. B. E. E. V.: If you are well, it is well. I am well.

FORTUNE-TELLING   The practice of fortune-telling by reading the palm of the hand is one of the most general activities of Gypsy women in every century. It became the subject of literary mention by the poets Clément Marot and Ronsard in France, by the dramatist Molière, by Gil Vicente in Portugal. Molière, in fact, makes quite an elaborate scene of it.

In England Samuel Pepys records in his *Diary* that he consulted a Gypsy fortune-teller.

FORTUNE-TELLING PLEA

Cross the poor old Gypsy's hand now
    With a little bit of gold:
You've the best of luck, my lady,
    That the stars have ever told.
There is a fair young man as loves you
    And you love him fond and true.
There is a dark young fellow also,
    Dying all for love of you.
And you'll marry him you love, miss,
    And you will make a first-rate wife.
You will be mother of two children,
    And be happy all your life.
And if I can read the stars right,
    You will meet him here today.

142

Look! Here's someone just coming
As will bear out all I say.

FRATERNAL FEELING As a proof of the fraternal feeling which is not infrequently displayed among the Gitános, George Borrow relates an incident that occurred in Cordova:

One of the poorest of the Gitános murdered a Spaniard. For this crime he was seized, tried, and found guilty. The life of the culprit is seldom taken, provided he can offer a bribe sufficient to induce the honorary public to report favorably on his case. But in this instance money was of no avail. The murdered individual left behind him powerful friends who were determined that justice should take its course. One of the richest Gitános offered for his own share of the ransom the sum of five thousand crowns; but it was of no avail. The Gypsy was executed. The day before the execution the Gitános one and all left Cordova, shutting up their houses and taking with them their horses, their mules, their wives and families. No one knew where they directed their course, nor were they seen in Cordova for some months: a few, however, never returned. So great was the horror of the Gitànos at what had occurred that they were in the habit of saying that the place was cursed for evermore.

FRENCH DECREE At the Assembly of the States of Orleans, in 1561, all governors of cities received orders to drive out the Gypsies with fire and sword.

Throughout the Middle Ages and even later similar decrees were issued against the Gypsies.

FRENCH EYE-WITNESS A French eye-witness thus describes the arrival of Gypsies in Paris in the fifteenth century:

On the 17th of April 1427, appeared in Paris twelve

penitents of Egypt, driven from thence by the Saracens. They brought in their company one hundred and twenty persons. They took up their quarters in La Chapelle, whither the people flocked in crowds to visit them. They had their ears pierced, from which depended a ring of silver. Their hair was black and crispy, and their women were filthy to a degree, and were sorceresses who told fortunes.

FRENCH INTEREST IN GYPSIES Among the French writers of the nineteenth century who displayed a romantic interest in Gypsies were, notably, Victor Hugo, Charles Nodier, Théophile Gautier, Prosper Mérimée, creator of Carmen, and the poet Charles Baudelaire, who described the Gypsies in his *Bohémiens en Voyage.*

FRENCH KING'S PLAN So numerous did the Gypsies become in France that in 1545 King Francis I, sixteen years before the Gypsy expulsion from the kingdom, proposed to embody 4000 of them to act as pioneers in taking Boulogne, which was then in possession of England.

FRENCH PEASANTRY From the Carpathian Mountains, where the Gypsies had mined metal, they moved Westward into France, but here they aroused resentment and animosity among the French peasantry in the fifteenth century.

FRENCH PERIODICAL The *Société des Etudes* Tsiganes, with headquarters in Paris, publishes a Bulletin dealing with Gypsy items of information and issues.

FRENCH REVOLUTION Before the French Revolution, there were few Gypsies in France, for every one who could be apprehended fell a sacrifice to the police.

FRIARS In the nineteenth century, among the Andalusians of Spain, the friars of a convent at Xeres particularly sought the acquaintance of the Gitános. The friars possessed a celebrated breed of horses: hence the interest of the friars in the Gypsies. who were so knowledgeable about horses.

FRIENDSHIP George Borrow knew the Gypsies, in many countries, for more than twenty years. There was invariably a feeling of friendship with whatever tribe he encountered. There was never any hint or suggestion of ill-treatment or of deception. But he thought their motive for such tolerance and intimacy was their belief, encouraged by his linguistic ability, that he was a *Rom,* and that their love for 'the Gypsy blood' was their distinguishing characteristic.

FRYING-PAN FORTUNE Two servant girls went into the camp of some Gypsies in the south of England, to have their fortunes told by a Gypsy woman. When she observed that they appeared to be lowly, she said to her companion: "I shall not get my books or cards for them. They are only servants."
The cards would have been the Tarot cards which Gypsies have regularly used in telling fortunes. The Gypsy then called for a frying-pan and ordered the servants to fill it with water and hold their faces over it. Then she proceeded to flatter and to promise them exciting futures. This method is called the frying-pan fortune.

FUGITIVES Throughout their history, the Gypsies have always been on the march. The earliest Gypsy tribes who appeared in Europe declared that they were Christians fleeing from the Turks.

145

FUNERAL At the death of a Gypsy, all his possessions, his personal belongings, his knives and cup and plate, even his horse, are destroyed by fire. No material thing of his remains, but the memory.

FUNERAL PROCESSION Among Hungarian Gypsies a funeral procession is on occasion a musical performance, consisting of the processional mourners who follow the coffin while playing the violin, clarinet, flute, cello.

FUNERAL RITE In some instances, when an English Gypsy dies by accident, a cross consisting of stones is placed near the scene of the accident and pressed down until it is level with the ground.

G

GACHO This Spanish Gypsy term is a variant form for the more general expression *gorgio,* the Gypsy designation for a non-Gypsy. Another Spanish Gypsy term for the Gentiles, the non-Gypsies, is *busnó:* in the plural, *busnè.*

GAGINO Antony Gagino, Count of Little Egypt, was the tribal leader of a band of Gypsies who sailed from Scotland to Denmark early in the sixteenth century. A few years later they appeared in Sweden. There is extant a Swedish record, the *Swensk Croneka,* of Olaüs Petri, in confirmation.

GALLOWS FOR GYPSIES

One Morning in Epping Forest,
   Beside the ale-house door,
I talked with the Gypsy Rosa,
   As I often had done before.
When she whispered quick and softly,
   "Don't speak in Romany,
For there is a policeman,
   Who can hear as well as see."
"But if he hears us talking,
   He will not understand."
"Why, don't you know my master,
   It is against the law of the land?"
I have heard it from my father,
   It may not be spoken or writ,

And many have swung on the gallows,
  For nothing but talking it.
And it's still down in the law-book,
  And was never struck out, do ye see?
They may swing you off the crossbeam
  For a-talking, much more for a-writing
A book in the Romany.
  And though you are a gentleman truly,
Don't go in the way to be hung
  For I say it's a hanging matter
This talking the Romany tongue.
  (Charles G. Leland)

GANA In Gypsy mythology Gana is Queen of the Witches. She is a huntress too and an enchantress. In some respects she corresponds to the ancient classical Diana or Artemis. Gypsy folklore is pervaded by tales of witches, demons, werewolves, demoniac spirits that haunt the fields and the forests, the rivers and springs.

GARCIA LORCA, FEDERICO (1899-1936) Spanish poet and playwright. He is particularly associated with his native province of Andalusia. Andalusia has been for centuries Gypsy territory. Lorca's *Romancero gitano,* Gypsy balladeer, made him nationally popular.

He describes the Gypsies of Granada, huddled in their caves, in conflict with society.

GARLIC In Gypsy folklore garlic was regarded at a witch-antidote. Hence the Gypsy proverb:

  Bizi ko vistica od biloga luka — She runs from it like a witch from white garlic.

GAROFALO, BENVENUTO DA (1481-1559) Italian painter who has depicted the Gypsy type in his *La Zingarella.* Among other painters who have treated the Gypsy theme are Frans Hals, Jacques Callot, Goya, Joseph Pennell.

GAUL   When a Gallic chief died, his favorite horse, as Julius Caesar relates in Book 6 of his *De Bello Gallico,* is buried along with his master. So, when the body of a deceased Gypsy is dug out from the grave and then burned, his horse too is destroyed along with the Gypsy.

GAUTIER, THEOPHILE   The noted French novelist who belongs in the nineteenth century. In his *Voyage en Espagne* he describes the Gypsies as he found them in Spain.
English, French, Portuguese, German, Italian, and Hungarian literature has depicted the Gypsy in both narrative and verse.

GENTILES   To the Gypsies all people not of their own blood are called *Gentiles* or *gorgios* or *busné.*
Despite their sojournings of variable duration in many countries, the Gypsies have remained essentially a self-contained, exclusive ethnic entity.

GENOCIDE   In World War II the Gypsies under the Nazis were exposed to genocide. Thousands of them were assassinated at Auschwitz. Survivors joined various resistance groups. The fate of the Gypsies in all Nazi-occupied territory is still undergoing investigation.

GEORGE II   In the reign of George II of England many Gypsy women, accused of stealing girls, were scorched and branded. This same accusation was directed against the Gypsies in many European countries, but it appears that no conclusive evidence has been established.

GEORGE III   George III of England displayed friendly sympathy with the English Gypsies. He often listened to their petitions for clemency, and on occasion even commuted sentences of death.

During their extended wanderings for centuries over Europe, the Gypsies have made similar contacts with kings and princes, with popes and highly placed civic authorities. By these means they sometimes gained stays of execution, or protection, shelter, and food.

GEORGE BORROW'S PURPOSE In his journey through Spain and Portugal, George Borrow, the gypsiologist, had as his primary purpose to print and circulate the Scriptures throughout Spain:

> I went there on a somewhat remarkable errand, which necessarily led me into strange situation and positions, involved me in difficulties and perplexities, and brought me into close and continued contact with the Gypsies their habits, and language, and their manner of life.

GEORGE ELIOT AND LELAND When Charles Leland, the noted gypsiologist, once visited George Eliot and G.H. Lewes at their home, George Eliot at once turned the conversation to the Gypsies, in whom she was deeply interested. She talked of having visited the Zincali in Spain, while Lewes discussed the Romany tongue.

GEORGIAN MANUSCRIPT An early Georgian manuscript refers to a band of sorcerers called Atsincan. They were unquestionably Gypsies, who are to this day known in Greece as Atsinganoi.

In the course of their migrations, the Gypsies acquired various names of identification in terms of the putative country of their origin. Thus they were called: Bohemians, Egyptians, Karaki, Moors, Rom, Heiden, Tartars, Sintés, Zigeuner, Gitános, Zingari, Zincali.

GERIGONZA This Spanish term that denotes the Gypsy language was used in a decree issued in 1783 by Charles

III of Spain. All Gypsies who gave up the use of the right to adopt any trade.

GERMAN BURIAL In Weissenborn churchyard, in Saxony, there is an inscription relating to a Gypsy burial:
Here rests in God Dame Maria Sybilia Rosenberg, Gypsy, and wife of the honorable and valiant Wolfgang Rosenberg, Cornet of the Electoral and Brandenburg Army, who died at Weissenborn, 9th of October, 1632, age 52, to whom God be merciful.

GERMAN GYPSIES At the turn of the century small bands of German Gypsies, who had been harassed in that country, made their way to England.

GERMAN IMPERIAL DIET Late in the fifteenth century the German Diet declared that the Gypsies were the spies and scouts of the enemy of Christianity. It was consequently ordained that they could not enter or settle in the country. This decree had little effect, however, on the continued infiltration of Gypsies. Hence a later decree, promulgated in 1722 by the Count of Reuss, ordered all Gypsies found in the territory of Reuss to be shot down on sight.

GERMANS In early centuries in Spain the Gypsies were called Germanos. Either the generic name of Romany was misunderstood and mispronounced by the Spaniards among whom they came or the confusion resulted from the fact of their having passed through Germany on their way to south and bearing letters of safety and passports from the various German states.

GERMAN TRAVELERS German travelers in Greek territory, among them Felix Fabri, Bernard of Briedenbach, Alexander of Veldenz, Arnold von Harff, reported on the presence of Egyptian, that is, Gypsy, settlers.

GERMAN TREATMENT   For centuries the Gypsies of Germany were treated as dangerous or useless encumbrances. Periodically, wherever they appeared in Teutonic territory, particularly in Prussia, they were hounded, mutilated, or executed.

GERMAN VIEWS   The tradition is that the Gypsies appeared in Germany early in the fifteenth century. For some half century they were treated with tolerable indulgence. Then the Gypsies began to be regarded as vagabonds and imposters, as practitioners of magic spells and responsible for many natural disasters such as earthquakes, famine, and plague.

GERMANY   Continually moving Westward, the Gypsies reached Western Germany in the year 1417. They introduced themselves as pilgrims and for half century were treated with some indulgence. Then, as the Germans began to fear these intruding migrants and to suspect them of the occult arts, harsh measures were instituted against them, and persisted for centuries.

GERONIMO OF ALCALA   Seventeenth century Spanish writer. Author of *Historia de Alonso, mozo de muchos amos,* The Story of Alonso, servant of many masters. Alonso, the hero, gives a graphic account of the Gitánas and their fortune-telling practices:

> O how many times did these Gitánas carry me along with them, for being, after all, women, even they have their fears, and were glad of me as a protector. And so they went through the neighboring villages, and entered the houses a-begging, giving to understand thereby their poverty and necessity, and then they would call the girls, in order to tell them the buena ventura and the young fellows the good luck which they were to enjoy, never failing in the first place to ask for a cuarto

or real, in order to make the sign of the cross. And with these flattering words they got as much as they could, although, it is true, not much in money, as their harvest in that article was generally slight, but enough in bacon to afford subsistence to their husbands and bantlings. I looked on and laughed at the simplicity of those foolish people, who, especially such as wished to be married, were as satisfied and content with what the Gitána told them, as if an apostle had spoken it.

GESTURES A shake of the head on the part of a Gypsy denotes affirmation. Negation is expressed by a clicking sound with the tongue and a backward thrust of the head.

GETTING RELIGION Among the poor and destitute Gypsies who were encamped in the southern counties of England in the nineteenth century there was one Gypsy in particular. In a state of wretchedness bordering on despair he had been wandering for nearly forty years. In his last days someone directed him to the Bible. As he could not read, he gave a woman some money to read to him. During the last few years of his life he often prayed under the hedges. A Gypsy, father of three motherless children, had lived as an atheist all his life but died reformed.

A fiddler, who often moved with the worst and lowest of degraded characters in towns and villages, became involved in crime. As he lay dying of alcoholism, he called his family together and forbade his children to practice fiddling, as he thought it was for this reason that he himself had sunk so low.

GITANA A Spanish description of the Gitána runs thus:

The Gitana is distinguished by the same complexion, and almost the same features. In her frame she is as well-formed and as flexible as the Gitáno. Condemned to suffer the same privations and wants, her countenance when her interest does not oblige her to dissemble her feelings, presents the same aspect of melancholy, and shows besides, with more energy, the rancorous passions of which the female heart is susceptible. Free in her actions, her carriage and her pursuits, she speaks, vociferates, and makes more gestures than the Gitáno, and, in imitation of him, her arms are in continued motion, to give more expression to the imagery with which she accompanies her discourse. Her whole body contributes to her gesture, and to increase its force; endeavoring, by these means, to sharpen the effect of language in itself insufficient. And her vivid and disordered imagination is displayed in her appearance and attitude.

GITANA IN SEVILLE   In *The Zincali,* George Borrow presents a description of a typical Gypsy:

She is of middle stature neither strongly nor slightly built and yet her every movement denotes agility and vigour. As she stands erect before you she appears like a falcon about to soar and you are almost tempted to believe that the power of volition is hers; and were you to stretch forth your hand to seize her she would spring above the housetops like a bird.

GITANISMO   A term that denotes Gypsy villains of every description. Gitanismo flourished in direct proportion to the harsh measures of suppression imposed upon the Gitános of Spain.

GITANO AND MODIFICATIONS   The term Gitáno has been variously modified in Spanish, as follows:

Gitáno: a Gypsy, a flatterer
Gitanillo: a little Gypsy
Gitanismo: the Gypsy tribe

Gitanesco: Gypsy-like
Gitanear: to flatter, entice
Gitaneria: wheedling
Gitanamente: in a sly, winning manner
Gitanada: blandishment, wheedling, flattery

GITANO LANGUAGE According to the gypsiologist George Borrow, the Gitáno language of Spain was nearing its last stage of existence in the middle of the nineteenth century. The Gypsy language, however, and its various national dialects, still flourish.

GITANOS These Spanish Gypsies are considered by some gypsiologists to be descendants of the Guanches. Their origin is taken to be the Canary Islands. Ethnically they are thought to be a people of ancient Atlantis. According to other gypsiologists, the Spanish term Gitános is used as a synonym for Gypsies and Gitános is evidently an abbreviated form of Egyptanos.

GITANOS AS SMITHS A common occupation of the Gitános of Granada is working in iron, and it is not infrequent to find their caves scooped in the sides of the ravines, tenanted by Gypsy smiths and their families, who ply the hammer and forge in the bowels of the earth. To one standing at the mouth of the cave, especially at night, they afford a picturesque spectacle. Gathered round the forge, their bronzed and naked bodies, illuminated by the flame, appear like figures of demons: while the cave, with its flinty sides and uneven roof, blackened by the charcoal vapors which hover about it in festoons, seems to offer no inadequate representation of fabled purgatory. Working in iron was an occupation strictly forbidden to the Gitános by the ancient laws, on what ground does not exactly appear.

GIRL VIOLINIST Skill in the violin was usually associated with the Gypsy men. But there was a Gypsy girl who at the age of fourteen was so famous as a violinist that the most fashionable people of Hungary were accustomed to send twenty or thirty miles for her, to play at their balls and other entertainments.

GLAMOR Glamor, in a Gypsy context, means the hypnotic power of the eye that has been regularly attributed to the Gypsies. By their keen gaze it is said that they can cast a spell on bystanders, making them see what does not actually exist. Sir Walter Scott, in one of his ballads, refers to this power of bewitching or 'overlooking':

> He thought the warlocks o' the rosy cross
> Had fang'd him in their nets sae fast:
> Or that the Gypsies' glamor'd gang
> Had lair'd his learning at the last.

GLANVILL, JOSEPH (1636-1680) English philosopher and cleric. In his *Vanity of Dogmatising* he introduced a poor Oxford student who joins a band of Gypsies. This incident is the source of Matthew Arnold's *The Gypsy Scholar.*

GOD AND SATAN The Russian Gypsies designate God as Deval and their name for Satan is Bengel. The Spanish Gypsy dialect, Caló, refers to God as Debel and the name for Satan is Bengi. A common variant name for Bengi is Beng. Beng appears frequently in Gypsy legend and folklore as the evil genius, the supreme malefic spirit.

GOLD WASHERS One of the more privileged occupations in which the Gypsies engaged was gold washing, especially in Rumania, Wallachia, and Transylvania. They washed the sand in the streams and rivers and received a share in the gold dust. These Gypsies were the Zlatari, the

Rudani. They also had other variant names associated topographically with locations in Rumania: Zlataressa, Rudari, Rudaria. The Rudars were licensed by the College of Mons, established by Maria Theresa of Austria, to practice their trade. The Ursar and the Lajaschen, also goldwashers, had to pay a tribute to the government.

GOODBYE   The Gypsy formula for leave-taking is:
Dza devlesa! — God go with you! This expression corresponds exactly to the Spanish *Va con dios!*

GOOD LUCK CHARMS   The Gypsies were accustomed to wear, as a luck charm, *bacht,* small sea-shells sewn in a leather bag. Silver thalers were also regarded as good luck amulets, as well as knives.

GORGIOS   A Gypsy expression that denotes persons who are not Gypsies. *Busné* is another term for *gorgios.* The singular form is *busnó.*
In a more general sense, all those who are not Gypsies are designated as Gentiles.

GOSPEL IN GYPSY DIALECT   Coton Ye Gabicote Majaro
Y soscabando dicando dicó los Barbalós sos techescában desqueros mansis on or Gazofilacio; y dicó tramisto yesque pispiricha chorroritam sos techescába duis chinorris sarraballis, y peneló: en chachipé en peneló, sos caba chorrorri pispiricha á techescao bus sos sares los evéles: persos saros ondobas han techescan per los mansis de Ostebé de lo sos les costuña; bus caba e desquero chorrori á techescao saro or susalo sos terelaba. Y pendó á cormuñis, sos pendában del cangaripé, soscabelaba uriardao de orchiris berrandáñas, y de dénes: Cabas buchis sos dicais, abillarán chibeles, bus ne muquelará berrandañá costuñé berrandañá, sos ne quesesa demarabeá. Y le

prucháron y pendáron. Docurdó, bus quesa ondaba? Y sos simachi abicará bus ondaba presimáre?

Specimen of the Gospel

And while looking he saw the rich cast their treasures into the treasury; and he saw also a poor, widow, who cast two small coins, and he said: In truth I tell you that this poor widow has cast more than all the others: because all those have cast, as offerings to God, from that which to them abounded; but she from her poverty has cast all the substance which she had. And he said to some, who said of the temple, that it was adorned with fair stones and with gifts: These things which ye see, days shall come, when stone shall not remain upon stone, which shall not be demolished. And they asked him and said: Master, when shall this be? And what sign shall there be when this begins?

GRATITUDE   In the opinion of George Borrow, whose experiences with Gypsies extended for over twenty years, of all beings in the world the Gypsies were the least susceptible of gratitude. Walter Simson, on the other hand, a Scottish gypsioligst, relates in his History of the Scottish Gypsies a number of episodes in which the Gypsy sense of gratitude is extremely marked.

GRAVES   The graves of deceased Gypsies are kept in good order in the various churchyards, by means of annual remuneration. Sometimes the English Gypsies expend large sums of money on head-stones.

GREAT TRICK   In the course of their wanderings in many countries, the Gypsies developed a shrewdness that was employed in cutwitting the *gorgio,* the non-Gypsy, and relieving him of his money. One of these Tricks involved the coining game. Another was a kind of confidence stratagem known as the Hidden Treasure. In every instance

158

the gullible victim, the busnó, was the dupe. To triumph over the non-Gypsy was a regular practice, a routine achievement.

GREECE In Greece the Gypsies celebrate the advent of spring with a feast on St. George's Day April 23. Greece was one of the first countries where the Gypsies settled on their way from India. They absorbed many Greek practices, as well as many linguistic elements.
In the fifteenth and sixteenth centuries, according to travelers and records such as the *Chronicle of Cyprus,* several Greek islands and other locations as well — Cyprus, Rhodes, Candia, Euboea — were settled by the Gypsies.

GREEK There is a striking similarity between certain Gypsy and Greek numerals, suggesting the traditional belief that Gypsies had settled in Macedonia centuries ago. The numbers 7, 8, 9, 10 are, in Greek: hepta, octo, ennea, deka. In Gypsy dialects they are: efta, ofto, enea, deca.

GREEK CHURCH The religion which these Russian Gypsies professed externally was the Greek, and they mostly wore crosses of copper or gold, but when I questioned them on this subject in their native language, they laughed and said it was only to please the Russians. Their names for God and his adversary are Deval and Bengel, which differ little from the Spanish Un-debel and Bengi, which signify the same.

GREEK ELEMENTS All the Gypsies who reached Europe in their migrations retain in their speech many Greek words: an indication of their comparatively lengthy settlement in Greece and Macedonia.

159

GREEK LANGUAGE   In the Middle Ages the Gypsies who had settled in Greek territory, on the mainland and in the islands, absorbed the Greek language to such an extent that it became for some time the only means of communication with non-Gypsies. The scholar Lorenzo Palmiréno, for instance, who belongs in the sixteenth century, could communicate with them only in Greek.

GREEK ORTHODOXY   The Gypsies of Russia nominally professed Greek Orthodoxy, but they made light of their actual faith.

As a rule the Gypsies assumed the external forms of the religion of the country where they settled. Thus they have been nominally Christians and Moslems.

GREEK ROMANY   The Romany language as spoken by the Gypsies who had settled in Greece and had absorbed into their own tongue a large body of Hellenic forms, idioms, and vocabulary, before the Gypsies spread throughout Europe early in the fifteenth century, is considered the purest form of the Romany Tongue.

GREETING   One Gypsy greeting consists in touching the breast and the forehead. A verbal salutation may be: Te traís! — May you live long!

An invitation is confirmed with: Misto avilean! — Welcome!

In Afghanistan Pathans greet a person with the Pushtu expression: Ta jôr ye? Are you well?

To which the response is: Zah jôr yum — I am well. Similarly, Turkish Gypsies ask: Zoraló san? — To which the answer is: Zoraló — I am well.

GREGARIOUSNESS   By the very conditions of their tribal organizations, the Gypsies are a naturally gregarious people. What is quite and dreaded is for a Gypsy to be abandoned, left to himself. This happens only when he has been outlawed for some unpardonable misdeed or violation of the *kris,* the Gypsy law.

GRELLMANN, HEINRICH M. G. Eminent German gypsiologist who flourished in the eighteenth century. Grellmann was the first gypsiologist to determine the Indian origin of the Gypsies. His book, *Die Zigeuner,* published in 1783 in Leipzig, is virtually the first major historical survey of this people.

GRELLMANN COMPARED Heinrich M. G. Grellmann, the noted philologist and gypsiologist, belongs in the eighteenth century. His monumental work on the Gypsies of Europe made, and still makes, notable history on the Gypsies.

James Crabb, a gypsiologist and also a minister of religion who published *The Gypsies' Advocate* in 1832, wrote: Whoever has read Grellmann's Dissertation on the Continental Gypsies, and supposes that those of England are equally immoral and vicious, are greatly mistaken. The former are banditti and robbers, without natural affection, living with each other almost like brutes, and scarcely knowing, and assuredly never caring about, the existence of God. Some of them are even supposed to be cannibals. The Gypsies of this country are altogether different, as monstrous crimes are seldom heard of among them.

The author is not aware of any of them being convicted of house-breaking, or highway robbery. Seldom are they guilty of sheep-stealing, or robbing hen-roosts. Nor can they be justly charged with stealing children: this is the work of worthless beggars, who often commit far greater crimes than the Gypsies.

GROUSZINI In Moscow, as in many other cities throughout Europe, there was a special quarter relegated exclusively for the Gypsies. This area was known as Grouszini. Granada, Seville, London, Budapest, Istanbul have similar Gitanerías.

GUILDS Among the Gypsies there are guilds, whose members have particular occupations, such as musicians, masons, carpenters, tinsmiths, cobblers, gardeners, basket makers, bear-trainers, horse-dealers.

GURBETI A term applied in Serbia to the Mohammedan Gypsies who live in tents. Religiously, the Gypsies accepted the religion of the country of their sojourn, but as a rule only in a superficial sense.
They have thus been Catholics, Protestants, Lutherans.

GUY MANNERING This is the title of a novel by Sir Walter Scott in which Gypsies appear without malice. Meg Merrilies is the prominent Gypsy character. John Keats was so interested in the locale of the novel that he produced a poem on Meg Merrilies herself.

GYP This expression, listed in some dictionaries with the meaning of *to deceive, to steal, to cheat,* is a traditionally prejudicial use of the term. It is in line with other such terms, of an ethnic origin, that have been discriminatingly used in a markedly pejorative sense.

GYPSIES AND AGRICULTURE The Gypsies, throughout their long and troubled history, had a fixed dislike for agriculture and had rather hunger, or any other privation, than follow the plough. Still, early in the nineteenth century, there were Gypsies in Hungary who were cultivators.

Since the year 1768 the Empress Maria Theresa of Austria had ordered the Hungarian and Transylvanian Gypsies to be instructed in husbandry: but these orders were very little regarded. In Spain, and in other countries, Gypsy farmers are quite rare.

GYPSIES AND CHRISTIANS In the Preface to his *The Zincali* George Borrow, who was intimately acquainted with the Gypsies of Spain, England, and Wales, categorically declares: The Gypsies are not a Christian people, and their morality is of of a peculiar kind, not calculated to afford much edification to what is generally termed the respectable portion of society.

GYPSIES AND THE AUTHORITIES In England, the relation between the Gypsies and the police was for from friendly. Charles G. Leland, the folklorist and gypsiologist, illustrated the situation thus:
Where There Isn't Police
Talk between two Gypsies
"What is luck for the day?" I asked and he said,
"very bad luck again to me."
It is very bad luck, that never will cease and all along these here police.
When I am sound asleep in our little camp,
The pigs come down and they make as tramp.
They roots me and I gets no peace.
For it's allen 'move on!' with them 'ere police.
If my missus gets in a house, you know,
To tell a bit of fortune or so
They scare her almost to her decease.
For they're natural devils, is their police.
I had a fellow preaching to me,
All this is land of liberty.
But I tells him my liberty is peace,
And there is none o' that there, where you has police

Oh, I had enough o' this land I say,
With all its Lords and parsons and sitch as they say,
And it is over the water I goes like geese,
To a land where there isn't no police.
There you can tell a fortune or so.
There you can clear out the things, you know.
There you are free as the blowing breeze:
Fearlessly from them vile police.
The Merican land, I think may hap,
Is just the spot for a Romany chap:
For from all I hear, there they lives at peace,
As if the people don't care for no police.

GYPSIES AND THE INQUISITION The Inquisition, which burned so many Jews and Moors and conscientious Christians, at Seville and Madrid, and in other parts of Spain, seems to have exhibited the greatest clemency and forbearance in their treatment of the Gitános. Indeed, we cannot find one instance of its having interfered with them. The charge of restraining the excesses of the Gitános was abandoned entirely to the secular authorities. The Inquisition always looked upon the Gitános with too much contempt to give itself the slightest trouble concerning them. For as no danger either to the state or the church of Rome could proceed from the Gitános, it was a matter of perfect indifference to the holy office whether they lived without religion or not. — *George Borrow*

GYPSIES AND WITCHES The Gypsy woman was often regarded as a witch, as is clear from the following lines:
Of Fairies, Witches, Gypsies,
My nourrice sang to me.
So Gypsies, Fairies, Witches,
I also sing to thee.

GYPSIES AS METAL-WORKERS Gypsies are known to have been skilled in the use of the common metals as well as gold. They are credited with the introduction of bronze into Europe. Their association with the Asian continent is also to some extent confirmed by the fact that the expression *tzigane* has been connected with the Tartar word *schegan,* which means a hammer.

GYPSIES IN ABERYSTWITH   In the 1880's when Charles Leland visited Wales, he came across a Gypsy settlement in Aberystwith.
The most monumental study of the Gypsy language in Wales was made by John Sampson, in his *The Dialect of the Gypsies of Wales,* published in 1926.

GYPSIES IN ASIA In Russian Central Asia the Gypsies were divided into Luli and Mazangs. The Luli were nomadic, like the European Gypsies. They lived in tents and made baskets and similar articles. The Mazangs were considered by some to be aborigines of the Turks of Constantinople. They professed Islam, and spoke Persian and Turki.

GYPSIES IN BALUCHISTAN   Early in the nineteenth century an Englishman, Sir Henry Pottinger, traveled in Baluchistan and Sind, where he found a nomadic people known as Luris. In them he observed a remarkable affinity with the European Gypsies. They spoke a language of their own. They had a leader or 'king' in each group. They were reputed to be plunderers. They were fond of animals and trained monkeys and bears and also practiced fortune-telling. They were also fond of dancing and music.

GYPSIES IN BARBARY   George Borrow, the nineteenth century gypsiologist, was inclined to believe that Gypsies existed, in his time, in Barbary:
> There are, however, many sects of wanderers in Barbary who might appear legitimate Gypsies. Among them are the Beni Aros, a Moorish sect, whose home is near

Tetuan. Another sect is that of Sidi Hamed au Muza, another roving people who dwell on the confines of the Sahara.

Another sect, that Borrow believed to be Gypsies, was called by the Moors *Those of the Darbushi-fal,* that is, those who are fortune-tellers. Their fixed dwelling or village was called *Char Seharra,* witch hamlet. Their manner of life, their guarded language closely corresponded to those of the Gypsies.

GYPSIES IN EARLY NETHERLAND Among the more exhaustive and scholarly surveys and accounts of Gypsy life in a historical setting or in a particular country are Mille Ans d'histoire des Tsiganes, by François de Vaux Foletier: published in Paris in 1970: and O. van Kappen's account of the Gypsies in the Netherlands, entitled Geschehnisse der Zigeuner in Nederland.

Also François de Vaux de Foletier's work on the Gypsies in medieval France: Les Tsiganes dans l'ancienne France.

GYPSIES IN EARLY ENGLAND It is easy enough, declared a gypsiologist of note, to conceive the manner in which the Gypsies lived in England for a long time subsequent to their arrival. Doubtless in a half-savage state, wandering about from place to place, encamping on the uninhabited spots, of which there were then so many in England; feared and hated by the population who looked upon them as thieves and foreign sorcerers; occasionally comfitting acts of brigandage, but depending chiefly for subsistence on the practice of the 'arts of Egypt', in which cunning and dexterity were far more necessary than courage or strength of hand.

GYPSIES IN EASTERN EUROPE An eighteenth century gypsiologist declared that the Gypsies were dispersed all over Moldavia, where every baron had several families

166

subject to him. In Wallachia and the Slavic countries they were quite as numerous. In Transylvania the Gypsies were grouped under four categories: the city Gypsies, who maintained themselves by music, smith-work, selling old clothes, horse-dealing: the next class consisted of gold-washers: the third division embraced the tent Gypsies: the fourth, the Egyptian Gypsies. These last were more filthy and more addicted to stealing than any of the others. Those who were gold-washers in Transylvania and the Banat had no intercourse with other tribes: nor did they like to be called Gypsies. They sifted gold sand in summer and in winter made trays and troughs, which they sold in an honest way.

Bessarabia, all Turkey, Bulgaria, Greece, and Rumania swarmed with Gypsies. Even in Constantinople they were innumerable. In Rumania, a large tract of Mount Haemus, which they inhabited, acquired the name of Tschenghe Valken—Gypsy Mountain. This district extended from the city of Aydos to Phillippopolis, and contained more Gypsies than any other province in the Turkish Empire.

In Poland and Lithuania, as well as in Courland, there were an amazing number of Gypsies. Even Sicily and Sardinia were not free of them. In the north of Eyria they were to be found in great numbers, passing for Mohammedans, living in tents or caravans. They dealt in milch cows and manufactured coarse carpets. A missionary, traveling in India in the eighteenth century, discovered a Gypsy encampment on the banks of the Ganges.

GYPSIES IN EGYPT   Charles Leland, the noted gypsiologist and folklorist, when traveling in Egypt to discover whether there were any Gypsies settled there, had a conversation with the Khedive Ismael. Leland was informed that there were many people in Egypt known as Rhagarin or Ghagarin, who were probably Gypsies. They were

167

wanderers who lived in tents, and were regarded with contempt even by the peasantry. Their women told fortunes, did tattooing, and sold small wares. The men worked in iron. They were all considered adroit thieves and noted as such. The men might sometimes be seen going around the country with trained monkeys. In fact, they appeared to be in all respects the same people as the Gypsies in other countries.

GYPSIES IN EUROPE   Tentative dates have been assigned to the appearance of Gypsies on the European continent. In the ninth century they are known to have been in Byzantium. In Bohemia, during the thirteenth century or possibly later in the fourteenth their sojourn became more extensive and ranged from Transylvania and Moldavia to Saxony, France, Denmark, Italy, Wales, Spain, and Scotland. They were in Russia, Poland, and Sweden early in the sixteenth century.

GYPSIES IN GREECE   Early in the twelfth century Gypsies arrived on Mount Athos. In the fourteenth century other Gypsies reached the islands of Crete and Corfu.
The Gypsies remained in Greece over such an extended time that the Greek language infiltrated largely into the Gypsy language.

GYPSIES IN PHILADELPHIA   Charles Leland the gypsiologist met with Austrian Gypsies in Philadephia during the 1880's:

> They were singularly attired, having very good clothes of a quite theatrical foreign fashion, bearing silver buttons as large as hen's eggs.
> In addition to Romany, they could speak Serb, Illyrian, German, Italian.

168

GYPSIES IN SEVENTEENTH CENTURY With respect to the English Gypsies, George Borrow the English gypsiologist, states that they probably lived a life tolerably satisfactory to themselves. They are not an ambitious people, and there is no word for glory in their language, but next to nothing is known respecting them. A people called Gypsies are mentioned, and to a certain extent treated of, in a remarkable work, a production of the seventeenth century entitled The English Rogue, or The Adventures of Merriton Latroon. But this work, though clever and entertaining, and written in the raciest English, is entirely valueless, the writer having evidently mistaken for Gypsies the Pikers or Abrahamites.

GYPSIES IN SWEDEN The primary home of the Gypsies has for centuries been a matter of debate among philologists and anthropologists. That they came from the Orient was and still is regarded in Sweden as definitive: for in that country the Gypsies are known as Tartars.

GYPSIES IN THE NINETEENTH CENTURY In the earlier decades of the nineteenth century the origin of the Gypsies had not been conclusively determined nor had their language been exhaustively studied. One gypsiologist at that time collated the hypothetical data on the Gypsies' original home, concluding that there was no decisive evidence of their descent from an Egyptian source. Not more than some fifty Hebrew words appeared in their language. Few words were of Coptic origin: few of Persian provenance. In every country that they adopted as their home, in Europe, Asia, and Africa, they spoke a language that was peculiar to themselves.

GYPSIES IN THE PYRENEES An early account of the Gypsies in the Iberian Peninsula runs as follows:

There exists, in the department of the Eastern Pyrenees, a people distinct from the rest of the inhabitants of a foreign origin, and without any settled habits. It seems to have fixed its residence there for a considerable time. It changes situation, multiplies there, and never connects itself by marriage with the other inhabitants. These people are called Gitanos, a Spanish word which signifies Egyptians. There are many Gitanos in Catalonia who are very strictly watched. They have all the vices of those Egyptians, or Bohemians, who formerly used to wander over the world, telling fortunes, and living at the expense of superstition and credulity. These Gitanos, less idle and less wanderers than their predecessors, are afraid of publicly professing the art of fortune-tellers; but their manner of life is scarcely different.

GYPSIES IN THE USSR In 1930 the USSR began publishing a Gypsy newspaper entitled *O novo Drom* — the New Way. In Moscow formerly there was a Gypsy theatre. At Uzhord in Ruthenia a Gypsy school for boys was founded: another similar institution in Kygor, in South Morovia.

GYPSIES IN TURKEY In Istanbul the Gypsy women used to enter the harems, pretending to cure children of the Evil Eye. At the same time they offered to interpret the dreams of the odalisques. In the coffee houses they danced lasciviously.
Some of the Zingari, the Gypsies, dealt in precious stones and also in drugs and poisons.

GYPSIES NOT JEWS In his *The Gypsies in Spain* George Borrow the gypsiologist categorically asserted that the Jews and the Gypsies were two distinct peoples:

I took the Jew of Fez, even Hayim Ben Attar, by the hand, and went up to Mr. Petulengro, exclaiming: "Sure ye are two brothers." Anon the Gypsy passed his hand over the Jew's face, and stared him in the eyes. Then turning to me he said: "We are not two brothers. This man is no Romano. I believe him to be a Jew. He has the face of one. Besides, if he were a Rom, even from Jericho, he could rokra a few words in Romany."

Now the Gypsy had been in the habit of seeing German and English Jews, who must have been separated from their African brethren for a term of at least 1700 years. Yet he recognized the Jew of Fez for what he was — a Jew, and without hesitation declared that he was "no Roman." The Jews, therefore, and the Gypsies have each their peculiar and distinctive countenance, which, to say nothing of the difference of language, precludes the possibility of their having ever been the same people.

GYPSIES OF MIXED BLOOD   Heinrich Grellmann, the noted eighteenth century gypsiologist, wrote as follows:

Experience shows that the dark color of the Gypsies, which is continued from generation to generation, is more the effect of education and manner of life than descent. Among those who profess music in Hungary, or serve in the imperial army, where they have learned to pay more attention to order and cleanliness, there are many to be found whose extraction is not at all discernible in their color.

GYPSIES OF THE STEPPES   In the late 1880's there were Gypsies wandering over the Russian steppes, wrapped in sheep-skins who called themselves *Mi Dvorane Polaivii*, Lords of the Waste.

171

GYPSIES OF WALES The Welsh Rom or Gypsy preserves many of the picturesque traits of his race which are now so rapidly vanishing. Time will yet show that before all time, or in its early dawn, there were root-born Romany itinerants singing, piping, and dancing.

The primary authority on the dialect of the Welsh Gypsies is John Sampson, author of The Dialect of the Gypsies of Wales, published in 1926.

GYPSIES ON THE MOVE The English Gypsies also travel in Scotland, relates a Scottish gypsiologist, with earthenware in carts and wagons. A body of them, to the number of six tents, with sixteen horses, encamped, on one occasion, on the farm of Kingledoors, near the source of the Tweed. They remained on the ground from Saturday night till about ten o' clock on Monday morning, before they struck their tents and wagons.

At St. Boswell's fair, continues the chronicler, I once inspected a horde of English Gypsies, encamped at the side of a hedge, on the Jedburgh road as it enters St. Boswell's Green. Their name was Blewett, from the neighborhood of Darlington. The chief possessed two tents, two large carts laden with earthenware, four horses and mules, and five large dogs. He was attended by two old females and ten young children. One of the women was the mother of fourteen, and the other the mother of fifteen, children. This chief and the two females were the most swarthy and barbarous looking people I ever saw. They had, however, two beautiful children with them, about five years of age, with light flaxen hair, and very fair complexions. The old Gypsy women said they were twins; but they might have been stolen from different parents, for all that, as there was nothing about them that had the slightest resemblance to any of the horde that claimed them. Apparently much care was taken of them, as they were very cleanly and neatly kept.

GYPSIOLOGISTS Among noted gypsiologists who have both studied the Gypsies and have written about them are: Ainsworth, W. H. *Rookwood*

Block, Martin. *Gypsies*
Cuttriss, Frank. *Romany Life*
Groome, F. *In Gypsy Tents*
Leland, C. G. *The Gypsies*
McCormick, Andrew. *The Tinkler-Gypsies*
Sampson, J. *The Dialect of the Gypsies of Wales*
Simson, Walter. *A History of the Gpysies*
Smith, Hubert. *Tent Life with English Gypsies in Norway.*
Vesey-Fitzgerald, Brian. *Gypsies in Britain*
Woodcock, Henry. *The Gypsies*
Yates, Dora, E. *My Gypsy Days*
Yoors, Jan. *The Gypsies*

GYPSY ADMISSION A Gypsy song, translated by George Borrow, reveals the Gypsy skill in extracting money from the *gorgio,* the non-Gypsy:

Britannia is my name;
I am a swarthy Lovel;
The Gorgios say I be
A witch of wondrous power;
The silly, foolish fellows,
For often I bewitch
The money from their pockets.

GYPSY AFFECTION Gypsies retain an affectionate remembrance of their deceased relatives. They are even attached to the horse or donkey, to a ring or a silver spoon that had belonged to the deceased.

GYPSY AMULETS Continental Gypsies, wrote a gypsiologist, are notable believers in amulets. Being in a camp of very

173

wild Cigany in Hungary a few years ago, I asked them what they wore for *bakt,* or luck. Whereupon they all produced small sea-shells which, I was assured, were potent against ordinary misfortunes.

GYPSY AND CHRISTIAN   George Borrow, the gypsiologist, states categorically in *The Gypsies in Spain* that the Gypsies are not a Christian people, and that their morality is of a peculiar kind, not calculated to afford much edification to what is generally termed the respectable portion of society.

GYPSY AND HINDU   In many instances Gypsy and Hindu practices and customs coincide in a remarkable way: a further confirmation of the accepted view that the Gypsies' original home was Northern India.
Childbirth customs in both races are similar. So too with marriage rites. Gypsy and Hindu dances show affinities. Funeral ceremonials in both races demonstrate ethnic relationships. Hindu numerology is closely linked to Gypsy numerals. Parallels are frequent between Gypsy and Hindu music.

GYPSY APOTHECARIES   The Gypsies are deeply versed, by their transmitted legends and folklore and domestic remedies, in treatments of an enormous variety of ailments, both human and animal. Medically and pharmaceutically, the Gypsies are self-reliant and have recourse to physicians in only highly exceptional cases.
An open wound, for instance, is simply treated with a dressing of snake's tongue, crushed and boiled in oil. Kidney trouble is also treated herbally with an infusion of barberries.
These treatments, and many similar ones, are all based on the Gypsies' knowledge of wood and field lore, of growing things and leaves, juices and wild berries, roots

174

and seeds, seaweed and flowers. All these ingredients are prepared as ointments or infusions, powders, decoctions, or poultices.

GYPSY APPEARANCE In *The Zincali,* George Borrow thus describes the appearance of a Spanish Gypsy:
Her complexion is more than dark, for it is almost that of a mulatto, and her hair which hangs in long locks on either side of her face is as black as coal and coarse as the tail of a horse, from which it seems to be gathered. There is no female eye in Seville that can support a glance of hers so fierce and penetrating and yet so artful and sly in the expression of their dark orbs.

GYPSY ASSEMBLY James V of Scotland issued an Order in Council declaring that, if three Gypsies were found together in assembly, in any part of Scotland, one was to be hanged or shot immediately. Such Orders and Decrees against the Gypsies were common throughout the Middle Ages and even later.

GYPSY AS SOLDIER On account of their migratory habits and of the fact of their non-absorption into any state organization, the Gypsy soldier was, until contemporary times, a great rarity. From the fifteenth on, however, Gypsies were at times enrolled as mercenary troops in the private armies of territorial dukes and princelings. Thus they were attached to the forces of Henry IV of France late in the sixteenth century.

GYPSY ATTITUDE The Gypsies always felt that the fruits of the earth, the grain of the fields, fish and fowl and the smaller animals belonged to man in general and were readily available, with some ruse or subtlety added.
Hence, to the Gypsy mind, petty pilfering, breaking into hen-roosts, poaching were regarded without criminal stigmata attached to them.

175

GYPSY BANK The Gypsies are not strangers to pawn-brokers' shops. But they do not generally visit these places for the same purpose as the poor. To the Gypsy, a pawn-shop is his bank. When the Gypsies acquire property illegally, as by stealing, swindling, or fortune-telling, they purchase valuable plate and sometimes in the same hour pledge it for safety. They keep such

property in store against days of adversity or trouble, as often occurs on account of their dishonest habits.
At other times, they carry their plate about with them, and when visited by friends they bring out from rags a silver teapot and a cream-jug and silver spoons. Their plate is by no means paltry, although considerable property in plate is not very generally possessed by the Gypsies.

GYPSY BELIEFS To the Gypsies, the earth, *phu,* is regarded as the supreme unchanging phenomenon in an otherwise unstable world. Gypsies also feel associated with the heavenly bodies. When the moon is visible, they pray with lowered head.

GYPSY BRAWL Writing of the Hungarian Gypsies, Heinrich Grellmann, the noted eighteenth century gypsiologist, says:
They are loquacious and quarrelsome in the highest degree. In the public markets, and before ale houses, where they are surrounded by spectators, they bawl, spit at each other, catch up sticks and cudgels, vapour and brandish them over their heads, throw dust and dirt; now run from each other, then back again, with furious gestures and threats. The women scream, drag their husbands by force from the scene of action; these break from them again, and return to it. The children, too, howl piteously.

GYPSY BREW In the Middle Ages Gypsies, when cooking a

stew in which a hedgehog was usually the main ingredient, were instantly associated by the villagers with demoniac concoctions like those prepared by The Three Witches. To a large extent, the food of the Gypsies depended on what they could secure for themselves in the fields, the woods, the farms, and the rivers.

GYPSY BURIAL   A peculiar burial custom was common among some Scottish Gypsies a century ago. Some of the Gypsies only put a paper cap on the head, and paper round the feet of the dead; leaving all the body bare, excepting that they place upon the breast, opposite the heart, a circle made of red and blue ribbons, in form something like the variegated cockade worn in the hats of newly-enlisted recruits in the army.

GYPSY CAMP ROUTINE   Gypsies usually prefer for pitching their tents the least frequented parts of the country, where they may have some convenient shelter. It is the business of the women to carry about and to dispose of the articles which they have for sale. The men, in the meantime, remain with their horses and carts, or occupy themselves in fishing or poaching, in both of which they show much dexterity. Occasionally two or more families travel together. They seldom remain longer than a few days in one place, and they very rarely or never travel on the Sabbath. They leave their headquarters very early in spring, probably the beginning of March, and return usually after the winter has fairly commenced, about the end of November. They seem to enjoy the best of health; and the older women of the tribe are supposed to possess much skill in the management of wounds and diseases. The only species of country work in which they engage with others is that of reaping and for this purpose many of them return about the beginning of autumn, to hire themselves to those farmers who will engage them. At home they usually conduct themselves in a quiet and peaceable manner, and their quarrels are chiefly among themselves. These are very violent while they last, and the occasion or ground of quarrel is seldom known but to themselves. On these occasions especially they are addicted to profane and dreadful imprecations. Their character for truth and honesty does not stand high. But they have enemies enough to proclaim their faults, and their faults it must be confessed are neither few nor small.

GYPSY CENTENARIAN Eppie Lundie was a Scottish Gypsy who lived to the age of one hundred. In ninteenth century Scotland she was a terror wherever she traveled. Without the least hesitation or scruple she frequently stripped defenseless individuals of their wearing apparel, leaving them sometimes naked in the open fields.

GYPSY CHARACTERS One Gypsy woman, who made many dupes by her 'treasure trove' devices, rode a good horse and dressed gaily and expensively. One of her saddles cost more than twenty pounds. It was literally studded with silver. For she carried on it the emblems of her profession wrought in that metal. There emblems consisted of a half-moon, seven stars, and the rising sun.

Her 'treasure trove' methods, by means of which she had accumulated these possessions, consisted in inducing gullible gorgios, non-Gypsies, to hand over to her a sum of money in return for which she would inform them of a treasure hidden somewhere in their home. No such treasure, of course, existed.

Another Gypsy likewise practiced similar deceptions. She persuaded an elderly man to put his notes and money in a wrapper and lock it up in a box. Then she asked permission to look at the box in his presence, in order, as she said, to pronounce a certain incantation over it. She was closely watched, but contrived to steal the box and put into it a parcel similar in appearance. On examination, the parcel revealed nothing but a bundle of rubbish. The money amounted to several hundred pounds. The Gypsy was immediately pursued and caught with the whole sum about her person. She was allowed to escape justice, because her covetous client did not wish to expose himself or to waste his money in prosecution.

The daughter of his Gypsy followed in the same practices as her mother: and the crime descended to her through several generations.

GYPSY CHIEFS The eighteenth century noted gypsiologist Grellman wrote of the Hungarian Gypsies:

They still continue the custom among themselves of dignifying certain persons, whom they make heads over them, and call by the exalted Slavic title of Voivode. To choose their Voivode, the Gypsies take the opportunity, when a great number of them are assembled in one place, commonly in the open field. The elected person is lifted up three times, amidst the loudest acclamation, and confirmed in his dignity by presents. His wife undergoes the same ceremony. When this solemnity is performed, they separate with great conceit, imagining themselves people of more consequence than electors returning from the choice of an emperor. Every one who is of a family descended from a former Voivode is eligible; but those who are best clothed, not very poor, of large stature, and about the middle age, have generally the preference. The particular distinguishing mark of dignity is a large whip, hanging over the shoulder. His outward deportment, his walk and air, also plainly show his head to be filled with notions of authority.

GYPSY CHILDREN In Scotland a person who cannot read

or write, is rarely to be met with. Still, there are many Gypsy children not sent regularly to school: and those are during the many months that they are traveling in the country, are extremely apt to forget all that they have been taught, and in the following winter must commence the same course of instruction again. Generally, they are remarked as clever children. Considering many disadvantages under which they receive instruction, the progress they make is surprising. The parents are in general very much attached to their children. This, in fact, is one of those features of their character which distinguish their tribe wherever it is found. Nevertheless, so anxious are they that their children should be instructed, that they have again and again expressed their utmost willingness to part with them for this purpose, and to leave them at home during the summer months, that they might attend school, but they lament their inability to maintain them.

GYPSY CHIROMANCY The noted gypsiologist Charles Leland declared that there was very little knowledge among the Gypsies of real chiromancy, such as was set forth in the literature of occult or semi-occult science.
But Leland adds that there are really Gypsies who have a very highly cultivated faculty of reading the mind.

GYPSY CODE To the Spanish Gypsies, the greatest crimes were a quarrelsome disposition and revealing the secrets of the brotherhood. By this code the members were forbidden to eat, drink, or sleep in the house of a Busnó, which signifies any preson who is not of the sect of the Gypsies, or to marry out of that sect. They were likewise not to teach the language of Roma to any but those who, by birth or inauguration, belonged to that sect. They were enjoined to relieve their brethren in distress at any expense or peril. They were to use a peculiar dress, which

is frequently alluded to in the Spanish laws, but the particulars of which are not stated. And they were to cultivate the gift of speech to the utmost possible extent, and never to lose anything which might be obtained by a loose and deceiving tongue, to encourage which they had many excellent proverbs, for example
— The poor fool who closes his mouth never wins a dollar. The river which runs with sound bears along with it stones and water.

GYPSY COLONY   In a letter written by a Scottish clergyman in the nineteenth century, he describes a unique Gypsy colony:

Kirk Yetholm, small village in the county of Roxburghshire, on the borders of the two kingdoms of England and Scotland, has been long known, and somewhat celebrated, as the favorite residence or headquarters of the largest colony in Scotland of that singular and interesting race of people the Gypsies, whose origin is involved in so much obscurity and doubt. It is not, perhaps, correct to say that the 'muggers' or 'tinkers' of Kirk Yetholm are the pure, unmingled Gypsy race, whose forefathers, upwards of four centuries ago, emigrated to Europe from the East. As in England, as also in Scotland. from their intermixture with the natives of the country, and with other wanderers like themselves, they are now less distinguishable as a peculiar race. Still, however, their language, their erratic and pilfering propensities, and, in general, their dark or dusky complexion, black piercing eyes, and Hindu features, sufficiently betray the original of this despised and long-neglected race.

At what period they first settled in Kirk Yetholm I have not been able to ascertain. The family of Fa or Fall (a name renowned in Gypsy story) seems to have been the first, which probably was about the beginning of the last century. Whether or not they have any inter-course with the Gypsies in other parts of the country, I am unable to say: I have at least no evidence that they have. That they have a peculiar language is a subject on which I have no doubt: though they themselves deny the fact, and seem astonished at the question. I do not mean to say that it is a regularly for-med and complete language, but they are able to con-verse with each other in words unknown to others, and accompany many of these words with the specimens furnished by Hoyland and Grellmann. I find that the slang or language used by the Kirk Yetholm Gypsies is very the same as the language spoken by the English and Turkish Gypsies, a fact which identifies the colony residing in Kirk Yetholm with the same people in other parts of the world.

The number of Gypsies in the parish of Yetholm is about 100. It would appear, however, that the Gypsy population of this place is fluctuating. In 1798, from the statistical report of the minister of the parish at that period, there were only 59. In 1818, there were 109. In 1831, upward of 100; and, in a few years more, this number may be considerably diminished or in-creased.

GYPSY CONCOCTS PHILTRE Two women, neighbors and friends, were tried some years since, in England, for the murder of their husbands. It appeared that they were in love with the same individual, and had conjointly, at various times, paid sums of money to a Gypsy woman to work charms to captivate his affections. Whatever little effect the charms might produce, they were successful in their principal object, for the person in question carried on for some time a criminal intercourse with both. The matter came to the knowledge of the husbands, who, taking means to break off this connection, were respectively poisoned by their vives. Till the moment of conviction these wretched females betrayed neither emotion nor fear, but then their consternation was indescribable: and they afterward confessed that the Gypsy, who had visited them in prison, had promised to shield them from conviction by means of her art.

GYPSY CONFESSION A few decades ago Petulengro was a noted Gypsy musician, with an international reputation. He was a typical roving, restless Gypsy personality. He was acquainted with the Amazon jungles, the South African gold fields, the Australian bush. He was a street musician and a soloist in the most luxurious theatres. He was the Gypsy Fiddler *par excellence,* a descendant of George Borrow's Petulengro, a descendant too of the Gypsy violinist Bihari. And his creed was summed up in his own words: I have never sought anything with much fervor or constancy except change.

GYPSY COURTS Henry VIII of England decreed that Gypsy courts were void and invalid and that only English law was to be administered in their case. Similar restrictive measures were directed against the Gypsies in many European countries, particularly in Spain and in Rumania.

GYPSY CRIME In the fifteenth century in England if a Gypsy, accused of a crime declared himself innocent, he was tried by a jury composed equally of Englishmen and Gypsies.
In other countries, particularly in the Balkans and in Spain, accusations against Gypsies were virtually tantamount to condemnation.

GYPSY DRESS During the sixteenth, seventeenth, and eighteenth centuries it was possible for Gypsy men to dress with elegance, in the manner of the country of their sojourn.

183

Doublets and hose and boots with adornments of collars and earrings, turbans and broad-brimmed hats, and capes gave them a distinction that was sometimes perpetuated in contemporary art. The women, on the other hand, maintained the traditional though colorful many-skirted costume that marked their Gypsy identity.

GYPSY ENTERTAINMENT   When the Gypsies first appeared in England, very early in the sixteenth century, they were regarded with great curiosity as exotic strangers from rémote coutries. Some years later, however, they had reached the point of being invited by the Duke of Suffolk to his home.

GYPSY EXCURSIONS   The most remarkable feature connected with the habits of the Hungarian Czigany consists in their foreign excursions, having plunder in view, which frequently endure for three or four years, when, if no mischance has befallen them, they return to their native land — rich; where they squander the proceeds of their dexterity in mad festivals. They wander in bands of twelve and fourteen through France, even to Rome. Once, during my own wanderings in Italy, I rested at nightfall by the side of a kiln, the air being piercingly cold. It was about four leagues from Genoa. Presently three individuals arrived, to take advantage of the warmth — a man, a woman, and a lad. They soon began to discourse — and I found that they were Hungarian Gypsies. They spoke of what they had been doing, and what they had amassed — I think they mentioned three hundred crowns. They had companions in the neighborhood, some of whom they were expecting. They took no notice of me, and conversed in their own dialect.

GYPSY EXPLANATION   The term *patrin* or *patteran* is thus explained in Gypsy terms:

184

You ask me what are *patrins. Patrin* is the name of the signs by which the Gypsies who go before show the road they have taken to those who follow behind. We flings handfuls of grass down at the head of the road we takes, or we makes with the finger a cross-mark on the ground, or we sticks up branches of trees by the side of the hedge. But the true patrin is handfuls of leaves flung down; for *patrin* or *patten* in old Roman language means the leaf of a tree.

GYPSY FAITH "What will gain thy faith?" said Quentin Durward, in Sir Walter Scott's novel of that name.
"Kindness," answered the Gypsy, Hayradden Maugrabbin.

GYPSY FEAR One of the principal fears that beset Gypsies is illness. Illness, they conceive, is in the control of malefic spirits, demons who must be appeased by incantations, by apotropaic spells, magic rituals, supplications.

GYPSY FEMALE If there is one being in the world who, more than another, deserves the title of sorceress, it is the Gypsy female — the Gypsy wife, the mother of two or three children. She can at any time, when it suits her, show herself as expert a jockey as her husband. But she can do much more. She is a prophetess, though she believes not in prophecy. She is a physician, though she will not taste her own philtres. She is a procuress, though she is not to be procured. She is a singer of obscene songs, though she will suffer no obscene hand to touch her. And though no one is more tenacious of the little she possesses, she is a cut-purse and a shop-lifter whenever opportunity shall offer.

GYPSY FETISH Among the Gypsies all sorts of objects were treated as fetishes that would bring good luck or avert misfortune. For instance, sea-shells were regarded as favorable amulets. Among the Gypsies of Serbia, nuts, especially those that were heart-shaped, that is, double, were carried about the person as fetishes or amulets.

In Bosnia, in the Balkans, the Gypsies prepared a fetish in the form of a cradle. It was made of nine kinds of wood, and its purpose was to bring good luck to the child who slept in it.

GYPSY FICTION   The Gypsy theme, in the genre of the short story, has appealed to many writers. In some cases the motif is romantic, while other tales cleave close to the realities. There are stories by French, Spanish, and English writers. Among the authors stand out such notable names as Cervantes, Alarcón, John Galsworthy, Maxim Gorky. Appended is a selective list of such tales:

Alarcón, P. A. de, *The Gypsy's prophecy*

Anderson, L. W. D., *Kiss and the queen*

Bacon, J. D. D., *The Gypsy*

Barr, A. E. H., *Gypsy Lady*

Benoit, P., *Night round*

Bercovici, K., *Gypsy blood that tells*

,,　　　,, *Youth to youth*

,,　　　,, *The Stranger*

,,　　　,, *Ghitza* : nine stories .

,,　　　,, *Singing winds* : twelve stories

,,　　　,, *Murdo* : nine stories

,,　　　,, *Luca*

,,　　　*Drought*

Boyd, D., *Romany child*

Byrne, D., *Tales of my uncle Cosimo and the fair girl of Wu*

Caldwell, E., *My old man and the gypsy queen*

Cervantes, Saavedra, M. de, *The little Gypsy girl*

Christie, A. M., *The Gypsy*

Coppard, A. E., *Cheese*

Demetrios, G., *Salt and Gypsies*

186

Dillon, E. J., *Among the Gypsies in Transylvania*
Donn-Byrne, D. C., *The turn of the wheel*
Ellner, J. ed. *Gipsy patteran* : twelve stories
Falkenberget, J. *Gipsy girl*
Galsworthy, J. *The Runagates*
Golding, L. *Vicar of Dunkerly Briggs*
Gorky, M. *Makar Chudra*
Goudge, E. *Diccon*
Hardwick, E. *People on the railway coaster*
Hughes, R. A. W. *Cornelius Katie*
Kaye-Smith, S. *Fear of streets*
    ,,   ,, *The moockbeggar*
Kliewer, W. *The prince of Egypt*
Lafferty, R. A. *Land of the great horses*
Lawrence, D. H. *The virgin and the Gypsy*
Lehmann, R. *Gypsy's baby*
Lewis, A. *Wanderers*
Lofts, N. R. *Bride of Christ*
Lory, J. van. *Death of my cat*
Mallet-Joris, F. *Cordelia*
McAlmon, R. *Potato picking*
Mansfield, K. *How Pearl Button was kidnapped*
Mérimé, P. *Carmen*
Mitchell, J. *King of the Gypsies*
Moravia, A. *The spell*
Mulhoffer, D. B. *Last year*
Neagoe, P. *Holy remedy*
   ,,   ,, *Ill-winds from the wide world*
O'Brien, F. J. *The wondersmith*
Penney, J. *Welka is stolen by Gypsies*
Quiller-Couch, A. T. *Yorkshire Dick*
Rice, L. G. *Lubbeny kiss*
Salten, P. *Mako, the little bear*
Scott, C. A. D. *Blasted oak*
Sharp, W. *Gipsy Christ*
Smith, Lady E. F. *Candlelight*

„	„	*The hurdy-gurdy*
„	„	*Sweet Spanish ladies*
„	„	*Tamar*

Smith, H. B. *Gypsy blood*
Stankovic, B. *Christmas comes after all!*
Thompson, V. *My Lady Greensleeves*
Van Doren, C. C. *The Gipsy*
Blicher, S. S., *Gypsy life*

GYPSY FOOD HABITS   To the Gypsies many types of food are unclean or defiled — machrimé. Cat-flesh or the flesh of a dog is rejected even in extreme circumstances. On the other hand, Gypsies will eat the meat of a dead mule.

GYPSY GESTURE   In greeting a Gypsy, the right hand is raised, with the palm opened outward, while the gorgio, the non-Gypsy, adds: San shan? How are you?

GYPSY GLANCE   It is very curious that Hindus, Persians, Gypsies have in common an expression of the eye which distinguishes them from all other Oriental races, and chief in this expression is the Romany. Captain Newbold, who first investigated the Gypsies of Egypt, declares that, however disguised, he could always detect them by their glance, which is unlike that of any other human being, though something resembling it is often seen in the ruder type of the rural American. I believe myself that there is something in the Gypsy eye which is inexplicable, and which enables its possessor to see farther through that strange mill-stone, the human soul, than I can explain. Any one who has even seen an old fortune-teller of 'the people' keeping some simple-minded maiden by the hand, while she holds her by her glittering eye, like the Ancient Mariner, with a basilisk stare, will agree with me. — *Charles Leland*

GYPSY GRATITUDE   A Scottish farmer was sent to prison

for non-payment of a small debt. Whenever a certain Gypsy used to come to this farmer, he, together with his family, was invited to stay on the farm. Hearing that his friend was in prison, the Gypsy, after great difficulty, was allowed to see the farmer. There were tears in his eyes as he offered fifty pounds, and more, if that were necessary, to set him free. The farmer, however, declined the offer. The Gypsy then brought his wife and family to visit the prisoner. All of them were overwhelmed with grief, particularly the father. It was known that the Gypsy was called King of the Gypsies, that is, he was a tribal chief. He was popular in the countryside, for his conduct and honesty.

GYPSY HABITAT In the late 1890's many Gypsies in Hungary lived in huts burrowed deep into the ground, with walls and roof of wood and mortar, thatched with corn-shucks. The Gypsies living in them had given up for-ever the old free life. They had come, many years ago, to squat upon the lord's estate, and he had let them stay, only exacting for payment a day's work in every week from each grown man.

GYPSY HAUNTS For the information of those who may wish to visit the Gypsies in London and Bristol, during the winter, the streets where they generally reside are as follows:

Tottenham Court Road, Bolton Srteet. Tothill Fields, White Street. The commons near London are places on which they constantly encamp. On Wimbledon common alone there were sevenyt of them at the Christmas of 1831.

Plum Street, near Woolwich: the Achbishop's Well, near Canterbury. In Bristol they are principally found in Saint Philip's, Newfoundland Street, Bedminster, and at the March and September fairs.

GYPSY HELPFULNESS Fifty years ago, wrote James Crabb the gypsiologist, in 1832, the Gypsies had their regular journeys in England, and often remained one or two months in a place, when they worked at their trades. And as access to different towns was more difficult than at the present time, partly from the hardness of the roads and partly from the paucity of carriers, they were considered by the peasantry and by small farmers, as very useful branches of the human family. At that period they usually encamped in the farmers' fields, or slept in their barns. They seldom robbed hedges, for their fires were replenished with dead wood procured, without any risk of fines or imprisonment, from decayed trees and wooded banks. And it may rightly be assumed that, at such a time, their outrages and depredations were very few.

GYPSY-HINDU CUSTOMS Many customs observed by the Gypsies, particularly those relating to childbirth and marriage, are remarkably similar to the corresponding Hindu customs. Another confirmatory demonstration of the kinship between the Gypsies and the Hindus.

GYPSY HISTORY To the Gypsies themselves, their past does not extend far historically. Their legends and folk-lore are largely oral and traditional. Until recently they were not literate in the accepted sense, although they could communicate in writing by formulaic symbols and signs and hieroglyphics.

GYPSY HUT Description of a Gypsy hut in Central Europe, at the beginning of the nineteenth century:
Air and daylight are excluded. The hut is very damp, having more the appearance of wild beast's dens. Rooms or separate apartments are not even thought of. All is one open space. In the middle is the fire, serving both for the purpose of cooking and warmth.

The father and mother lie half naked, the children entirely so, round the fire. Chairs, tables, beds, bedsteads find no place here. They sit, eat, sleep on the bare ground, or at most spread an old blanket or a sheep-skin under them. Every fine day the door is set open for the sun to shine in, which they continue watching so long as it is above the horizon. When the day closes, they shut their door and rest. When the weather is cold, or the snow prevents them opening the door, they make up the fire and sit round it until they fall asleep, without any more light than it affords.

GYPSY IMAGE IN GERMANY The phenomenon of the Gypsies in Germanic territory was reflected in several directions. They are referred to by Martin Luther. They were frequently represented in carnival shows. Hans Sachs, the famous Meistersinger, became the spokesman for the general attitude toward the Gypsies.

In his novel *Simplicissimus,* Hans Grimmelshausen, who belongs in the seventeenth century, has his heroine marry a Gypsy.

Schiller, the poet and dramatist, used a Gypsy as a character in his *Die Räuber.*

GYPSY IN ART The Gypsy has been represented pictorially in many instances, sometimes with notable effect. Joseph Pennell, the American artist (1857-1926) executed a a large number of etchings of Gypsy types and scenes in Transylvania and other areas of the Balkans. Spanish Gypsies have been vividly depicted in the sketches of José Porta. Arthur Rackham, the English artist, illustrated from the books of Walter Starkie the gypsiologist. There is a Dutch representation, belonging in the sixteenth century, of a flagellation scene in which the victims are Gypsies.

In La Bohémienne Frans Hals (c. 1580-1666) the Dutch

painter depicts a Gypsy with her characteristic smile. Zuloaga, too, the modern Spanish artist, portrayed on his canvasses many Spanish Gypsy types such as bull-fighters and beggars. Among his notable works is the Gypsy Bullfighter's Family.

GYPSY INCOGNITO   In *The Bible in Spain,* George Borrow the gypsiologist mentions:

> having met several cavalry officers from **Granada,** Gypsies *incog.,* who were surprised at being discovered to be Gypsies. They had been impressed, but carried on a trade in horses, in league with the captain of their company.
>
> They said: 'We have been to the wars, but not to fight: we left that to the *busné.* We have kept together, and like true Caloré, have stood back to back. We have made money in the wars.'

GYPSY INGENUITY   Forming from pre-historic times a caste or distinct class, it is very probable, wrote Charles Leland, that these Gypsies, roamed from India to Spain, possibly here and there all over Europe. The extraordinary diplomatic skill, energy, and geographic knowledge displayed by the first bands of Gypsies who, about 1417, succeeded in rapidly obtaining permits for their people to wander in every country in Europe except England, indicate great unity of plan and purpose.

GYPSYISM   With regard to the significance of this term, Walter Simson, the gypsiologist who belongs in the earlier decades of the nineteenth century, stated:

> It rests upon the broadest of all bases — flesh and and blood, a common and mysterious origin, a common language, a common history, a common persecution, and a common odium, in every part of the world. Remove the prejudice against the Gypsies,

make it as respectable to be Gypsies, as the world, with its ignorance of many of the race, deems it dis-reputable.

GYPSY JOURNALS   Various Gypsy journals are published, as follows:

In France: *Etudes tsiganes*: a quarterly published by the Association des Etudes Tsiganes, Paris.

In Italy: Lacio Drom.

In Finland: Zirickli.

Also in France: Monde gitan.

        Vie et lumière.

        Romano Pral.

Sweden: Zigenaren.

Spain: Pomezia.

Switzerland: Zigeunerfreund.

        La voix mondiale.

        Tzigane.

GYPSY KINGDOM   Kirk Yetholm, a large Gypsy colony in Roxburghshire, Scotland, was sometimes called the metropolis of the Gypsy kingdom of Scotland. It was their favorite settlement, according to the following verses by John Leyden (1775-1811), Scottish poet and Orientalist:

On Yets's banks the vagrant Gypsies place
Their turf-built cots, a sun-burnt swarthy race;
Through Nubian realms their tawny line they bring,
And their brown chieftain vaunts the name of king.
With loitering steps from town to town they pass,
Their lazy dames rocked on the panniered ass.
From pilfered roost or nauseous carrion fed,
By hedge-rows green they strew the leafy bed.
While scarce the cloak of tawdry red conceals
Their fine-turned limbs which every breeze reveals.
Their bright black eyes through silken lashes shine,

Around their neck their raven tresses twine,
But chilling damps and dews of night impair
Its soft sleek gloss and tan the bosom bare.
Admit the lines of palmistry to trace,
Or read the damsel's wishes in her face.
Her hoarded silver store they charm away,
A pleasing debt for promised wealth to pay.

GYPSY LAMENT

I'm sailing across the water,
A-stealing bread and meat so free,
Along with a precious harlot,
And she has been the ruin of me.

I slept one night within a barn,
A-stealing bread and meat so free,
Along with a precious harlot,
And she has been the ruin of me.

Next morning she would have me go,
A-stealing bread and meat so free,
To see with her the wild-beast show,
For she would be the ruin of me.

I went with her to see the show,
A-stealing bread and meat so free,
To steal a purse she was not slow,
And so she was the ruin of me.

They took us up, and with her I,
A-stealing bread and meat so free:
Am sailing now to Botany,
So she has been the ruin of me.

I'm sailing across the water,
A-stealing bread and meat so free,
Along with a precious harlot,
And she has been the ruin of me.

GYPSY LAW   Gypsy law may be divided into three headings:

(a) Do not separate from the husbands. The Rom is enjoined to live with his brothers, the husbands and not with the busné, the gorgios.
He must live in a tent, not in a house.

(b) Be faithful to the husbands. This precept applies particularly to the Gypsy women. The women must not associate with gorgios.

(c) Pay your debts to the husbands. In Romany the state of being in debt is called Pazorrhus. The Rom who did not try to extricate himself from this condition was regarded as infamous, and was finally turned out of the tribe.

GYPSY LAWS   With the best intentions, Charles III of Spain promulgated a law in 1783 that made the Spanish Gypsies New Castilians and required them to settle down in fixed locations. They were to change their peculiar dress and their language and adapt themselves to some trade. Their children, too, were to be taken from parents and educated by the State.
To the Gypsies in Spain this law, if implemented, would mean the annihilation of all Gypsy life. They coined an expression to meet the occasion: El krallis ha nicobado la liri de los Calés — The King has destroyed the law of the Gypsies: signifying that the Gypsies would no longer be able to maintain their own ethnically identifiable unity and their independence.

GYPSY LEGEND The Holy Family of Bethany consisted mainly of the three Marys — two sisters of the Virgin Mary, Marie Jacobé and Marie Salomé, and their servant Sara, who became the patron saint of the Gypsies.

The three Marys were bought by ship from the Holy Land to Provence. In 1448 the crypt of the shrine that had been dedicated to Les Saintes Maries were discovered at the sea shore in the Camargue country of Provence.

At the shrine where the Marys had originally landed a town was later built. Since the middle of the nineteenth century it has been known as Les Saintes Maries de la Mer.

This is a pilgrim spot for Gypsies. Here they foregather annually to do reverence to their patron saint and to celebrate with a great festival on May 23 and May 24.

GYPSY LETTER Illiteracy is common among the wandering Gypsies. Charles Leland, the gypsiologist, however, received a letter, well expressed, written by a Gypsy woman, Britannia Lee, in the late 80's.

GYPSY LOCATIONS In their migrations the Gypsies frequently settled in quarters that were allocated exclusively to them. Hence throughout many European cities, in Spain and Hungary, in France and Germany, there are streets and areas that bear the identifying addition "of the Bohemians," "of Egypt": as, for instance, Street of the Bohemians, Little Egypt Quarter. Sometimes entire villages or hamlets were identified as completely Gypsy: Tsiganca, Cikanda, Tsiganova.

GYPSY LOGIC It happened once that Billy Marshall, the Gypsy chief in Gallowayshire, attacked and robbed the laird of Bargally, and in the tussle lost his cap. A respectable farmer, passing by, some time afterward, picked up the cap, and put it on his head. The laird, with his mind confused by the robbery and the darkness combined, accused the farmer of the crime: and it would have gone hard with him at the trial, had not Billy come to his rescue. He seized the cap in the open court, and, putting it on his head, addressed the lair: 'Look at me sir, and tell me, by the oath you have sworn, am I not the man that robbed you?' — 'By heaven! You are the very man.' — 'You see what sort of memory this gentleman has,' exclaimed the Gypsy. 'He swears to the bonnet, whatever features are under it. If you yourself, my lord, will put it on your head, he will be willing to swear that your lordship was the person who robbed him.' The farmer was unanimously acquitted.

GYPSY LORE SOCIETY   The purpose of this Society, which was founded in 1881, is to improve the conditions of Gypsy study, to promote the investigation of Gypsy problems, and to collate the results obtained from various sources.

The Society publishes an annual *Journal* devoted to Gypsy vocabulary, texts of folk-tales and folk-songs, in various Romany dialects, as well as ethnographical, historical, and topical articles. In addition to the *Journal,* the Society has published five monographs: A Gypsy Bibliography, The Position of Romani in Indo-Aryan, A Grammar and Vocabulary of the Language of the Nawar or Zutt, the Nomad Smiths of Palestine. The headquarters are at the University Library, Liverpool, England.

GYPSY LOVE LYRIC

To Trinali

Now thou art my darling girl,
    And I love thee dearly;
Oh, beloved and my fair,
    Lov'st thou me sincerely?
As my good old trusty horse
    Draws his load or bears it:
As a gallant cavalier
    Cocks his hat and wears it;
As a sheep devours the grass
    When the day is sunny;
As a thief who has the chance
    Takes away our money;
As strong ale when taken down
    Makes the strongest tipsy;
As a fire without a tent
    Warms a shivering Gypsy;
As a Gypsy grandmother
    Tells a fortune neatly;
As the Gentile trusts in her,
    And is done completely, —
So you draw me here and there,
    Where you like you rake me;
Or you sport me like a hat, —
    What you will you make me.
So you steal and gnaw my heart,
    For to that I'm fated!
And by you, my Gypsy Kate,
    I'm intoxicated.
And I own you are a witch.
    I am beaten hollow;
Where thou goest in this world
    I am bound to follow, —
Follow thee, where'er it be,
    Over land and water,

Trinali, my Gypsy queen!
  Witch and witch's daughter!

GYPSY LOVE POEM

My mother's gone awandering
  Away to yonder town:
My father is in the ale house,
  Is safely settled down.
There is not a lad at home.
I'm all alone and waiting —
So come my darling, come!
  Tell me what I'm doing
By the fire-light here,
All for you, love, all for true love,
  All for luck, my dear!
I told a lady's fortune
  In that big house hard by.
No Gypsy could have done it
  More cleverly than I.
I promised that she'd marry
A lord with heaps of gold.
She filled my hand with silver,
As much as I could hold.

I can chatter, flatter
Gorgios far and near,
All for you, love, all for true love,
  All for luck, my dear!
  I bought some flour last evening —
  I bought it secretly.
Come now the cake is ready
  And nobody to see.
Meal so white money bright,
  Baked together here.
All for you, love, all for true love,
  All for luck, my dear!

Wait near the hedge awhile, lad,
    Stay yet a moment, stay —
I'm coming now to meet you.
In our old Gypsy way
I will throw the cake right over,
Although the hedge is high.
Go, drink to me, my lover,
Go, drink the tavern dry!
What is this, just a kiss?
Plenty, never fear.
All for you, love, all for true love,
    All for luck, my dear!

Janet Tuckey

GYPSY LUCK Luck is a commodity which the Gypsies are always selling to everybody while they protest they themselves have none. This attitude is illustrated in these Gypsy verses:

I've seen you where you never were
    And where you never will be;
And yet within that very place
    You can be seen by me.
For to tell what they do not know
    Is the art of the Romany.

GYPSY MAGPIE To English Gypsies the water-wagtail is known as the *Romano chiriklo* — the Gypsy magpie.

The Greeks had a saying, dating back at least to the fifth century B.C., 'Poorer than a kinklos: that is, a water-wagtail. Peasants in the third century A.D. gave the name *kinkloi* to homeless vagabonds.

The water-wagtail, described in Greek as 'much-wandering,' may have thus been associated with the much-wandering Gypsy people.

GYPSY MELODIES Traces of Gypsy music appear in Haydn,

Mozart, Beethoven, Schubert. Liszt wrote on the musical characteristics of Gypsy music and its widespread influence.

GYPSY MELODY   The Gypsies have such a sense of melody and harmony that many eminent musicians, including Beethoven, Brahms, and Haydn, have made use of Gypsy motifs.

It has been debated, on the other hand, whether Gypsy music is an original contribution or whether the Gypsies adapted the melodies of the countries where they settled.

GYPSY MEMORIAL   On their arrival in Europe, the Gypsies bestowed on themselves many honorific titles: Prince, Duke of Little Egypt, Count of Egypt. The practice continued among them. In contemporary times there are still Gypsies who are crowned as King or Queen of tribal groups. An interesting record was preserved on a gravestone dating in 1445, in the town of Furnstneau. On the stone is a dedication to the noble Lord Sir Panuel, Duke of Little Egypt and Lord of the stag's horn. The latter phrase refers to a coat of arms, presumably bestowed for services by the 'lord of the manor.'

GYPSY MINSTRELS   The Gypsy minstrels in Hungary have retained their musical traditions since their famous Czinka Panna, who flourished in the eighteenth century. She was the first Gypsy woman who became celebrated for her playing.

GYPSY MIXED BLOOD   On the question of intermarriage between Gypsy and *gorgio* or non-Gypsy, a gypsiologist wrote:

> Even remove the prejudice that exists against the Gypsies, as regards their color, habits, and history; what then? Would they, as a people, cease to be? Would

they amalgamate with the natives, so as to be lost?
acter, and creed, they might 'become confounded with
the residue of the population.' In that respect, they
are the most exclusive people of almost any to be
Mashurdálo-help!
Assuredly not.
They may mix their blood, but they preserve their
mental identity in the world; even although, in point of
physical appearance, habits, manners, occupation, char-
found in the world.

GYPSY MONSTER Mashurdálo, in Gypsy folklore, is a
monstrous giant who lurks in rocky places and forests in
order to catch animals and men and women and devour
them.

Mashurdálo appears in a magic invocation. To cure a
fever, a Gypsy goes to a running stream and casts pieces
of wood nine times backward into the running water,
at the same time repeating:

Fever go away from me.
I give it, water, unto thee.
Unto me thou art not dear.
Therefore go away from here
To where they nursed thee,
Where they shelter thee,
Whey they love thee,

GYPSY MUSIC Gypsy music has made a strong appeal in
many countries. It has become incorporated into the
music of Hungary and Spain in particular. Noted composers
have made this Gypsy music highly popular throughout
Europe and in the entire Western Hemisphere. Among
such musicians are Sarasate, Brahms, Schubert, and Liszt.

GYPSY MYSTICISM There is a deep, strange element in the
Gypsy character, which finds no sympathy or knowledge

in the German, and very little in other Europeans, but which is so much in accord with the Slavonian and Hungarian that he who truly feels it with love is often disposed to mingle them together. It is a dreamy mysticism; an indefinite semi-supernaturalism, often passing into gloom; a feeling as of Buddhism which has glided into Northern snows, and taken a new and darker life in winter-lands. It is strong in the Czech or Bohemian, whose nature is the worst understood in the civilized world.

GYPSY MYTH One of the most notable legends among the Gypsies involves Sara the Egyptian. She is reputed to have come as a hand-maiden to the two sisters of the Virgin Mary, Sainte Marie-Jacobé and Sainte Marie-Salome. The two sisters, together with others, constituted the family of Bethany, and settled in Provence in 42 A.D. Sara is the patron saint of the Romanichals.

GYPSY NAMES Common names for Gypsy boys include: Yerko, Frinkelo, Yakali, Ilika, Yanali, Stevo, Anaro, Pepindorio, Euri, Soner, Bendigo. Girls may be called: Savina, Terlina, Oraga, Dunicha, Vadoma, Djidjo, Oste-Linda, Leander, Mumeli, Mozol, Sinfai, Fezenta, Rawnie. Among the English Gypsies the following names are in use: Jasper, Colvato, Morella, Ercilla, Curlanda, Sanpriel, Pakonovina, Camilla, Orlanda.

GYPSY OATH A powerful oath among the Gypsies is Apo miro dadeskro vast! — By my father's hand!
To the Gypsies oaths are traditionally binding.

GYPSY OCCUPATIONS Among the various trades and occupations in which Gypsies have been engaged are: grastari, farriers: kastari, carpenters: anasori, tinsmiths: miyeyesti, traders: loautari, musicians.

They have been snake-charmers and acrobats, chimney sweeps and house painters, fishermen and mole-catchers, wrestlers, makers of clothes-pegs, boxes. In an exclusively feminine domain, the Gypsy women have concentrated their talents on fortune-telling.

GYPSY ORPHANS A clergyman was asked to put four Gypsy children, orphans, under the care of a Benevolent Committee:

> He visited their tent the following day. It was winter, and the weather was unusually cold, there being much snow on the ground. The tent, which was only covered with a ragged blanket, was pitched on the lee side of a small hawthorn bush. The children had stolen a few green sticks from the hedges, but they would not burn. There was no straw in the tent, and only one blanket to lay between six children and the frozen ground. The youngest of these children was three, and the eldest seventeen years old. In addition to this wretchedness, the smaller children were nearly naked. The youngest was squatted on the ground, gnawing a frozen turnip which had been stolen from an adjoining field. None of them had tasted bread for more than a day. Some money was given to the older sister to buy bread with. Straw was also provided to sleep on. Four were measured for clothes and after a few days they were placed under the care of one of the reformed Gypsies.

GYPSY PHILOLOGY Philologists, anthropologists, and historians have since the eighteenth century studied and collated the varieties of languages and dialects spoken by the Gypsies. In the course of their migrations the Gypsies have incorporated elements from the languages of the countries where they have sojourned for any length of time: Turkey and Greece, Egypt, the Baklans, England, the Iberian Peninsula.

The general consensus is that the origin of the Gypsies lies in India and that their primary language was Sanskrit, from which stemmed Hindi.

Among the philologists who been been notably associated with the linguistic sources of the Gypsies are Stephen Valyi, the German scholar Grellmann, Rüdiger, August F. Pott, Alexander Paspati of Greece, Beames, Miklosich, Jan de Goeje, Bataillard, E. Pittard, Sir Richard Burton, Pierre Meile, John Sampson, Jules Bloch, E. O. Winstedt.

GYPSY PHYSIQUE   The Gitános are, for the most part, of the middle size, and the proportions of their frames convey a powerful idea of strength and activity united. A deformed or weakly object is rarely found among them in persons of either sex. Such probably perish in their infancy, unable to support the hardships and privations to which the race is still subjected from its great poverty, and these same privations have given and still give a coarseness and harshness to their features, which are all strongly marked and expressive. Their complexion is by no means uniform, except that it invariably darker than the general olive hue of the Spaniards. Not unfrequently countenances as dark as those of mulattos present themselves, and in some few instances of almost negro blackness. Like most people of savage ancestry, their teeth are white and strong. Their mouths are not badly formed, but it is in the eye more than in any other feature that they differ from other human beings.

Another description, from a Spanish angle, runs as follows:

The Gitános have an olive complexion and very marked physiognomy. Their cheeks are prominent, their lips thick, their eyes vivid and black. Their hair is long black, and coarse, and their teeth very white. The general expression of their physiognomy is a compound of pride, slavishness, and, cunning. They are, for the most part, of good stature, well formed, and support with facility fatigue and every kind of hardship. When they discuss any matter, or speak among themselves, whether in Catalan, in Castilian, or in Germania, which is their own peculiar jargon, they always make use of much gesticulation, which contributes to give to their conversation and to the vivacity of their physiognomy a certain expression, still more penetrating and characteristic.

GYPSY PLUNDER Writing of the Gypsies in 19th century Scotland, Walter Simson, the gypsiologist, said:

These Gypsies were extremely civil and obliging to their nearest neighbors. But the farmers and others at a distance, who frequented the markets at Falkirk, and other fairs in the neighborhood, were always a plentiful harvest for the plundering Tinklers. Their plundering on such occasions spread a general alarm over the country. They even formed strong attachments to certain individuals of the community and afforded them protection. The fiery Tinklers, however, often fell out among themselves, on dividing, at home, the booty which they had collected at fairs and their astonished neighbors were horrified when they observed the hurricanes of wrath and fury exhibited by both sexes, and all ages, in the heat of their battles.

The children of these Gypsies attended the principal school at Linlithgow, and not an individual at the school dared to cast the slightest reflection, or speak a disrespectful word, either of them or their parents, although their robberies were everywhere notorious yet always conducted in so artful a manner that no direct evidence could ever be obtained of them. Such was the fear of the audacious conduct of these Gypsies inspired that the magistrates of the royal burgh of Linlithgow stood in awe of them, when any matter relative to their conduct came before them.

GYPSY POEM   In Spain, George Borrow encountered a person who recited a poem on the plague that had broken out in Seville in 1800. Translated from the Gypsy, the poem follows:

I'm resolved not to tell
In the speech of Gypsy-land
All the horror that befell
In this city huge and grand.
In the eighteenth hundred year
In the midst of summertide,
God, with man dissatisfied,
His right hand on high did rear,
With a rigor most severe.
Whence we well might understand
He would strict account demand
Of our life and actions here.
The dread event to render clear
Now the pen I take in hand.
At the dread event aghast,
Straight the world reform'd its course;
Yet is sin in greater force.
Now the punishment is past.
For the thought of God is cast
All and utterly aside,
As if death itself had died.
Therefore to the present race
These memorial lines I trace
In old Egypt's tongue of pride.
As the streets you wander's through
How you quail'd with fear and dread,
Heaps of dying and of dead
At the leeches' door to view.
To the tavern O how few
To regale on wine repair.
All a sickly aspect wear.

Say what hearts such sights could brook —
Wail and woe and ghastly care.
Plying fast their rosaries,
See the people pace the street,
And for pardon God entreat
Long and loud with streaming eyes.
And the carts of various size,
Piled with corpses, high in air,
To the plain their burdens bear.
O what grief it is to me
Not a friar or priest to see
In this city huge and fair.

GYPSY PRACTICE   The Gypsy fortune-teller is accustomed for years to look keenly and earnestly into the eyes of those whom she *dukkers* or "fortune-tells." She is accustomed to make ignorant and credulous or imaginative girls feel that her mysterious insight penetrates 'with a power and with a sign' to their very souls. As she looks into their palms, and still more keenly into their eyes, while conversing volubly with perfect self-possession, before long she observes that she has made a hit — has chanced upon some true passage or relation to the girl's life.

GYPSY PRANKS   The pranks and tricks played by a certain Scottish Gypsy named McDonald were numerous. He took great pains in training some of his horses to perform various evolutions and tricks. At one time he had a piebald horse so efficiently trained that it assisted him in his depredations. By certain signals and motions he could make it clap close to the ground, like a hare in its furrow. It would crouch down in a hollow piece of ground, in a ditch, or at the side of a hedge, so as to hide itself. With the assistance of one of these well-trained horses, McDonald on one occasion saved his wife, Ann Jamieson, from prison, and perhaps from the gallows. Ann was apprehended near Dunfermline for some of her unlawful practices. As the officers of the law were leading her to prison, McDonald rode up to the party and asked permission to speak with the prisoner. Permission was readily granted. McDonald then drew her aside, under the pretence of conversing with her in private. In an instant, Ann, with his assistance, sprang upon the horse, behind him, and bade goodbye to the officers who were amazed at the sudden escape of their prisoner.

GYPSY PRESENCE IN SPAIN   In the fifteenth century, when the Gypsies advanced into Spain, they were divided into numerous bodies, frequently formidable in point of number. Their presence was an evil and a curse in whatever quarter they directed their steps. As might be expected, the laborers, who in all countries are the most honest, most useful, and meritorious class, were the principal sufferers. Their mules and horses were stolen, carried away to distant fairs, and there disposed of, perhaps, to individuals destined to be deprived of them in a similar manner; whilst their flocks of sheep and goats were laid under requisition to assauage the hungry cravings of these thievish cormorants.

It was not uncommon for a large band or tribe to encamp in the vicinity of a remote village scantily peopled, and to remain there until, like a flight of locusts, they had consumed everything which the inhabitants possessed for their support; or until they were scared away by the approach of justice, or by an army of rustics assembled from the surrounding country. Then would ensue the hurried march: the women and children, mounted on lean but spirited asses, would scour along the plains fleeter than the wind. Ragged and savage-looking men, wielding the scourge and goad, would scamper by their side or close behind, while perhaps a small party on strong horses, armed with rusty matchlocks or sabres, would bring up the rear, threatening the distant foe, and now and then saluting them with a hoarse blast from the Gypsy horn. They traversed the country in gangs. They were what the Spanish law has styled Abigeos and Salteadores de Camino, cattle-stealers and highwaymen.

GYPSY PRESTIGE   In the Middle Ages the Gypsy tribal leaders brought their clans and companies through the length and breadth of Europe. They acquired such prestige on account of their putative Egyptian origin that even royalty acknowledged them. For example, in 1505 James IV of Scotland commended to the King of Denmark Anthony Gawin, Earl of Little Egypt.

Somewhat later, in 1540, James IV's successor granted letters under the Great Seal to 'our loved John Faw, Lord and Earl of Little Egypt . . . to assist him in execution of justice upon his company and folks, in coformity with the laws of Egypt.'

GYPSY QUARTERS   In the Middle Ages there were Gitanerías or quarters intended for Gypsies, in many Spanish towns. In a number of instances particular districts are still known by this name, although the Gitános themselves have long since disappeared. Even in Oviedo, in the Asturias, there is a place called Gitanería, though no Gitáno has been known to reside in the town within the memory of man. In the Gitanería the Gypsies lived in squalor. Here they worked as blacksmiths, a forbidden occupation. Here too they discussed plans for theft and plunder, in the Romany tongue, a language which was forbidden under severe penalties.

GYPSY RAIDS There were, in the eighteenth century, Gypsy sorties, plundering raids, into Germany and Switzerland. They swept over the Northern plains, through the Black Forest. Among the notorious chiefs of these marauding bands that included all kinds of outlaws were Johann Hassler and Hannikel.

GYPSY REFUGE A French decree, issued in 1538, prohibited the French people from offering a refuge to any Gypsy found in French territory.
Throughout their restless history the Gypsies in most European countries have been exiled or initially excluded from entrance.

GYPSY REFUSAL According to Gypsy legends, the ancestors of the Gypsies are doomed to wander because they refused to give shelter to the Virgin and Child. Another proposed explanation of their migrations is that the Gypsies foreswore the Christian faith and were required to do penance by roaming the world.

GYPSY REPUTATION The Gypsies have repeatedly been accused of having no religious feelings whatever. But they believe in a God, in a devil, in diabolic spirits that have an influence on their lives. In some countries they are believed to be Mithraics, worshipping fire and the sun like the ancient pagans devoted to the Persian Sun-God Mithra. And in many countries where they have infiltrated among the native populations they are credited with practicing the occult arts, black magic, sorcery, and diabolic rites.

GYPSY RHYMES Such rhymes relate to the popular reputation of Gypsies for fortune-telling and pilfering:
  For every Gypsy that comes to toon,

A hen will be a-missing soon,
And for every Gypsy woman old
A maiden's fortune will be told.
Gypsy hair and devil's eyes,
Ever stealing, full of lies.
Yet always poor and never wise.

GYPSY RITUAL   There is a remarkable echo of the theme
in ancient mythology relating to Pandora's box.
On Easter Monday Hungarian Gypsies made a wooden
box, wrapped it in white and red wool, and threw it
into a running stream. By sympathetic magic the Gypsies
conceived that prospective sicknesses were enclosed in the
box and would be carried off in the stream.

GYPSY RONDO   The title of a composition on a Gypsy theme
by Hayden.
Many noted musicians have been deeply interested in
Gypsy music, notably Franz von Liszt, who wrote on
Gypsy music in Hungary and who regarded such music
as original, not adapted from the Hungarians.

GYPSY SAYING   With regard to the laws imposed on the
Gypsy of Spain, the Gypsies themselves had a proverbial
saying: El Crallis ha nicobado la liri de los Cales: The
law of the King, Carlos III, has superseded Gypsy Law.
This law, in its human and generous provisions, opened
the schools to the Gypsies offered them the arts and
sciences, if only they were willing to advance. As late as
the mid-nineteenth century, however, the Gypsies had
availed themselves to a very little extent of these lawful
rights.

GYPSY SCAPEGOAT   With regard to the various magic methods of averting plague in Modern Greece, a Greek writer
related, in 1890:

sen slightly later. From the year 1417 on, which is the
siologists that there were settlements of Gypsies at Hil-
desheim early in the fifteenth century, at Basle and Mais-

The plague during the last terrible epidemic in Greece
spared Livartzi, because, as tradition says, many years
ago, when the disease attacked the Peloponnese, the
then inhabitants of Livartzi, with a view to the warding
off of all future danger from the plague, buried a Gypsy
boy alive as a propitiatory sacrifice.

GYPSY SCENE   In Hungary in the nineteenth century the Gypsies had more freedom than the peasants who were under
feudal serfdom. But the Gypsies had habits that were
far from attractive. Their hovels were sinks of poverty
and filth. Their dress was rags. Their food was occasionally
carrion. But their encampments often echoed with music
and song, and the Gypsies danced away their plight.

GYPSY SETTLEMENTS   It has been established by gyp-
accepted date of the appearance of Gypsies in Europe,
and in successive years, many chronicles and official
records, in Germany and Spain, in Rumania and England,
testify to this historical fact.

GYPSY SMITH   One of the most unique characters among the
Gypsies. Although the Gypsies have invariably been
regarded as non-Christian, and although their nomadic
life, detached from city ways, has by its very nature
rarely been in harmony with Christian practices, yet
there is the remarkable case of Gypsy Smith, the evangelist
to refute the general and long-maintained view of Gypsy
unconcern with the spiritual life.

Gypsy Smith wrote his autobiography, entitled Gypsy
Smith, His Life and Work, by Himself. The book was

published in 1903, under the auspices of the National Council of the Evangelical Free Churches, London.

From a typical Gypsy encampment Smith emerged as a famous evangelist. In England, in his day, the Gypsies were virtually foreigners, encamped on hostile ground, overlooked by Christian Churches, apart from the work of Crabb in the middle of the nineteenth century, among the Gypsies of Hampshire and the New Forest.

Gypsy Smith was neither a scholar, nor a theologian, nor a trained orator. His effectiveness as an evangelist lay in his simplicity and in the sincerity of his appeal. Rodney Smith was was born in 1860, in a Gypsy tent, in Wanstead near Epping Forest. The Gypsies care little for religion, yet they always take care to have their children baptized. Rodney Smith was baptized.

As a boy he experienced all the varieties of life as a Gypsy. Then he 'got religion.' He learned to read and write. He preached in the turnip-fields. He sang hymns in rustic cottages. In 1877 he became professionally an evangelist and devoted the rest of his life to his activities in this field. He became a Captain in the Salvation Army. He became known throughout Britain and in other countries. In his missions he toured England, Australia, and America.

GYPSY SONGS These songs were translated into English by George Borrow, the famous gypsiologist:

The Youthful Earl (English Gypsy)
Said the youthful earl to the Gypsy girl,
As the moon was casting its silver shine:
Brown little lady, Egyptian lady,
Let me kiss those sweet lips of thine.
   The Romany Songstress (Russian Gypsy)
Her temples they are aching,

As if wine she had been taking;
Her tears are ever springing,
Abandoned is her singing!
She can neither eat nor rest
With love she's so distress'd;
At length she's heard to say:
"Oh here I cannot stay.
Go saddle me my steed.
To my lord I must proceed;
In his palace plenteously
Both eat and drink shall I;
The servants far and wide,
Bidding guests shall run and hide.
And when within the hall the multitude I see,
I'll raise my voice anew, and sing in Romany."

The Friar (Spanish Gypsy)

A Friar
Was preaching once with zeal and with fire;
And a butcher of the town
Had lost a flitch of bacon;
And well the friar knew
That the Gypsies it had taken.
So suddenly he shouted: "Gypsy, ho!
Hie home, and from the pot
Take the flitch of bacon out,
The flitch good and fat,
And in its place throw
A clout, a dingy clout of thy brat,
Of thy brat,
A clout, a dingy clout of thy brat."

GYPSY SORCERESSES It is customary for all Gypsy sorceresses to take those who are to be fortune-told aside and, if possible, into a room by themselves. This is done partly to enhance the mystery of the procedure, and partly to avoid the presence of witnesses to what is really an illegal act.

GYPSY SORCERY-LORE   Gypsy sorcery-lore is of great value according to a gypsiologist, because all over the Aryan world Gypsies have in ancient or modern times been, so to speak, the wandering priests of that form of popular religion which consists of a faith in fortune-telling.

GYPSY STATUS   In Scotland the Gypsies often rose to high prominence in the mercantile field, and were connected by marriage with Scottish families of the rank of baronet. In another case, in 1734, a certain Gypsy Captain James Fall of Dunbar was elected Member of Parliament for Dunbar.

This same Gypsy family of Fall produced provosts and baillies and other civic officials. It was said that when these civic notables were in their cups they reminisced about their Gypsy origin.

GYPSY STIGMA   In the seventeenth century, in the days of Judge Hall, thirteen English Gypsies were hanged at Bury St. Edmonds, for no other cause than that they were Gypsies. At that time it was death without benefit of clergy for anyone to live among them for a month.

Lately, wrote a nineteenth century friend of the Gypsies, two of the most industrious of these Gypsies had a small pony and two donkeys taken away, merely on suspicion that they were stolen. The Gypsies were apprehended and brought before a magistrate, to whom they proved that the animals were their own and that they had obtain them legally. The animals were then pounded for trespassing on the common. It was fortunate that their owners had money to defray the expenses. Otherwise, one of the animals would have been sold for that purpose.

GYPSY STRATAGEM Whenever the Gypsies entered a new city in their migrations through Europe, the citizens would hesitate to accept the large bands that came clamoring for food and shelter. The tribal leaders therefore frequently managed to persuade the chief magistrate or the burgomaster to issue a proclamation of civic welcome to the Gypsies, since they were Christian pilgrims who had, as they alleged, been driven forth by the infidel Saracens.

GYPSY SURVIVAL Despite George Borrow's gloomy prognostication that by the end of the nineteenth century the Gypsies would be a disappearing people, the contrary, by the general consensus of many gypsiologists, is the considered view. The Gypsies seem to have an innate resilient buoyancy that has already enabled them to survive long centuries of persecution and that may well be an earnest of their persistent tenacity.

GYPSY TALES The folktales of the Gypsies, particularly of the Rumanian Gypsies, are traditional stories transmitted from one generation to another. The material is basically identically in each case, merely varied by the emotional recital. These tales deal with visitations of ghosts and werewolves, with sorcery, fleet-footed horses, battle conflicts with Turks and Russians and other enemies.

GYPSY THEME In the nineteenth century, in France, the Gypsy theme became highly popular among writers and poets, whether their characters were depicted romantically or with harsh realism. So George Sand, Eugène Sue, Théophile Gautier, Prosper Mérimée, among others, described the Gypsy phenomenon, although in many cases the writer had little if any actual contact with Gypsies themselves.

In his fiction and also in his historical themes and his

poetry, Victor Hugo often etched his characters with sharp, distinctive precision. In his novel *Le Roi s'amuse,* a Gypsy named Saltabadil, a killer, lives with his sister Maguelonne, a dancer, who is equally vicious. In his romantic novel *Hans l'Islande,* also, there is a hangman, whose wife is a Gypsy.

GYPSY TO THE GALLEYS! A Spanish Gypsy incident was turned into popular verse. A miquelet, a Spanish armed policeman, is conducting a Gypsy to the galleys. Coruncho Lopez, the Gypsy, had committed a robbery:

> Coruncho Lopez, gallant lad,
>   A smuggling he would ride;
> He stole his father's ambling prad,
> And therefore to the galleys sad
>   Coruncho now I guide.

GYPSY TRAIL Like the Afghans, like the Bedouin or the pastoral people of the Iranian uplands, the Gypsies, wherever possible, prefer to dwell in tents, like the Biblical peoples, or in caravans. In their migrations, they formerly were forced on occasion to travel on foot. Then by pony or donkey, by mule or horse. Or, in more comfortable circumstances, in ox-drawn wagons. Now, in many cases, where a tribal community has achieved some wealth, they use the automobile.

GYPSY TREATY King James V of Scotland, in 1540, made a kind of treaty with the Scottish Gypsies. He signed a writ that gave the Gypsies the privilege of jurisdiction over their own people, their traditions and laws.

GYPSY TRIBES Gypsies are classified into three categories: (a) The Kalerash Gypsies. They are predominantly metal

Rumanian Gypsy Coppersmiths (1911)

Rumanian Gypsies (1911)

workers. They are sub-divided into five units. This group has its milieu in Central Europe.

(b) The Gitanos. They are associated with the Iberian Peninsula, Provence, and North Africa.

(c) The Manush. The name, which is Sanskrit, denotes 'true men'. There are three sub-divisions.

Non-Gypsies who follow the trades and occupations of Gypsies are termed Barengré.

GYPSY TRIBES IN BULGARIA Among these tribes in the North-East of Bulgaria, there are both sedentary and nomadic groups. Some are Christians, others have adopted Islam. There are special terms for each classification of craft or occupation, while particular areas or towns are associated with such crafts.

DIVISION OF TRIBES

A. Sedentaries.

1. Moslems.

(a) Kalburdjís or sieve-makers: habitat — Varna, Dobritch, and surrounding villages. Chief centre Dobritch.

(b) Kalaidjís or tinners: habitat — Baltchik, Kavarna, Varna, Rustchuk. Chief centre Baltchik.

(c) Demirdjís or workers in iron, of which two subdivisions, the first known as the Yerlis, or 'locals,' speaking no Gypsy, the second referred to as Ustalar, the 'artisans,' speaking Gypsy.

(d) Sepetdjís or basket-makers of Shumla, to which are closely allied the rush-carpet makers or Hasîrdjís.

(e) Calgidjís or musicians, whose ancestors were wool cleaners, known as Dríndaris, found in

Kotel and surrounding villages, in Dobritch, Varna, Shumla, Slivna, Eski-Djumaya, and generally at all fairs. Centre Kotel.

(f) Demirdjís or iron workers of Kazanlik.

(g) Dawuldjís and Mehtéris, or drum and pipe players. Speak no Gypsy.

2. Christians.

(a) Sieve-makers of Dobritch and environs.

(b) Djezvedjís or coffee-pot makers of Shumba.

(c) Rustchuk Sedentaries (originally a tribe of Rumanian Gypsies, formerly Nomads). Highly criminal tribe.

(d) Nalbandjís or horse-shoe makers.

B. Nomads.

1. Moslems.

(a) Sieve-makers, now mostly horse-dealers. Half sedentary. Original centre Silistria. Wander in summer from village to village along the river Kamtchia. Same race as Sedentary sieve-makers.

(b) Zágundjis, origin of appellation unknown. Carrion eaters; no trade; converts to Islam two generations ago. Chief centres Varnas, Rustchuk, and Burgas, and chief beat the intervening district.

(c) Demirdjís or Nomad iron workers, speaking the purest dialect yet recorded in the Balkans, and indistiguishable from the best Nomad dialects recorded by Paspati. Wander in the Eastern Balkans. Called by other tribes and perhaps by themselves Aidía. Claim Slivna as their chief centre.

(d) Dinikovlárs. Rear buffaloes, by which their carts are drawn. Men, horse-dealers. Women, great thieves: wear the *feredza*. Have no tents. Sleep in carts covered or tilted with rush matting.

220

Found along the Danube.

2. Christians.

(a) Grebenáris or comb-makers. Beat — the whole of Eastern Bulgaria. No chief centre. Winter in villages, rarely the same one for two successive winters. Most criminal tribe in Bulgaria. Chiefly horse-thieves along the Rumanian frontier. Known to other tribes as Zavrakcía.

(b) Recent Rumanian invasion of a tribe practically identical with the comb-makers, and equally criminal.

(c) Burgudjís or gimlet-makers, known to other tribes as Párpulia. Make also shepherd's crooks. Speak an exceedingly pure dialect, and are otherwise interesting, owing to the strangely elaborate form of their tents. Are honest.

(d) Kashikdjís or spoon-makers, who call themselves Rudáris, i.e., makers of small articles in wood, known also to the Bulgarians as makers of wooden troughs, Kopanáris or Koritáris. Rear buffaloes. Speak no Gypsy. Native language Rumanian, but know also Bulgarian and Turkish. The most honest tribe in Bulgaria, and perhaps the most numerous. Of very pure blood, and exceedingly dark.

Journal, Gypsy Folk-Lore Society

GYPSY TROOPS When Napoleon invaded Spain, there were not a few Hungarian Gypsies among his troops. Gypsies were also to be found in many national armies, in the imperial Austrian army, in the Spanish forces at various times, and with the French and English armies.

GYPSY UNITY Whatever tribal groups there may be and

whatever ethnic distinctions may appear the Gypsies regard themselves as one people, all designated under the term *Rom,* Men. Adoption into a tribe, however, is possible though not too common. The only way to enter into the life of the Gypsies, sharing tent and food and talk, is to become a 'brother.'

GYPSY VICES Whatever crimes the English Gypsies commit, their vices are few, for the men are not drunkards, nor are the women harlots. There are no two characters which they hold in so much abhorrence, nor do any words when applied by them convey so much execration as these two.

GYPSY WANDERER Matthew Arnold (1822-1888), the English poet and critic, in his poem *The Scholar Gypsy,* described the Scholar thus:
(he) went to learn the Gypsy lore
And roam'd the world with that wild brotherhood.

GYPSY WELCOME Sir Walter Scott the novelist relates an anecdote about his grandfather. This grandfather was riding over the Scottish moors when he fell among a band of Gypsies. They stopped his horse and exclaimed that since they had often dined at his expense (by poaching), he must now share their good cheer. The grandfather, though rather alarmed because he was carrying a considerable sum of money, sat down at the feast. It consisted of game, poultry, and pig. When the festal hilarity grew high, at a hint from one of the Gypsies, Scott's grandfather mounted his horse and rode off.

GYPSY WITCH In Gypsy folklore, to banish the presence of a witch, repeat:
Jasa tu chovihani!
Begone, witch!

GYPSY WOMAN A very singular kind of women are the Gitánas, far more remarkable in most points than their husbands, in whose pursuits of low cheating and petty robbery there is little capable of exciting much interest. But if there is one being in the world who, more than another, deserves the title of sorceress, it is the Gypsy female in the prime and vigor of her age and ripeness of her understanding — the Gypsy wife, the mother of two or three children. She can any time, when it suits her, show herself as expert a jockey as her husband, and he appears to advantage in no other character, and is only eloquent when discanting on the merits of some particular though she believes not in prophecy. She is a physician, though she will not taste her own philtres. She is a procuress, though she is not to be procured. She is a singer of obscene songs; though no one is more tenacious of the little she possesses, she is a cut-purse and a shoplifter.

H

HAIR A Gypsy superstition, of which there are many among
the Gypsies of all countries, runs as follows:
  Should birds find any human hair and build
  them into their nests, the person who lost
  the hair will suffer from headaches until,
  during the wane of the moon, he rubs his
  head with the yolk of eggs and washes it
  in running water.

HAIR TONIC When a new-born Gypsy infant is first bathed,
the forehead and neck are marked with a lunar crescent
compounded of a salve called *barcali*. This salve is reputed to promote the growth of the hair.

HABITAT In addition to their usual custom of camping out
in the open spaces in tents made of canvas or tree bark
or in caravans, the Gypsies sometimes find temporary
shelter against winds and rain in caves, in disused pits,
in abandoned huts. Few live in houses, except Gypsies
who have shed some of their wandering tendencies and
settled into a semi-town life.
ship and misery. These were the views of an early nineteenth century Gypsiologist.

HALS, FRANS (c. 1580-1686) The Dutch painter has represented a Gypsy girl in his notable *La Bohémienne*. Among
other painters who have depicted the Gypsy type are:

Benvenuto da Garofalo, Jacques Callot, Robert Henri, Joseph Pennell.

HAM, JOHN   Bishop Ham of Hungary, who was sympathetic to the condition of the Gypsies in that country, established a school for Gypsies at Szatmar, in 1857: it was, however, of short duration.

HANGING GYPSIES   In 1782 over 200 Gypsies in Hungary, under orders from Joseph II, were hanged, without a shred of conclusive evidence, on the charge of cannibalistic practices.

HANSEATIC TOWNS   In the Hanseatic towns along the North Sea and on the Baltic littoral large bands of Gypsies appeared as early as the beginning of the fifteenth century. They had evidently come from Asia Minor and still more Eastward.

HAPPY PEOPLE   The traditional apothegm that the people who have no history are a happy people does not quite apply to the Gypsies. For although for hundreds of years the history of the Gypsies has been rather the history of their environment, of the countries of their stay, they themselves have experienced all kinds of trials and diabilities, massacre and persecution. For their history has essentially been a history of constant migrations, of no settled history, so to speak.

HARBORING GYPSIES   In most periods of their history in Europe, the Gypsies were rarely accepted with goodwill. In many European countries, in fact, the natives were officially forbidden to harbor any Gypsies. Polish laws decreed such a prohibition. In the Netherlands, giving shelter to the Gypsies was punished. Similarly in France and Spain. In Denmark it was illegal to convey Gypsies as passengers by boat.

Frequently, when captured, the Gypsies, male and female, were executed or hanged on sight.

HARDINESS The Gypsies are lean, since they are seldom guilty of excess in eating or drinking. They have iron constitutions, because they have been brought up hardily. A mother takes her child on her back, wandering about in fair and foul weather, in heat and cold. Children live a rough open-air life. They acquire good health by hard-

HAT Gypsy women normally wear a scarf over the head. In the Balkans the men often wear a fur cap. In England, a cloth cap is the usual headgear. In Spain, the men wear the sombrero when they want to merge with the native customs.

HATVAN In Hungary Gypsies were regularly to be found in public places of entertainment, performing dexterously and with verve, particularly on the violin. Their reputation in this field was already well established in 1525, when they participated at Hatvan in musical celebrations.

HAUNTED MURDERER George Borrow the English gypsiologist tells a gruesome Gypsy tale:

He told me once that when he was a chap of twenty he killed a Gentile, and buried the dead meat under ground. He was taken up for the murder, but as no one could find the cold meat, the justices let him go. He said that the job did not sit heavy upon his mind for a long time, but then all of a sudden he became sad, and afraid of the dead Gentile's ghost; and that often of a night, as he was coming half-drunk from the public-house by himself, he would look over his right shoulder and over his left shoulder, to know if the dead man's ghost was not coming behind to lay hold of him.

HAYDN, FRANZ JOSEPH (1732-1809) The famous Austrian composer was interested in the evolution of Gypsy music and produced a piece entitled *Gypsy Rondo.*

HEALTH MEASURES Among Gypsies health is of primary importance in conditioning the continuity of their treks. Hence sick and weakly children are not regarded with affection, while adults who are undesirable in other respects are excluded from the tribe.
To ensure healthy children, Gypsy women tie a string of bear's claws and children's teeth round their neck.

HEATHENS In a religious sense, the Gypsies, in their wanderings, have often accepted the faith of the country of their sojourn. In the Netherlands, however, and in parts of Germany they are called "heathens."

HEBER, REGINALD (1783-1826) English prelate. Bishop of Calcutta. In his *Journal* he wrote:
On the other side of the river was a large encampment of wretched tents of mats, with a number of little packeries, paniers, ponies, goats, etc., so like Gypsies, that on asking what they were, I was not surprised to hear Abdallah say they were Gypsies: that they were numerous in the Upper Provinces, living exactly like the Gypsies in England: that he had seen the same people both in Persia and Russia: and that in Persia they spoke Hindustani, the same as here. In Russia he had no opportunity of ascertaining this fact, but in Persia he had spoken with some of the wandering tribes, and found that they understood and could answer him.

HEDGEHOG The favorite dish of the Gypsies is the hedgehog — the *nigló,* or, in English Gypsy, the *hotchi-witchi.* The animal is wrapped in clay and placed on white-hot stones. When the roasting is completed, the prickles attached to the clay are pulled off and the hedgehog is served wrapped in leaves.

HEIDEN In Scandinavia, especially in Norway, Gypsies are called Heiden, Heathens or Pagans. In Denmark and Sweden they are usually called Tartars, identifying them thus with an Asiatic origin.

HEIDENJACHTEN This term signifies *Hunt of the Heathens:* that is, hunting the Gypsies. In the United Provinces of the Netherlands the relentless pursuit of Gypsies was in the hands of the army and the police. The result was complete banishment of Gypsies from these provinces.

HELL In Gypsy mythology the *beng* or *bengui,* the devil, is conceived as dwelling in a Hell compounded of mud. Gypsy tales are pervaded by fanciful concepts relating to heaven and hell and the spirits that haunt the woodlands and the rivers.

HELP YOURSELF

If the Gypsy man is weary,
    There is a horse in the farmer's stall.
If the Gypsy child is hungry,
    There is a hen near the granary wall.
If the Gypsy lads are thirsty,
    There is beer enough for them all.
And if there's naught in the Gypsy hand
    There are wealthy Gorgios in all the land.

                                                Janet Tuckey

HENRI, ROBERT (1865-1929) American painter who has depicted a *Spanish Gypsy*: now in the Metropolitan Museum of Art, New York.

Gypsies, and Gypsy scenes have attracted many artists and etchers: Pennell, Callot, Goya, Frans Hals, Garofalo.

HENRY IV   King Henry IV of Castile granted letters of safe-conduct to the Gypsy tribal leaders who appeared in Jaen and in Andujar late in the fifteenth century.

HENRY VIII   In the reign of Henry VIII, King of England, an edict termed the Gypsies "an outlandish people, calling themselves Egyptians, using no craft nor feat of merchandise, who have come into this realm, and gone from shire to shire and place to place in great company; and used great subtlety and crafty means to deceive the people — bearing them in hand that they, by palmistry, could tell men's and women's fortunes; and so, many times, by craft and subtlety, have deceived the people for their money; and also have committed many heinous felonies and robberies."

HERBAL LORE   These Gypsy inhabitants of the fields and forests, the lanes and the moors, wrote a gypsiologist, were not without a knowledge of the medicinal qualities of certain herbs. In all slight disorders they have recourse to these remedies. Frequently they use the inner bark of the elm — star-in-the-earth, pellitory-of-the-wall, wormwood, and parsley. There are numerous similar herbs, roots, leaves, juices of plants that reputedly contribute to allay fevers and to ease rheumatic conditions and analogous situations to which the Gypsies are subject.

HEAT   Gypsies are fond of a great degree of heat. Their supreme luxury is to lie day and night near a fire. At the same time they can bear to travel in the most severe cold bareheaded, with no other covering than a torn shirt, or some old rags carelessly thrown over them, without fear of catching cold, cough, or any other disorder.

HEREDITARY COMPLEXION   The Gypsies, in general, are of a tawny or brown color, but it was not thought that this characteristic was wholly hereditary. The chief cause, it was suggested, probably lay in the lowness of their habits. For they very seldom washed their person, or the clothes they wore, except their linen. Their alternate exposures to cold and heat, and the smoke surrounding their small camps, perpetually tended to increase those characteristics of complexion and feature by which they were distinguishable.

HIDDEN TREASURE   One of the devices used by the Gypsies against the guillible *gorgio,* the non-Gypsy, was the Hokano baró, the Great Trick.
A Gypsy would inform a *busno,* a non-Gypsy, of a treasure hidden either in the *busno's* own house or in some remote cottage. For information regarding the whereabouts of the actual treasure the Gypsy asked for a sum in advance. That was the end of the matter. The *busnó* departed not any the wiser.

HIERARCHY   Despite popular opinion, there is no final and highest authority in Gypsy tribes who is actually the King or Queen. The term Duke and similar title are merely honorific designations applied to a chief or leader of a tribe.

HIGHLANDER AND GYPSY   The Scottish gypsiologist Walter Simson makes a comparison between the conduct of the Scottish Gypsies, far from commendable, and the analogous conduct of the Scottish Highlanders themselves:
And what shall we say of our Highland thieves? High-

landers may be more touchy on this point, for their ancestors were the last of the British race to give up that kind of life. Talk of the laws passed against the Gypsies! Various of our Scottish monarchs issued decrees against 'the wicked thieves and limmers of the clans and surnames, inhabiting the Highlands and Isles,' accusing 'the chieftains principal of the branches worthy to be esteemed the very authors, fosterers, and maintainers, of the wicked deeds of the vagabonds of their clans and surnames.' Indeed, the dowries of the chiefs' daughters were made up by a share of the booty collected on their expeditions.

The Highlands were, at one time, little better than a nest of thieves; thieving from each other, and more particularly from their southern neighbors. It is notorious that robbery in the Highlands was 'held to be a calling not merely innocent, but honorable'; and that a highborn Highland warrior was 'much more becomingly employed the lands of others than in tilling his own.' In the case of the Gypsies, however, the Gypsy's ordinary pilfering was confined to such petty things as 'hens and peats at pleasure, cutting a bit lamb's throat and a mouthful o' grass and a pickle corn, for the cuddy — things that a farmer body ne'er could miss.' But your Highlanders did not content themselves with such 'needles and pins.' They must have horned cattle.

HINDU FILMS In Belgrade Indian films were highly popular among the Gypsies. One Gypsy informed the Indian Ambassador that the Gypsies had understood 70% of the words in a Hindu film: evidence of their affinity with India.

HINDU SONGS The Zaurachis, a Gypsy community that has settled in the United States, have traditional songs that recall Hindu melodies.

HINDU SUDER ORIGIN   The nineteenth century was not yet quite categorical about the Hindu origin of the Gypsies, although the testimony, particularly the linguistic evidence, was soon to approach definitive finality.

James Crabb, the clergyman and gypsiologist, whose primary interest in the Gypsies was their spiritual amelioration, declared that:

> Those who suppose these wanderers of mankind to be of Hindu or Suder origin have much the best proof on their side. A real Gypsy has a countenance, eyes, mouth, hands, and quickness of manners strongly indicative of Hindu origin. This is more particularly the case with the females. The testimony of the most intelligent travelers, many of whom have long resided in India, fully supports this opinion. And, in fact, persons who have not traveled on the Asiatic continent, but who have seen natives of Hindustan, have been surprised at the similarity of manners and features existing between them and the Gypsies.
>
> The Hindu Suder delights in horses, tinkering, music, and fortune-telling: so does the Gypsy. The Suder tribes of the same part of the Asiatic continent are wanderers, dwelling chiefly in wretched mud huts. They imitate these erratic tribes in this particular. They wander from place to place, and carry their small tents with them, which consist of a few bent sticks and a blanket. The Suders in the East eat the flesh of nearly every unclean creature: nor are they careful that the flesh of such creatures should not be putrid. How exactly do the Gypsies imitate them in this abhorrent choice of food! They have been in the habit of eating many kinds of brutes, not even excepting dogs and cats: and, when pressed by hunger, have sought after the most putrid carrion. It has been a common saying among them: That which God kills is better than that killed by man. But of late years, with a few

exceptions they have much improved in this respect. For they now eat neither dogs nor cats, and but seldom seek after carrion. But in winter they will dress and eat snails, hedgehogs, and other creatures not generally dressed for food.

HINDU VOCABULARY The Gypsies, whose original home was India, have in their various dialects thousands of words stemming from Hindi, Punjabi, Gujarati and many dialects in other parts of India.

HISPANIC Walter Simson, the nineteenth century historian of the Gypsies declared that in Spain the generality of the Gypsies are the settled inhabitants of considerable towns, and although the occupations of some necessarily lead them to a more vagrant life, the proportion is small who do not consider some hovel in a suburb as a home. 'Money is in the city — not in the country' is a saying frequently in their mouths. In the vilest quarters of every large large town of the southern provinces there are Gitanos living together. Their principal occupation is the manufacture and sale of articles of iron. Their quarters may always be traced by the ring of the hammer and anvil. An inferior class have the exclusive trade in second-hand articles, which they sell at the doors of their dwellings or at benches at the entrance of towns, or by the sides of frequented walks. A still inferior order wander about, mending pots, and selling tongs and other trifling articles. In Cadiz, they monopolize the trade of butchering and frequently amass wealth. Others, again, exclusively fill the office of Matador of the Bull Plaza, while the Toreros are mostly of the same race. Others are employed as dressers of mules and asses: some as figure dancers, and many as performers in the theatre. Some gain a livelihood by their musical talents. Dancing, singing, music and fortune-telling are the only objects of general pursuit for the females. Sometimes they dance in the inferior theatres, and sing and dance in the streets. Palmistry is one of their most productive avocations. In Seville, a few make and sell an inferior kind of mat. Besides these, there is a class of Gypsies in Spain who lead a vagrant life — residing chiefly in the woods and mountains, and known as mountaineers. These rarely visit towns, and live by fraud and pillage. There are also others who wander about the country — such as tinkers, dancers, singers, and jobbers in asses and mules.

HISTORICAL RECORD *The Chronicle of Dalimil,* a Czech record dating the fourteenth century, mentions the strange language of the Gypsies.

HOAX The Gypsies have been notorious for their wiles and tricks imposed on the gorgios. In this respect, the terms hoax and hocus, George Borrow asserts, are immediately derived from the language of the Gypsies who first introduced their deceptions into Europe.

HOGARTHIAN SCENES The Gypsy musicians usually attended fairs, wakes, private parties in England, and also houses notorious for immorality and vice. To these places their children too were taken, as soon as they could perform on any instrument or in any other way help their parents.

HOKKANO BARO A Gypsy term meaning The Great Trick. The expression refers to the various Gypsy methods of duping credulous gorgios. Such practices include:
La Bahi: the Gypsy term for the technique of fortune-telling.
Ustilar pastésas: various kinds of theft.
Chiving drawo: poisoning cattle.
La Bar Lachi: the loadstone. Miraculous properties

are attributed by the Gypsies to the loadstone. It is regarded as a powerful aphrodisiac. It is reputed to induce a cloud of mist, producing invisibility, when a Gypsy is pursued by revenue officers and others. La Rais del Buen Baron: The root of the good Baron. The Gitánas sell various roots and herbs to women. The roots are boiled in white wine and the concoction is taken fasting. The good Baron is a euphemism for his Satanic majesty.

HOLYROOD Holyrood Palace in Edinburgh, Scotland, the royal residence of many Scottish kings, was in the early sixteenth century the scene of a dancing performance given by Gypsies.

HOMAGE In Gypsy folklore and mythology, many customs and practices are associated with the invisible world of spirits and demons, that must be appeased by means of incantations, charms, amulets, invocations.
Among the Rumanian Gypsies it is a custom to do homage to the Rumanian *Wowna zena,* the Water-woman: in Hungarian Gypsy dialect, the *Nivashi.* A few drops of water are spilled on the ground after filling a jug. It is regarded as an insult to offer drink to anyone without observing this ceremony.

HOMELAND In Czechoslovakia a Hindu writer, Chaman Lal, found in Gypsy quarters and villages many Gypsies who declared a kinship with India and spoke of its nostalgic associations, as the home of their ancestors.

HOMERIC LEGEND Numerous hypotheses have been proposed with regard to the original home of the Gypsies. In the Homeric epics, Vulcan, driven from Olympus, the home of the gods, by Zeus, was rescued on the island of Lemnos by a people called Sinti. These Sinti have been identified by some gypsiologists as the Gypsies.

HONORIFICS In earlier centuries, particularly in Europe, the Gypsy tribal leaders assumed self-imposed titular designations, such as Earl, Duke, Marquis, Count, Lord, King. These titles implied, however, neither power beyond their communities nor wealth. The terms king, nevertheless, and queen are still in occasional use to denote the head of a tribe. In the case of a woman, queen is bestowed on the oldest woman in the clan.

HOP PLANTATIONS In the 1830's several English clergymen visited the hop-plantations in the south of England, where many Gypsies were engaged in hop-picking. Public meettings were held with a view to directing such Gypsies along spiritual lines, as they were regarded as quite irreligious.

HORSE-COPING Gypsies have been traditionally known to be skilled in presenting to a buyer a horse that appears in sound condition. By the use of certain drugs and other means known exclusively to the horse-trader he can eliminate all kinds of equine defects. This is a practice employed largely by the Gypsies in the Balkans, in England, in the Ukraine, and wherever there is a Gypsy settlement.

HORSE LANGUAGE A peasant tradition credits the Gypsies with the ability to understand the language of horses.

HORSE-SHOES The superstition regarding the good luck that accompanies horse shoes is expounded by an old Gypsy woman whom Charles Leland the gypsiologist met:
That's the way the Gorgis always half does things. You see 'em get a horse-shoe off the roads, and what

236

do they do with it? Goes like idiots and nails it up with the p'ints down, which, as is well beknown, brings all the bad luck there is flyin' in the air into the house, and draws witches like anise-seed does rats. Now common sense ought to teach that the shoe ought to be put like horns, with the p'ints up. For if it's lucky to put real horns up, of course the horse-shoe goes the same road.

HORSE-STEALING Horse-stealing was one of the principal crimes of the English Gypsies. When disposed to steal a horse, they selected one a few miles from their tent and made arrangements for disposing of it at a considerable distance: to which spot they would ride in a night. A certain old and infirm Gypsy was known to have ridden a stolen horse nearly fifty miles in that time. The Gypsies would pass through by-lanes, well known to them, and thus avoid turnpikes, and so they would often escape detection.

HOSPITALITY Gypsy tradition retains the age-old sense of hospitality to any stranger or guest. The offering may be meagre, but it is given with readiness and warmth. Nor is there ever any question of payment. The Gypsies, in this regard, have continued the ancient Homeric tradition, when a friend, a stranger, even an avowed enemy, was treated like a welcome guest.

HOUSEHOLD SLAVES In Central Europe, in the early nineteenth century, many Gypsies were subjected as serfs to the wealthy landowners, particularly in Hungary and Rumania.

HOW GYPSIES BECAME SORCERERS The Gypsies from the mere fact of being wanderers and out-of-doors livers in wild places, became wild-looking, and when asked if they did not associate with the devils who dwell in the desert places, admitted the soft impeachment, and being further questioned as to whether their friends the devils, fairies, elves, and goblins had not taught them how to tell the future, they pleaded guilty, and finding that it paid well, went to work in their small way to improve their "science", and particularly their pecuniary resources. It was an easy calling; it required no property or properties, neither capital nor capitol, shiners nor shrines, wherein to work the oracle.

HUDSON, WILLIAM HENRY (1841-1922)   Famous naturalist and writer. He felt a great kinship with the Gypsies and praised their close contacts with the life of Nature.

HUMAN MEMBERS   It must not be forgotten, warned James Crabb, the gypsiologist whose purpose was to redeem the Gypsies spiritually, that they are members of the same family as ourselves. They are capable of being fitted for all the duties and enjoyments of life. Their condition, therefore, at once commands our sympathies, energies, prayers, and benevolence.

HUNGARIAN ACCOUNT   With respect to the traditional and unfounded tales of cannibalism among the Gypsies, there is the following record:

On the 21st. of August, 1782, there was a dreadful execution at Frauenmark in the Hortenser country. Thirteen delinquents, Gypsies, who had existed twelve years by robbing on the highway and were accustomed to eat the bodies of those they had murdered, were brought to punishment. Four of them were women. Of the remaining nine men, six were hanged, two were broken on the wheel, and the leader of this inhuman gang was quartered alive. It is said that one hundred and fifteen more remain in the county gaols.

HUNGARIAN ACADEMY OF SCIENCES Since the foundation of this Academy in the nineteenth century, the study of the Hungarian Gypsies, in relation to their traditions, language, history, folk poetry, customs, ethnology, has been pursued with the most intense interest.

HUNGARIAN ACCUSATIONS Cases of cannibalism were said to have occurred in Hungary among the Gypsies. In fact, the whole race, in that country, was accused of cannibalism. It is very probable, however, that they were quite innocent of this odious practice, and that the accusation had its origin in popular prejudice.

HUNGARIAN GYPSIES In 1782 the Gypsies of Hungary were accused of cannibalism, with the result that many Gypsies, unwarrantably suspected, were exterminated.

HUNGARIAN GYPSY DRESS We are not to suppose however that they are indifferent about dress. On the contrary, they love fine clothes to an extraordinary degree. Whenever an opportunity offers of acquiring a good coat, either by gift, purchase, or theft, the Gypsy immediately bestirs himself to become master of it. Possessed of the prize, he puts it on directly, without considering in the least whether it suits the rest of his apparel. If his dirty shirt had holes in it as big as a barn door, or his breeches so out of condition that any one might, at the first glance, perceive their antiquity; were he unprovided with shoes and stockings, or a covering for his head; none of these defects would prevent his strutting about in a laced coat, finding himself of still greater consequence in case it happened to be a red one. They are particularly fond of clothes which have been worn by people of distinction, and will hardly ever deign to put on a boor's coat. They will rather go half naked, or wrap themselves up in a sack, than condescend to wear a foreign garb. Green is a favorite color with the Gypsies, but scarlet is held in great esteem among them. It is the same with the Hungarian female Gypsies.

HUNGARIAN LOVE POTION The Hungarian Gypsies prepared a certain love philtre as follows:

On St. John's Day they catch a green frog and put it in a closed earthen receptacle full of small holes, and this they place in an ant-hill. The ants eat the frog and leave the skeleton. This is ground to powder, mixed with the blood of a bat and dried bath-flies and shaped into small buns, which are, as the chance occurs, put secretly into the food of the person to be charmed.

HUNGARIAN MAXIM Working in metals was for centuries the occupation common to many Gypsy tribes. In Central Europe, particularly in Hungary, this occupation was so widespread that a Hungarian proverb ran as follows:

So many Gypsies, so many smiths.

HUNGARIAN RECOGNITION The skill of the Gypsies in working wth metals was so remarkable that the Hungarian King Uladislaus issued an order in 1496, as follows:

Every officer and subject, of whatever rank or condition, is to allow Thomas Polgar, leader of twenty-five tents of wandering Gypsies, free residence everywhere, and on no account to molest either him or his people; because they had prepared musket bullets, and other military stores, for the Bishop Sigismund, at Fünfkirchen.

HUNGARY In Hungary, in the fifteenth century, Gypsies, known as Egyptians, were serfs in the personal possession of the ruling monarch. They were often the object of assault on the part of the government officials. The alleged crimes of the Gypsies included cannibalism, kidnapping, and rape. Punishment consisted of cutting off the ears and even the head.

HUNGARY AND THE GYPSIES Two classes are free in Hungary to do almost what they please — the nobility and the Gypsies. The former are above the law — the latter below it.

HYPNOTIC EYE The peculiarity of the Gypsy eye consists chiefly in a strange staring expression, which to be understood must be seen, and in a thin glaze, which steals over it when in repose, and seems to emit phosphoric light. That the Gypsy eye has sometimes a peculiar effect, we learn from the following stanza:

A Gypsy stripling's glossy eye
Has pierced my bosom's core;
A feat no eye beneath the sky
Could e'er effect before.

HYPOTHETICAL MIGRATION James Crabb the author of *The Gypsies' Advocate,* published in 1832, conceived the Gypsy migration westward in these terms:

In the years 1408 and 1409 Timur Beg ravaged India, to convert India to Islam. Hundreds of thousands of Hindus were slain, but some survivors fled from their native country and became wandering strangers to each other. If the Gypsies were of the Suder caste of Asiatic Indians, the question might have been asked: why did not some of the other castes of India accompany them? The reason lies in the hatred and contempt that all the other castes of India felt for the Suders. The Brahmans, Kshatriyas, Vaisyas and other castes, also, regarded their country as God-given and would on no account have abandoned it. On the other hand, the

Suders had no particular attachment to their native soil. They were a degraded people: looked on as the lowest of the human race; and, with an army seeking their destruction, they had every every motive to leave.

It cannot be determined, continues Crabb, by what route the ancestors of the Gypsies found their way from India to the European countries. But it may be presumed that they passed over the southern Persian deserts of Sigiston, Makran, and Kirman: along the Persian Gulf, to the mouth of the Euphrates: thence to Basra into the deserts of Arabia: and thence into Egypt by the Isthmus of Suez.

The Gypsies, he remarks, dislike being so called, except by their real friends. The reason for this dislike is that the Gypsies are suspected and hated as the perpetrators of all crime, and they are almost universally prosecuted as vagrants.

HYPOTHETICAL ORIGINS Many hypotheses have been advanced in the last few centuries with regard to the territorial and ethnic origins of the Gypsies. Some gypsiologists have attributed to them an intermixture of Judaic elements. Others have suggested that they were descendants of the Moors of Spain. Still others have conceived them as a mixed breed. Or that they sprang from Iberia. Or from Allachia. Or from Nubia. Or from the Pyrenees. Or from Greece. Or from the Babylonians. Or from the fabled submerged Atlantis. Or from the Phoenicians. Or the Canary Islands. Or Baetica, Farther Spain. Or Ethiopia.

I

IDENTIFICATION Among the hundred and fifty wandering tribes of India and Persia, some of them Turanian, some Aryan, and others mixed, it is of course difficult to identify the exact origin of the European Gypsy. One thing we know: that from the tenth to the twelfth century and probably much later on, India threw out from her northern half a vast multitude of very troublesome indwellers.

Now there are many historical indications that these outcasts, before leaving India, became Gypsies, which was the most natural thing in a country where such classes had already existed in very great numbers from early times. And from one of the lowest castes, which still exists in India, and is known as the Dom, the emigrants to the West probably derived their names and several characteristics. The Dom burns the dead, handles corpses, skins beasts, and perfoms other functions, all of which were appropriated by, and became peculiar to, Gypsies in several countries in Europe, notably in Denmark and Holland, for several centuries after their arrival there. The Dom of the present day also sells baskets, and wanders with a tent; he is altogether Gypsy. It is remarkable that he, living in a hot climate, drinks ardent spirits to excess, being by no means a 'temperate Hindu' and that even in extreme old age his hair seldom turns white, which is a noted peculiarity among our own Gypsies of pure blood. I know, declares the Gypsiologist Charles Leland, and have often seen a Gypsy woman,

243

nearly a hundred years old, whose curling hair is black, or hardly perceptibly changed. It is extremely probable that the Dom, mentioned as a caste even in the Shastras, gave the name to the Rom. The Dom calls his wife a Domni, and being a Dom is 'Domnipana.' In English Gypsy, the same words are expressed by *Rom, romni,* and *romnipen.* D, be it observed, very often changes to *r* in its transfer from Hindu to Romany.

IDENTIFICATION OF ANIMALS When the Gypsies first came to Europe from their home in Northern India, they named animals after those which resembled them in Asia. A dog they called *juckal*, from a jackal: a swan, *sakku* or pelican, because it so greatly resembled it. The Hindu *bandarus,* or donkey, they changed to *bombaros.*

IDENTIFICATION OF GYPSIES In Syria and Persia a Gypsy is known as a Dom. In Baluchistan, the Dom was a poet, a minstrel who was the oral transmitter of the Baluch folklore, history, and traditions.
In Armenia, the Gypsy is called a Lom.
I think, wrote Charles Leland the American gypsiologist, it will be found difficult to identify the European Gypsy with any one stock of the wandering of India. Among those who left that country were men of different castes and different color, varying from the pure northern invader to the negro-like southern Indian.

IDENTIFICATION WITH LUMINARIES Charles Leland the American gypsiologist reflects:
It was very natural that the Gypsies, observing that the sun and moon were always apparently wandering, should have identified their own nomadic life with that of these luminaries. That they have a tendency to assimilate the idea of a wanderer and pilgrim to that

of the Romany, or to *Romanipen,* is shown by the assertion once made to me by an English Gypsy that his people regarded Christ as one of themselves, because he was always poor, and went wandering about on a donkey, and was persecuted by the Gorgios.

IMITATIVE MUSIC The Gypsies have been regarded not as creative musical composers of their own, but as versatile adapters and imitators of the indigenous national music with which, in their wanderings, they have become acquainted.

IMMIGRATION INTO SWEDEN In 1914 the Swedish authorities forbade the entrance of Gypsies into Sweden. The first infiltration came from the Scottish Gypsies, in 1512.

IMPORTANCE OF GYPSY CHARACTER The origin of the Gypsies, according to one gypsiologist, was not so important in his view as the knowledge of their character, manners, and habits, for the purpose of improving their condition and their spiritual life.
Through the centuries, however, the Gypsies had a reputation for being totally irreligious. For expediency, they assumed but only nominally, the religion of the country in which they settled.

IMPORTATION OF GYPSIES In the 27th Statute of King Henry VIII's reign, a law was promulgated against the importation of Gypsies into England, under a fine of forty pounds for the importer.
Throughout the Middle Ages, the Gypsies were regularly forced, by harsh decrees and royal edicts, to move from country to country.

IMPOSITION OF FINE   In the reign of Henry VIII of England an Act imposed a fine of forty pounds for every Gypsy imported into England. Somewhat later, an Act passed in Queen Elizabeth's reign made it a felony for strangers to associate with Gypsies.

IMPOSITION ON THE GYPSIES   Not infrequently the Gypsies have been wrongfully accused, or the actual perpetrators of a crime have 'framed' the Gypsies.
Such a case occurred last century, in England. Instances have been known of house-breakers leaving some of the stolen goods near the tents of the Gypsies. When the articles were picked up by the Gypsy children and were found on them, they were taken to be real culprits. The grandfather of three orphans was charged with stealing a horse and was condemned and executed; although the farmer of whom he had bought it swore to the horse being the same as he had sold him. His evidence, however, was rejected on account of some slight mistake in the description that he gave of the horse.

INCANTATIONS   Among the Gypsies there are ancient chants, invocations, and formulaic appeals to certain spirits that will divert or exorcise bodily disorders and afflictions. By such incantations the evil spirits depart and leave a person in sound health.
Legends and folk-lore involving such practices are common to Gypsies, from Hungary to Spain, from the Balkans to England. They uniformly stress the element of assumed mystic and miraculous efficacy of the curative virtues of the incantations.
A Gypsy incantation, recited as a skin remedy, runs as follows:

Duy yákhá hin mánge
Duy punrá hin mánge
Dukh ándrál yákhá

246

Já ándre punrá
Já ándrál punrá
Já ándre pçuv
Já ándrál pçuv
Andro meriben!
I have two eyes
I have two feet
Pain from my eyes
Go into my feet!
Go from my feet
Go into the earth!
Go from the earth
Into death!

IN DEFENSE OF GYPSIES A Scottish gypsiologist, defending the conduct and character of the Gypsies in Scotland in the early nineteenth century, has this to say in their behalf:

The Scottish Highlands were a nest of marauding thieves, and the Borders are little better. Or society at the present day — what is it but a compound of deceit and hypocrisy? People say that the Gypsies steal. True: some of them steal chickens, vegetables, and such things; but what is that compared with the robbery of widows and orphans, the lying and cheating of traders, the swindling, the robberies, the murders, the ignorance, the squalor, and the debaucheries of so many of the white race? What are all these compared with the simple vices of the Gypsies? What is the ancestry they boast of, compared, point of antiquity, with ours? People may despise the Gypsies, but they certainly despise all others not of their own race. The veriest beggar Gypsy, without shoes to his feet, considers himself better than the queen who sits upon the throne. People say that Gypsies are blackguards. If some of them are blackguards, they are at least illustrious blackguards as regards descent, and so in fact; for they never rob each other, and far less do they rob or ruin those of their own family.

INDIAN GYPSIES   Charles Leland the gypsiologist declared: I have definitely determined the existence in India of a peculiar tribe of Gypsies, who are *par excellence* the Romanys of the East, and whose language is there what it is in England, the same in vocabulary, and the chief slang of the road. This I claim as a discovery, having learned it from a Hindu who had been himself a Gypsy in his native land.

INDIAN SURVIVALS   Dr. M. J. Kounavine, a Russian physician and philologist who belongs in the nineteenth century, found that the Gypsies in Russia preserved Indian legends relating to Brahma, Vishnu, Lakshmi, and Indra.

INEFFECTIVE EXPULSION   Although from the fifteenth century on the Gypsies were officially banished and outlawed from one European country after another, they still managed to persist in European territory. For banishment from one country merely meant that the Gypsies again became a mobile unit and proceeded into another region from which they had not yet been officially excluded. Thus they perpetuated a kind of cycle of unending migrations until late in the nineteenth century. From that time on more humane measures and treatment began to be accorded to them by the state.

INFIDELITY   A faithless Gypsy woman, in the Balkans, was judged by a secret tribunal called *manlaslo*. In Hungary, she was flogged, left naked tied to a stake, for twenty-four hours, then banished from the tribe.

248

Bodily chastity, in fact, was held in the highest esteem among the Gypsies.

INFORMERS   Very lately, recounts one who worked among the English Gypsies, in the nineteenth century, a vile informer swore to having seen a Gypsy on a horse that had been stolen. Although it came out at the trial that it was night when he observed the man, and that he had never seen him before — which ought to have rendered his evidence invalid — the prisoner was convicted and condemned to die. His life, however, was afterward spared by other facts having been discovered and made known to the judge.

INGRATITUDE   A clergyman, interested in working among the English Gypsies, said that he seldom met with instances of ingratitude among the Gypsies, although he was obliged to record one. He was interested in the reformation of a Gypsy family that encamped, a short time since, about five miles from Southampton, whom he visited early on a Monday morning. Reaching the camp, accompanied by an old Gypsy, he said to them: Since you would not come to see me, I am come to see you.
The camp, consisting of eight persons, gave him a cordial reception, the husband excepted, who said he did not want company.
"You certainly do not mean what you say," said his friend.
To which he replied: "I never speak words without meaning."
In a good-natured way he was questioned as to the truth Gypsies were seldom ungrateful for favors shown to them. Half an hour after, he left the camp very angrily.
This man had been released from many years' imprisonment: but having associated with thieves so long, the

worst principles of his heart were drawn out. Before he left the camp, he said he had no care about his children but to clothe and feed them.

INHERITANCE   Despite many changes within the tribal context, Gypsy inheritance is traced basically in a matrilineal sense. This, despite the 'official' standing of the male as a Gypsy tribal leader. For the mother was long the acknowledged source of the tribe, in an economic sense. She was the financial support of the entire family.

INN SIGNS   Throughout England there are quite a number of Gypsy signs in country taverns, an indication of the presence of Gypsy encampments or activities or associations in the neighborhood. In Hagley, Stourbridge, there is *The Gipsies' Tent,* while *The Gipsy Queen* swings over the entrance of an inn at Highbury. *The Queen of the Gipsies* appears in Norwood. Here there lived a Gypsy 'Queen' named Margaret Finch, who died in Norwood in 1760, at the age of 109.

INSIGNIA   In Central Europe a Gypsy tribal chief, a *yataf,* was distinguishable particularly by the metal buttons on his jacket. He also carried a silver staff, called a *Bareshti rovli rupui,* the chief's silver stick.

INTERMARRIAGE   Intermarriage between Gypsies and gorgios, non-Gypsies, is rare. It is contrary to Gypsy law. Only in extremely rare cases does a Gypsy girl marry outside the tribe.
On the other hand, there have been instances where a wealthy landowner in the Balkans falls in love with a Gypsy and tranferred her to a new and different life, without incurring the hostility and resentment of the tribe.

INTERPRETATION OF DREAMS   The Gypsies of Central

Handsome samovars and silver cups are frequent possessions of the Nomads and Coppersmiths; but they count their children as their chief riches

*The typical Coppersmith anvil is driven
into the ground. The gypsies are
skilled handicraftsmen*

Russia made their own dream interpretations, as follows:
To dream of dead persons signifies a hard frost.
To dream of honey means wealth.
To dream of worms means many children.
I saw a wolf in a dream — that's luck.
To dream of a rope means prison; cutting a rope, escape.
To dream of a perch means a boy.

INTERPRETERS Among the most eminent scholars and travelers who have studied the Gypsies and their traditions and culture was George Borrow, who lived for many years with the Gypsies of Spain, during the nineteenth century. Alexandre Paspati, a Greek physician, studied Turkish Gypsies. Andriano Amerigo, Marquis de Colucci, was an Italian scholar who lived with the Gypsies in the Balkans and studied their ways. In 1889 he produced an account of Gypsy life, with an Italian-Gypsy vocabulary, entitled *Storia d'un popolo errante.*

INVASION OF SPAIN When Napoleon invaded Spain there were not a few Hungarian Gypsies in his armies. Some strange encounters occurred on the field of battle between these people and the Spanish Gitános. When quartered in the Spanish towns, the Czigány invariably sought out their peninsular brethren, to whom they revealed themselves, kissing and embracing most affectionately. The Gitános were astonished at the proficiency of the strangers in thievish arts, and looked upon them almost in the light of superior beings.

INVENTIVE WRITERS Over half a century ago a writer on Gypsy life deprecated the passion that newspaper men, equipped with only a brief and superficial acquaintance, had for inventing mysterious ceremonies, strange beliefs, and scandalous practices and crimes and imputing them to the Gypsies.

251

INVITATION TO A SPIRIT   Gypsy folklore contains references to ceremonies by means of which spirits may be attracted to come to people in dreams:

There was a young man who lived near Monte Lupo, and one day he found in a place among some old ruins a statue of a *fate,* a fairy or goddess, all naked. He set it up in its shrine, and admiring it greatly he embraced it with love. And that night and ever after the *fate* came to him in his dreams and lay with him, and told him where to find treasures, so that he became a rich man. But he lived no more among men, nor did he after that ever enter a church. And I have heard that anyone who will do as he did can draw the *fate* to come to him, for they are greatly desirous to be loved and worshipped by men as they were in the Roman times.

INVOCATION   To punish an enemy, Russian Gypsies invoked fire. The Gypsy faced the burning hearth and recited:

Fire, who punishest the evil-doer, who hatest falsehood, who scorchest the impure, thou destroyest offenders; thy flame devoureth the earth. Devour X if he says what is not true, if he thinks a lie, and if he acts deceitfully.

IRELAND   Gypsies, in the early nineteenth century, were infrequent in Ireland. Some districts of Scotland were free of them, while in others they were as numerous as in the English counties.

IRRELIGIOUS REPUTATION   The Gypsies as a people have long been regarded as quite irreligious. Possibly the reason lies in their race history. Traditionally, they had been the lowest caste in India itself, their original home. Hence they were never formally or in any other sense brought

252

into the religious atmosphere of rituals, festivals, ceremonials, liturgies of the other, higher castes. Furthermore, according to another tradition, they were forced to migrate Westward on account of the massacres inflicted on them by Timur Beg. They were therefore totally and exclusively absorbed in mere survival, as they moved from India through Persia to Eastern Europe. The spiritual life, in consequence, was completely alien to them, totally crushed for centuries.

ISHMAELITES   In the eleventh century Ladislaus I of Hungary ordered the Gypsies, who were known as Ishmaelites, to be baptized, as they were not regarded as Christians.

ISOLATED CLANS   The Gypsies of England did not have much knowledge of the tribes and clans in counties that were distant from them. They were very particular about keeping to their own family and tribal units.

ISTANBUL   In the quarter called Sulukule, in Istanbul, there is a large colony of Turkish Gypsies, known locally as Cingiane. Some of them have settled into some kind of permanency, while others still continue to roam. Among the sedentary settlers are Gypsy fishermen, smiths, musicians.

ITALIAN DECREES   Throughout the Middle Ages, from the Iberian Peninsula to Eastern Europe and north in the Scandinavian countries, laws were repeatedly promulgated to the detriment of the Gypsies. In the sixteenth century the Gypsies were banished from Milan, Venice, and Parma. They had appeared in Italy as early as 1427.

ITALIAN LEGEND   The Gypsies annually assemble at Les Saintes Maries de la Mer, in the Camargue, in Provence.

There they do ceremonial reverence to their patron saint Sara, the servant of the Marys.

There is another legend associated with this Sara, who is believed to be buried in the Italian town of Veroli.

ITALIAN SONGS During the Renaissance, in the field of popular entertainment, many Italian songs were entitled *Zingaresche,* that is, songs of the Zingari or Gypsies.

ITALIAN THEATRE In the seventeenth century numerous theatrical pieces, particularly comedies, dealt with the Gypsy theme, in a light-hearted but sometimes not too complimentary vein.

ITALY There was a general law throughout Italy, in the sixteenth century, that no Gypsy should remain more than two nights in any one place.

Throughout their migratory history the Gypsies were rarely permitted to settle for long in any one country, except under harsh restrictions or conditions that negated their Gypsy mode of life.

J

JATS An Indian people with whom, as with the Doms, the origin of the Gypsies has been equated. Various gypsiologists have proppored a variety of the possible original home of the Gypsies, in addition to India. Among these are Ethiopia, Persia, the Canary Islands, the continent of Atlantis.

JEWELS However poor the Gypsies may be and however difficult their task to sustain themselves, the Gypsies in the Balkans usually have gold and silver ornaments, left to them as heirlooms, rings and necklaces, silverwork. With currency that has long been out of circulation — silver thalers, gold coins — they make a necklace, all the coins strung together, with additions of rings and bangles. That is the basic investment of the women. That constitutes their bank, their savings, their future.

JEWISH AFFINITIES Among those who investigated the Gypsies and studied their possible origin, there was an unwarranted and erroneous theory that, on account of certain similarities — such as facial configuration, complexion, nomadic habits — the Gypsies were ethnically of Judaic origin.

JEWISH THEORY In the nineteenth century a theory was prevalent that the Gypies were the descendants of the lost tribes of Israel. In George Borrow's view, there was no warrant for such an assumption.

ITALIAN TERRITORY   At the beginning of the nineteenth century Gypsies were to be found in considerable numbers in Italy, in Sicily, and in Sardinia. There was a general law throughout Italy that no Gyspy should remain more than two nights in any one place. But no sooner had one group gone, than another came in their place. It was a continuous cycle, but it was more or less tolerated by the authorities.

JOHN AUGUSTUS   (1879-1961) An eminent English portrait painter who displayed a profound interest in Gypsy lore. He was President of the Gypsy Lore Society. Many of his paintings depict Gypsy scenes and subjects.

JOKAI, MAURUS   (1823-1904) Hungarian dramatist and novelist. Author of *Der Zigeunerbaron,* which deals with Gypsy life in Hungary.

JOLLY BEGGARS   During the wars with the French, Gypsies often accepted the bounty for recruits; but took French leave of the service. Robert Burns the Scottish national poet illustrates this propensity in the Jolly Beggars:

> My bonny lass, I work in brass,
>   A Tinkler is my station:
> I've travell'd round all Christian ground,
>   In this my occupation.
> I've ta'en the gold, and been enroll'd
>   In many a noble squadron:
> But vain they search'd when off I march'd
>   To go and clout the caudron.

JONSON, BEN   (c. 1573-1637) The English poet and playwright who became Master of the Revels at the court of King James I of England. One of his masques is *The Gypsies Metamorphosed,* which depicts, without malice, the Gypsies as pedlars and tricksters.

JOSEPH II'S REGULATION   Joseph II of Austria issued a regulation in 1783 requiring Gypsy children to be taken to church and school. Those over four years of age were to be assigned to various neighboring communities. Adults were prohibited from wandering. Horse-dealing was also prohibited. The use of the Gypsy language was forbidden, as was inter-marriage among the Gypsies.

JUDAS   According to one tradition, the ancestors of the Gypsies advised Judas to betray his Master. Hence the punishment inflicted on the Gypsies of being everlasting wanderers on the face of the earth.

JUDGMENT ON GYPSIES   Walter Simson the gypsiologist explained why the Gypsies had such an ill reputation:
> Here, then, we have one of the principal reasons for everything connected with the Gypsies being hidden from the rest of mankind. They have always been looked upon as arrant vagabonds, while they have looked upon their ancestors as illustrious and immortal heroes. How, then, are we to bridge over this gulf that separates them, in feeling, from the rest of the world? The natural reply is that we should judge them, not by their condition and character in times that are past, but by what they are today.

JULIAN THE APOSTATE   Among fanciful conjectures on the original home of the Gypsies was the assumption that they were fugitives who were driven out of the city of Singara, in Mesopotamia, by the Emperor Julian the Apostate.

JUMPING THE BROOMSTICK   This expression, relating to the Gypsies, denotes a marriage ceremony in which the bride and groom jump over a broom in the presence of their families.

Another Gypsy practice, common among English Gypsies,

is for the young couple to join hands, in the presence of witnesses.

Still another ceremony consisted of the bride and groom putting a drop of their blood on a piece of bread and then eating each other's bread. Marriage in church, or in a registry office, has latterly become more common.

JURISDICTION OF TRIBAL COUNT Among the Gypsies the tribal chief often assumed the honorific title of Duke or Earl or King or Count.

With the Counts rested the management of the Gypsies. It was they who determined their marches, countermarches, advances, and retreats: what was to be attempted or avoided; what individuals were to be admitted into the fellowship and privileges of the Gitános, or who were to be excluded from their society. They settled disputes and sat in judgment over offenses.

By this code the members were forbidden to eat, drink, or sleep in the house of a busnó, which signifies any person who is not of the sect of the Gypsies. They were were likewise not to teach the language of Roma to any but those who, by birth or inauguration, belonged to that sect. They were enjoined to relieve their brethren in distress at any expense or peril.

K

KAKO A Gypsy term denoting a tribal chief. Such chiefs or leaders were, in the Middle Ages and later, designated as Dukes or Counts, often as the Duke of Little Egypt.

KALI As confirmatory testimony to the early association of Gypsies with India, it is remarkable that Kali, the malefic goddess of death and evil, is currently an object of worship by Gypsies.

KALUS This Gypsy term means *sticks*. These sticks are used in a dance in which each participant is equipped with a stick. Smeared with garlic, the stick is assumed to have an apotropaic effect in warding off sickness.

KANT, IMMANUEL (1724-1804) The German philosopher was of the considered opinion that the Gypsy language was of Indian origin.

KARMAN, DEMETRIUS A nineteenth century Gypsy who was noted for his violin playing. The violin is the supreme musical instrument to the Gypsies.

KASTARI A Gypsy term applied to Gypsies who work in wood and produce agricultural tools. Each occupation group has its own designation. The bear-trainers, for instance, are *oursari*.

KAULIYAH A term applied to the Gypsies who roam the Syrian desert. It is believed that, in origin, they are kin to the pariahs of India.

259

KEATS, JOHN (1795-1821) English poet. In a letter he wrote to Fanny Keats from Auchencairn, in 1818, he said: We are in the midst of Meg Merrilies country, of whom I suppose you have heard. Keats composed the following poem on the occasion:

Old Meg she was a Gipsy,
And liv'd upon the Moors:
Her bed it was the brown heath turf,
And her home was out of doors.

Her apples were swart blackberries,
Her currants pods o'broom;
Her wine was dew of the wild white rose,
Her book a churchyard tomb.

Her Brothers were the craggy hills,
Her Sisters larchen trees —
Alone with her great family
She liv'd as she did please.

No breakfast had she many a morn,
No dinner many a noon,
And 'stead of supper she would stare
Full hard against the Moon.

But every morn of woodbine fresh
She made her garlanding,
And every night the dark glen Yew
She wove, and she would sing.

And with her fingers old and brown
She plaited Mats o'Rushes,
And gave them to the Cottagers
She met among the Bushes.

Olg Meg was brave as Margaret Queen
And tall as Amazon:

An old red blanket cloak she wore;
A chip hat had she on.

God rest her aged bones somewhere —
She died full long agone!
Meg Merrilies is a Gypsy character who appears in
Sir Walter Scott's novel entitled *Guy Mannering.*

KEKKONO MUSH'S POOV A Gypsy expression meaning
No man's land, where the Gypsies might be allowed to
encamp for a short while. As a rule, their encampments
were very temporary, and depended on the good-will or
hostility of the local authorities.

KENNIK A Gypsy term meaning one who lives in a house.
This expression is more or less a word of contempt, as
the Gypsies are essentially a nomadic, non-sedentary
people.

KIDNAPPING The popular conception of the Gypsies as
customary kidnappers of children has prevailed for centuries, particularly in country districts, among the illiterate, and in legends and folklore. But it has also been
exploited in literature, in drama and fiction. In Victor
Hugo's *Notre Dame de Paris* Esmeralda is the victim of
Gypsies. Alexandre Hardy's tragi-comedy *La Belle Egyptienne* repeats the theme: Molière's *L'Etourdi* and *Les
Fourberies de Scapin* make it a dramatic subject. *L'In-
nocente Egyptienne,* a seventeenth century novel by Jean-
Pierre Camus, uses the same notion. Eugène Scribe, in
La Bohémienne, employs the same motif. Many contemporary short stories, too, have taken Gypsy kidnapping
as a dramatic and effective technique. In actuality, there
have been comparatively few authenticated cases of
child kidnapping by the Gypsies.

KILMER, JOYCE (1886-1918) The American poet who characterized the Gypsy's wanderlust as being linked with the Gypsy's sense of family unity:

> If you call the Gypsy a vagabond,
> I think you do him wrong;
> For he never goes a-traveling
> But he takes his home along.

KIND TREATMENT In Bristol, Southampton, and other areas in England committees were formed in the 1830's to help the Gypsies to become self-reliant and to devote themselves to sedentary occupations. The children were cared for, fed and clothed and sent to elementary schools. The elders were likewise dealt with sympathetically. Private citizens, men and women, professors, landowners, clergymen all took a share toward the amelioration and education of the hitherto abandoned Gypsies.

KING The term king or chief of a Gypsy tribe or clan is becoming rare. In the eighteenth century, the German Gypsies of Pennsylvania had two kings. In the later decades there was a King Kis Mihajlo. A Gypsy queen, Matilda II, was about the same time crowned in Ohio.

KING GEORGE V King George V of England once received a request from a Gypsy 'King' to help in founding a Gypsy colony in North Africa. The form *King,* among the Gypsies, is merely a tribal honorific. Similarly with the corresponding designation of *Queen.*

KING JAMES V OF SCOTLAND King James V of Scotland, as he was traveling through part of his dominions, disguised under the character of the Gaberlunzie-man, or Guidman of Ballangiegh, prosecuting, as was his custom, his low and vague amours, fell in with a band of Gypsies, in the midst of their carousals, in a cave, near Wemyss, in Fifeshire. His majesty heartily joined in their revels, but it was not long before a scuffle ensued, wherein the king was very roughly handled, being in danger of his life. The Gypsies asserted that the king attempted to take liberties with one of their women; and that one of the male Gypsies "came crack over his head with a bottle." The Gypsies, perceiving at last that he was none of their people, and considering him a spy, treated him with great indignity. Among other humiliating insults, they compelled his royal majesty, as a humble servant of a Tinkler, to carry their budgets and wallets on his back, for several miles, until he was exhausted; and being unable to proceed a step further, he sank under his load. He was then dismissed with scorn and contempt by the merciless Gypsies. Being exasperated at their cruel and contemptuous treatment of his sacred person, and having seen a fair specimen of their licentious manner of life, the king caused an order to be drawn up stating that if three Gypsies were found together, one of the three was instantly to be seized, and forthwith hanged or shot, by any one of his majesty's subjects that chose to put the order in execution.

KING JOSEPH LEE He was a Gypsy tribal chief who had official jurisdiction over the Gypsies of Scotland. The last of such 'kings' — merely a nominal title, an honorific — , Lee died in 1884.

KING OF THE GYPSIES Bamfylde Moor Carew, (1693-c. 1770), was an Englishman who led a strange nomadic life. As a boy, he left school and joined the Gypsies, by whom he was subsequently chosen as king. Transported to Maryland, he managed to escape and resume his vagabondage in England.

He wrote *The Life and Adventures of Bamfylde Moor Carew, the King of the Beggars*: a book that traces the

263

origin and describes the customs and the language of the Gypsies of England.

KING RENE   In the mid-fifteenth century the relics of Les Saintes Maries de la Mer, Sainte Jacobé and Sainte Salomé, who had providentially been cast ashore on the Camargue coast in Provence, were transferred from Italy, where they had been believed to be buried, to Provence. Here they were under the sponsorship of King René. From that time on the Gypsies, to whom Sara, the servant of the two Marys, was the patron saint, made reverence, at the spot where a shrine had been built. This spot is now known as Les Saintes Maries de la Mer. Annually, throngs of Gypsies assemble from many countries to pay their respects to Sara and to hold a grand festival on May 24.

KING VIKRAM AND THE VAMPIRE   This is a Sanskrit humorous romance. It consists of twenty-five disconnected stories that collectively serve to illustrate in the most painful manner the highest lesson of wisdom. In this book the Gypsies, and the scenes that surround them, are intended to teach the lesson of freedom and nature.

KLINGSOHR   He is the reputed author of the Germanic epic the *Niebelungen Lied*. He was regarded as a Gypsy wizard, who, like Odin the Norse god, rode upon a wolf.

KNIFE   The knife occurs frequently among the Hungarian and Italian Gypsy charms or spells. It is sometimes stuck into a table, while a spell is muttered, protesting that it is not the wood which one wishes to hurt, but the heart of an enemy. Here the knife is supposed in reality to have an indwelling spirit, which will pass to the heart or health of the one hated. In Robert Burns' *Tam O'*

Shanter there is a knife on the witches' table, and in Transylvania, as in Tuscany, a new knife, not an old one, is used in diverse ceremonies. Sometimes an old and curious knife becomes an amulet and is supposed to bring luck, although the current belief is that any pointed gift causes a quarrel.

KNOWING THE GYPSIES James Crabb, a clergyman who was interested in proselytizing among the Gypsies of England produced in 1832 *The Gypsies' Advocatem* or *Observations on the Origin, Character, Manners and Habits of the English Gypsies.*
He stressed the fact that his knowledge of these people was not derived from the testimony of others, for instance, from two prominent gypsiologists, Grellmann and Hoyland, but from close personal investigation. He made frequent visits to the Gypsy tents. He gave the Gypsies free access to his home when they were encamped near Southampton. He gave them help and advice.
By these means, he continued, he gained a general knowledge of their vicious habits, their comparative virtues, and their unhappy mode of life. His desire was to correct popular misconceptions about the Gypsies, which had given rise to many unjust and injurious prejudices against them.
Furthermore, his intention was to arouse his countrymen to an energetic benevolence toward this despised people. He called the Gypsies an unhappy race, poor English heathens.

KOCHANOWSKI, JAN A contemporary gypsiologist who is himself a Gypsy postulates that the Gypsies stem from the Rajputs of India, from the Romane Chave, that is, the Sons of Rama. In the twelfth century they escaped a massacre by the Moslems and crossed through Afghanistan into Europe.

KOROS In Transylvania the River Körös is associated with the Gypsies. Formely they gathered the alluvial mud in the river bed and washed out the gold. In return for this labor, in the eighteenth century the Empress Maria Theresa granted these Gypsies special privileges. Occupationally, such Gypsies were designated as Orari or Zlatari, gold-washers.

KOUVANINE, M. J. Nineteenth century Russian physician and gypsiologist. For over three decades he devoted himself to collecting the mythology of the Russian Gypsies, folksongs, tales, rituals. He traveled among the Gypsies of Germany and Austria, the Arab countries, India, Iran, Kurdistan, Central Asia, Caucasia. In all his investigations he found that the core of Gypsy life is its Indo-Aryan origin.

KRIS This Gypsy term denotes a body of law and custom, a composite of usage, oral traditions and magic practices. Kris may also designate a trial conducted by a judge. As a rule, the Gypsies have administered their own tribal laws throughout the centuries. In some instances the tribal chief has been granted the royal permission to act in cases relating to family, tribal, and clan matters.

KRSTNIKI This Greek term signifies: one who has been baptized. In Gypsy folklore the krstniki is the youngest of twelve brothers, all sons of the same father. The krstniki protect the world from the machinations of witches. But on St. John's Eve they are in great danger for the witches then assail them with sticks and stakes. A krstniki is also defined as one who has gained the love of a Vila, a beautiful witch.

KUKAYA A Hungarian Gypsy tribe that regards itself as descendants of Pçuvushi, earth spirits. These earth spirits constitute a part of a large corpus of Gypsy mythology.

KUMPANIA   A Gypsy expression that denotes a group consisting of several family units, independent of other units of the same type.

The basic organization of Gypsy life comprises the family, the tribe, the clan, in that sequence.

KUSHTO BACHT   A Gypsy expression meaning *good luck,* a notion that is constantly in the Gypsy mind.

Bacht is secured by the possession and wearing of certain amulets and charms and the recitation of incantations.

L

LACE ROMNI A Gypsy expression used in Hungary to signify "good women." Such women derive their magic powers from the Nivasi or Pçhuvusi, the spirits of water and earth.

Gypsy mythology and folklore are full of imaginative concepts relating to good and evil spirits that haunt the woodlands, the rivers, the fields and the underground.

LACHA A Gypsy term referring to the physical chastity of the Gypsy women. A Gypsy woman may be obscene in gesture, in speech, in look, but her *lácha* is never sullied or questioned.

This notion of chastity is a vital issue in the event of a Gypsy marriage.

LACK OF COLORS Among many common terms that cannot be expressed in Romany, the Gypsy language, are some colors. There is no word, for example, for gray, or for green, or blue. This was the view expressed by George Borrow, the noted gypsiologist. A later gypsiologist, however, Charles Leland, found that there was a Gypsy term denoting green: namely, *shelno,* in use among the English Gypsies.

LAESHI A Gypsy group in Rumania who are intensely independent. They have very little association even with other Gypsy tribal units. Their camping grounds are in the mountains and forests.

LA GITANILLA   This is the title — The Little Gypsy Girl — of a short story, one of his Exemplary Novels, by Cervantes, in which he expressed the contemporary Gypsy life and the attitude of the Spaniards. He describes the Gypsies as innately addicted to thievery. Cervantes, who knew his Gypsies well, also describes an interesting ceremony of admission into a Gypsy tribal community.

LALERE SINTI   A Gypsy expression meaning 'stupid Gypsies.' The term was used by the Germans when mentioning the Gypsy people.
Many expressions of contempt have been applied to the Gypsies as they infiltrated in the European countries. They have been called, in official records and edicts, heathens, thieves, idlers, vagabonds, sorcerers.

LAMBADIS   A people of India who have been identified with the Gypsies. A variant name for the Lambadis is Banjaras, or Vangaris.
In the course of their wanderings from Asia to Europe, the Gypsies have been identified with different territorial origins: among them, Persia, Ethiopia, Portugal, Greece, lost continent of Atlantis.

LAMENT FOR A GYPSY   William Faa, a Scottish Gypsy, had been engaged in smuggling on the coast of Northumberland. Armed with a cudgel only, he had defended himself against one of a party of dragoons. Using his sword, the dragoon attacked William Faa and compelled him to surrender.
The death of this King of Little Egypt was commemorated in the *Scotsman,* the Scottish national newspaper, in 1847:
A Lament for Will Faa
The daisy has faded, the yellow leaf drops;
The cold sky looks grey o'er the shrivelled treetops;

And many around us, since Summer's glad birth,
Have dropt, like the old leaves, into the cold earth.
And one worth remembering hath gone to the home
Where the King and the Kaiser must both at last come,
The King of the Gypsies — the last of a name.
The cold clod ne'er pressed down a manlier breast
Than that of the old man now gone to his rest.
In the old house of Yetholm we've sat at the board,
The guest, highly honored, of Egypt's old lord,
And mark'd his eye glisten as oft as he told
Of his feats on the Bordes, his prowess of old.
It is meet, when that dark eye in death has grown dim,
That we sing a last strain in remembrance of him.
The fame of the Gypsy has faded away
With the breath from the brave heart of gallant Will Faa.

LANGUAGE The lingua franca, the fundamental linguistic medium of communication of the Gypsies, is known as Romany. Every group or community or tribe, however, has its own individual vocabulary, its own pronunciation, an amalgam of ancient word-roots attached to terms taken from a diversity of languages and dialects.

Hence, even among Gypsies, there is sometimes difficulty in communication for tribal clans or disparate areas.

LANGUAGE PROHIBITION Maria Theresa, Empress of Austria, late in the eighteenth century, forbade the Gypsies to use Romany. In Spain, too, in earlier centuries, royal edicts repeatedly prohibited the Gitános, the Spanish Gypsies, from using the Romany language, the Gypsy dress, and the practice of fortune-telling.

LARGE FAMILIES Children are treated with such affection by the Gypsies that one of their characteristic proverbs runs: many children, much luck.

differences, at any level, within the tribal context. The term for law is *kriss,* which is in the hands of the council and child. But the judge was adamant, declaring that he

LAW Whenever possible, the Gypsies prefer to settle all their of the tribal elders. The law is a body of oral customs and secret traditions. There is no written record. All customs, rules, ceremonials are transmitted orally.

LEE, LUCY A celebrated English Gypsy fortune-teller whose headquarters were located at The Devil's Dyke, near Brigton, England. Throughout their wandering for centuries, fortune-telling remained the characteristic occupational practice of the Gypsy women.

LEGAL DISCRIMINATION At the Lent Assizes, in March 1827, in England, a judge was passing sentence of death on two men. He was merciful to one. but to the other, a young Gypsy convicted of horse-stealing, he gave no hope. The convicted man pleaded in behalf of his wife and his fellow-judges had determined to execute horse-stealers, especially Gypsies, on account of the increase in crime.

LEGEND OF THE SINTI There are many fanciful and imaginative legends that are associated with the origin and provenance of the Gypsies. They came from Eastern India, and as *Sinti* advanced to Chaldea, where they showed their skill in bronze and gold. They also acquired a knowledge of astronomy and astrology. Then they set out with the Patriarch Abraham into Canaan. Finally they reached Egypt.

LEIS PRALA A Gypsy expression that signifies the law of brotherhood, the tribal morality. According to this code an unfriendly act on the part of one tribe may involve the total extermination of that tribe.

LEISURE   When a Gypsy is free of any assigned or undertaken task, he plays cards, goes to the inn to join his fellows in talk, sings, dances traditional steps, relates old folktales around the camp fire.

LELAND, CHARLES GODFREY (1824-1903) American writer who had an enthusiastic and scholarly interest in the Gypsies, especially in their legends and activities relating to witchcraft and fortune-telling. He lived among them in England and elsewhere, and learned Romany. He is the author of some seven books on the Gypsies and their ways. Among these are *The English Gypsies and their Language* and *Gypsy Sorcery and Fortune-Telling.*

LELAND AND FORTUNE-TELLING   In Russia, Charles Leland the gypsiologist asked a number of Gypsy girls in Moscow whether they could tell fortunes. To his amazement, they admitted their inability to do so. Turning the tables, as it were, Leland himself proceeded to read the palms of the Gypsies themselves.

LELAND ON BULWER LYTTON   Charles Leland the American gypsiologist chats about his meeting with Bulwer Lytton, the famous English novelist:

I have talked with Lord Lytton on Gypsies. He, too, was once a Romany rye in a small way, and in the gay May heyday of his young manhood once went off with a band of Romanys, and passed weeks in their tents, — no bad thing, either, for anybody. I was more than once tempted to tell him the strange fact that, though he had been among the black people and thought he had learned their language, what they had imposed upon him for that was not Romany, but cant, or English

272

thieves' slang. For what is given, in good faith, in "Paul Clifford" and the "Disowned" is only the same old mumping *kennick* which was palmed off on Bampfylde Moore Carew; or which he palmed on his readers, as the secret of the Roms.

LELAND ON GYPSY FOOD   Charles Leland, the gypsiologist and folklorist, wrote of the food of the Gypsies:
The Gypsy eats everything and anything except horse-flesh. Among themselves, while talking Romany, they will boast of having eaten nullo baulors, pigs that have died a natural death.

LELAND ON MOSCOW GYPSIES   As for the Gypsies of Moscow, I can only say that, after meeting them in public, and penetrating to their homes, where I was received as one of themselves, even as a Romany, I found that this opinion of them was erroneous, and that they were altogether original in spite of being clean, deeply interesting although honest, and quite attractive in most respects, notwithstanding their ability to read and write.

LELAND ON SHELTA   Charles Leland, the gypsiologist, who discovered the secret language of Shelta, the tinkers' talk, wrote:
The question which I cannot solve is, On which of the Celtic languages is this jargon based? My informant declares that it is quite independent of Old Irish, Welsh, or Gaelic. In pronunciation it appears to be almost identical with the latter; but while there are Gaelic words in it, it is certain that much examination and inquiry have failed to show that it is contained in that language. That it is "the talk of the old Picts — thim that built the stone houses like bee-hives" — is, I confess, too conjectural for a philologist. I have no doubt that when the Picts were suppressed thousands

273

of them must have become wandering outlaws, like the Romany, and that their language in time became a secret tongue of vagabonds on the road. This is the history of many such lingoes; but unfortunately Owen's opinion, even if be legendary, will not prove that the Painted People spoke the Shelta tongue. I must call attention, however, to one or two curious points. I have spoken of Shelta as a jargon; but it is, in fact, a language, for it can be spoken grammatically and without using English or Romany. And again, there is a corrupt method of pronouncing it, according to English, while correctly enunciated it is purely Celtic in sound. More than this I have naught to say.

Shelta is perhaps the last Old British dialect as yet existing which has thus far remained undiscovered. There is no hint of it in John Camden Hotten's Slang Dictionary, nor has it been recognized by the Dialect Society. Mr. Simson, had he known the 'Tinklers' better, would have found that not Romany, but Shelta, was the really secret language which they employed, although Romany is also more or less familiar to them all. To me there is in it something very weird and strange. I cannot well say why; it seems as if it might be spoken by witches and talking toads, and uttered by the Druid stones, which are fabled to come down by moonlight to the water-side to drink, and who will, if surprised during their walk, answer any questions.

LELAND ON THE ORIGIN OF THE GYPSIES Charles Leland the gypsiologist delivered papers on the origin of the Gypsies before the London Philological Society and the Oriental Congress at Florence. His summation ran as follows:

First, then, there appears to be every reason for believing with Captain Richard Burton that the Jats of Northwestern India furnished so large a proportion of the emigrants or exiles who, from the tenth century, went out of India westward, that there is very little risk in assuming it as an hypothesis, at least, that they formed the *Hauptstamm* of the Gypsies of Europe. What other elements entered into these, with whom we are all familiar, will be considered presently. These Gypsies came from India, where caste is established and callings are hereditary even among out-castes. It is not assuming too much to suppose that, as they evinced a marked aptitude for certain pursuits and an inveterate attachment to certain habits, their ancestors had in these respects resembled them for ages.

These pursuits and habits were that

They were tinkers, smiths, and farriers.

They dealt in horses, and were naturally familiar with them.

They were without religion.

They were unscrupulous thieves.

Their women were fortune-tellers, especially by chiromancy. They ate without scruple animals which had died a natural death, being especially fond of the pig, which, when it has thus been 'butchered by God,' is still regarded by prosperous Gypsies in England as a delicacy.

They flayed animals, carried corpses, and showed such aptness for these and similar detested callings that in several European countries they long monopolized them.

They made and sold mats, baskets, and small articles of wood.

They have shown great skill as dancers, musicians, singers, acrobats; and it is a rule almost without exception that there is hardly a traveling company of such performers or a theatre, in Europe or America, in which there is not at least one person with some Romany blood.

Their hair remains black to advanced age, and they retain it longer than do Europeans or ordinary Orientals They speak an Aryan tongue, which agrees in the main with that of the Jats, but which contains words gathered from other Indian sources. This is a consideration of the utmost importance, as by it alone can we determine what was the agglomeration of tribes in India which formed the Western Gypsy.

LELAND'S INTEREST IN GYPSIES The American gypsiologist Charles Leland explains his interest in Gypsies:

Why do I love to wander on the roads to hear the birds; to see old church towers afar, rising over fringes of forest, a river and a bridge in the foreground, and an ancient castle beyond, with a modern village springing up about it, just as at the foot of the burg there lies the falling trunk of an old oak, around which weeds ands flowers are springing up, nourished by its decay? Why love these better than pictures, and with a more than fine-art feeling? Because on the roads, among such scenes, between the hedgerows and by the river, I find the wanderers who properly inhabit not the houses but the scene, not a part but the whole. These are the Gypsies, who live like the birds and hares, not of the house-born or the town-bred, but free and at home only with Nature.

LENAU, NIKOLAUS (1802-1850) Hungarian poet. Author, among other works, of a poem entitled *The Three Gypsies.* Poems on Gypsy themes have been written by John Keats, Matthew Arnold, Charles Leland, and George Borrow.

LENGTH OF STAY Gypsiologists and philologists who have concerned themselves with the problem of the Gypsies' origin, particularly Miklosich and Sampson, have analyzed the various Gypsy dialects in relation to the countries where the nomads settled. The gypsiologists have been able to estimate with some precision the duration of Gypsies' settlement in any particular country in terms of the size of the indigenous vocabulary absorbed into the Gypsy language.

LEO AFRICANUS Famous Arab traveler and geographer, who belongs in the sixteenth century. He produced a Description of Africa. He refers to the merchants of Agades, whose caravans were frequently harassed by bands of marauders commonly called Bohemians or Egyptians.

LESAGE, ALAIN RENE (1668-1707) French novelist and dramatist. In his picaresque novel entitled *Gil Blas de Santillane,* he presents Coscolina, a Gypsy fortune-teller. Sir Walter Scott's novel Guy Mannering has Meg Merrilies, a Gypsy, as a prominent character. The French novelist, Prosper Mérimée, also, has a novel entitled *Carmen* with a Gypsy heroine.

LETTERS OF SAFE-CONDUCT During their Westward march through Europe, in the Middle Ages and later, the Gypsy leaders, the tribal chiefs who called themselves Dukes and Counts of Little Egypt, presented to the authorities of the towns where they arrived certain letters of protection, recommendations for charitable treatment, from the Pope, from Sigismund of Hungary, from Alonso V of Aragon, from James V of Scotland, from European rulers and princelings and from civic authorities. On occasion, it was difficult to confirm the authenticity of such protective passports, but in most cases the Gypsies were able to profit from the welcome they received in consequence of the latter.

LIBERATION   After long efforts, a bill was passed in 1855 that freed some two hundred thousand Gypsies in Rumania. In the Balkans, the Gypsies had been feudal serfs under the local landowners and the ecclesiastical authorities.

LICENTIOUSNESS   Despite the general view of Gypsy habits, some authorities have considered that the Gypsies are more free from licentiousness than any other race in the world.
Although the Gypsy women may dance and sing in an obscene and lewd manner, their personal chastity has been a traditional characteristic in the family and the tribe.

LIFE AT STAKE   If a member of a Gypsy tribe was brought before the court, charged with a crime that was likely to cost him his life, or to transport him, every article of value was sacrificed to save the accused from death or banishment.

LIGHT WORK   In the early nineteenth century the Gypsies of Central Europe were reluctant to undertake heavy work in metals. They seldom went beyond making horse-shoes. In general, they confined themselves to small articles such as rings and nails. They mended old pots and kettles, made knives, needles, and also worked trifles in tin or brass.

LILITH   Lilith was the legendary first wife of Adam. She was the demon-mother of all witchcraft. The Slavic Gypsies practiced spells to avert her evil influence. Gypsy mythology is full of such fanciful tales and beliefs.

LIMITED VOCABULARY   The English Gypsies have of course words of their down only for the most common objects and ideas. As soon as they wish to express something beyond these, they must have recourse to English. And even to express some very common objects, ideas, and feelings, they are quite at a loss in their own tongue, and must either employ English words or very vague terms.

LINGUISTIC COMPOSITE   In the view of authoritative philologists, Romany is derived from Sanskrit. In addition, Romany contains thousands of words stemming from various Indian languages: Punjabi, Hindi, Gujarati, and the dialects of Rajputana and Malwa.

LINGUISTIC DISTINCTIONS   In a linguistic sense there are two groups of Hungarian Gypsies:
  (a) Hungarian Gypsies (romungro)
  (b) Wallachian Gypsies (vlasiko rom)
In the various countries where the Gypsies have settled, They have absorbed the native idiom to a large extent into their own Romany linguistic pattern: as in Greece and Spain.

LINGUISTIC ENCOUNTER   A linguistic coincidence is related by James Crabb, the nineteenth century gypsiologist:
  A well-known nobleman, who had resided many years in India, taking shelter under a tree during a storm in this country near a camp of Gypsies, was astonished to hear them use several words he well knew were Hindustani. Going up to them, he found them able to converse with him in that language.
  Not long ago, a missionary from India, who was well acquainted with the language of Hindustani, was at the author's house when a Gypsy was present. After the conversation which he had with her, he declared that her people must once have known the Hindustani language well. Gypsies, in fact, often expressed surprise when words were read to them out of the Hindustani vocabulary.
  Lord Teignemouth once said to a young Gypsy woman,

in Hindustani, *Tue burra tschur,* that is, You are a great thief. She immediately replied: No. I am not a thief I live by fortune-telling. He also conversed with an old Gypsy at Norwood.

It can be no matter of surprise that this language, as spoken among this people, is generally corrupted, when we consider that, for many centuries, they have known nothing of elementary science, and have been stranger to books and letters. Perhaps the secrecy necessary to effect many of their designs has been the greatest mean of preserving its scanty remains among them. But an attempt to prove that they are not of Hindu origin because they do not speak Hindustani with perfect correctness, would be as absurd as to declare that our Gypsies are not natives of England because they speak very incorrect English.

LINGUISTIC GROUPS   In Hungary there are two groups of Gypsies, from a linguistic viewpoint:
(a) Hungarian (Carpathian) Gypsies — romungro.
(b) Wallachian Gypsies — vlasiko rom.

LINGUISTIC INVESTIGATIONS   The first attempts to determinate the origin of the Gypsies through philological and linguistic study and examination began toward the end of the seventeenth century. Late in the eighteenth century more thorough investigation was continued, particularly through the efforts of Stephan Vályi. He discovered that the language of the Hungarian Gypsies corresponded largely to the language of India as spoken on the Malabar coast. In 1844 August Friedrich Pott made still more thorough and revealing researches. He published his findings in *Die Zigeuner in Europa und Asien.*

LIQUIDATION   Under the Nazis, at the instance of Hitler, Himmler, and Heydrich, the order was given for the liquidation of all Gypsies. They were, at the beginning sterilized. Finally, in 1945, those Gypsies who had been confined in concentration camps were gassed.

LISZT, FRANZ VON (1811-1886)   In addition to being a noted Hungarian pianist and composer, Liszt was also keenly interested in Gypsy music. On this subject he wrote his *Gypsies and their Music in Hungary.* "The rhythms," he declared, "swell out powerfully, like a potent love-charm, then again they die away in sighs like sweet haunting farewells." Liszt regarded Gypsy music as completely and essentially original, totally their own in the triumphal melodies they produced, the fire and frenzy they extracted from their instruments, the romantic waves of melancholy, the jubilation alternating with brooding gloom and despair. But Liszt had his opponents, particularly among the Hungarians themselves, who rejected any Gypsy contributions to their own native music.

LITERACY   Few Gypsies in England could either read or write in the nineteenth century. Yet a correspondence was kept up between members of families or tribes who had some modicum of writing practice. Friends often became the scribes, as in antiquity, in the Middle Ages, and often in the Orient at the present times, for those who lacked writing knowledge.

LITERARY HOSTILITY   In the nineteenth century, among writers, there existed violent hostility to the Gypsies:
> The greater number of writers, in Scotland at least, when speaking of or alluding to this unfortunate race, seem scarcely able to discover expressions sufficiently strong to manifest their abhorrence of them. This in some respects is unjust. It is granted that they are idle, disorderly, vicious, and unrestrained; without almost any knowledge of religion. But it might also be recollected that this will always be the character, more or

less, of those who live as they do — a very wandering life, and it becomes therefore the duty of society to inquire what they can do to reclaim them from their erradic mode of life — the grand source of almost all their vicious habits.

The Gypsies are not destitute of good qualities. They have a species of honor, so that if trusted, they will not deceive or betray you. They are grateful for any attention that is shown them; so that I believe there are few instances of those who have treated them with kindness receiving any injury at their hands. Many pleasing instances could be mentioned of their grateful sense of favors conferred. They are very sensible of the dislike which is generally entertained against them, and would frequently conceal the fact that they belong to a separate race; whereas, formerly, it would appear that they were rather proud of being regarded as a peculiar tribe, and this feeling is not altogether extinct among them.

LITERARY IMAGE IN ENGLAND   For the first time Gypsies appeared as dramatic characters in 1578, in England. The play was George Whetstone's *Promos and Cassandra*. In Shakespeare's dramas *Othello, Antony and Cleopatra,* and in *Romeo and Juliet,* references to the Gypsies occur. The Gypsies were well enough known in a literary sense for Shakespeare to use the name of Caliban in *The Tempest*: for Caliban is a Gypsy term signifying *blackness.* Again, in *As You Like It,* in Act 5 a page says:

I' faith, i' faith; and both in a tune, like two Gypsies on a horse.

The *Spanish Gypsy,* a romantic comedy by Thomas Middleton, was performed in 1623.

Henry Fielding (1707-1754), the noted English novelist, in *Tom Jones,* has the hero himself mingle with a Gypsy assembly. He meets their king and talks with him. Fielding comments on the well organized Gypsy society, with its own laws and restrictions and its chief authority, the king.

LITERARY IMAGE IN ITALY   In the seventeenth century Italy was well acquainted with the Gypsies. They were made the subject of Gypsy motifs in the drama, in comedy, in poetry. Florido de Silvestris presented *Signorina Zingaretta,* Miss Gypsy. It contained Gypsy expressions, dancing scenes, guitar playing, and a kidnapping theme.

In the seventeenth century Giovanni Briccio produced several comedies all dealing with Gypsy manners.

LITERARY IMAGE IN PORTUGAL   Portugal in the sixteenth century, like Spain, took active cognizance of the phenomenon of the Gypsies in their midst. They became the subject of poems, or scenes in farces and other theatrical spectacles. For they were news, something strange and exotic and hence of exciting interest to the general public. Diego Camacho produced a poem containing references to Gypsy dances. Another poet, Garcis de Resende, presented a Grega, a Gypsy woman. Grega actually means a Greek woman: Gypsies were called Greek because their speech was interspersed with Greek words.

Gil Vicente, founder of the Portuguese drama, produced for the stage *La Farça das Ciganas,* which was performed before King John III. The spectacle presented Gypsies who danced and sang and begged, asked for clothes, and told fortunes. Evidently a theatrical reflection of the actual life of the Tsiganes as the Portuguese observed them.

Miguel Leitao, also, in his *Miscellanea,* makes references

to the Gypsy dances that were already popular in the Iberian peninsula.

LITERARY IMAGE IN THE NETHERLANDS In the seventeenth century the Gypsies were well known in the Netherlands as an exotic element in the context of the state. They were the subject of a versified comedy entitled *The Life of Konstance,* by Tengnagel, that appeared in 1643. There followed, in 1658, *The Spanish Gypsy,* a novel by Catharina Verwers.

LITHUANIA AND POLAND Late in the fifteenth century the Gypsies appeared in Lithuania and Poland. At the beginning of the sixteenth century King Alexander I granted a charter to a Gypsy tribal leader named Vasil, a *woyi cyganski,* that is, a Gypsy *voivode* or chief.

LITTLE EGYPT In the Middle Ages the Gypsies, moving westward from India, settled in Modon, in the Greek Peloponnesus, near a Mount Gype. This spot was identified as Little Egypt.

LIVELIHOOD OF ENGLISH GYPSIES Half a century ago, Gypsy families, forced by weather conditions to occupy themselves in their tents or caravans, engaged in producing all sorts of more or less useful small articles and wares. The raw material they usually procured from neighboring fields and woods. The resultant objects included fern baskets, doormats, grass baskets, clothes pegs, heather brooms, artificial flowers, bottles containing wooden artifacts.

LIVELIHOOD OF RUSSIAN GYPSIES In most of the provincial towns of Russia they were to be found in a state of half-civilization, supporting themselves by trafficking in horses, or by curing the disorders incidental to those animals. But the vast majority rejected this manner of life, and crossed the country in bands, like the ancient Hamaxobioi; the immense grassy plains of Russia affording pasturage for their herds of cattle, on which, and the products of the chase, they chiefly depend for subsistence. They are, however, not destitute of money, which they obtain by various means, but principally by curing diseases amongst the cattle of the mujiks or peasantry, and by telling fortunes, and not infrequently by theft and brigandage.

LIVING IN THE PRESENT The Gypsies live intensely in the present. Of the next day, they say: O Delore zanel — God knows what tomorrow will bring.
Their migratory habits have of course intensified this attitude.

LOADSTONE The Gypsies are addicted to a superstition associated with the loadstone, which they call *La Bar Lachi*. The Spanish Gypsies believe that he who is in possession of it has nothing to fear from steel or lead, from fire or water, and that death itself has no power over him. Extraordinary things are related of its power in exciting the amorous passions, and, on this account, it is in great request among the Gypsy hags. All these women are procuresses and find persons of both sexes weak and wicked enough to make use of their pretended knowledge in the composition of love-draughts and decoctions. In the case of the loadstone, however, there is no pretence, the Gitános believing all they say respecting it, and still more. This is proved by the eagerness with which they seek to obtain the stone in its natural state, which is somewhat difficult to accomplish.
In the museum of natural curiosities in Madrid there is a large piece of loadstone originally extracted from the

American mines. There is scarcely a Gitána in Madrid who is not acquainted with this circumstance and who does not long to obtain the stone. Pepita, an old Gitána, informed me that a priest who was in love proposed to her to steal the loadstone, offering her all his sacerdotal garments in the event of success; but she appears to have declined the attempt. According to the Gypsy account, the person in love, if he wishes to excite a corresponding passion in another quarter by means of the loadstone, must swallow, in *aguardiente,* a small portion of the stone pulverized, at the time of going to rest, repeating to himself the following magic rhyme:

> To the Mountain of Olives one morning I hied.
> Three little black goats before me I spied.
> Those three little goats on three cars I laid.
> Black cheeses three from their milk I made.
> The one I bestow on the loadstone of power,
> That save me it may from all ills that lower.
> The second to Mary Padilla I give,
> And to all the witch hags about her that live.
> The third I reserve for Asmodeus lame,
> That fetch me he may whatever I name.

LOCATIONS   In England, Gypsies have allocated to themselves certain areas or circuits. Devonshire, for instance, is the locale of the Stanley Gypsies. Derbyshire is associated with the Boswell tribe, while the Smiths cling to the New Forest.

LOM   This term, with its variant *dom,* is used by the Gypsy tribes in the Near East, in Syria and Persia, to identify themselves. The Gypsies have been identified by a large variety of names: Manouches, Zingari, Zigeuner, Heiden, Bohemians.

LONGEVITY OF GYPSIES The Gypsies often live to a considerable age. Margaret Finch, who was known as Queen of the Gypsies, died in 1740, at the age of 109. In his tent at Launton, Oxfordshire, James Smith, called by the public King of the Gypsies, died in 1830, at the age of more than one hundred. His body was followed to the grave by his widow, who was herself more than a hundred years old. At the funeral the widow tore her hair, uttered the most frantic exclamations, and begged to be allowed to throw herself on the coffin to be buried with her husband: in the manner of the Hindu custom of suttee.

A Gypsy woman lived to the reputed age of a hundred and twenty years, and up to that age she was accustomed to sing gaily. Many events in her life were rather remarkable. In her youth she had been a notorious swindler. At one time she extracted a large sum of money and other valuable effects from a lady. For which and other offences she was condemned to death. A petition, however, was presented to King George III, to use the Gypsy's own expression, 'just after he had set up business.' The sentence was reversed. But the Gypsy continued her ways. She taught her daughter the same crimes for which she had been condemned.

LONG HAIR Like Samson, the Gypsy men like to keep the hair long. It lends a certain prestige to their appearance. Few, on the other hand, wear beards.

LONG SETTLEMENTS A study of Romany, the Gypsy language, tends to show that the Gypsies settled for a longer period in Persia and Greece than in other countries.

LORD OF THE FOREST In Gypsy folklore there are many spirits and demons that haunt the woodlands and streams and can inflict injury on human beings. Some of these spirits, however, are benevolent.

The Lord of the Forest, for instance, once taught a hunter that if he loaded his gun on New Year's Night with a live adder he would never miss a shot during the ensuing year.

LORD-PARAMOUNT   In the region of James V of Scotland, in the year 1540, John Faw, a Scottish Gypsy, had such prestige that he was made lord-paramount over the Gypsies of Scotland.

LORD'S PRAYER   English Gypsy Dialect
Moro Dad, savo djives oteh drey o charos, to caumen Gorgio tu Romany Chal tiro nav, to awel tiro tem, to kairen tiro lav aukko prey puv, sar kairdios oteh drey o charos. Dey men to-divvus moro divvuskoe moro, ta fordey men pazorrhus tukey sar men for-denna len pazorrhus amande; ma muk te petrenna drey caik temptacionos; ley men abri sor doschder. Tiro se o tem, Mi-duvel, tiro o zoozlu vast, tiro sor koskopen drey sor cheros. Avali. Tachipen.
Spanish Gypsy Dialect
Batu monro sos socabas oté enré ye char, que camele Gacho ta Romani Cha tiro nao, qu'abillete tiro chim, querese tiro lao acoi opré ye puve sarta se querela oté enré ye char. Dinaños sejonia monro manro de cata chibes, ta estormenanos monrias bisauras sasta mu estormenanos a monrias bisabadores; na nos meques petrar enré cayque pajandía, lilanos abri de saro chungalipen. Persos tiro sinela a chim. Undevel, tiro ye silna bast, tiro saro lachipen enré saro chiros. Unga. Chachipé.
Literal English Translation
Our Father who dwellest there in heaven, may Gentile

288

and Gypsy love thy name, thy kingdom come, may they do thy word here on earth as it is done there in heaven. Give us today our daily bread, and forgive us indebted to thee as we forgive them indebted to us, suffers not that we fall into no temptation, take us out from all evil. Thine is the kingdom my God, thine the strong hand, thine all goodness in all time. Aye. Truth.

LORRAINE   In Alsace-Lorraine there were great numbers of Gypsies dwelling in the forests before the French Revolution of 1790.
On occasion, the Gypsies have made their homes in caves, like troglodytes, as in Granada.

LOUIS XII   Louis XII of France in 1504 ordered all Gypsies to be banished from the country under penalty of hanging in the case of those who persisted in remaining in France.

LOUIS XIV   In France, Louis XIV was the first king to try to settle the nomadic Gypsies on the land. He hoped to give then a sense of security and permanence, but his effort was futile. In 1675 he decreed the extermination of all Gypsies in French territory by fire and sword.

LOUISIANA   In the nineteenth century France sent Gypsies to colonize Louisiana and settled them in New Orleans and elsewhere.
England also deported the Gypsies to the American colonies.

LOUISIANA GYPSIES   Walter Simson, the nineteenth century gypsiologist, wrote:
It is stated that in Alexandria, Louisiana, when under Spanish rule, there were French and Spanish, Egyptians and Indians, Mulattoes and Negroes. . . These Egyptians came from 'some of the Northern islands.' . . .

They spoke a language among themselves, but could talk French and Spanish too. They were black, but not very black, and as good citizens as any, and passed for white folk. They married mostly with mulattoes, and a good many of the mulattoes had Egyptian blood in them too. These Egyptians had disappeared since the State became part of the Union . . . The Egyptians were probably Spanish Gypsies.

LOVE CHARM On St. John's Day a frog is put into an earthen vessel full of small holes. The vessel is placed on an ant hill. Ants eat the frog and leave the skeleton. This skeleton is then ground to a powder, mixed with the blood of a bat, and dried. The mass is shaped into small buns and secretly inserted in the food of the desired lover.

LOVE PHILTRE In the Hungarian novelist Maurus Jokai's novel *The Yellow Rose,* one passage refers to Gypsy plant-lore. An inn-keeper's daughter, having lost her lover's affection, wonders how to regain his love:

> Suddenly the girl remembered about a gipsy woman, who had once told her fortune for some old clothes, and, out of pure gratitude, had said to her as well, "Should your lover's heart grow cold, my dear, and you wish to make it flame again, that is easily managed. Give him wine mixed with lemon juice, and drop a bit of this root called 'fat minnikin' into it. Then his love will flame up again, till he would break down walls to reach you."

> She administered the concoction, including 'fat man-nikin,' which was really the mandrake, but the result was almost fatal, as the dose had been excessive.

LOVE POTIONS In order to induce amorous feelings, young lovers, of both sexes, appeal to a Gypsy woman versed in herbal lore. She is the *drabarni* and, like the ancient Roman and medieval beldames, she is experienced in concocting philtres and other types of love stimulants. A girl may also fashion a small figure representing the object of her love and use formulas that were identical with those in Theocritus' idylls and in Vergil's bucolics. In addition to potions, the *drabarni* makes use of other means as well: charms, spells, incantations, and traditional magic rituals.

LUKE   The Gospel of St. Luke was translated into Basque by George Borrow and published in Madrid in 1838.
In this capacity he was an agent of the British Bible Society. Borrow also translated the Gospel of St. Luke in 1837.

LURI   Traditionally, the first known Gypsies were the Luri, musicians who were skilled in flute-playing. The Persian poet Firdusi (c. 1000 A.D.) in his epic *The Shah Nameh* states that Behram Gur, a king of Persia, sent for some thousand minstrels from India. After a year however as they were unwilling to adapt themselves to an agricultural life, the king banished them, and they became wanderers over the world.

LUTHER, MARTIN   The German Reformer had no great affection for the Gypsies. He regarded them as Tartars and attributed to them all the vices, particularly the practice of frequent baptisms for the same infant in order to increase the number of gifts received.

M

MACEDONIA   Macedonia is a kind of crossroads for Gypsy migrations. In this territory Gypsies appear on their exodus from the Middle East, or on their way to the Balkans of Central Europe.

Macedonia was one of the very early settlements of Gypsy tribes. Here, in all probability, particularly in the Middle Ages, they absorbed many Greek expressions into their own dialects.

It is said that the purest form of the Gypsy language is spoken in Macedonia.

MADRID   In Madrid the Gitános, the Spanish Gypsies, chiefly resided in the neighborhood of the *mercado,* the place where horses and other animals were sold. The Gypsies spoke the dialect of Valencia, but among themselves they used the Romany language.

MADRILENIAN GYPSY   The Madrilenian Gypsy women are indefatigable in the pursuit of prey, prowling about the town and the suburbs from morning till night, entering houses of all descriptions, from the highest to the lowest; telling fortunes, or attempting to play off various kinds of Gypsy tricks, from which they derive much greater profit.

MAGIC POWERS   In Gypsy belief, the last of seven girls born in succession without the birth of a boy, is credited with remarkable skill in magic practices. She is also said to possess second sight and to perceive hidden treasure.

In the case of a boy, the corresponding situation holds good for the ninth boy in a consecutive series. He will presumably become a gifted seer. There was also a belief that a Christian child, kidnapped by the Gypsies, gave the Gypsy tribe a magic virtue.

MAGNASCO, ALESSANDRO (1677-1749)   Italian painter who specialized in genre scenes and landscapes. He also produced a Gypsy wedding procession.

MAGPIE   The magpie, notorious for its thieving propensities, is the name given by the Gypsies to the little finger. The little finger is often instrumental in withdrawing surreptitiously desired objects in a shop or market.

MAHALA   A quarter in Tangier exclusively inhabited by Gypsies. Many European cities have such Gypsy settlements: Seville, Granada, Budapest, Istanbul.

MAHMUD   Mahmud of Ghazni, in Afghanistan, who belongs in the eleventh century, ruled over a domain that extended from Persia to the Punjab. According to one tradition, he forced the Gypsy people, whose homeland was India, to migrate westward on account of his invasions of North and Northwest India.

MALEFIC ANIMALS   For the Gypsies, there are certain animals that reputedly bring misfortune. Their approach and contact must be avoided. Such creatures are: the ferret, the rat, the fox, the weasel, the serpent, the lizard.

MALOS MENGUES   A Gypsy curse directed against Beng or Benguc, who is the Satanic Archfiend. The Gypsy god is *O Del*, the God.

MANG, PRALA   This Gypsy expression means *Beg on, brother.*

293

An anecdote, related by the Gypsies in every part of Continental Europe, is associated with the phrase:

A Gypsy brat was once pestering a gentleman to give him a halfpenny. The mother, who was sitting nearby, cried in English: Leave off, you dog and come here! Don't trouble the gentleman with your noise. Then she added in Romany: Beg on, brother! And so the brat did, till the gentleman flung him a sixpence.

MAN OF LOGROÑO   In the middle of the sixteenth century, in the city of Logroño, chief town in a Spanish province, there dwelt an old bookseller, versed in many obscure languages. In earlier days he had traveled widely in Spain, and even as far as Italy and Barbary.

One day he revealed to a priest who visited him the secret of his earlier life. He had studied at Salamanca. Later, he supported himself by playing the guitar. He was captured by a band of Gitános, to whom his musical skill made a strong appeal. Later, he was initiated into Gypsy society, with many strange and horrifying ceremonies.

As a member of the tribe, he plundered and killed along with the other Gypsies. Now the Count or leader had a daughter whom the young man married. After the Count was killed in conflict with troopers, the bookseller and his wife took over the reins of tribal authority. The bookseller finally tired of such a life, but his wife, perceiving his intentions to withdraw from the tribe, formed a conspiracy against him. He was bound and delivered into slavery among the Moors of Morocco. Finally, a missionary paid his ransom. Free, he left for Italy and then returned to his native Spain. But he lost his way and came upon a Gypsy encampment, where he heard mention of drao, a poison that destroys cattle.

The day following the priest's visit, sickness broke out all over the town, causing the death of most of the inhabitants. The priest himself, the only survivor in his house, was one night visited by the bookseller. The latter explained that he knew of the Gitános' plans to sack the town after the inhabitants had perished. Through his intervention, however, and with the help of troopers, the town was saved. In the conflict, the streets were strewn with the corpses of the Gitános, men and women and children.

The tale is told in a summary fashion by a certain Francisco de Cordova in his *Didascalia.* Therein he mentions the aid given by a certain bookseller: bibliopolae opera.

MANOUCHES A French term currently in use in France to designate the Gypsies. The word stems from Sanskrit and has the same significance as *Rom,* man. Another French term for Gypsies is *Bohémiens.*

MARCHING THROUGH THE BALKANS In the fifteenth century the Gypsies, with their tribal leaders at the head, with horses and wagons, with families and clans, spread through Moldavia and Hungary, Transylvania, Saxony and Bavaria, through Belgium, Switzerland, France and Spain. Their ostensible reason for their compulsive and continuous nomadic advance was the fact that they were penitent pilgrims, punished for once foreswearing the Christian faith.

MARCH TO ANDALUSIA In their infiltration into Spain, The Gypsies found the province of Andalusia the most suitable. It had three kingdoms: Jaen, Granada, and Seville. Andalusia was the land of the proud steed and the stubborn mule, the land of the savage sierra, and the fruitful and cultivated plain. To Andalusia they hied, in bands of thirties and sixties. Of all the provinces of Spain, Andalusia was the most frequented by the

Gitáno race, and in Andalusia they most abound at the present day.

MARCINKIEWICZ, JAN He was the last Gypsy King in Poland. His position was confirmed by the King of Poland himself. Marcinkiewicz died near the close of the eighteenth century.

MARIA THERESA Empress of Austria and Queen of Hungary, Maria Theresa issued a decree during her reign in the eighteenth century, that the Gypsies residing in her territory should be designated as Uj Magyars — New Magyars, and thus be absorbed into the national life. Her effort, however, was abortive.

MARINA ROTZE This is a kind of sylvan garden on the outskirts of Moscow. In the summer time, in the nineteenth century, it was the favorite place of resort of the Russian Gypsies.

MARRIAGE As in many primitive societies, there are still vestiges of ancient ways among Gypsies. Purchase is still in force. The boy and the girl may be as young as thirteen or fourteen. The tribal chief acts as a priestly officiant.

MARSHALL The name of a Scottish Gypsy, 'the old man' of the race, who died at the age of 107. Longevity among the Gypsies is not uncommon. One Gypsy 'Queen', Margaret Finch, died in 1740 at the age of 109.

MARTIN DEL RIO Del Rio was a Spanish priest and a demonographer who flourished in the sixteenth century. He is the author of Disquisitionum Magicarum Libri Sex. He describes the Gypsies of Spain and their leaders or Counts as follows:

When in the year 1584 I was marching in Spain with the regiment, a multitude of these wretches were infesting the fields. It happened that the feast of Corpus Domini was being celebrated, and they requested to be admitted into the town, that they might dance in honor of the sacrifice, as was customary; they did so, but about midday a great tumult arose owing to the many thefts which the women committed, whereupon they fled out of the suburbs, and assembled about St. Mark's, the magnificent mansion and hospital of the knights of. St. James, where the ministers of justice attempting to scize them were repulsed by force of arms; nevertheless, all of a sudden, and I know not how, everything was hushed up. At this time they had a Count, a fellow who spoke the Castilian idiom with as much purity as if he had been a native of Toledo; he was acquainted with all the ports of Spain, and all the difficult and broken ground of the provinces. He knew the exact strength of every city, and who were the principal people in each, and the exact amount of their property. There was nothing relating to the state, however secret, that he was not acquainted with; nor did he make a mystery of his knowledge, but publicly boasted of it.

The Count was invariably responsible for planning and excecuting plundering sorties in town and villages. But if his venture failed, the condemnation of the tribe fell upon him.

MASHMURDALO A Gypsy expression that means a meat-killer. In Gypsy mythology, Mashmurdálo is a rustic giant. He is anthropophagous, and is fond of devouring men. He is also the guardian of treasure.

MATADOR The famous Spanish matador Gitanillo de Triana is a Gypsy. Many Spanish Gypsies have been associated with bullfighting: for instance, El Gallo, Chamaco, Joselito.

MATRIARCHY Gypsy tribes are largely matriarchal and the women have a decisive control over the family unit and not rarley over the tribe, despite the authority of the leader or Count or Duke.

MATRILINEAL CLAN When a Gypsy became the husband of a Gypsy woman, it was he who was absorbed into the clan, joining the wife's family, becoming part of this unit, and traveling and working within its circuit.

MAXIMOFF, MATEO Maximoff is a contemporary novelist who is himself a Gypsy. He is the author of *The Ursitory,* a novel published in Englnd in 1948.

MAXIMS Among gnomic sayings common to Gypsy life are the following:

Sacais sos ne dicobélan calochin ne bridaqué-lan.

Eyes which see not break no heart.

Coin terelare trasardos e dinastes nasti le bu-chare berrandañas a desquero contiqué.

He who has a roof of glass let him not fling stones at his neighbor.

Bus mola yes chirriclo on la ba sos grés ba-logando.

A bird in the hand is worth more than a hundred flying.

Bus mola quesar jero de gabuño sos manpo-ri de bombardo.

It is worth more to be the head of a mouse than the tail of a lion.

| Aunsos me dicas vriar-dao de jorpoy ne sirlo braco. | Although you see me dressed in wool I am no sheep. |
| Len sos sonsi bela pani ó reblandani teréla. | The river which makes a noise has either water or stones. |

McPHERSON'S FAREWELL James McPherson, the reputed son of a Gypsy, was a daring robber who was hanged at Banff in Scotland in 1700. It is said that, under sentence of death, he composed his own Lament or Farewell. There was, notes Robert Burns the famous Scottish poet, a tradition that McPherson played the Lament on his violin on the way to the gallows or at the foot of it. But that, adds the poet, was absurd. Robert Burns' poem follows:

Farewell, ye dungeons dark and strong,
    The wretch's destinie!
McPherson's time will not be long
    On yonder gallows-tree.
O, what is death but parting breath?
    On many a bloody plain
I've dar'd his face, and in this place
    I scorn him yet again!
Untie these bands from off my hands,
    And bring to me my sword,
And there's no man in all Scotland
    But I'll brave him at a word.
I've liv'd a life of sturt and strife;
    I die by treacherie:
It burns my heart I must depart,
    And not avengèd be.
Now farewell light, thou sunshine bright,
    And all beneath the sky!
May coward shame disdain his name,
    The wretch that dare not die!
      Chorus

Sae rantingly, sae wantonly,
      Sae dauntingly gaed he,
He play'd spring, and danc'd it round
      Below the gallows-tree.

MEALS During meals Gypsies are accustomed to sit on their heels, without any feeling of discomfort. In many parts of India, the primary home of the Gypsies, the custom still prevails. Turkish Gypsies may sit cross-legged, like the Turks themselves.

MEANING OF ZINCALI In Spain, the Gypsies were known as Zincali. It is believed that the meaning of this ethnic term is *The Black men of Zend or Ind.*
This expression points to their Oriental origin, Ind or India.

MECCA In the Ottoman Empire many Gypsies who reached Turkish territory turned to Islam and even made the pilgrimage to Mecca.
Such adherance to any particular religion was merely nominal, and was conditioned by the country in which they settled.

MEDICINE The Gypsies have a vast and traditional knowledge of herbal remedies of all kinds. This knowledge is usually transmitted in the female line. The Gypsy woman, normally the elder in the tribe, is the repository of medicinal drugs and concoctions, simples and unguents, infusions and potions, roots and leaves and plants that are effective in a multitude of cases. For coughs and colds, for ague and stings, fevers, erysipelas, kidney conditions, ulcers, convulsions, toothache, dropsy, rashes, stomach trouble, weak eyes, colic, jaundice, epileptic fits, gout, inflammation of the lungs, pleurisy. The list is almost endless and embraces a large number of conditions to which people are generally subjected, from rheumatism to sore throat, and all the many ailments that afflict man. The pharmacopoëia includes agrimony and alder, bettony, bindweed, blackberry, bracken and broom, bogbean and burdock. The juice of celandine, centaury, camomile, henbane. The impression one receives is of the contents of an Elizabethan herbal. And of course these plants and roots were largely used not only in the Middle Ages, but in antiquity as well.

Honeysuckle too is efficacious in treating ulcers. Then there are pellitory and mistletoe, marshmallow and lime, horsehound and pennyroyal, scabious and dittany.

In the case of animal ailments, particularly ailments common to horses, the Gypsies have an entire remedial treasury. They can effectively treat colic and foot thrush, spavin, sprains and sores and staggers.

MEDIEVAL CHRONICLE In *The Diary of a Burgher of Paris,* an anonymous chronicle belonging in the fifteenth century, the author refers to the Gypsies:

> They called themselves good Christians, natives of Lower Egypt. They also added that they had formerly been Christians. Some time after they had accepted Christianity, the Saracens attacked them. Hence they surrendered, turned Saracens, and rejected Christianity.

MEDIEVAL CONCEPT If a person in the Middle Ages looked on at some of the performances of Spanish or Syrian Gypsy women executing their sarabands, he would readily have believed that they were dancing to the devil's music as witches and sorceresses.

MEDIEVAL DESIGNATION In the Middle Ages harsh laws were enacted against the Gypsies in England, who were regarded as "people using the manner of Egyptians."

301

MEDIEVAL NAME In the Middle Ages the Gypsies, in chronicles and other historical documents, decrees, edicts, are termed: Acingani, Cingeri, Cingani. These Latin terms corresponded to the Atcinganoi, the Zingari, and the Tsiganes all three variant designations for Gypsies.

MEG MERRILIES A Gypsy witch who appears in the novel by Sir Walter Scott entitled *Guy Mannering.*
John Keats also showed an interest in this character by writing a poem about her.

MEISTERSINGER Hans Sachs, the chief Meistersinger of the sixteenth century, knew the Gypsies and wrote and sang of their inherent mystery and the strangeness of their ways against the European background.

MELALO This Gypsy term, which means *unclean,* is used in the case of a Gypsy who has broken any of the tabus of Gypsy law or tradition or morality. Among such tabus are adultery, eating horse flesh, or stealing from another Gypsy.

MENDICITY Often the Gypsies, deprived of the means of sustenance, were forced to beg their way from one area to another. The concomitant of this practice was theft, as Cervantes pointed out for the Gypsies in Spain: It appears that the Gypsies are here on earth for the sole purpose of being thieves. Their fathers were thieves. They are brought up on thievery.

MERIMEE, PROSPER (1803-1870) French historian and novelist. Some of his fiction deals romantically with Gypsy life, especially his novel *Carmen.*

MERINAO A Spanish Gypsy term that signifies an immortal. Gypsy legend is compacted of belief in spirits, earth fairies and similar beings who are immortal and appear, sometimes malefically and on occasion with a beneficent purpose, to human beings.

MESMERIC POWER   The piercing, hypnotic gaze of the Gypsies became such a widespread phenomenon that in Scotland, in 1579, an Act of Parliament attacked 'the idle people calling themselves Egyptians,' who used their spellbinding power on innocent victims.

MESOPOTAMIA   It is generally accepted that Gypsy tribes inhabited the Mesopotamian region in the ninth century A. D.
Thence large bands moved Westward and settled in the Peloponnese, in Greece.

MEXICO   There was a strange, unfounded theory that the Gypsies who reached Mexico centuries ago had succeeded in building massive, towering structures.

MICHEL OF EGYPT   This Gypsy tribal leader, nominally Duke Michel of Egypt, came to Bologna in 1422 with the members of his clan. According to contemporary accounts, they created disturbance and havoc in the city by their abandoned pilfering ways.

MIGRATION   Driven by periodical persecution, discrimination, and antagonism, the Gypsies migrated from Spain and settled in colonies in Chile, Brazil, and Peru.

MIGRANTS   In the early years of the nineteenth century many Gypsy tribes roamed from one region to another area, making no permanent home in any one country. Their habitations were tents, or holes in the rocks, or caves. In Germany and Spain, many did not even carry tents with them. They sheltered themselves from the heat of the sun in forests, or behind hedges.

In Hungary, even those who had discontinued their rambling way of life and managed to build some kind of house for themselves were off again in spring to wander through fields and forests.

MIGRATION OF GYPSIES   After crossing the Danube, the Gypsies settled largely in Rumania. From Rumania some went North-east, overrunning Russia, while others advanced Westward, as far as Spain and England.

MIKLOSICH, RANZ VON   A German gypsiologist who, late in the nineteenth century, tried to prove a linguistic affinity between Gypsy and African dialects. His two monumental works, published between 1874-1881, deal comprehensively with the folklore, mores, and dialects of the Gypsies.

MILITARY MUSICIANS   In the eighteenth century among the troops enrolled in the French regiments were Gypsy drummers and fifers.
The Gypsy people, in general, have always been highly skilled in music and are noted for the violin playing in particular.

MILITARY SERVICE   In the reigns of Louis XIV and Louis XV of France, Gypsies appear in military service, in the infantry, cavalry, dragoons, artillery. Often their musical ability assigned them to bands as drummers and trumpeteers. As soldiers they proved efficient. What irked them was barrack life and its confinements. The Gypsy wives and daughters often followed the army as vivandières. One Gypsy, Jean de La Fleur, made a career of the army, fighting in many European campaigns, late in the sixteenth century.
Some Gypsies fought in the Spanish armies, in the Portuguese forces, with the English troops, in the Swedish

army. They fought in the Thirty Years War, One Gypsy, calling himself Christian Resenberg von Gröningent, became captain of the bodyguard of the Duke of Saxe-Lauenburg. But Denmark, under Christian V, prohibited Gypsies from entering the army.

MILK Gypsies drink milk that is mixed with the blood of a calving cow.

Among the English Gypsies, berries and raw milk and potatoes are staples.

MILLER, THOMAS (1807-1874) English poet and novelist. In his novel *Gidoen Giles, the Roper,* published in 1840, he describes the Gypsies from first hand knowledge, for since boyhood Miller had associated with Gypsies.

MINIONS OF THE MOON This expression is used to describe the Gypsies who retain old superstitious beliefs in connection with the influence of the Moon goddess, variously represented as Diana or Hecate or Semele, upon human affairs.

MINOR CLANS Some English Gypsy clans comprise not more than a dozen members. Among such groups are the Browns, the Bosvils, the Chilcotts, the Grays, Lees, Taylors, Whites.

MINSTRELS In medieval Europe the troubadours and wandering minstrels composed and sang songs and poems depicting the life of the warrior barons, the feuds and conflicts between princelings, courtly love, and heroic deeds. These songs were absorbed into the life of the people. The Gypsies made use of these songs and melodies. In village and manor and castle they sustained themselves by singing ballads and folk-songs to the accompaniment of guitar or fiddle.

MIRACULOUS SALVES The wise wives among the Gypsies in Hungary have many kinds of miraculous salves for sale to cure different disorders. These they declare are made from the fat of dogs, bears, moles, frogs. As in all fetish remedies they are said to be of strange or revolting materials, like those used by the ancient Roman witch Canidia, the witches of Shakespeare and Ben Jonson, and of Burns in *Tam O'Shanter.*

MISTRAL, FREDERIC (1830-1914) Famous Provençal poet. In his *Mémoirs* he refers to his visit to Les Saintes Maries de la Mer, in the Camargue, in Provence, where the Gypsies make their annual pilgrimage in memory of their patron Saint Sara.

MITHRA There is a tradition that in the crypt of a shrine at Les Saintes Maries, in the Camargue, in Provence, the Gypsies sacrificed to the ancient cult-god Mithra, the god of the sun, of fire and water.

MITHRAIC ALTAR Some gypsiologists consider that the Gypsy worship of Sara as their patron saint in a shrine in the Camargue, in Provence is a survival of paganism. The annual dedicatory ceremony on May 24, it is argued, is a long-retained mythical tradition among the Gypsies. At the shrine there is a fresh water spring with a stone around it. The spring and the stone are putatively associated with the cult of the ancient Persian god Mithra, the stone once forming a sacrificial altar.

MIXED BLOOD A full-blood English Gypsy, said Walter Simson the gypsiologist, looks upon himself with all the pride of a little duchess while in the company of young male mixed Gypsies. A mixed Gypsy may reasonably be assumed to be more intelligent than one of the old stock. Still, a full-blood Gypsy looks up to a mixed Gypsy. The two kinds will readily marry.

MIXED MARRIAGES Marriage between Gypsies and *busné* or *gorgios,* non-Gypsies, was in early days very rare. In more recent times it occurs with greater frequency. Many cases have occurred especially in England. In the nineteenth century a Rumanian or Russian nobleman often became enamoured of a Gypsy girl and made her his wife.

MIYEYESTI A Gypsy term applied to Gypsies who are engaged in itinerant trading. Occupational groups have distinctive descriptive designations: *costorari,* tinsmiths: *oursari,* bear-trainers.

MOCHARDI This Gypsy expression means *unclean,* usually in a ritualistic sense. Certain animals, for instance, are regarded by the Gypsies as mochardi: particularly cats and dogs. A woman may be ritually mochardi. There are many tabus with respect to women's deportment. Infants are mochardi. Women's clothes are likewise mochardi. There are tabus, too, associated with the menstrual periods. Not all tabus, however, are uniformly observed by all Gypsies. A variant term for mochardi is marhimé.

MODERN USAGE The common designation for Gypsy, which is becoming rare and is usually employed in a pejorative sense, is Romany or traveler.

MOLDAVIA In Moldavia, according to an early nineteenth century writer, every baron had several families of Gypsies subject to him. In Moldavia and also in Wallachia the Romanys were frequently in the service, as serfs, of a landowner. In some cases, such owners had hundreds of Gypsies under their command.

MOL-DIVVUS This Gypsy term signifies Christmas. Literally, the expression means Wine-day. In the course of their restless history, the Gypsies have adopted many customs and festivals from other countries. They have at times adapted themselves to Christian beliefs and to Moslem practices as well.

MOLIERE Molière, the noted French playwright who belongs in the seventeenth century, introduces in his comedies, among a variety of other characters, Gypsies or, as he calls them, "Egyptian women." They appear in *L'Etourdi, Les Fourberies de Scapin,* and *Le Mariage forcé.*

In *Le Malade Imaginaire,* second Interlude, we also have 'Egyptians dressed like Moors, who mingle songs with dance.'

MONCADA, SANCHO DE In a speech addressed to King Philip III of Spain by Sancho de Moncada, Professor of Theology at the University of Toledo, the Gitanos appear in a highly sinister light:

> They are foreigners, though authors differ much with respect to the country whence they came ... They are called Cingary or Cinli, because they in every respect resemble the bird cinclo, the wagtail, which is a vagrant bird and builds no nest ...
>
> There is not a nation which does not consider them as a most pernicious rabble. Even the Turks and Moors abominate them ... In all parts they are considered as enemies of the states where they wander, and as spies and traitors to the crown ... They are an idle and vagabond people, who are in no respect useful to the kingdom, without commerce, occupation, or trade of any description. . . Gitanas are public harlots, common, as it is said, to all the Gitanos, and with dances, demeanor, and filthy songs are the cause of continual detriment to the souls of the vassals of your Majesty. it being notorious that they have done infinite harm in

many honorable houses by separating the married women from their husbands, and perverting the maidens ... They are enchanters, diviners, magicians, chiromancers, who tell the future by the lines of the hand ... Some think that they are called Cingary, from the great Magician Cincus, from whom it is said they learned their sorceries ... They sucked the vitals of the state, without being of any utility whatever.

MONOGAMY Among the Gypsies monogamy is the prevalent custom, although polygyny appears among the Balkan Gypsies.

As a rule the family is a close-knit unit, self-reliant and devoted.

MOON WORSHIP Gypsies regard the moon as a mysterious power affecting their lives. A pregnant Gypsy, for instance, does not leave her tent by full moonlight.

In many Gypsy incantations the moon has a phallic significance.

MOORS Even before the fall of Granada in 1492, the Gitanos lived among the Moors in Spain, and became acquainted with their language and customs.

MORAL DISTINCTIONS A moral estimate of the Gypsies, particularly in the nineteenth century, by George Borrow the gypsiologist:

The Gypsies are almost entirely ignorant of the grand points of morality. They have never had sufficient sense to perceive that to lie, to steal, and to shed human blood violently, are crimes which are sure, eventually, to yield bitter fruits to those who perpetrate them. But on one point, and that one of no little importance as far as temporal happiness is concerned, they are in general wiser than those who have had far better opportunities than such unfortunate outcasts, of regulating their steps, and distinguishing good from evil. They know that chastity is a jewel of high price, and that conjugal fidelity is capable of occasionally flinging a sunshine even over the dreary hours of a life passed in the contempt of almost all laws, whether human or divine.

MORALITY   One writer, himself a Gypsy, declared that Gypsy girls rarely went astray. Respect for women is inculcated from boyhood. In courtship, an elder, usually the prospective mother-in-law, accompanied the young couple on a stroll. There are few spinsters or old bachelors. Practically all Gypsies get married. Respect for old age is quite general. With regard to the gorgio or non-Gypsy, the Gypsy feels that he is mistrusted or suspected or that the gorgios are uniformly hostile. One of their major weaknesses is drink, particularly beer. They are also self-confessed pilferers when the occasion arises, as well as poachers. But these latter characteristics may be conditioned by the nature of their economy in the context of society. Pre-marital chastity is the regular situation among Gypsy girls. Adultery and infidelity of the women are punished harshly. Prostitution is uncommon, as girls marry early and remain within the tribal circle: exceptions occur in large urban areas.

MORAL TALE   The Prize-fighter and the Gentleman
Once a prize-fighter was to fight, and a gentleman asked him: Will you sell the fight for twenty pounds?
Said the prize fighter: Will you let me break your leg for one hundred pounds?
"No," said the gentleman, "for if I did, I should never

walk well again."

"And if I lost a fight," said the prize-fighter, "I could never 'run' again."

MOSCOW   In the middle of the nineteenth century there were Gypsies in Moscow who had attained a secure and acceptable civic status. Some possessed stately houses and elegant carriages. This position they reached through their musical abilities. They sang in public halls and at private parties and achieved a wide reputation throughout the entire country.

Some Gypsies intermarried with Russians. One countess, a member of the Tolstoi family, was a Zigáña by birth and was originally one of the principal attractions of a Romany choir in Moscow. The majority of Gypsies, however, sang and danced in the taverns and inns, while the men occupied themselves with horse-dealing.

In summer, these Gypsies spent their time at the Marina Rotze, a rustic garden near Moscow. George Borrow visited this group and, speaking the English form of Romany, addressed the Gypsies, who hailed him as a brother. Their greeting was: Kak camenna tute prala! — How we love you, brother!

MOSCOW GYPSIES   George Borrow wrote of the Gypsies he found in Moscow on his visit there in the nineteenth century:

Those who have been accustomed to consider the Gypsy as a wandering outcast will be surprised to learn that, amongst the Gypsies of Moscow, there are not a few who inhabit stately houses, go abroad in elegant equipages, and are behind the higher order of Russians neither in appearance nor mental acquirements. The sums obtained by the Gypsy females, by the exercise of their art (singing in the choirs of Moscow), enable them to support their relatives in affluence and

311

luxury. Some are married to Russians; and no one who has visited Russia can but be aware that a lovely and accomplished countess, of the noble and numerous family of Tolstoi is, by birth, a Zigana, and was originally one of the principal attractions of a Romany choir at Moscow.

MOUNTAIN GYPSIES In the sixteenth century Mountain Gypsies, as they were called, appeared in the Kingdom of Poland. The Gypsy leader or *voivode* was granted in Poland letters of safe-conduct.

MOUNTAIN MONK In Gypsy mythology, this Mountain monk is a mischievous spirit. He extinguishes lamps; he overturns water-pails. In a ruthless mood, he sometimes strangles workmen.

MULE In Gypsy mythology the mulé are the souls of the dead. They return to life precisely at the moment of midday. Their function is to harass the living, often driving them to suicide.

MULLA DUDIA In Gypsy folklore this expression means *dead lights,* that is, spirits or goblins. Gypsy mythology contains many allusions to evil spirits, good fairies, water sprites, spirits of the dead, witches.

MUNSTER, SEBASTIAN (1489-1552) German theologian and cosmographer. Author of *Cosmographia Universa,* the first detailed description of the world. Of the Gypsies, he wrote:

> The Christians who are wanderers throughout the world and are called Egyptians, fortune-tellers, and Saracens. In the year 1417 A.D. there began to appear in

Germany a strange people, black, sun-burned, in ordinary clothes, unclean in all their ways, expert thieves, particularly the women, who support their husbands by pilfering. The common people in Germany call them Tartars, or Pagans, and in Italy they are known as Zingani. They honor the Duke and the Counts among them. These are well dressed. They keep dogs, like the nobles, but they do not have the means for hunting, except by stealing. They often change horses, although most of them go on foot. The women ride on horses or mares, bearing their beds and children with them. Wherever they go they carry letters of King Sigismund and some other princes, to give them permission to pass freely, and without danger, through the towns and countries. They say that a penance was imposed on them to roam the world as wandering pilgrims; and that originally they come from Lower Egypt. But these are stories. For they are people (in so far as one may judge from experience) who wander and migrate, addicted to idleness, acknowledging no country as theirs, and thus they advance from one country to another, and from city to city, living on the thefts committed by their children, as we said. They have no religion but live like dogs, in spite of having their children baptized when they are among Christians.

MUSIC Although the Gypsies are a musical people, there is no written Gypsy musical score. At all times the Gypsies have been largely illiterate, partly on account of their constant forced or even voluntary migrations, and partly on account of their great reluctance to regimented and to submit to scholastic routine.

In the eighteenth century laws were promulgated in Transylvania prohibiting the Gypsies from practicing their dances and music and singing, except in prescribed festivals.

MUSICAL INSTRUMENTS   The Gypsies, who are a naturally musical people, are adepts with a variety of instruments. Their favorite is the violin, but they also use flutes of willow or aspen wood, tambourines, bagpipes, the clarinet, the cymbal. Brass instruments are not used. In the larger cities, they rehearse in groups, and sometimes even attend instructional schools. But their musical passion springs from their own ethnic and traditional consciousness.

MUSICAL TALENT   The marked musical talent characteristic of the Slavonian and other European Gypsies appears to link them with the Luri of Persia. These are distinctly Gypsies; that is to say, they are wanderers, thieves, fortune-tellers, and minstrels. The Shah-Nameh of Firdusi tells us that about the year 420 A.D. Shankal, the Maharajah of India, sent to Behram Gur, a ruler of the Sassanian dynasty in Persia, ten thousand minstrels, male and female, called *Luri*. Though lands were allotted to them, with corn and cattle, they became from the beginning irreclaimable vagabonds. Of their descendants, as they now exist, Sir Henry Pottinger says:

"They bear a marked affinity to the Gypsies of Europe. They speak a dialect peculiar to themselves, have a king to each trope, and are notorious for kidnapping and pilfering. Their principal pastimes are drinking, dancing, and music. They are invariably attended by half a dozen of bears and monkeys that are broken in to perform all manner of grotesque tricks. In each company there are always two or three members who profess modes of divining, which procure them a ready admission into every society."

MUSICAL RUSSIAN GYPSIES   The Gypsies of Russia are noted for a Gypsy choir composed only of women. The choir has attained a wide international reputation. As a people, the Gypsies have had a reputation throughout all Europe for their musical ability and their dancing and singing.

MUSICIANS AND DANCERS   Among noted Gypsy musicians may be mentioned Djano Reinhardt, the guitarist, Gyorgy Csiffra, the pianist, and Ion Voicu. Among dancers Carmen Amaya has acquired an international reputation.

MUSIC, SONG, DANCE   The Gypsies are by nature a music-loving people, passionately attached to their folksongs, to the melodies produced by lute and guitar and particularly violin. These melodies are largely of Gypsy origin, but in their more prolonged contacts with other nations, especially the peasants, they have absorbed or adapted the national melodies. So with their chants and coplas and songs. So too with their dances that they perform their tribal circles. Later they borrowed rhythms and movements and motifs from other native dances. The result was a harmonious synthesis of Gypsy dances touched with Spanish sarabands, pervaded by Balkan peasant tempos.

The Gypsies have always had the faculty of taking a Moorish theme and stamping it with the distinctive Gypsy imprint: taking a Hungarian csárdás and merging it with their own interpretation, their assimilative concept of balance and liveliness and agility. The terms Gypsy music, then, Gypsy songs, Gypsy dances are generic expressions that postulate infusion of foreign elements into the Gypsy texture. Nowadays Gypsy music is accepted as music played by Gypsies. So Gypsy songs, although there may be strains and echoes of other nationals in them, mean songs as sung by the Gypsies. Such songs are now their own, and it would be hazardous and ultimately futile to investigate and determine the elements that are essentially Gypsy, and those factors that, in the course of time and by habituation, have become integrated into the woof and warp of Gypsy musicality. Similarly, a Gypsy dance may have reminiscences of Rumania, or of Andalusia, but a Gypsy dance means a dance as performed in a typically and distinctively Gypsy manner.

With reference to musical instruments, the Gypsies perform on the naiou, the Panpipes, on the zimbal, a small piano, and with tambourines and drums. They play the lute, an instrument of Asiatic origin.

The Spanish flamenco dance is associated with the Gypsies. In Rumania the Gypsy women dance the Dance of the Kalus: the Dance of the Sticks. The women also perform sinuous and seductive snake dances.

In contemporary times, celebrated dancers are Carmen Amaya and La Chunga.

MUSTAPHA The skill of Gypsy smiths was so well-known throughout Europe that they were often employed by the Turkish Regent of Bosnia, besieged Crupa and the Turks

MYRTLE STEMS When a baby is teething, a Gypsy mother puts round its neck a necklace made of myrtle stems. In the case of a boy, the myrtle must be cut by a woman. In the case of a girl, a man cuts the stem.

MYSTERY OF THE GYPSIES In his study of the Gypsies of Spain, entitled *The Zincali,* George Borrow says that the Gypsies are certainly a very mysterious people who come from some distant land, no mortal knows why, and who made their first appearance in Europe at a dark period when events were not so accurately recorded as at the present time.

MYTHOLOGICAL FEATURES   Characteristic figures in Gypsy mythology include:
urme — fairies who decide human fate, like the three deities, Clotho, Lachesis, and Atropos in classical antiquity.
nivasi — water fairies
phuvus — underground spirits
kesali — forest fairies

MYTHOLOGICAL LEGEND   One of the three Hungarian tribes of Gypsies, the Kukuya, believes that it is descended from the Pçuvushi, the earth-fairies.

N

NAMES OF TURKISH GYPSIES As in other cases where the Gypsies have adopted Spanish or French names, according to the country of their sojourn, so among the Turkish Gypsies the women have assumed Turkish names, such as Leila, Sultana, Selamet, Cherife.

NANO, JOHN Charles Leland the gypsiologist tells of his encounter with John Nano, a Mahometan Hindu Gypsy from Calcutta:

> I was going one day along the Marylebone Road when I met a very dark man, poorly clad, whom I took for a Gypsy; and no wonder, as his eyes had the very expression of the purest blood of the oldest families. To him I said, *"Rakessa tu Romanes?"* (Can you talk Gypsy?) "I know what you mean," he answered in English. "You ask me if I can talk Gypsy. I know what these people are. But I'm a Mahometan Hindu from Calcutta. I get my living by making curry powder. Here is my card." Saying this he handed me a piece of paper, with his name written on it: *John Nano.*
>
> "When I say to you, *'Rakessa tu Romanes?* what does it mean?"
>
> "It means, 'Can you talk Rom?' But rakessa is not a Hindu word. It's Punjabi."
>
> I met John Nano several times afterwards and visited him in his lodgings, and had him carefully examined and pumped by Professor Palmer of Cambridge, who is proficient in Eastern tongues. He conversed with John

in Hindustani, and the result of our examination was that John declared he had in his youth lived a very loose life, and belonged to a tribe of wanderers who were to all the other wanderers on the roads in India what regular Gypsies are to the English — Gorgio hawkers and tramps. These people were, he declared, 'the real Gypsies of India, and just like the Gypsies here. People in India called them Trablus, which means Syrians, but they were full-blood Hindus, and not Syrians."

And here I may observe that this word Trablus which is thus applied to Syria is derived from Tripoli. John was very sure that his Gypsies were Indian. They had a peculiar language, consisting of words which were not generally intelligible. 'Could he remember any of these words?' Yes. One of them was *manro,* which meant bread. Now *manro* is all over Europe the Gypsy word for bread. John Nano, who spoke several tongues, said that he did not know it in any Indian dialect except in that of his Gypsies. These Gypsies called themselves and their language *Rom.* Rom meant in India a real Gypsy. And Rom was the general slang of the road, and it came from the Roms or Trablus.

NAPOLEON   Early in the nineteenth century, when Napoleon invaded Spain, there was a considerable quota of Hungarian Gypsies in his armies.

Gypsies were to be found in the Austrian, Spanish, French armies in various campaigns.

NASAL LOSS   Lizzie Brown was a Scottish Gypsy who lost her nose in a battle fought in the shire of Angus:

In this encounter the Gypsies fought among themselves with Highland dirks. When this woman found that her nose was struck off, by the sweep of a dirk, she put her hand to the wound and, as if little had befallen her, called out, in the heat of the scuffle, to those nearest her: "But, in the middle o' the meantime, where is my nose?"

NATIONALITY Although the Gypsies have encamped in virtually all of Europe as well as on other continents, they are a people without a nationality.

NATIONAL RELIGION The Gypsies have no national unifying religion. It is asserted, in fact, that they have no formal religion whatever. They assume superficial and conventional religious attitudes in the various countries of their sojourn, But they are merely conciliatory gestures, without any profound significance. Magic, folklore, myths take the place of any formal religious system.

Still, the Gypsies use two expressions that somehow recall the ancient pagan cult of Mithra. O Del in Romany means God, that is, Spirit, in a wide sense. Beng is the adversary, the Devil, Satan. So in Mithraism Ahura Mazda is the beneficent Spirit of Light, of Goodness, while his adversary the Genius of Evil, is Ahriman.

As attendants to Ahura Mazda there are good spirits, Yazatas, while malefic agents are associated with Ahriman. So to the Gypsies there are, in the unseen, invisible world, spirits of goodness and satellites of wickedness.

NATS The Nats or Buzegurs of India have been identified with the Gypsies who anciently migrated from their home in India. The Nats were believed to be descendants of an aboriginal race prior even to the Hindus. Under the name of Dacoits the Nats were, it seemed, guilty of frequently sacrificing victims to the goddess Kali under circumstance of atrocity and horror. A Scottish Gypsy dialect term in use in the nineteenth century was Nawken, with the meaning of traveler, wanderer. One gypsiologist saw an affinity between Nat and Nawken.

NATURAL FOODS Many Gypsies, particularly in England, sustain themselves as well as possible on non-processed foods. They eat wild berries, drink milk straight from the cow and water from the brooks.

NAZI MASSACRES During World War II the Gypsies, despite the fact that their Aryan origin as natives of Northern India had long since been established by the gypsiologist Heinrich Grellmann, were massacred or sent to the German crematoria by the thousands: in Germany itself, in the Ukraine and other regions of Russia, and in Bosnia.

NAZIS As a culmination to the centuries of persecution experienced by the Gypsies, in Germany they were interned in concentration camps even before World War II. In 1945 all Gypsies in internment camps were gassed, as was revealed to the Commission of the United Nations for War Crimes.

It is estimated that some 400.000 Gypsies died in the gas-chambers and the concentration camps. Those who escaped fought with the Allied partisan forces.

NETOTSI A Gypsy expression that denotes "Men of the Woods." They were Gypsy serfs who, as late as the nineteenth century, escaped from the Balkans into the mountains and forests of Transylvania.

NETTLES The nettle has its own peculiar association. According to the Gypsies it grows chiefly in places where there is a subterranean passage to the dwellings of the Earth-fairies, the Pçuvus. It is therefore consecrated to them and called Pçuvus-wood. Hence the Gypsy children while gathering nettles for pigs sing:

Nettle, nettle do not burn.

In your house no one shall go.

No one to the Pçuvus goes.
Drive, drive away the worms!

NEW TENT To protect a new tent from any malefic force, Gypsies sprinkle it with a few drops of a child's blood. There are many such superstitions in the traditions and folklore of the Gypsies, particularly the Gypsies of the Balkans.

NICKNAMES Among the Gypsies nicknames are added to a person's regular name when he has reached his maturity and has achieved some form of reputation or notoriety in the tribe.

NIGHT To the Gypsies the night time is fraught with menace and danger, when the *mulos,* the spirits of the dead, walk abroad. Among the Gypsies, there are strong beliefs in both benevolent and malefic spirits who can affect the lives of the living.

NINETEENTH CENTURY In France during the nineteenth century the Gypsies became particularly notorious for their treatment of animals and their reputation as kidnappers of children.

NINETEENTH CENTURY AND AFTER The study of the Gypsies, notably their language and their provenance was a major interest in the nineteenth century. Among such gypsiologists should be mentioned: Baudrimont, Predari, G. Borrow, Campuzano, Mayo, Jiménez, Kalina, d'Ascoli, Paspati, Wlistocki, Artout, Miklosich.

Since the beginning of the twentieth century, the work has been continued unabatedly, under the impulse of these notable names:

In Great Britain: Sampson and Turner
In Germany: Wolf.

In France: Pierre Meile, Jules Bloch, Georges Calvet. Also: Tineo Rebolledo, Popp Serboianu, Ragnvald Iversen, Carlo Clavería.

NOAH In accordance with a Gypsy legend, after the Biblical Flood, Noah lived with his sons. One of them, Ham, was the ancestor of the Gypsy race.

NOBILITY Among the Gypsies. From as early as the fifteenth century in Europe, titles were employed by certain Gypsies. Some tribal leaders assumed the title of Duke. Others were known as Count. Still others proclaimed themselves as King. These honorifics, however, were misleading. They were merely equivalent to the designation of tribal chief, but the practice stemmed from the assumed origin of the Gypsies as of Egyptian descent and their pretentions of distinguished ancestry.
The tribal chief might have, within his jurisdiction, a few hundred families, or even fewer. The Duke or Count or King was also the spokesman, the representative of his Gypsy bands, whenever there were disputes or clashes or negotiations of any kind between the Gypsies and the officials of a particular country.

NOCTURNAL THEFT When a Gypsy is driven by hunger or poverty to steal food, he never does so at night, for fear of the *mulé,* the evil spirits, the souls of the dead that haunt the darkness and harass the living.

NOMADIC AND SEDENTARY In the nineteenth century in Hungary the Gypsies who had settled down into some form of sedentary life were called *gletecore;* those who remained nomadic were termed *kortorar.* There was no friendship between the two classes. Even their language had distinctive differences.

323

NOMADIC NAMES   Among the Arabs, Gypsies are designated as Bokharni and Harami — terms which signify their propensities to steal and rob in their migratory marches.

NOMADS   Although the Gypsies are essentially a migratory people, they have in many instances settled into some form of permanence, in huts, houses, caves. In Spain, for instance, there is a well-known colony of Gypsy cave-dwellers.

NOMENCLATURE   On account of the migratory habits of the Gypsies, from the fifteenth century on, throughout Europe and the Middle East, and also on account of the uncertainty of their racial origin, the designation of the Romanys has varied with the country of their more or less temporary settlement. They were Bohémiens to the French because they presumably came from Bohemia. In the Low Countries they were known as Heydens, that is, Heathens, because they did not conform religiously to the established orthodoxy. In Smyrna their appellation was Madjub. In Bokhara they were termed Diajii. And, variantly, in different European countries, they were Gypsies, Zigeuners, Gitanos, Cyganis.

NO POACHING   James Crabb, who worked among the English Gypsies during the nineteenth century, wrote of them:

> In England, the Gypsies avoided poaching, knowing that the sporting gentlemen would be severe against them, and that they would not be permitted to remain in the lanes and commons near villages. But sometimes they took osiers from the banks and coppices of the farmers, of which they made their baskets.
>
> And occasionally they have been known to steal a sheep, when they had not anything to eat, or money to buy it with.
>
> James Crabb recollected an incident of the sort in the

county of Hants. Eight Gypsy men were united in stealing four sheep. Four men were chosen by lot for the purpose. They sharpened their knives, rode to the field, and perpetrated the act, and before daybreak brought to their camp the sheep they had engaged to steal. Before the evening of the same day, they were thirty miles distant.

NORTH SEA According to German records, the Gypsies appeared as early as the year 1417 in the vicinity of the North Sea.

NOTABLE GYPSIES In recent times the Gypsies have achieved reputations in several directions, in music, dancing, and other fields. Jacob Richard and Torino Xigler are painters. Lola Flores is a distinguished dancer. Among pianists and violinists are Nemeth, Horvath, Babai. In poetry the names of Jane Kieffer and Bromislawa Wajs are notable.

NOTED MUSICIANS Throughout the Hungarian plains and the Transylvanian fields the music of the Gypsy for centuries went echoing in harmony with their constant wanderings. Many musicians thus became outstanding performers: among them Bihari and Patikasus, Barna, Berkes, Salamon, Racz, and the remarkable female violinist Zinka Panna.

NUBIA Bonaventura Vulcanius, a Dutch gypsiologist of the sixteenth century, proposed Nubia as the original home of the Gypsies. In the seventeenth century Gisbertus Voetius, a Dutch Calvinist, made a similar suggestion.

NUMBER OF GYPSIES No exact census has even been taken of the Gypsy population in any country, for the obvious reasons of their mobile tendencies and the difficulty of

NO POACHING James Crabb, who worked among the English identification and distinction between Gypsies and others who are merely migratory. Some gypsiologists, however, have estimated that the total number of Gypsies throughout the world must be in the neighborhood of six million.

NUMBERS A study of the numerals in Hindi, the original language of the Gypsies, indicates that, in the course of their wanderings, they absorbed the numbers in Armenian, Syrian, Greek, Rumanian. For example, the Hindi term for one is ek. In Armenian Gypsy it is yaku: in Syrian, yoka: in Greek, yek: in Rumanian, ék.

NURI This term refers to the Gypsies of Asia Minor. A philological comparison between the language of the Nuri and Hindustani shows remarkable analogies suggestive of the Indian origin of the Gypsies.

NURI TALE The Nuri are nomads found at the present time in Egypt and Asia Minor. In Arabic, *Nuri* is the plural form of *na war,* which means Moslem Gypsies. The *Nuri* are also called *Nawar.*

There came to us once on a time Nawar seeking a woman. An Egyptian had taken her, her mother wept for her. The men betook themselves and went with their tents, and their sheikh with them. They came to us, from us they descended to Jaffa, from Jaffa they got on a ship, they and their sons and their tents, and made to Haifa. From there they came, rode to Tiberias. They went to the bedawin: from the bedawin they went to the country of Hauran. From there they went to the Druses. They searched all that place and went to Damascus. They did not see them. They came further. They betook themselves, rode, encamped with the bedawin, from the Arabs they went to Jerich, slept there a night. Two donkeys and a mare were stolen from them. They went and complained to the *mamur*:

'That village has stolen our donkeys and our mare: seek for them, O *mamur.*' They gave two pounds to the *mamur.* He imprisoned the people of the village till they fetched the donkeys and the mare. They went from there, camped at that village which is on the way. The rain kept them two nights there, and today their people came to us with their tents and their sheikh. They were in the villa. He was in the town. Their sheikh came. We made for him bitter and sweet coffee. We went, set before him a sheep and four *rotls* of rice. We made food for him. They ate, drank. They betook themselves in the morning, departed and went to their own place.

O

OBSERVANCE OF SABBATH   A writer declared that although Gypsies dwell in the deepest heathen darkness, the law of the Sabbath is rigidly observed. Gypsy Smith the evangelist wrote that his father would go a mile on Saturday to get a bucket of water so that he should not have to travel for it on Sunday. The bundles of sticks for the Sunday fire were likewise gathered the day before. Even whistling a song was not permitted on Sunday.

OCCULTISM AND GYPSIES   During the Renaissance the Gypsies in Europe were regarded as gifted with magic powers, with hypnotic faculties, and experienced in the occult arts. Hence they attracted the interest of Paracelus (c.1490-1541), the pre-eminent occultist of his age. In his travels through Europe as physician and magus, he encountered the exotic wandering people, the Gypsies who were generically known as Egyptians.

OCCUPATIONAL ADHERENCE   In their original home in India, as pariahs or outcasts, the Gypsies were required, according to Hindu caste laws, to adhere to certain trades such as smiths. Such crafts have thus been traditionally followed by them in whatever country they have sojourned.

OCCUPATIONAL DESIGNATIONS   Trades and occupations have their specialized descriptive names among the Gypsies. These occupations are usually traditionally followed by a group or tribe. The **oursari** are the bear-trainers.

Musicians are called *ghilabari.* Cobblers are *ciobatori.* *Zlatari* wash gold from the rivers in the Balkans. Gardeners are *vatraschi,* a sedentary occupation. Bricklayers are *salahori.* Those who make objects and articles of wood are the *radari.* Horse-dealers are *lovari. Cerhari* are nomads — tent-dwellers. *Colari* are blanket handlers.

OCCUPATIONS Traditionally the Gypsies have been blacksmiths and coppersmiths, basket-makers, acrobats, jugglers, bear-trainers, horse-dealers, tinkers, fiddlers, and, in the case of women, fortune-tellers. But they have equally been branded, from one century to another, as vagabonds, idlers, thieves, parasites.

OCCUPATIONS OF SCOTTISH GYPSIES The occupations of these Gypsies are various. Two of the families are 'horners' or 'spoonmakers', who manufacture horn into spoons; one a traveling tinker; another a traveling cooper; the rest are 'muggers' or 'potters', as they prefer being called, who carry earthenware about the country for sale. The spoons fabricated by the horners are very generally used by the poor, and farmers purchase a considerable number of them before autumn, for the use of the reapers. With the exception of the individuals of this profession, whose occupation is better attended to at home, all the others are absent from home, with their families, from eight to nine months in the year.

OCULAR POWER The Gypsies are said to have a peculiarly piercing, penetrating gaze, almost hypnotic, which affects onlookers. The following stanza illustrates the impact of such a look:

A Gypsy stripling's glassy eye
   Has pierced my bosom's core,
A feat no eye beneath the sky
   Could e'er effect before.

O DEL ORO DEVEL   Gypsy expressions that denote the (one) God.

This concept of god is equated with the sky: it is not the traditionally established acceptance of a Supreme Being as found in the major religious faiths.

OLDEST SPECIMEN   The oldest specimen of the English Gypsy language at present extant, and perhaps the purest, dating back at least to the Elizabethan Age, is contained in these three lines of a Gypsy ballad. Two strangers, Gypsies, meet suddenly, put questions to each other, and return answers:

Coin si deya, coin se dado?
Pukker mande drey Romanes,
Ta mande pukkeravava tute.

OMREN   In Gypsy mythology the Om Ren or wild man is a malevolent spectre indigenous to the forests. He is the terror of hunters and shepherds. Usually he appears in winter. He can tear up pine trees by the roots and destroy anyone who approaches his haunts.

OPHIOLATRY   This term means the worship of snakes. In early centuries the Gypsies were dedicated to snake worship. In Greece, in antiquity, the snake was similarly a cult deity. In modern Greece, and the Gypsies know Greece, the snake is still a domestic creature.

OPPIDUM PRISCUM RA   This Latin expression means the Ancient Town of Ra, the Egyptian Sun-god. Near this spot, in the Camargue, in Provence, Les Saintes Maries de la Mer — Sainte Jacobé and Sainte Salomé — who, with their servant Sara, were miraculously cast ashore in the Camargue, built a shrine. Now this spot is the annual meeting place for Gypsies who assemble from many distant countries to do reverence to Sara, whom they regard as their patron saint.

OPPRESSION An English Gypsy named Stanley was indicted at Winchester for house-breaking. But for his friends who at great expense proved an alibi, he might have been executed. In this way the Gypsies have been suspected and persecuted ever since the days of Henry VIII. They have been hunted. Their property has been taken from them. They have been frequently imprisoned, and in many cases their lives taken. Or, which to many of them is much worse, they have been transported to another part of the world, for ever separated from their families and friends.

ORIGIN The precise area of Gypsy provenance has long been a matter of debate, of conjecture, of fanciful and imaginative hypotheses among ethnologists, philologists, and gypsiologists. Countless conflicting legends and vague myths and surmises have obscured the primary historical truths about their origin.

Gypsies have at times been regarded as the descendants of Cain, destined to global vagabondage, bound to labor with iron and brass and other metals.

Another legend, equally stemming from Biblical sources, associates the Gypsies with the workmen who made the nails for the Crucifixion. They have furthermore been considered as of Phoenician race. Again, scholars have identified them as of early Egyptian ancestry. The term Gypsy, it was pointed out, is itself derived from *Egyptian*. Many Gypsy tribal chiefs, too, actually call themselves Duke of Egypt. But these are far from conclusive interpretations.

Still other historians assign the Gypsies to Babylonia, or to Abyssinia, or to Assyria. Another conjecture involves an attempt to equate Gypsies and Jews, on account of certain similarities, both in personal characteristics and in historical tradition, between the two peoples. Both races have experienced excessive intolerance racially. Both have undergone a diaspora, an ethnic dispersal over the continents. Under the Nazis, in fact, for extermination purposes, Gypsies and Jews were classified conjointly.

These and similar traditional and hypothetical accounts have, however, little basis in factual testimony. The general consensus is that the original home of the Gypsies lies in India.

Philological investigations of Hindu expressions resulted in the discovery of similar words, with similar meanings in use by European Gypsies. Further research postulated that the tribes of the Luri, indigenous to Baluchistan, or the Dom, whose tribal area also is Northern India, are our Gypsies.

It is generally accepted, therefore, that the Gypsies, in their tribal nomadic migrations, inhabited parts of Northern India. This area, in the course of centuries, was subjected to a series of invasions by Greeks and Scythians, Persians and Moslems. In consequence, approximately in the year 1000 A.D., the Gypsies of India were dispersed. One wave of migration reached Russia and spread to Scandinavia. Another advanced into Egypt. From Turkey in Asia one stream crossed into the Balkans and Central Europe.

ORIGIN OF BOHEMIAN An ancient people that inhabited Gaul were the Boii. They are described by Julius Caesar in his *Gallic War*. Later, they gave their name to the territory of what was Bohemia. The Gypsies who made their settlement in Bohemia were consequently called Bohemians.

ORIGIN OF NAME It is supposed that the Faws or Faas, a Gypsy family whose headquarters were at Yetholm in Scotland in the early nineteenth century, acquired this appellation from Johnnie Faw, Lord and Earl of Little Egypt. That is, Johnnie Faw was a Gypsy tribal leader. With him King James IV and Queen Mary, sovereigns of Scotland, saw not only the propriety, but also the necessity of entering into a special treaty.

ORIGIN OF ROM Rom, the basic Gypsy language, is of Indian origin, a composite of many dialects or linguistic families such as Murathi, Gujarati, Hindi. The vocabulary and syntax, too, stem from Sanskrit. There is, in addition, a large element of Greek in the Romany tongue.

In their wanderings, too, the Gypsies have absorbed linguistic elements from Syrian, Armenian, Ukrainian, Serbian, Russian, Persian. There are, furthermore, some seven or eight major dialects spoken by the Gypsies in England, Hungary, Andalusia and other areas where the Gypsies have been located.

ORIGIN OF ROMANY In George Borrow's *Lavengro* there is a discussion on the origin of Romany and the Roma-nichals:

> Indeed, many obscure points connected with the vocabulary of these languages, and to which neither classic nor modern lore afforded any clue, I thought I could now clear up by means of this strange broken tongue, spoken by people who dwelt among thickets and furze bushes, in tents as tawny as their faces, and whom the generality of mankind designated, and with much semblance of justice, as thieves and vagabonds. But where did this speech come from, and who were they who spoke it? These were questions which I could not solve, and which Jasper himself, when pressed, confessed his inability to answer. "But, whoever we be,

brother," said he, "we are an old people, and not what folks in general imagine, broken gorgios; and, if we are not Egyptians, we are at any rate Romany Chals!"

"Romany Chals! I should not wonder after all," said I, that these people had something to do with the founding of Rome. Rome, it is said, was built by vagabonds, who knows but that some tribe of the kind settled down thereabouts, and called the town which they built after their name: but whence did they come originally? ah! there is the difficulty."

But, abandoning these questions, which at that time were far too profound for me, I went on studying the language, and at the same time the characters and manners of these strange people. My rapid progress in the former astonished, while it delighted, Jasper.

"We'll no longer call you Sap-engro, brother," said he, "but rather Lav-engro which in the language of the gorgios means Word Master."

"Nay, brother," said Tawno Chikno, with whom I had become very intimate, "you had better call him Co-oro-mengro. I have put on the *gloves* with him, and find him a pure fist master; I like him for that, for I am a Cooro-mengro myself, and was born at Brummagem."

"I likes him for his modesty," said Mrs. Chikno, "I never hears any ill words come from his mouth, but, on the contrary, much sweet language. His talk is golden, and he has taught my eldest to say his prayers in Romany, which my rover had never the grace to do."

"He is the pal of my rom," said Mrs. Petulengro, who was a very handsome woman, "and therefore I likes him, and not less for his being a rye. Folks call me high-minded, and perhaps I have reason to be so. Before I married Pharaoh I had an offer from a lord — I likes the young rye, and, if he chooses to follow us, he shall have my sister. What say you, mother? Should not the young rye have my sister Ursula?"

"I am going to my people," said Mrs. Herne, placing a bundle upon a donkey, which was her own peculiar property. "I am going to Yorkshire, for I can stand this no longer. You say you like him. In that we differs. I hates the gorgio, and would like, speaking Romanly, to mix a little poison with his waters. And now go to Lundra, my children, I goes to Yorkshire. Take my blessing with ye, and a little bit of a gillie to cheer your hearts with when ye are weary. In all kinds of weather have we lived together; but now we are parted. I goes broken-hearted — I can't keep you company. Ye are no longer Romany. To gain a bad brother, ye have lost a good mother."

OTHELLO In connection with the traditional belief that the Gypsies were knowledgeable in love charms, there is the testimony of Shakespeare's *Othello*:

Othello:
That is a fault.
That hankerchief
Did an Egyptian to my mother give.
She was a charmer and could almost read
The thoughts of people. She told her, while she kept it,
'Twould make her amiable and subdue my father
Entirely to her love, but if she lost it
Or made a gift of it, my father's eye
Should hold her loathly, and his spirits should hunt
After new fancies. She dying gave it me;
And bid me, when my fate would have me wive,
To give it her. I did so — and take heed on't,
Make it a darling like your precious eye.
To lose or give't away were such perdition
As nothing else could match.
Desdemona:
Is't possible?

Othello: 'Tis true. There's magic in the web of it.
A sibyl, that had number'd in the world
The sun to course two hundred compasses,
In her prophetic fury sew'd the work.
The worms were hallow'd that did breed the silk,
And it was dy'd in mummy which the skilful
Conserv'd of Maidens' hearts.

OTTOKAR II   This King of Bohemia, writing to Pope Alexander VI, mentions the presence of Zingari, Gypsies?, in the year 1260, in the Hungarian Kingdom of Bela IV.

OURSARI   This name is applied to Gypsies who exhibited performing bears and other animals at fairs and country shows and other public places of entertainment. The Gypsies have designations that classify their trades and skills and occupations.

OUTCASTS   On account of their perpetual roving, from century to century, through the countries of Asia Eastward from their source in India, the Gypsies, as an ethnic entity, have consistently been regarded as outcasts, beyond the frontiers of human society. They have been the universal desposed and rejected of men. They, and their children likewise, have been treated as the disiecta membra — the scattered limbs, the offscourings of humanity. Their lot has been compounded of resentment and intolerance, of active hostility that reached its climax in torture, continuous persecution, massacre, and extermination. As recently as World War II the Nazis, in their frenzied attempts to 'purify' the Teutonic race, massacred thousands of Gypsies throughout the entire area of their occupation in Central and Eastern Europe.

OUTLAWS   If a Gypsy serf succeeded in escaping from the *voivode,* his master the landowner, in the Balkans, the Gypsy made for the mountains of Transylvania and became a member of other similarly outlawed Gypsies. Such outlaws were known as *Netotsi,* men of the woods, like the French resistance fighters of the maquis.

OUTWITTING THE WEATHER There was a Gypsy, named Dighton, encamped near Brighton, who told the story of a Gypsy, who was inspired with anything but the inner glowing glory of God, but who was, on the contrary, cram full of pure cussedness, being warmed by the same, — and the devil, — when chased by a constable, took refuge in a river full of freezing slush and broken ice, where he stood up to his neck and defied capture; for he verily cared no more for it than did Saint Peter of Alcantara, who was both ice and fire proof.

"Come out of that, my good man," said the gentleman, whose hen he had stolen, "and I'll let you go."

"No, I won't come out," said the Gypsy. "My blood be on your head!"

So the gentleman offered him five pounds, and then a suit of clothes, to come ashore. The Gypsy reflected, and at last said: "Well, if you'll add a drink of spirits, I'll come; but it's only to oblige you that I budge."

OVIEDO In Spain many towns have districts called Gitanerías, reserved exclusively for Gypsies. Even in the town of Oviedo, in the heart of the Asturias, there was a place called the Gitanería, though no Gitáno had been known to reside in the town within the memory of man, nor been seen, except perhaps as a chance visitor at a fair.

P

PAINTING GYPSY SCENES Among European painters who have depicted domestic or nomadic Gypsy scenes are Lucas van Leyden (1494-1533), Dutch painter and engraver: in the seventeenth century, the etcher Jacques Callot; a century later, Varin: and Denis Raffet (1804-1860), French lithographer.

PALMIRENO, LORENZO A sixteenth century Italian scholar who was also a gypsiologist. During this century great interest was aroused in Italy and France by the exotic hordes of Gypsies who had come from 'Egypt.'

PALMISTRY Gypsy women are skilled in reading the palm and interpreting the significance of the fingers. Fortune-telling, in fact, has through the centuries been the only exclusively female occupation among the Gypsies.

PAL, PEN When speaking to each other, the English Gypsies say *Pal* or *Pen;* that is, brother or sister.
Pralo, meaning *brother,* is used between a Rom, a Gypsy, and a gorgio or non-Gypsy.

PAPAL DECREE In the Middle Ages the prestige of the Gypsies in Europe, who were regarded as religious pilgrims bound for Rome, was protected by papal decree. Other pilgrims were designated to make a pilgrimage to Spain, to the shrine of James of Compostela.

PARACELSUS Famous Swiss physician and alchemist, who flourished in the sixteenth century. He took a deep interest in the traditional beliefs that the Gypsies were sorcerers and magicians.

PARAMITSCHA   In their traditional folklore the Gypsies have a large corpus of tales that they relate in the long winter months at their camp fires or in their caravans and tents. The tales are usually recited by the same person in the tribe or family, always in the same formulaic sequence, as was the case in Homeric times: or among the Doms of Baluchistan. The stories sometimes have an Oriental flavor: often too they incorporate matter from the countries that the Gypsies have known in their wanderings.

PARENTAL CONCERN   Gypsy mothers are hesitant about permitting a daughter to take up an occupation away from the family encampment, unless she can be assured of the daughter's morals being protected. Sometimes a grown daughter is punished with lashes by a parent for repeating some lascivious tale she has heard.

PARIS   In 1427 the entry into Paris of a group of Gypsies, men, women, and children, caused great consternation and excitement and aroused numberless conjectures about them. A medieval text describes their swarthy appearance, their dress, their cajoling manners, and also their fortune-telling practices.

PARNO   This Gypsy term which means *white,* is applied to all non-Gypsies. Among themselves, Gypsies are called *calo,* black, on account of their swarthy complexion.
Other terms used by Gypsies to denote non-Gypsies are gorgio, busnó, Gentile.

PASSION FOR THE VIOLIN   The traditional Gypsy love for violin music is expressed in this Gypsy song:
I've known no father since my birth,

I have no friend alive on earth;
My mother's dead this many day
The girl I loved has gone her way;
Thou violin with music free
Alone art ever true to me.

PATIV A Gypsy term meaning *a feast*. The expression is used by the Gypsies of Rumania to celebrate the acquittal of an innocently accused person.

PATRIN OR PATTERAN *Patrin* is the name of the signs by which the Gypsies who go before show the road they have taken to those who follow behind. 'We fling handfuls of grass down at the head of the road we take, or we make with the finger a cross-mark on the ground, or we stick up branches of trees by the side of the hedge. But the true *patrin* is handfuls of leaves flung down: for *patrin* or *patten* in old Romany language means the leaf of a tree.

PATRONS Among eminent names that have shown concern and made efforts in behalf of the Gypsies are the late Professor Walter Starkie of Dublin University and Europe. He was the Romany Rye par excellence whose revealing adventures throughout the Europe of the Gypsies have added few aspects to Gypsy life. Other such patrons: the Abbé Fleury of Poitiers, the Abbé Barthélemy of Verdun, C. H. Tellhagen of the Nordiska Museum of Stocolm, and Ivar Lo-Johannson.

PATTERAN Variants of this word are pateran and patrin. The term denotes a Gypsy trail sign. As they wander through the countryside they leave certain marks and symbols that enlighten the Gypsies who follow the same road. The marks refer to the attitude of the neighborhood, the possible welcome they may expect, the hope of food. The signs may be a few handfuls of leaves lying in a particular way on the roadside, or a cleft stick, or a cross drawn at the entrance of a road, and many other similar ideographic and traditional items of information for the migrant Gypsies.

PAUCITY OF ROMANY VOCABULARY The English Gypsies have no specific words for stars. There are no words for the less positive colors like gray, yellow, green. Some terms have dual meanings: for instance, *collico* means both yesterday and tomorrow. *Merripen* means life and also death. The English Gypsy can count to six. There are numbers for seven, eight, nine but these are known only to a few Gypsies. To express seven, for example, the Gypsy will say: Two threes and one: dui trins ta yek.

PAUCITY IN CERTAIN COUNTRIES Early in the nineteenth century Gypsies were very scarce in many parts of Germany, as well as in Switzerland and the Low Countries.
In Upper Saxony, in Hanover and in Brunswick it was such a rare occurrence to see a Gypsy that the appearance of a Romany caused quite a stir among villagers or burghers.

PECULIAR CHARACTERISTICS OF GYPSIES From the Dom, a Hindu caste, it is asserted, the migratory Gypsies derived their name, in its variant form of Rom, and several characteristics as well. The Dom burned the dead, handled corpses, skinned beasts, and performed other functions, all of which were appropriated by and became peculiar to, Gypsies in several countries in Europe, notably in Denmark and Holland, for several centuries after their arrival there.

PECULIARITY OF DRESS What can be said of the Gypsy

dress, of which such frequent mention is made in the Spanish laws, and which is prohibited together with the Gypsy language and manner of life? Of whatever it might it is almost impossible to describe the difference. They consist in former days, it is so little to be distinguished from the dress of some classes among the Spaniards, that generally wear a high-peaked narrow-brimmed hat, a zamarra of sheep-skin in winter, and, during summer, a jacket of brown cloth; and beneath this they are fond of exhibiting a red plush waistcoat, something after the fashion of the English jockeys, with numerous buttons and clasps. A faja or girdle of crimson silk surrounds the waist, where, not infrequently, are stuck the cachas. Pantaloons of coarse cloth or leather descend to the knee. The legs are protected by woolen stockings, and sometimes by a species of spatterdash, either of cloth or leather. Stout high-lows complete the equipment.

It is still more difficult to say what is the peculiar dress of the Gitanas. They wear not the large red cloaks and immense bonnets of coarse beaver which distinguish their sisters of England. They have no other headgear than a handkerchief, which is occasionally resorted to as a defense against the severity of the weather. Their hair is sometimes confined by a comb, but more frequently is permitted to stray dishevelled down their shoulders. They are fond of large ear-rings, whether of gold, silver, or metal, resembling in this respect the poissardes of France. There is little to distinguish them from the Spanish women save the absence of the mantilla, which they never carry. Females of fashion not infrequently take pleasure in dressing à la Gitána; but this female Gypsy fashion, like that of the men, is more properly the fashion of Andalusia, the principal characteristic of which is the saya, which is exceedingly short, with many rows of flounces.

PELOPONNESUS This peninsula in Greece is said to have

harbored Gypsies in the Middle Ages. Certain ruins appear to support this view. The Greek designation for such a ruin is *Gyphtokastron,* Gypsy fortress.

PENETRATION INTO AFRICA Gypsiologists have disputed the question whether the Gypsies ever penetrated into Africa. The Gitános, asserted, George Borrow:

would have been compelled to pass through the tribes who speak the Shilhah language, and who are the descendants of the ancient Numidians. These tribes are the most untamable and warlike of mankind, and at the same time the most suspicious, and those who entertain the greatest aversion to foreigners. Now the Gitanos, such as they arrived in Barbary, could not have defended themselves against such enemies, had they even arrived in large divisions, instead of bands of twenties and thirties, as is their custom to travel. They are not by nature nor by habit a warlike race, and would have quailed before the Africans, who, unlike most other people, engage in wars from what appears to be an innate love of the cruel and bloody scenes attendant on war.

Neverthless, concludes Borrow, I repeat that I am inclined to believe that Gypsies virtually exist in Barbary.

PENGA In Gypsy folklore King Penga is a legendary monarch. In the same mythological category belongs the story of Swarga, which is paradise. Gypsy legends are packed with such imaginative tales dealing with the forests, the heavens, and the spirits that haunt these places.

PERMANENT SETTLEMENTS At various times and in different countries — in Prussia in the eighteenth century, in Austria late in the nineteenth century, in Poland in the eighteenth century — land was offered by the state so that the Gypsies would settle down into more or less

343

permanent homes. The offers showed that the state was concerned about the status of the Gypsies and obviously proposed to ameliorate it. But the suggestions and plans were largely failures on account of the inherent wanderlust of the Gypsies themselves.

PERSIA In the exodus from India, the Gypsies are believed to have reached Persia by the year 1000 A.D. From that point some moved eastward toward Greece, while others advanced to Central Europe.

PERSIAN ASSOCIATIONS The saddle-makers and leather-workers of Persia are called Tsingani. They are, in their way, low caste, and a kind of Gypsy, and it is supposed that from them are possibly derived the names Zingan, Zigeuner, Zingaro, etc., by which Gypsies are known in so many lands.

PERSIAN LEGEND In his epic poem the *Shah Namah,* the Persian poet Firdusi, who belongs in the eleventh century, relates that a Persian king, Bahram Gur, brought from India some 10,000 lute-players, who were called in Persian Luris. These were Gypsies: for the term Luri is still used in Persia to denote a Gypsy.

PERSIAN VIEW Do what you may, say what you can. No washing e'er whitens the black Zigan.
This view of the Zingans, the Gypsies, appears in Firdusi, the Persian poet of the eleventh century, in his *Shah Nameh,* The Book of Kings.

PERSISTENCE OF ROMANY WAYS A notable feature about the Romanys is that neither time, climate, nor example of other peoples made any alteration in their inherent way of life. For the space of between three and four hundred years they went wandering like pilgrims

344

and strangers. They were to be found in Eastern and Western countries, among peasants and burghers, among the indolent as well as the active inhabitants.

Yet they remained, and still remain, what their fathers were — Gypsies. Africa makes them no blacker, nor Europe whiter. They neither have to be lazy in Spain nor diligent in Germany. In Turkey, Mohammed, and among Christians Christ remain equally without religious veneration. On every side around them they observed fixed and stable dwellings, with settled inhabitants.

The Gypsies, nevertheless, proceed in their own way, and continue, for the most part, as unsocial wayfarers.

PERVERSIONS Among Gypsies sexual perversions are tabu and never countenanced, while prostitution itself is rare. In the case of alleged infidelity, a wife is required to undergo certain tests in which talismans play a prominent part.

When, in rare cases, sexual perversions do occur, they are treated with the utmost harshness. The punishment is either annulment of the marriage or banishment from the tribe.

PESTILENCE In the Middle Ages, wherever the Gypsies appeared in Europe, they were regarded as a curse, a pestilence, carriers of plague and cholera. They came, it was said, like flights of wasps, to prey upon the fruits of others.

In France, they were attacked by the peasants, or by armed bands. Some were massacred on the spot; or, without a trial, were hanged on the next tree, or sent for life to the galleys. Women and children were scourged or mutilated.

PHARAO NEPEK A Gypsy expression meaning *Pharaoh's people.* The Gypsies who reached Central Europe in the Middle Ages announced themselves thus. The term is still in use in Hungary.

PHARAVONO A Gypsy term denoting the Gypsies' ancestors: evidently the association is with Pharaoh and Egypt.
The Gypsies, according to some early gypsiologists, conceived Egypt as the original home of the Gypsies. Hence in the Middle Ages the tribal leaders often styled themselves as Count or Earl or Duke or King of Little Egypt. And in many official records and edicts these Gypsy chiefs were accepted as such.

PHARON This term is applied to the Gypsies in the Balkans and in Macedonia. The word probably stems from Pharaoh, and indicates the putative origin of the Gypsies in Egypt.
Many gypsiologists debated the question of the original home of the Gypsies. They were assigned to Persia, Greece, Bohemia, Portugal. Philological investigations definitively determined India as the primary home of the Gypsies.

PHILADELPHIA In the later decades of last century Philadelphia was a haunt of Gypsies. Their tents were pitched in woodland or field outside the city, in Oakland Park, or in Camden. According to the seasons, these Gypsies moved on to Maine, or went south.

PHILIP IV Philip IV of Spain decreed in 1633 that the Gypsies who had settled in the country should be absorbed by the native inhabitants and should intermarry with the Spaniards.

346

The characteristic tserXe *which they still use in Europe have been given up for tents of many forms. The shade of a tree, however, remains the favorite living room*

The hair is usually braided and oiled, sometimes in four braids, with coins and pieces of silk woven into the strands

PHILIP V   Philip V of Spain, like most of the Spanish kings, decreed harsh measures against the Spanish Gypsies. In 1726 he forbade Gypsy complaints against the administration of Spanish justice. He likewise banished all the Gypsy women from Madrid and from all the towns where royal audiences were held. The justices were particularly commanded not to permit the Gitános to leave their places of domicile except in cases of very urgent necessity.

PHILOLOGICAL ELEMENTS   One peculiar feature of the speech of the Gypsies is the considerable number of Slavic words that it contains. These words appear in the Gypsy dialects of Germany and Spain, England and Italy. Such words were probably absorbed when the Gypsies passed through and even settled in Bulgaria. Another considerable element incorporated into Romany is modern Greek. The Spanish Gypsies in particular understood Greek well, until far into the sixteenth century.

PHOTOGRAPHY   At the Hampton Races, in England, Charles Leland the gypsiologist was talking with a Gypsy, when she suddenly arose and went away. An itinerant photographer was going to take her photograph. The Gypsy, who was of the real old kind, believed it was unlucky to have her portrait taken.

PHURI DAÏ   A Gypsy expression meaning a wise counselor, a tribal leader. He was often regarded as endowed with occult power.

PHYSICAL CHARACTERISTICS   The Gypsies, according to a nineteenth century European Gypsiologist, were well shaped, muscular, active physically. They were neither giants nor dwarfs, Humpbacks, blindness, corporeal defects were rare among them. Their health was consistently good. Neither wet nor dry weather, heat nor cold, seemed to have any untoward effect on them. In sickness, when it does appear, they employ old traditional remedies of theirs transmitted from tribe to tribe, from one family to another, through countless generations.

PILGRIMAGE As ostensible and expedient Christians in Christian countries, the Gypsies participated in the many pilgrimages that attracted bodies of devout and penitent Christians from many regions. Such pilgrimages, moreover, were in harmony with the Gypsies' migratory tendencies. They made a pilgrimage, in the Middle Ages, to Mont St. Michel, to the Shrine of the Archangel, to St. Galien in Tours, to the Shrine of Sainte-Reine in Burgundy, to the Shrine of the Madonna of Reggio, in Italy, to Granada in Spain, to the Feast of Saint Anne in Madrid. One of the most notable pilgrimages was the annual pilgrimage to Saintes Maries de la Mer, in the Camargue country in Provence.
Other pilgrimages involve Gracanica, in Serbia and elsewhere in the Balkans: the ceremonials include sacrifices of pigs, hens, lambs.

PILGRIMAGE TO CAMARGUE The annual pilgrimage of the Gypsies to Les Saintes Maries de la Mer, in the Camargue, in Provence, is assumed to have begun in the mid-nineteenth century. The pilgrimage is made by Gypsies who gather on May 25 and 25 from all over Europe to pay homage to their traditional patron Saint Sara.

PIPERS In the eigteenth and nineteenth centuries the courts of Europe had their own Gypsy musicians, choirs, bands. Janczy was a famous Gypsy musician who acted as court piper to Ladislas III of Poland. Another Gypsy, James Allan, made a name for himself as a bag-piper in Scotland.

PITTARD, EUGENE Professor Pittard, of the University of Geneva, is a dedicated gypsiologist who made important anthropometric researches on the Gypsies in the Balkans. He published his findings in *Les Tziganes ou Bohémiens dans le Péninsule des Balkans,* 1932.

PIUS II Aeneas Silvius Piccolomini, who became Pope Pius II, propounded the theory that the Gypsies originated on the slopes of the Caucasus.

PLAGUR The Bishop of Forli, as far back as 1422, insinuated that the Gypsies carried the plague with them: as he observed that it raged with peculiar violence the year of their appearance at Forli. The Latin text reads as follows:
Eodem anno praecipue fuit pestis seu mortalitas For-livio: that same year there occurred a peculiarly deadly plague at Forli.

PLANTS Gypsies are deeply versed in plant lore, and have a vast and miscellaneous knowledge of the properties and efficacy of numberless herbs and spices that are used in potions for apotropaic, or medicinal or erotic purposes.

PLATONIC CONCEPT In a Gypsy tribe the children belong not to the individual family but to the community as a whole.

POACHING The Gypsies have long had a popular reputation as poachers. Whatever they secured was used for their own food. not for commerce. They were particularly knowledgeable with rabbits, hares, fish, poultry, game.

POETRY Like the poetry of other peoples, Gypsy poetry

349

represents the character of the race. The general themes of Gypsy poetry are the incidents of Gitáno life and the feelings and attitudes of the Gypsies. The subjects themselves may be very slight or incidental: a lover's lament, a sick Rom.

In structure, Gypsy poetry consists of quartains or couplets, with two usually imperfect rhymes. Another but rare metrical arrangement consists of six-line stanzas. The essential point is usually contained in one stanza.

George Borrow declared that the Gypsy poetry which he included in his *The Gypsies in Spain* might have little literary merit but the verses were free from affectation and they were different from the poetry "of those interesting personages who figure, under the names of Gypsies, Gitanos, Bohemians, etc. in novels and on the boards of the theatre."

POGADO JIB A Gypsy expression that means: broken language: that is, Romany interlarded with English words. Pogado jib is a common medium among the English Gypsies. Romany, interspersed with Hungarian or Spanish or Rumanian is similarly used in these countries respectively. Pogado jib corresponds exactly to the macaronic verse that was so popular in the Middle Ages: e.g., poems in Latin and Italian, or Latin and English.

POISONING THE PORKER The Gypsies had a practice of using *drab* or *drao* on a pig, a poison that did not affect the blood of the animal. When the pig was dead, a Gypsy would appeal to the farmer for the carcass. The Gypsies cleared up the *drab* and feasted on the pig. A Gypsy song on this theme was translated by George Borrow as follows:

> Listen to me, ye Romany lads,
> who are seated in the straw about the fire,
> and I will tell how we poison the porker,

I will tell how we poison the porker.
We go to the house of the poison-monger,
where we buy three pennies' worth of bane,
and when we return to our people we say
we will poison the porker;
we will try and poison the porker.

We then make up the poison,
and then we take our way to the farmer's house,
as if to beg a bit of victuals,
a little broken victuals.

We see a jolly porker,
and then we say in Roman language,
'Fling the bane yonder amongst the dirt,
and the porker soon will find it,
the porker soon will find it.'

Early on the morrow
we will return to the farm-house,
and beg the dead porker,
the body of the dead porker.

And so we do, even so we do;
the porker dieth during the night;
on the morrow we beg the porker;
and carry to the tent the porker.

And then we wash the inside well,
till all the inside is perfectly clean,
till there's no bane within it,
not a poison grain within it.

And then we roast the body well,
send for ale to the alehouse,
and have a merry banquet,
a merry Roman banquet.

The fellow with the fiddle plays, he plays;

the little lassie sings.
She sings an ancient Roman ditty;
now hear the Roman ditty.

POMEZIA   This is the title of a Spanish periodical published in Barcelona. It covers Gypsy life and conditions throughout Spain and also dwells on the history of the Romany people in that country.

POLAND   In the sixteenth century the Gypsies were exposed to official hostility. From that time onward, however, they were treated with marked tolerance. Similar acceptance of the Gypsies prevailed in the Balkans, and in Latvia and Lithuania.

POLGAR   Vladislav II of Hungary granted a charter in 1496 to the voivode, the tribal chief, Thomas Polgar. He was the leader of twenty-five tents of wandering Gypsies. The royal order decreed that the Gypsies were to receive free residence everywhere, and on no account was anyone to molest the leader or his people, because they prepared musket balls and other military stores for the Bishop Sigismund at Fünfkirchen.

POLICE   In domestic affrays, in fights and conflicts and attacks between rivals or rival tribes or between one encampment and another, the Gypsies involved in the disturbances rarely appeal to the local police. All such acts of violence are considered within the jurisdiction of the Gypsies themselves. It would be a marked breach of Gypsy mores and tradition to call in the police, the gorgios, the non-Gypsies to settle their disputes.

POLIGARI   A Gypsy term for Gypsies who made arms and weapons in the Middle Ages.
Occupational groups had their distinctive trade desig-

nations: for instance, *costorari,* tinsmiths; *oursari,* bear-trainers.

POLYGAMY Polygamy has not been uncommon among the Gypsies, although it is rather rare now. George Borrow, the nineteenth century gypsiologist, refers to a certain Riley Boswell, who had two wives. Another Gypsy was credited with three wives. Still another married, in sequence, seven wives. On the other hand, pre-marital chastity among the Gypsies has traditionally been very high, possibly as the result of early marriage. Girls married as early as the age of twelve. Such a custom has been for centuries in force in India, the original home of the Gypsies.

POLYGLOT Many Gypsy tribes are polyglot. The Sintés, for instance, speak Sinto, Polish, Russian, German, Yiddish.
In any case, the Gypsies are at least bi-lingual: they speak Romany, and the language of the country where they are settled.

POLYGYNY Polygyny occurs among Bulgarian, Serbian, and English Gypsies. In Serbia, the first wife may ask a divorce if the husband takes a second wife.

POMENA In Gypsy Romany, this term means a *feast in memory of the dead.* The feast is repeated at intervals until the anniversary day. On such occasions the Gypsies do not wear black for mourning.

POPULAR FOOD Among foods that are regularly used by the Gypsies are: potatoes, beans, celery, tomatoes, cucumbers, pimento, pepper, rice, maize, spices, vinegar. Salt and eggs are used sparingly. Water is the usual drink. At a special feast, they have wine, whisky, beer.

POPULAR MUSICIANS   In Egypt, as in Austria or Syria, or Persia or India, the Gypsies are the popular musicians, wrote a gypsiologist. In Hungary, and particularly in Spain, the Gypsy musician achieved a remarkable reputation.

POPULATION   It is estimated that at the present time there are some six million Gypsies dispersed throughout the entire world. These are rarely settlers in urban communities. Mostly they appear in small numbers or bands, in encampments or caravans on the peripheral of remote villages, in the open fields, by river banks, or at the outskirts of forest. Virtually, despite the changes they have observed in their hundreds of years of wandering, the Gypsies have retained their essential identity.

POSHRATT   A Gypsy term that signifies a half-caste Gypsy. A complete non-Gypsy is called a *busnó* or a *gorgio.*

POSSESSION   To the Gypsies the concept of accumulations of material possessions is markedly absent. For such a migratory people, of course, possessions in large bulk would be cumbersome. This indifference gives Gypsies a remarkable sense of freedom that has for centuries been the mainspring of their existence. They belong to no delimited national frontiers. Yet they belong everywhere. They are virtually *cives orbis,* not *cives urbis* — citizens of the world, not citizens of a city.

POTIONS   In the sixteenth century the Gypsies often prepared and sold potions to the *busné,* the non-Gypsies. The philtres and concoctions were compounded of miscellaneous and often nauseating ingredients, and were intended as an effective means of arousing erotic inclinations.

POVERTY   In the fifteenth century the poverty of the Gypsies in Spain was so marked that a proverb was current on this term: más pobre que cuerpo de Gitano: poorer than a Gypsy body. Hence the Moors, seeing their abject condition, did not molest them.

POWER OF MUSIC The Gypsies of Eastern Europe regard their dances as means of inducing rain. They also have a belief that their musical ability is to be ascribed to the collaboration of the Archfiend himself.

As in ancient mythology, when Orpheus by his music could charm wild beasts and make stones rise into walls, so music in the Gypsy tradition is a potent remedy for sickness. For sickness is produced by malignant spirits and music alone can banish them.

POWER OF WATER If a Gypsy has a child who is suspected of having the Evil Eye, she takes the child to a stream and presses its face close to the water. Then she recites:

Water, water, hasten:
  look up, look down.
Much water hastens,
  may as much come into the eye
which looked up on thee
  and may it now perish.

PRACTICING SORCERY Dabbling in sorcery is in some degree the province of the female Gypsy. She affects to tell the future, and to prepare philtres by means of which love can be awakened in any individual toward any particular object. And such is the credulity of the human race, even in the most enlightened countries, that the profits arising from the practices are great.

PRALO A Gypsy term signifying brother. This expression is symbolic of the ethnic kinship between members of one tribe and another, and of a Rom and a gorgio, a Gypsy and a non-Gypsy.

PRAY The Hungarian chronicler considered that the primary home of the Gypsies had been the Seljuk Kingdom of Rum, whence the Gypsy term for themselves as Rom.

PRAYER A common prayer among the Gypsies of Hungary and Transylvania runs as follows:

Gula Devla,
da me saschipo.
Swuntuna Devla,
da me bacht
t'aldaschis cari me jav;
te ferin man,
Devla, sila ta niapaschiata,
chungalé
manuschendar, ke
me jav andé drom
ca hin man traba;
ferin man, Davla;
ma mek man
Devla, ke manga
man tre Devleskey.
Sweet Goddess,
give me health, Holy Goddess,
give me luck and grace wherever I go;
and help me, Goddess, powerful and
immaculate, from ugly men,
that I may go in the road
to the place I purpose;
help me, Goddess;
forsake me not, Goddess,
for I pray for God's sake.

The strange feature in this prayer is that the Gypsies are declared to be non-Christians, certainly not observing or pious Christians: merely nominally so, to accord with the circumstances where they are settled.

PRAYER TO THE VIRGIN   Appended is a specimen of the Gypsy language, together with a translation:

Ocanajimia a la Debla

O Débla quirindía, Day de sarós los Bordeles on coin panchabo: per los duquipénes sos naquelástes á or pindré de la trejúl de tute Chaborro majarolísimo te manguélo, Débla, me alcorabíses de tute chaborró or estormén de sares las dojis y crejétes sos menda udicáre aquerao on andoba. — Anarania, Tebléque.

Ostebé te berarbe Ostelinda! perdoripe sirles de sardaña; or Eraño sin sartute c bresban tute sirles enré sares las rumiles, y bresban sin or frujero de tute po. — Tebléque.

Manjari Ostelinda, day de Ostebé, brichardila per gabéres crejetaóres, aocaná y on la ocana de nonrra beribén! — Anarania, Tebléque.

Chimuclani or Bato, or Chabal, or Chispero manjaró; sata sia on or presimelo, aocana, y gajeres: on los sicles de los siclos. — Anarania.

Prayer to the Virgin

O most holy Virgin, Mother of all the Christians in whom I believe; for the agony which thou didst endure at the foot of the cross of thy most blessed Son, I entreat thee Virgin, that thou wilt obtain for me, from thy Son, the remissions of all the crimes and sins which I may have committed in this world. — Amen, Jesus.

God save thee, Maria! full art thou of grace: the Lord is with thee; blessed art thou amongst all women, and blessed is the fruit of thy womb. — Jesus.

Holy Mary, Mother of God, pray for us sinners, now and in the hour of our death! — Amen, Jesus.

Glory to the Father, the Son, the Holy Ghost; as was in

the beginning, now and for ever: in the ages of the ages. — Amen.

PREDARI'S THEORY   Francesco Predari, an Italian gypsiologist, published in 1841 his *Origine e vicende dei Zingari con documenti alle proprietà ásiche e morali*, in which he conceived that the Gypsies were descended from a prehistoric people who were forced by a geological or political catastrophe to become wanderers.

PREDATORY HABITS   In Spain the Gypsies would encamp near some remote village and not rarely remain there until they had consumed whatever the villagers possessed for their support.

PRESTIGE   Those who have been accustomed, wrote George Borrow, the gypsiologist, to consider the Gypsy as a wandering outcast, incapable of appreciating the blessings of a settled and civilized life, or — if abandoning vagabond propensities, and becoming stationary — as one who never ascends higher than the condition of a low trafficker, will be surprised to learn that among the Gypsies of Moscow there are not a few who are behind the higher orders of the Russians neither in appearance nor mental acquirements.

PRIESTS AMONG GYPSIES   Throughout the reign of Elizabeth there was a terrible persecution of the Gypsy race; far less, however, on account of the crimes which they actually committed, than from a suspicion which was entertained that they harbored amidst their companies priests and emissaries of Rome, who had come to England for the purpose of sowing sedition and inducing the people to embrace again the old discarded superstition. This suspicion, however, was entirely without foundation. The

Gypsies call each other brother and sister, and are not in the habit of admitting to their fellowship people of a different blood and with whom they have no sympathy.

PRIZE-FIGHTING The Gypsies, laments a nineteenth century gypsiologist, have long been encouraged by many of those in high life in the savage practice of prize-fighting. Pugilism has been the disgrace of our land, and our nobility and gentry have not been ashamed to patronize it.
Not long ago a fight took place in this county, which will be a lasting disgrace to the neighborhood. One of the pugilists, a Gypsy in the pride of his heart, said, during the fight, that he would never be beaten so long as he had life. The poor wretch fought till not a feature of his countenance could be seen, his head and face being swollen to a frightful size, and his eyes quite closed. He attempted to tear them open, that he might see his antagonist; and was at last taken off the stage. Not satisfied with this brutal scene, the spectators offered a purse of ten guineas for another battle. This golden bait caught the eye of another Gypsy who, a few months before, had 'ruptured a blood-vessel in fighting. Throwing up his hat on the stage, the sign of challenge, he was soon met by a fellow as degraded as himself, but with much more strength and activity. The Gypsy was three times laid prostrate at the feet of his antagonist, and was taken away almost lifeless. His conqueror put a half-crown into his hand as he was carried off, saying it was something for him to drink. Three months later, the Gypsy was in the last stage of consumption.

PROCESSIONAL When the Gypsies assemble annually in their thousands at Les Saintes Maries, in the Camargue country of Provence, they carry their patron saint Sara's image, together with a model of the ship that brought the Marys to Provence, in procession and then advance off shore, into the sea. The procession finally returns to the ancient crypt of the dedicated shrine at Les Saintes Maries.

PROCESSIONS During the Corpus Christi processions in Granada, the Spanish Gypsies performed traditional dances.

The Gypsies regularly adapted themselves, in dance and music, to the customs of the country where they settled.

PROFESSIONAL GYPSIES In some countries the Gypsies have risen in status from their unsettled, nomadic life. There are, for example, Gypsy writers, physicians, lawyers. In Bulgaria, some 350 municipal councillors are Gypsies. In addition, twelve members of parliament are also Gypsies.

PROFESSION OF FAITH Charles Leland, visiting Russia in the nineteenth century, wrote of the Gypsies:

I found, on inquiry, that the Russian Gypsies profess Christianity; but, as the religion of the Greek church, as I saw it, appears to be practically something very little better than fetish-worship, I cannot exalt them as models of evangelical piety.

PROFILE OF SPANISH GYPSIES A little over a century ago a Scottish gypsiologist named Walter Simson wrote the following harshly and sharply etched description of the Gypsies in Spain:

They scatter themselves among villages and lonesome farms, where they steal fruit, poultry, and often even cattle; in short, everything that is portable. They are almost always abroad, incessantly watching an opportunity to practice their thievery. They hide themselves with much dexterity from the search of the

360

police. Their women, in particular, have an uncommon dexterity in pilfering. When they enter a shop, they are watched with the utmost care. But with every precaution they are not free from their rapines. They excel, above all, in hiding the pieces of silver which are given in exchange for gold, which they never fail to offer in payment, and they are so well hidden that they are often obliged to be undressed before restitution can be obtained.

The Gitanos are disgustingly filthy, and almost all covered with rags. They have neither tables, chairs, nor beds, but sit and eat on the ground. They are crowded in huts, pell-mell, in straw. And their neglect of the decorum of society, so dangerous to morals, must have the most melancholy consequences on wretches and vagabonds, abandoned in themselves. They consequently are accused of giving themselves up to every disorder of the most infamous debauchery, and to respect neither the ties of blood nor the protecting laws of the virtues of families.

They feed on rotten poultry and fish, dogs and stinking cats, which they seek for with avidity; and when this resource fails them, they live on the entrails of animals, or other aliments of the lowest price. They leave their meat but a very few minutes on the fire, and the places where they cook it exhales an infectious smell.

They speak the Catalonian dialect, but they have, besides, a language to themselves, unintelligible to the natives of the country, from whom they are very careful to hide the knowledge of it.

The Gitanos are tanned like the mulattoes, of a size above mediocrity, well formed, active, robust, supporting all the changes of seasons, and sleeping in the open fields, whenever their interest requires it. Their features are irregular and show them to belong to a transplanted race. They have the mouth very wide, thick lips, and high cheek-bones.

PROPHECY   The Prophet Ezekiel predicted: I shall scatter the Egyptians among the nations. This has been interpreted by Gypsies and gypsiologists alike, as proof that the wandering Gypsies are equated with those Egyptians.

PROTEAN GYPSIES   Through the centuries, the Gypsies have been protean or chameleon-like in assuming the outward formalities of whatever religion they have encountered on their continental peregrinations. Even as early as the beginning of the seventeenth century a Spanish theologian who inveighed against the Gypsies, a certain Sancho de Moncado, declared that with the Turks the Gypsies were Turkish Moslems, with the heretics, they were heretical.
In the Crimea and in Turkey there are still Gypsies who are Moslems nominally: they are known as Nawar or Chorachaja.

PROTECTED CATTLE   In all the South Slavic country the peasants on St. George's Day adorned the horns of cattle with garlands, in Gypsy-Indian style, to protect them from evil influences.

PROTECTION OF ENGLAND   In Henry VIII's reign the Gypsies were considered so dangerous to the morals and comfort of the country that many of them were sent back to Calais, whence they had embarked.

PROTECTION OF HORSES   One Hungarian Gypsy tribe protects its horses by placing the animal beside the fire. A hole is dug into which are thrown ninefold grass and some hairs from the horse's tail and mane. The left fore-foot is then traced on the ground, and the earth is then extracted and shaken into the hole, to the accompaniment of an incantation containing the formula:

A straw, a hair!
May you never be hungry!
May he who steals you die!

PROVENCE In parts of Provence the Gypsies are termed *caracaio*, fowl-callers: *caraco* means a rooster.
The term *caracaio* may conceivably stem from *Karaki*, by which name the Gypsies were known in Persia.

PROVERBS The general opinion of Gypsies is illustrated in these Hungarian and Wallach proverbs:

False as a Tzigane.
Dirty as a Gypsy.
No entertainment without Gypsies.
With a wet rag you can put to flight a whole
village of Gypsies.
Every Gypsy woman is a witch.

Proverbial sayings used by the Gypsies of themselves include the following:

Svaka vracara svrazje strane: every witch belongs
to the Devil's gang.
Kud ce vjestica dou svoj rod?: where should a witch
go if not to her kin? Birds of a feather flock together.
Izjele te viestice!: may the witch eat you!
A common curse.
Svake baba viestica, a djed vjestac: every old woman
is a witch and every old man a wizard.

Among maxims relating to the Rumanian Gypsies are the following:

They made us eat with the dogs and sleep with the

horses, and wonder why we prefer animals to people. When you fix a pot, make sure not a single wire is loose. That one loose wire can ruin a day's work.

The dance makes us free — at least for a while.
We love children: they are our only good neighbors.
Beware of the written word! It always reads against our people.
They rape our women and then apprehend them for immorality.

The Germans broke our fiddles but our music lived on.
Boyars speak to the people. To us they let their dogs speak.
If the gilding is done well, who cares what is underneath?
A wagon will hold more people when there is peace among them.

Stealing from a thief is no theft.
The Germans burned our women and children but they said Christian prayers when they buried their ashes.

The Boyars kept us in pig sties and then said we were dirty.
We cannot plant. We are never certain who will take in the harvest.
God is in the forest, not in the church.
Not until we find love among people will we abandon our horses.

Modest Gypsies don't eat.
Who cares if we come from the blacklands of Africa or the blacklands of India, our blackland is Europe.
The darkness of the forest is the light of the Gypsy.
Eat while you can. Tomorrow you may be on the run.
A Gypsy's house is always harnessed, ready to leave.
A Gypsy's heaven looks like a forest. It's safe.

Beware of your neighbors: strangers will not harm you.
The forest is safer than the market-place.

The German killed us because we were Jews: the Turks chased us because we were Christians: and the English because we were poor.

The Boyars made us slaves: only the trees are our friends.

The best friends a Gypsy has are a fast horse and a watchful dog.

A Gypsy never knows his tomorrow.

Their schools teach learning: but they also teach hating.

They say there is Jewish blood in us: so it is in Mother Mary and Holy Joseph.

We saved many Jews from the Christians for a thousand years not because we love them but because we hate persecution.

When one's pitched up one's little tent, made one's little fire before the door, and hung one's kettle by the kettle-iron over it one doesn't like an inspector or constable to come and say: What are you doing here? Take yourself away, you Gypsy dog.

The true way to be a wise man is to hear, see, and bear in mind.

A tramp has more fun than a Gypsy.

When the Gentile way of living and the Gypsy way of living come together, it is anything but a good way of living.

It is not a wise thing to say you have been wrong. If you allow you have been wrong, people will say: You may be a very honest fellow, but you are certainly a a very great fool.

Behind bad luck comes good luck.

Don't ask for a thing when you can't get it.

The best is soonest gone.

You can do a thing better if you go about it secretly.

Nice reeds make nice baskets.

A cloudy morning often changes to a fine day.

Many of these proverbs illustrate the Gypsy mentality. Others are applicable, in a wider sense, to all people. There is no startlingly profound wisdom in these maxims, but there is always a sense of pragmatic reality. Sometimes the apothegm is harsh and bitter and cynical, particularly when it condenses the essence of the Gypsy experience in relation to the contacts with the *gorgios*, the *busne*. On occasion, again, there appears a resilient tone, a buoyancy that shrugs off the hostilities of the Gentiles, that almost sees the whimsical aspect of the frustrating situations that they encounter.

PROVOCATION A nineteenth century historian of the Gypsies says: It must not be supposed that the whole of Christendom had been so provoked by the conduct of the Gypsies as to have attempted their expulsion, or rather their extermination merely because they were jugglers, fortune-tellers, astrologers, warlocks, witches and imposters. The true cause of the promulgation of sanguinary laws and edicts lay in their thefts and robberies, and living upon the inhabitants of the countries through which they traveled.

PRUSSIAN EDICT Germany always laid a heavy hand on the Gypsies in their territory. They were invariably regarded as an incumbrance to the state. Frederick William I of Prussia, for instance, decreed in 1725 that all Gypsies, male and female, over the age of eighteen, should be hanged if they were discovered on Prussian territory after the promulgation of the edict.

PSEUDO-GYPSY NARRATIVE In the seventeenth century

366

a narrative appeared under the name of *The Gypsy Rogue,* or *The Adventures of Merriton Latroon.* It purported to be an account of Gypsy life, but actually the author confused a body of vagrants and beggars, called Abraham men, with the Gypsies.

PUNJAB When a Hindu writer came to visit a lawyer in Belgrade, a Gypsy, he was greeted with the words: Punjab, Punjab! He explained that as a Gypsy he knew that his ancestors had come from the Punjab. The affinity between the Gypsy and the Hindu was expressed in the words: Tu main ek rakta — You and I have the same blood.

PUPPETRY In the Balkans the Gypsies used to make an occupational practice of presenting mobile puppet shows at fairs, carnivals, and festivals.

PURE GYPSY DIALECTS George Borrow, the gypsiologist, declared:

> In the foremost class of the purer Gypsy dialect, I have no hesitation in placing those of Russia, Wallachia, Bulgaria, and Transylvania. They are so alike that he who speaks one of them can make himself very well understood by those who speak any of the rest. Whence it may reasonably be inferred that none of them can differ much from the original Gypsy speech: so that when speaking of Gypsy language, any of these may be taken as a standard.

PURO JIB A Gypsy term for *the old language*: that is, the Romany tongue spoken by all Gypsies, with differences in dialect and vocabulary, according to the country in which they have settled.

PURO ROM In Gypsy idiom, this expression denotes the leader of a tribe.

In the Balkans he was usually termed, in the local idiom, the *voivode*.

Q

QUAIL Gypsies regard the quail as the Devil's bird. In their mythology the daughters of the Nivasi, the spirits of the earth, appear as quails in the fields. At night they steal the corn.

QUAINT CONCEIT There is current in the Balkans a quaint conceit relating to the Gypsies' religion. It is said that they never built a church, that their church was composed of cheese and pig-fat, and that they had eaten all this long years ago. The legend also appears in other areas of Gypsy settlements.

QUEEN BRIDGET In England, in the eighteenth century, many Gypsy colonies were in existence under a tribal leader commonly called a King. His wife, or sometimes the oldest woman in the tribe, was nominally the Queen. There is a record of a certain Queen Bridget who died in 1768.

QUEEN OF THE FAIRIES In Gypsy mythology Ana is the Queen of the Fairies. She has a son, Melalo, an obscene bird with two heads. Another child is Lilyi, a demon. Her other offspring are likewise demoniac creatures.

QUEEN OF THE WITCHES In Gypsy folklore and mythology, Gana is queen of the witches. She rushes in headlong hunt over the heavens or through the skies, followed by a throng of witches and fairies. People point to the places where she has passed, and where the grass and leaves are dry.

Her name, Gana, is probably a variant for Diana, the ancient huntress-goddess.

QUENITES They are Gypsies who are skilled in metal-work. Their locale is on the Syrian frontiers. Their name is equated with Cainites, who appear to be associated with the descendants of Cain, doomed to wander.

QUERELAR NASULA A Spanish Gypsy expression signifying *Casting the Evil Eye*. Some Spanish Gypsies pretend to have the power of casting the evil eye. Likewise they sell remedies to dispel the influence of the evil eye. These remedies consist largely of various drugs and charms known only to themselves.

In the East, the usual remedy for the evil eye is the sputum of the person who has cast the spell.

QUIÑONES, DON JUAN DE In 1632 he published an account of the Spanish Gypsies. He was the principal accuser of the Gypsies as cannibals. Put to the rack, the accused Gypsies confessed that they had murdered and eaten a female pilgrim in a forest. On being again tortured, they admitted that they had likewise murdered and eaten a Franciscan monk. On their own admissions, declared Quiñones, they were excecuted. Those and similar anecdotes are presented by the writer. Borrow dismisses them as being without foundation. But he does add that in ancient times acts of cannibalism have been committed, when the Gypsies lived in a semi-savage state or under the pressure of famine.

R

RABBLE   In 1422 the Bishop of Forli described Gypsies as a 'raging rabble, of brutal and animal propensities.'
On their first appearance in the European countries the bands of wandering Gypsies, with their strange dress and their peculiar language, created at first a sensation, then hostility and finally active persecution, banishment, torture, massacre.

RACE-COURSE   The English Gypsies are regular attendants at the race-course: what jockey is not? Perhaps jockeyism originated with them, and even racing, at least in England. Jockeyism properly implies the management of a whip, and the word jockey is neither more nor less than the term, slightly modified, by which they designate the formidable whip which they usually carry.
In Romany, *chuckni,* means a whip.

RACOCZY   The name of the national Hungarian favorite orchestral composition, fashioned by Gypsy musical art. Into Hungarian music a great deal of Gypsy music has infiltrated. On the other hand, some musicologists have asserted that Hungarian music is virtually all Gypsy music.

RAGGED DRESS   The first Gypsies who came to Europe, declared a Gypsiologist in the nineteenth century, appeared ragged and miserable. Their descendants similarly continued for hundreds of years and still remain so. This is particularly remarkable in the countries about the mouth of the Danube, which abound in Gypsies: namely Transylvania, Hungary, and Turkey in Europe.

RAGGLE-TAGGLE GYPSIES An English ballad well illustrates the Gypsy roving spirit:

> What care I for my house and land?
> What care I for my treasure, O?
> What care I for my new-wedded lord, —
> I'm off with the raggle-taggle Gypsies, O!

Walter Starkie, the professor of Spanish at Dublin University and the noted gypsiologist, felt the same urge and went wandering over Europe, from Spain to Transylvania, from Provence to Rumania. He made his way by playing the violin and singing Gypsy songs.

RAI, BAUOR These two Gypsy expressions refer to *gorgios,* the non-Gypsies. A *rai* is a gentlemanly person, but not a Gypsy. A *Bauor* is just a person, a fellow.

RAINBOW A Gypsy superstition. English Gypsies believe that if, on seeing a rainbow, you cross two sticks, the colors of the rainbow will fade away. Many such traditional beliefs occur in Gypsy folktales.

RAIN DANCES In Eastern Europe the Gypsies perform dances to induce rain, as is the custom with many primitive tribes.

RAINMAKERS In Bulgaria Gypsy women who perform the dance called *paparuda* are sprinkled with water. This practice is an old form of sympathetic magic to induce rain.

RAKLO   A Gypsy term that denotes a boy who is a non-Gypsy. An adult non-Gypsy is termed a *busnó* or a *gorgio*. In a general sense, to the Gypsies, the non-Gypsies are the Gentiles.

RAMA   Alexander Paspati, a noted Greek gypsiologist, associated the term Rom, the original Gypsy designation, with the Sanskrit Rama, the incarnation of the god Vishnu.

RANJICIC, GIMA   A Serbian Gypsy who died in 1891. She was noted for her poetic talent, and left some 250 Gypsy poems. Her work has been translated into German. Many Gypsies have distinguished themselves in various fields, as editors, lawyers, musicians, dancers.

RASVAN   This name refers to a prince of Moldavia who was a Gypsy. In the course of their history the Gypsies often gave themselves honorific titles: as The Duke of Little Egypt, or Count, or King.

REAL GYPSYLAND   Hungary has been called so by many gorgios, non-Gypsies, who have seen the Romanychals in situ. There:

> Free is the bird of the air,
> And the fish were the river flows;
> Free is the deer in the forest,
> And the Gypsy wherever he goes.
>   Hurrah!
> And the Gypsy wherever he goes.

REALISM   In *The Gypsies in Spain,* George Borrow the gypsiologist declared that he had depicted the Gypsies as he found them, neither aggravating their crimes nor gilding them with imaginary virtues.

REASON FOR ILLITERACY A Gypsy legend relates that the Gypsies' ancestors, the Pharavono, were drowned in the sea. The disaster deprived the Gypsy people of homeland, religion, and the power of expression through the written word.

REASON FOR MIGRATION One gypsiologist suggested that the primary reason for the migration of the Gypsy people from India westward, was their desire to participate in the wealth and abundance of the European El Dorado. But their advance was not instantaneous. It was pondered for generations. Spies and advance groups were sent ahead to reconnoitre the prospects. When the Gypsies did begin their Westward march they came in small groups, to avoid investigation and surmise and suspicion. When a location had been determined, the small companies merged into larger tribal units, under their own leaders. Despite their numbers, there was a decided unity among them, in motive, in language, in traditional customs.

RECKONING In whatever country they are, Gypsies count in Greek numbers.
This is an indication of their long sojourn in Greek-speaking countries. As they passed through other countries, both in Asia and Europe, they absorbed many elements of the native language.

RECOLLECTIONS Sir Walter Scott, whose novel *Guy Mannering* presents Meg Merrilies the Gypsy, wrote:

> I remember to have seen one of her grand-daughters; that is, as Dr. Johnson had a shadowy recollection of Queen Anne — a stately lady in black, adorned with diamonds. So my memory is haunted by a solemn remembrance of a woman, of more than female height,

dressed in a long, red cloak, who commenced acquaintance by giving me an apple, but whom, nevertheless, I looked on with as much awe as the future doctor could look upon the Queen.

RECORDS Extant records testify that early in the sixteenth century there were Gypsy settlements in Poland, Russia, and Sweden.
They had already appeared in many other countries of Europe.

RECURRENT THEME In the sixteenth and seventeenth centuries, etchings and landscapes and tapestries depict the Gypsy theme under various aspects. Representations of camp life, with Gypsies feasting on game and rabbits and chickens, of Gypsy women telling fortunes, of Gypsies in their peculiar distinctive dress, appear in Hieronymus Bosch, in Garofalo, in Caravaggio's *The Gypsy Fortune-teller,* in Lucas Leyden.

RED DRESS GYPSIES This was a Gypsy organization founded by a Gypsy named Steve Kaslov in New York. It had however no appreciable duration.

REDEMPTION OF GYPSIES The Rev. James Crabb in 1827 formed a Committee to aid the English Gypsies who were encamped in his vicinity. Some became sedentary and secured regular employment. Their children were placed in elementary schools. Their manners and habits improved. When a horse, for instance, strayed from a field, a Gypsy woman retrieved it but refused any reward. Another Gypsy gave up the practice of begging. Some who were widows were taught suitable work, such as making shoes. Occasionally a Gypsy would disappear, disdainful of the well-meant efforts to redeem her. A young Gypsy, apprenticed to a coach-maker, gave up his employment and wandered off with his father. Among the reclaimed Gypsies who came under the aegies and guidance of the reformers were fiddlers and fortune-tellers. They were taught to read, encouraged in regular domestic habits and given training to make them self-dependent.

RED HAIR   Among the Gypsies a child born with red hair is assured of good fortune. Red hair is called balá kameskro, sun-hairs.

RED STRING   It's lucky to pick up a red string in the morning, said Old Liz de Gypsy, yes, or at any time. But it's sure love from a girl if you do, — specially silk. And if so be she gives you a red string or cord, or a strip of red stuff, that means she'll be bound to you and loves you.

REFUGEES   During World War II many Gypsies who escaped the holocaust of the Nazis succeeded in finding a new haven in the United States, England, South América, and the Near East.

REJECTED   In the sixteenth century the migratory Gypsies were banished politically and socially from one country in Europe to another. Furthermore, they were equally rejected by the Church, both Catholic and Protestant.

RELIGION   In Spain the Gypsies were styled atheists, heathens, idolaters, Moors. Quiñones, who wrote of them in the sixteenth century, says:

> They do not understand what kind of thing the church is, and never enter it but for the purpose of committing sacrilege. They do not know the prayers. For I ex-

amined them myself, males and females, and they knew them not, or if any, very imperfectly. They never partake of the Holy Sacraments, and though they marry relations they procure no dispensations. No one knows whether they are baptized. One of the five whom I caused to be hanged a few days ago was baptized in the prison, being at the time upward of thirty years of age. Don Martin Fajardo says that two Gitanos and a Gitana, whom he hanged in the village of Torre Perojil, were baptized at the foot of the gallows.

RELIGIOUS ADHERENCE In the Crimea and in Turkey there are Gypsies who are Moslems. In Finland are to be found Gypsies who are of the Protestant faith. In Bessarabia they are Greek Orthodox. In the USSR and in Italy the Sintés are Catholic. But essentially the Gypsy prefers to remain himself, without any specific religious association.

RELIGIOUS AND MORAL HYPOCRISY The Gitanos affect, externally, a great attachment to the Catholic religion. And if one were to judge from the number of relics they carry about with them, one would believe them exceedingly devout. But all who have well observed them assure us they are as ignorant as hypocritical, and that they practice secretly a religion of their own. It is not rare to see their women, who have been lately brought to bed, have their children baptized several times, in different places, in order to obtain money from persons at their ease, whom they choose for godfathers. Everything announces among them that moral degradation which must necessarily attach to a miserable, insulated caste, as strangers to society, which only suffers it through an excess of contempt.

RELIGIOUS BELIEFS The Gypsies of Spain, the Gitanos, have at all times, since their first appearance in Spain, been notorious for their contempt of religious observances: yet there is no proof that they were subjected to persecution on that account. The men have been punished as robbers and murderers, with the gallows and the galleys: the women, as thieves and sorceresses, with imprisonment, flagellation, and sometimes death: but as a rabble, living without fear of God, and, by so doing, affording an evil example to the nation at large, few people gave themselves much trouble about them.

REMEDIAL MEASURES In cases of sickness, the Gypsies use ingredients that are remarkably identical with those used by the ancients in magic and apotropaic concoctions. Such ingredients include excrementitious matter, the flesh of snakes, beetles, bear grease, menstrual blood, brains of birds.

REMENYI, EDE Famous Gypsy violinist of Hungary, who belongs in the nineteenth century. He appeared professionally in the United States and in European countries, and was official violinist to Queen Victoria. In the Hungarian War of Liberation in 1848 Reményi played the troops into battle with the exultant and stirring notes of his violin.

RENAISSANCE IMAGE OF THE GYPSIES Literary Europe, in the period of the Renaissance, was deeply interested in the phenomenon of a strange people who had evidently migrated from somewhere in the East and had come to settle in the European continent. The Gypsies presented a unique appearance in their picturesque costumes. They had new excitements to offer, particularly the techniques of predictions through the hand,

The Romanies doubtless came from India at various times, and from slightly different tribes; but the typical gypsy is Hindu in appearance as well as in language

Gypsy ornaments like those of Hindu nomads

from the facial configuration. They had their own idiosyncratic ways. And they spoke a strange language, evidently
compounded of many elements drawn from other tongues.
Hence they became the subject of the literate circles,
matter for description, for speculation, for description.
Pierre de Ronsard (1524-1585), the French poet, chanted
their divinatory abilities. Clément Marot, another French
poet of the same period, followed along similar lines.
A Gascon poet made the Gypsies the theme of his verse.
The Gypsies had come into their own. They were a
novelty. They were news. Montaigne, the French essayist,
wrote of them, while Rabelais the satirist wondered about
the Egyptian origin of the Gypsies. For then Egypt was
assumed to be the definitive home of those exotic nomads.
Italy was not far behind. There was a body of songs
called *Zingaresche,* on the Zingari, the Gypsies. A *Comedy of an Ugly Man and a fortune-telling Gypsy* was
written by Mateo Maria Bojardo, Count of Scandiano.
Another comedy, *La zingara,* was published by Gian-
carli in Mantua, in 1545.

In Ragusa, a Serbian poem by Cubranovic, entitled
Jegjupka, contained a scene in which an Egyptian fortune-teller appears.

More academic was the poem in Latin hexameters en-
titled Ruinae Pannonicae, published in 1571. The author,
Christian Chessaeus, took as his theme the Gypsies of
Rumania.

REPUTATION In the fifteenth century, when the Gypsies
first appeared in Europe, newcomers brought with them
a sense of mystery, coming as they reputedly did from
Egypt, or from India. And the East was a land of magic
and sorcery and the occult arts. Hence the advancing
Gypsies, reputed to be Eastern sorcerers and wizards
and spell-binders, were for a long time regarded as Sa-

379

tanic associates and were consequently an object of dread and compulsive respect.

RESTRICTIVE LAWS For some three centuries every ruler of Spain, on his accession to the throne, seems to have considered that one of his most immediate and most urgent duties was to suppress the enormities perpetrated by the Spanish Gitanos. But despite these repressions, the Gypsies continued to live in Spain, and still do so. They were supported in their resistance by many persons in important positions, including some who belonged to the nobility. To these Spaniards the Gypsies were known as Chalanes.

The first law promulgated against the Gypsies was that of Ferdinand and Isabella, in 1499. In 1539 Don Carlos confirmed the first edict. In 1586, in Madrid, Philip I added another decree requiring any Gypsy merchant to have a notary's permission to trade and also to have a fixed place of residence. At Belem, in Portugal, in 1619, Philip III ordered all Gypsies to leave the country within six months and not to return under penalty of death.

In 1633 Philip IV decreed severe penalties against the Gypties, enjoining them to become active members in the social frame and forbidding them to use the name of Gitanos. In 1695 the same ruler issued a new law, harsher than before, in terms of the persecution and punishment of the Gypsies. This law consisted of twenty-nine articles of the utmost severity. In 1726 Philip V banished all Gypsy women from Madrid and forbade Gypsies to leave their places of domicile, except in urgent cases.

That same year Philip V issued another law, requiring the Gitanos to be hunted down by fire and sword.

Further laws, directed against the Gypsies, were issued periodically, until the year 1780.

RETURN OF THE DEAD It is a common belief among the Gypsies that the spirit of a deceased person may return among the living, possibly to seek atonement for some evil act during life.

RHAGARIN The Rhagarin are Egyptian Gypsies. They are thus described by Charles Leland the gypsiologist who saw them in Cairo in the 1880's:

> They all resembled the one whom I had seen, and all were sellers of small articles and fortune-tellers. They all differed slightly from common Egyptians in appearance, and were more unlike them in not being importunate for money, nor disagreeable in their manners. But though they were as certainly Gypsies as old Charlotte Cooper herself, none of them could speak Romany.

RICHEPIN, JEAN (1839-1930) French novelist who was born in Algeria. Among his other works, he produced dramas and poems and *Les Chemineux,* the tramps who wandered over France. He is also the author of *Miarka, the Girl with the Bear,* a novel set against a Gypsy background.

RIDDLES Popular Gypsy riddles include the following:
Q. What is it God does not see?
A. Another like himself.
Q. Black as coal yet not coal: white as snow and yet not snow: it leaps here and there like a little foal.
A. A magpie.
Q. A little box, one can open it: a field full of men cannot shut it.

A. A nut.

Q. What grows head down and feet up?

A. An onion.

Q. What goes over the water and under the water, and over the wood and under the wood?

A. A young woman, crossing a wooden bridge, carrying a wooden pail of water on her head.

Q. How is it a man with one eye can see more than a man with two?

A. The man with one eye sees both the eyes of the other man.

Q. What is every living creature doing at the same time?

A. Growing older.

Q. Who thrusts his way into the queen's chamber and asks leave of none?

A. The Sun.

Q. What goes up white and comes down yellow?

A. An egg.

Q. Grows in a garden and never grows green.

A. A mushroow.

Q. Four white ladies run after each other but never catch each other.

A. A windmill.

It will be noted that most of these riddles deal with items of open-air life, what the objects most familiar to non-city dwellers.

RIMBAUD, ARTHUR (1854-1891) French poet and adventurer. Himself a restless nomadic character, he had exotic leanings that urged him to roam endlessly:

I shall rove with Love as my Guide,
As Gypsies wander, where they do not know.

ROBBER BANDS Early in the nineteenth century Gypsy robber bands terrorized and harassed the French-Spanish frontier. The year 1829 saw the end of these marauders.

ROBBER LANGUAGE The Gypsies who have to sustain themselves largely by breaches of the law and furtive operations, have devised particular jargons and dialects that are secretive by their very nature. Such dialects are unintelligible to those outside the Gypsy circle.
The name of the jargon varies. In Spain it is known as Germania. In France it is called argot. The Germans now it as Rothwelsch. In Italy, it becomes Gergo. In England, it is termed cant, thieves' Latin. These jargons have erroneously been confounded with the basic Gypsy language.

ROBBERS A Gypsy episode:
Los Chores

On grejelo chiro begoreó yesque berbanilla de chores á la burda de yes mostipelo a oleba rachi — Andial sos la prejenáron los cambrais presimeláron a cobadrar; sar andoba linaste changanó or lanbró, se sustiñó de la charipé de lapa, utiló la pusca, y niquilló platanando per or platesqueró de or mostipelo á la burda aos socabelába pandí, y per or jobi de la clichi chibeló or jundró de la pusca, le diñó perquibo á or languté. y le sumuqueló yes bruchasnó on la tesquéra á or Jojerían de los ostilaóres y lo techescó de or gráte á ostelé. Andial sos los debus quimbilos dicobeláron á desquero Jojerían on chen sar las canrriáles de la Beriben, lo chibeláron espusifias a los grastes, y niquilláron chapescando, trutando la romuy apála, per bausalé de las machas ó almedálles de liripió.

The Robbers

On a certain time arrived a band of thieves at the gate of a farmhouse at midnight. So soon as the dogs heard

383

them they began to bark, which caused the laborer to awake, he raised himself from his bed with a start, took his musket, and went running to the courtyard of the farmhouse to the gate, which was shut, placed the barrel of his musket to the keyhole, gave his finger its desire, and sent a bullet into the forehead of the captain of the robbers, casting him down from his horse. Soon as the other fellows saw their captain on the ground in the agonies of death, they clapped spurs to their horses, and galloped off fleeing, turning their faces back on account of the flies or almonds of lead.

ROM The Gypsies call themselves *Rom.* This term also denotes a man, a husband. A wife is called *romni.* Romanichal is a term used by the Gypsies to signify a *son of Rom.*

ROMAN CUSTOM In Roman antiquity, an adulterer had his nose cut off, and the epigrammatist Martial refers to this fact frequently as a mark of the degeneracy of his time. Similarly, the Gypsies perform the same mutilation in the case of a Gypsy woman taken in adultery.

ROMANES This is a variant Gypsy term for *Romany,* the language of the Gypsies. There is a basic Romany language, but the different dialects, with their absorption of the forms and vocabularies of the countries where the Gypsies settled, sometimes present to the non-Gypsy, the *busno* or *gorgio,* almost distinctive languages of their own. Among the purer dialects are those of Russia, Wallachia, and Transylvania. They are so alike that a person who speaks one of them can make himself very well understood by those who speak any of the rest.

The derivation of the term Romanes may come from the Hindu word *Ram* or *Rama,* which signifies a husband. Or from the town of *Rome,* which took its name from the Hindu *Ram*. Or from the Gallic word *Rom,* which is nearly tantamount to husband or man.

These are the suggested derivations offered by the gypsiologist George Borrow.

ROMANTIC   The Gypsies have been designated by many variant names, in an ethnic sense. Socially, wherever they have installed themselves, they have been branded with terms of contempt or hostility. But on occasion they have been regarded in a less repellent light: rather in a romantic, poetic context. Hence they have been called The Children of the Wind.

ROMANTIC GYPSY   In *Götz von Berlichingen,* the first tragic drama by the German dramatist and poet Goethe (1740-1832), there appears, on the stage a Gypsy encampment in a forest. It is a romantic picture, in line with the general view regarding the phenomenon of the Gypsies.

ROMANY CHIEFS   A Gypsy expression meaning Daughter of Rome. The English Gypsy women call themselves thus. The men are *Romany Chals,* Sons of Rome.

ROMANY KRALLIS   It would appear that the Gypsies were always divided into clans and tribes, each bearing a particular name and to which a particular district more especially they would exchange districts for a period and, incited by their characteristic love of wandering, would travel for a while. Of these families or groups each had a sher-engro, or head man. But that they were ever united under one Romany Krallis or Gypsy King, as some people have insisted, there is not the slightest ground for supposing.

ROMANY MORICLO   This expression signifies a Gypsy cake

baked by girls to arouse the erotic impulses of their lovers.

ROMANY OATH   A traditional oath among the Gypsies is: Ap i mulende! — By the dead! Traditionally, the Gypsies believe that there are evil spirits of the dead who have influence over the living.

ROMANY PECULIARITIES   The English Gypsy tongue is less deficient than several of the continental Gypsy dialects. It preserves far more of original Gypsy peculiarities than the French, Italian, and Spanish dialects, and its words retain more of the original Gypsy form than the words of those three. Moreover, however scanty it may be, it is far more copious than the French or the Italian Gypsy, though it is inferior in copiousness to the Spanish Gypsy. The Spanish Gypsy dialect is probably the richest in words of all the Gypsy dialects in the world, having names for very many of the various beasts, birds, and creeping things, for most of the plants and fruits, for all the days of the week and all the months of the year: whereas most other Gypsy dialects, amongst them the English, have names for only a few common animals and insects, for a few common fruits and natural productions, none for the months, and a name for only one day, Sunday, *Curkey,* which is a modification of the modern Greek *kuplakn.*

ROMANY RYE   To Gypsies he is a non-Gypsy who has intimate knowledge of Gypsy ways, language, and traditions, and is welcomed among them. The term Rye itself denotes a "gentleman" or "lord."
The Romany Rye is a novel that is virtually a sequel to George Borrow's *Lavengro.* Published in 1857, it was

described by a London reviewer as "a strange cross between a novel and an autobiography."

ROMANY TRICKS The Gypsies are adept at cheating the gorgios or non-Gypsies, particularly in buying and selling horses.
They are also known for practicing the *Hokkano Baro,* the Big Trick, which involves a kind of alleged treasure hunt.

ROMANY WIDELY SPOKEN James Crabb, the nineteenth century gypsiologist who worked among the Gypsies relates an anecdote that shows the widespread nature of the Romany tongue:

> One of our reformed Gypsies, while in the army, was with his regiment at Portsmouth. Being on garrison duty with an invalid soldier, he was surprised to hear some words of the Gypsy language, unintentionally uttered by him, who was a German. On inquiring how he understood this language, the German replied that he was of Gypsy origin, and that it was spoken by this race in every part of his native land, for purposes of secrecy.

ROM BARO A Gypsy expression that means The Big Man, the head of a *kumpania.*
A kumpania itself is a group consisting of several family units, independent of other units of the same type.

ROMMERRIN This Gypsy term denotes a Romany wedding. In contemporary times many traditional customs associated with Gypsy weddings have lapsed. But the yellow furze is still nailed over the caravan where the bridal couple stands. There is a comparatively elaborate ceremony, with introductory speeches followed by a feast.

387

ROMNI NASLĪ A Gypsy term meaning a runaway wife. Such a situation is not uncommon in a Gypsy tribe, and of course a runaway husband is equally possible. Reconciliation or judgment is determined usually within the tribal group, without recourse to a civil court.

ROSSETTI, DANTE GABRIEL (1828-1882) English artist. He depicted the Gypsy type of dancing girl in many of his paintings.

ROUMANI In Wallachia and Moldavia, two of the easternmost regions of Europe, are to be found seven millions of people calling themselves Roumani, and speaking a dialect of the Latin tongue much corrupted by barbarous terms, so called. They are supposed to be in part descendants of Roman soldiers, Rome in the days of her grandeur having established immense military colonies in these parts. In the midst of these people exist vast numbers of Gypsies, amounting to at least two hundred thousand. The land of the Roumani, indeed, seems to have been the hive from which the West of Europe derived the Gypsy part of its population. That is not to say that the Gypsies sprang originally from Roumaniland. It was merely their grand resting-place after crossing the Danube. They entered Roumani-land from Bulgaria, crossing the great river, and from thence some went to the north-east, overrunning Russia; others to the West of Europe, as far as Spain and England. That the early Gypsies of the West, and also those of Russia, came from Roumany-land is easily proved, as in all the western Gypsy dialects, and also in the Russian, are to be found words belonging to the Roumani speech.

ROYAL ASIATIC SOCIETY Colonel Herriot, of the Indian Army, read a paper last century, before the Royal Asiatic

Society in London. Giving an account of the Zingari of India, he added that the class of people he described were frequently met with in that part of India which was watered by the Ganges, as well as the Malwa, Gujurat, and the Deccan. These people were called Nath or Benia. Nath signifies a rogue, and Benia a dancer or acrobat. The speaker cited various authorities in demonstration of the resemblance between the Gypsies and their neglected brethren in Europe.

ROYAL DENUNCIATIONS   In the period of Henry the Eighth, Mary, and Elizabeth, the Gypsy issue in England had reached such a climax that the Gypsies were officially denounced in royal statutes.

RUDDIMAN, THOMAS (1674-1757) Latin grammarian. While on his way from his home in Banffshire, Scotland, to Aberdeen University, at the age of sixteen, he was 'plundered and stripped at a place called Starbrigs by a band of Gypsies.'

RUMANIAN CUSTOM   The Rumanian Gypsies show their grief at a funeral by lamentations, but also by singing, dancing, violin playing. The Gypsies also make holes in the coffins and to let the dead hear the litanies and the expressions of grief.

RUMANIAN GYPSIES   In Wallachian and Moldavian records dating from the ninth to the twelfth centuries, allusion is made to the Gypsies who pitched their tents in Rumania.

RUSKIN, JOHN (1819-1900)   English writer on art. Author period. when events were not so accurately recorded as of a eulogistic poem on the Gypsies, all the more remarkable on account of the contemporary contempt for the

Gypsies as whole. A great humanist himself, he said that the Gypsies were 'the honestest, harmlessest of the human race.'

RUSSIA Gypsies were known in Russia since the sixteenth century. They were permitted to live there without molestation. Their encampments were to be found as far South as the Ukraine and the banks of the Black Sea.

RUSSIAN DIALECT In the language of the Russian Gypsies there are Rumanian and Greek elements, along with Polish, Serbian, and German. These linguistic borrowings indicate the countries where the Gypsies have remained for any length of time.

RUSSIAN FOLKLORE Gypsies have been wandering and temporarily settling throughout Russia for years without end. Hence Russian folklore is filled with Gypsy tales and chants and traditions. The Gypsies have sung and danced and traded at the important fairs, in Nizhni-Novgorod, in Moscow, and elsewhere throughout the country.

RUSSIAN GYPSIES In the eighteenth century a certain Captain Sergei Plesheef, in a survey of the Russian Empire, commented on the Russian Gypsies:

> About the Don, as well as in almost every part of Russia, from time to time are found gipsies, a race well known every where by their cheating and pilfering. They have no fixed residence, but wander continually from one place to another, and exercise the trades of blacksmiths and farriers and horse-dealers, which last they generally do by exchanging instead of selling their horses. In order to collect the poll-tax with

more certainty, the greatest part of them are put under the inspection of different masters, of whom they are obliged to take their passports before they can go upon their peregrinations.

S

SABBAT   As a result of their seclusive and picaresque ways and their custom of living on the fringe of villages, in waste areas or woods, the medieval Gypsies were regarded as warlocks and witches in league with diabolic powers. The Gypsy women, as the populace readily assumed were members of covens that assembled in remote regions, on hillsides, or in groves. The convention invariably took place at night, usually on a Good Friday, or on any night ordained by Satan, the Master, the monstrous goat-shaped figure. Usually, however, unions were held on May Eve, in Midsummer, and on Hallowmass.

Some of the witches were said to set out on foot with their children. They were carried home by the Demon himself. Sinister and obscene rites were performed, and the entire atmosphere was marked by orgiastic frenzies. Upon the crowing of the cock everything was said to vanish, as light was regarded as inimical to the occult arts.

Goya, the eighteenth century Spanish artist, had a profound interest in these furtive byways.

When arrested, the Gypsies were subjected to a harsh interrogation. Almost invariably they were convicted of consorting with malefic agents and with practicing witchcraft. They were put to death by drowning or burning at the stake.

SACRAMENTAL BREAD Many Gypsies have a superstitious belief in the efficacy of the sacramental bread and wine. There are many instances of their stealing them for magical purposes.

SACRED DAY Among the Rumanian Gypsies, Friday was sacred to Paraschiva, that is, Venus. All infractions of this tradition were bound to be punished.
Many similar tabus affected the lives of the Gypsies: in their beliefs, their personal conduct, their relationships with tribal groups.

SAFEGUARDS Gypsies are prone to treasure amulets of all kinds and charms for protective purposes. Knives and sea-shells were regarded as potent periapts in assuring good luck. A mole's foot, too, was a safeguard against rheumatism. A hand-shaped ornament was regarded as a token of a good future. A bone from the side of a sheep's skull was also considered efficacious as a charm.

SAGAS Among the Gypsies there is a traditional, orally trans-mitted corpus of folklore and mythology, but there is no body of historical or legendary sagas: no remem-brance in the Gypsy consciousness of national figures, of heroic personalities: no dominant racial or communal or tribal episodes that form an integrated element in their ethnic mind. In so far as they have a personal social or political history, it is largely the history of the country of the sojourn, whenever that country impinges on their existence, with respect to tolerance and human rights and persecution and banishment.
Yet to some extent the Gypsies have absorbed or adapted or modified tales about their own origin that had been suggested or devised by the peoples they encountered in their wanderings. Thus they were identified at times with

Ezekiel's Biblical prophecy: I will scatter the Egyptians among the nations. In the Middle Ages the Gypsies appeared in Europe as Christians, repentant pilgrims. They took on, as it were, the views of their environment, the ideas of their milieu, and they readily accepted the varying and sometimes contradictory or fantastic opinions of their willing or unwilling hosts.

SAINT CYPRIAN   He is the patron saint of Gypsies. The legend ran that he became the King of Sorcerers with diabolic aid. He was the reputed author of *The Treasure of the Wizard,* from which the Gypsy fortune-tellers derived their knowledge.

SALMON   In Sir Walter Scott's novel *Guy Mannering,* Salmon was the inviolate oath of the Scottish Gypsies. If the word was pronounced like the fish, as it most probably was, it would closely resemble the term *serment,* the French word for oath. *Serment* itself stems from the Latin *sacramentum,* an oath.

The English Gypsies used the word sacrament to denote an oath: for instance, he took the sacrament to tell the truth. This quotation comes from F. H. Groome the gypsiologist.

SALVES   Among the Gypsies of Hungary many salves and unguents are concocted as remedies for various types of sickness. The ingredients of such concoctions are invariably of a revolting and scatalogical nature. They may include the fat of dogs, bears, wolves, frogs.

One recalls the witches' brew in *Macbeth,* or the sinister and obscene operations of the witches as described by the Roman poet Horace.

SANSKRIT   As linguistic evidence of the first home of the

Gypsies in India, it is estimated that in Caló, the common tongue used by the Gypsies from Spain to Rumania, about a third of the words have Sanskrit roots.

SARA Sara-Kali, Black Sara, the Black Virgin, is the patron saint of the Gypsies. With her worship are associated a vigil, certain ritualistic acts, and an annual procession to Saintes-Maries de la Mer, and participation in a rain-inducing ceremonial.

The fuller legend runs as follows: Marie-Jacobé, sister of the Virgin Mary, and Marie Salomé, the mother of James and John, together with Lazarus and his sisters Martha and Mary Magdalene, had been cast adrift from the Holy Land in a boat without sails or provisions. They had somehow survived and finally landed on the desolate coast of the Camargue country, in Provence.

SARACEN In the Middle Ages, throughout Europe, Gypsies, regarded as migrants from the East, were termed Saracens, in contrast with those who professed the orthodox Christian faith.

SARACENER Some Gypsiologists, in their conjectures relating to the original home of the Gypsies, conceived that their appellation of Zigeuner should really be Zigarener, a corruption of the term Saracener, or Saracens.

SARACENS IN PROVENCE The Saracens, as the Gypsies were called, appeared in Provence in 1410. They encamped outside the town of Sisteron and were welcomed with food and drink by the civic authorities.

SARA LA BOHEMIENNE This French phrase, used by the Gypsies of Provence, applies to Sara, the servant who traditionally accompanied Les Saintes Maries de la Mer

— Sainte Jacobé and Sainte Salomé — when they were all providentially cast ashore on the coast of the Camargue, in Provence. On May 24 the Gypsies go to the crypt in her shrine to pray. The Gypsy women consider that this act will assure good luck.

SARTORIAL ANECDOTE The time, the nineteenth century, in England: The Gypsy male is no less addicted to gay clothing than the female. A Gypsy orphan, ten years of age, was taken and fed and clothed. Although every care was taken of him, he would not remain with his friends. Instead, he returned to the camp from which he had have top boots. When he was asked how he would get them, he replied: by catching rats.

SCANDINAVIA It is believed that the Gypsies of Scandinavia are a branch of Russian Gypsies who migrated Westward. As they moved out from India, their original home, they passed through Persia, then Turkey, then into Greece and the countries of Eastern Europe, then into Central Eubeen taken. He explained that he wanted to be a real Gypsy, and would wear silver buttons on his coat and rope, and finally West as far as Portugal.
Branches of the tribes went North, to Scandinavia, to Scotland.

SCANDINAVIAN EXPULSION The Gypsies, who were termed Tartars as they were presumed to have migrated from the East, were expelled from Sweden in 1512, and, some twenty years later, from Denmark. The chief accusation launched against them was their alleged paganism.

SCANDINAVIAN TREATMENT Although they were threatened with expulsion from Sweden in the eighteenth century, the Gypsies spread into the Scandinavian countries.

The climate of Finland, however, which they ultimately reached, was inimical to their accustomed mode of life. In Norway their unusual habits linked them with the Finns, who already had a sinister reputation.

SCARRON, PAUL (1610-1660) French poet, dramatist, and novelist. Author of a picaresque novel entitled *Roman Comique,* in which he repicts Gypsy ways and particularly a Gypsy feast.

SCHOOLS In contemporary times the Gypsies are usually required to have their children attend school. Sweden has established 'traveling schools'. Spain has created special schools for Gypsies. Britain too requires school attendance.

SCOTT, SIR WALTER The famous nineteenth century Scottish novelist and poet, in his *The Lay of the Last Minstrel,* describes his countryman, Michael Scot, as a magician whose occult writings were buried in Melrose Abbey, Scotland. He has also presented a vivid picture of the Gypsy Meg Merrilies. In *Quentin Durward,* too, there is a dramatic Gypsy episode.

SCOTTISH GYPSIES A letter of King James IV of Scotland, addressed to the King of Denmark refers to Gypsies who appeared in Scotland as early as 1506. The letter recommends a certain Anthonius Gawino, Earl of Little Egypt, a Gypsy chief. But there is a tradition that a company of Gypsies or Saracens were committing depredations in Scotland in the first decades of the fifteenth century. The chronicler adds that, as he was unaware of Saracens ever having set foot in Scotland, England, or Ireland, he is convinced that the newcomers were Gypsies.

SCOTTISH GYPSY DANCE The Gypsies of Lochgellie had a dance peculiar to themselves, during the performance of which they sang a song, in the Gypsy language, which they called a "croon." A Gypsy however informed me that it was exactly like the one old Charles Stewart and the other Gypsies used to perform and which I will describe. At the wedding near Corstorphine, which Charles Stewart attended, there were five or six female Gypsies in his train. On such occasions he did not allow males to accompany him. At some distance from the people at the wedding, but within hearing of the music, the females formed themselves into a ring, with Charles in the centre. Here, in the midst of the circle, he danced and capered in the most antic and ludicrous manner, sweeping his cudgel around his body in all directions, and moving with much grace and agility. Sometimes he danced round the outside of the circle. The females danced and courtesied to him, as he faced about and bowed to them. When they happened to go wrong, he put them to rights by a movement of his cudgel. For it was by the cudgel that all the turns and figures of the dance were regulated. A twirl dismissed the females; a cut recalled them; a sweep made them squat on the ground. A twist again called them up, in an instant, to the dance. In short, Stewart distinctly spoke to his female dancers by means of his cudgel, commanding them to do whatever he pleased, without opening his mouth to one of them.

SCOTTISH GYPSY MARRIAGE In discussing the Gypsies of Scotland in the early nineteenth century, a gypsiologist relates:

> About one o'clock the oldest matron, accompanied by others advanced in years, conducts the bride into the bedroom. Tunc vetula, manu sua sponsae naturalibus admota, membranam, vulvae ori oppositam un-

guibus scindit et cruorem a plaga fusum linteolo excipit.

Then, as a mark of their respect for her remaining chaste till the hour of her marriage the bride receives a handsome present from friends.

SCOTTISH GYPSY NAMES In the early nineteenth century the Scottish Gypsies had assumed Scottish surnames. Among such characteristic names were: McDonald, Jameson, Young, Marshall, Stewart, Miller Smith, Ruthven, Fleckie, Fall, Bailie.

SCOTTISH LAIRD When the Scottish Parliament passed an Act in 1609 prohibiting the lairds or lords of the manor from entertaining the presence of the Gypsies, some lairds, who disregarded the Act, were subjected to a fine.

SCOTTISH SOCIETY Under the patronage of the Scottish Church, a society was formed in 1838 for the reformation of the Gypsies. Among the committee of management was a minister who said that he himself was a Gypsy.

SCRIPTURAL NAMES Some eighty per cent of the Gypsies have Biblical names. It is astonishing when it is considered that the Gypsies, as a people, do not have a Bible, and that they are largely illiterate. It has been suggested that the names were transmitted by some persistent though undefined tradition.

SCUDERY, GEORGES DE (1601-1667) French writer, dramatist, poet. In a sonnet entitled La Belle Egypticnnc hc eulogizes a Gypsy girl as a sultry goddess, the sorceress who foretells the future.

SEASONAL WORK   In the winter, the English Gypsies settle down temporarily in some town or village and occupy themselves with repairing cars, making baskets, mending pots and pans and such small jobs. But when the winter is over, they get ready to move on. Throughout the summer and autumn they help at the harvests, or gathering fruit and berries, or hop picking, according to the requirements of the local farmers. Thus they move around the country, from Hampshire to Kent. They still retain their caravans and work together as a family or tribal unit.

SECRECY   One of the reasons why the Gypsies are more or less unwilling to reveal themselves completely to the gorgios, the non-Gypsies, is their sense of the sanctity of their ways. Like the ancient Egyptians, the Gypsies are reluctant to disclose personal names, ceremonials and traditions to the busné, the Gentiles. They are a close people, and they prefer to keep their ethnic ways to themselves. That is why it is invariably the non-Gypsy who interprets the Rom to the Gypsies themselves.

SECRET LANGUAGE   The Gypsies have invariably been reluctant to communicate their language or dialect to gorgios or busné, that is, to non-Gypsies. In this respect Heinrich Grellmann the gypsiologist wrote:
> It will be recollected, from the first, how great a secret the make of their language, and how suspicious they appear when any person wishes to learn a few words of it. Even if the Gypsy is not perverse, he is very inattentive, and is consequently likely to answer some other rather than the true Gypsy word.

SEDENTARY GYPSIES   Although the Gypsies are essentially nomadic, they settle, for a tmie, in villages in Central

Europe. But their stay is never permanent, and periodically they set off into the open.

SEMNO A Gypsy term signifying The Sign of the Gypsies. This consists of a cross, a star, an axe, the sun and the moon.

SENSE OF HOSPITALITY The Gypsies have a traditional sense of hospitality. Any Gypsy is welcomed at the domestic board, whatever it may be, of any other Gypsy. The *busnó* or *gorgio*, the non-Gypsy is equally invited without restraint.

SERBIA In the late nineteenth century the laws of Serbia prohibited tribal groups to wander through the country. Hence many Gypsies migrated to the United States of America.

SERBIAN ARMY Serbian Gypsies have appeared in Eng-with the Serbian forces, singing eulogies of ancient Serbian warriors.
In various European campaigns the Gypsies have served with the German, Spanish, French, Austrian and English forces.

SERBIAN GYPSIES Serbian Gypsies have appeared in England. The children, who speak very little English, use Hungarian and Romany.

SERFDOM In Rumania, the Gypsies were under feudal serfdom from 1370 until 1856.
In the Balkans in general they were for centuries in this condition, subject to the *boyars*, the over-lords.
When Wallachia in the Balkans became a tributary to the Turks, the Gypsies who had migrated into Wallachia

moved into Hungary and Transylvania. The Gypsies who remained in Wallachia were not released from serfdom until 1856.

SERFS OF THE KING In the fifteenth century the Gypsies who had settled in Transylvania and Hungary came under royal protection as 'serfs of the king.' They were allowed to encamp on private property with the king's consent. As skilled workers in metal they were enlisted as armorers and munition makers.

SETTLED GYPSIES Many Gypsies in Europe were, a century ago, settled in regular dwellings, according to their personal circumstances. In Spain, some Gypsies maintained inns. In Transylvania and Hungary there were Gypsies who pursued a regular trade or business. They lived in huts near Hermanstadt, Cronstadt, Karchau, Debrezin, and other places.

SETTLEMENTS In the nineteenth century Bishop John Ham opened a school for Gypsies at Szatmar. Ferdinand Farkas, a priest, followed his example in Neuhausel. Both attempts were abortive.

SETTLING GRUDGES The Gypsies often fought with each other at fairs and other places where they met in great numbers. This was their way of settling old grudges. But as soon as one Gypsy yielded, the quarrel was made up, and they repaired to a public house to renew their friendship. This forgiving spirit was a pleasing trait in their character.

A certain Gypsy fought three times in one day with his brother-in-law, not in anger, but to try their pugilistic skill. At last he said: Brother, you have beaten me.

SEVEN LANGUAGES When Gypsies praise the proficiency of a person in own tongue, customarily add: He understands the seven languages. A gorgio or non-Gypsy who interests himself in Gypsy life and can speak Romany is called a Romany Rye, a Romany gentleman.

SEVENTH DAUGHTER In Gypsy tradition a seventh daughter is credited with second sight and is believed capable of seeing hidden treasure and spirits. In 1883 the chief of a Kukaya Gypsy tribe, named Danku Niculai, offered a Gypsy woman, Pale Boshe, one hundred ducats if she would persuade her seventh daughter to marry him.

SHAKESPEARE AND THE ROMANY In the fifth scene of the second act of *As You Like It* occur some expressions which have never been satisfactorily explained by any commentator. Solutions have indeed put forward in plenty, some of which seem to have been thought convincing by their authors alone; and not one has found universal acceptance among Shakesperean students. It is therefore with some deffidence that I venture — where so many have failed — to proffer yet another clue to these mysteries.

For the sake of clearness, it will be convenient to quote that portion of the scene in which the *cruces* occur. After hearing the song *Under the Greenwood Tree, Jaques* says —

>— I'll give you a verse to this note that I made yesterday in despite of my invention.
>*Amiens* — And I'll sing it.
>*Jaques* — Thus it goes —
>
>>If it do come to pass
>>That any man turn ass,
>>Leaving his wealth and ease,

> A stubborn will to please,
>
> Ducdàme, ducdàme, ducdàme:
>
>> Here shall he see
>> Gross fools as he,
>> An if he will come to me.

Amiens — What's that "ducdame"?
Jaques — 'Tis a Greek invocation, to call fools into a circle. I'll go sleep if I can; if I cannot, I'll rail against all the firstborn of Egypt.

The difficulties here are (1) the word *ducdame;* (2) *Jaques' explanation* thereof; and (3) his remark about the first-born of Egypt. The editor of the "Variorum" Shakespeare, after quoting the commentators who have proved to their own satisfaction that *ducdame* is either Latin, Italian, French, Gaelic, or Welsh, and one who says that it represents the twang of a guitar, cites with approval the verdict of Dr. Aldis Wright that it means nothing at all; is a mere "fol-de-riddle" (as it were) to to fill up space. Nobody has even tried to show why *Jaques* should suddenly make use of a Welsh or Gaelic word, or why he should call it Greek. His explanation only makes the puzzle more difficult. No one has explained what the "circle" into which fools are called may mean; and Dr. Johnson, who says that "the first-born of Egypt" is "a proverbial phrase for high-born persons," gives no example of a previous use of such a phrase, nor does he tell us why *Jaques,* at this particular point in the play, should express a wish to rail at those of high birth. It seems as though the most modern critics had made up their minds that an eccentric person like *Jaques* is capable of talking any kind of inconsequent rubbish, and that it is a waste of time to try and extract sense from it. But this is an unsatisfactory position to

404

assume, for *Jaques,* though a whimsical fellow, is made to talk nonsense in no other passage in the play.

I believe that *ducdame* is pretty good Romanes, and that all these locks open to one key. *Jaques,* in his remarks about a Greek invocation and the first-born of Egypt, is referring to the Gypsies. There were plenty of Gypsies in England at the end of the sixteenth century, and Shakspere must often have met with them. They were commonly called Egyptians. Now, what is more likely than that Shakspere in some country walk, or when travelling as a strolling player, should have come upon an encampment of these strange people: men, women, and children, sitting or sprawling round the cooking-pot, ready to predict the future of any foolish counrty-folk who could be enticed into their *circle?*

I do not maintain that Shakspere knew anything of the Romany tongue, but he might well pick up one word from the songs or pretended *invocations* which would go so far to impress the credulous with a belief in the "Egyptian's" occult power. A word so picked up and reproduced in a play some 300 years ago is not likely to correspond in appearance with the same word as known to modern experts in Romanes. But *ducdame* is very like *dukdom me* (I did harm), or *dukkerdom me* (I told fortunes, cast spells), or *dikdom me* (I saw). It resembles either of these words much more than the *duc ad me* of Hanmer, the *dusadam-me-me* of Phillipps, the *duthaich* of Dr. Mackay, or, indeed, the twanging of a guitar.

Dr. Mackay, however, although putting forward a Gaelic origin for the word, makes a shrewd guess when he says that by "Greek" *Jaques* means "Pedlar's Greek," the cant language of tramps and Gypsies. Why these people should talk Gaelic (unless in the form of Shelta) does not appear. But we know that the term "Greek" was applied to buffoons or persons of loose life, and has almost certainly been applied to Gypsies in England as well as on the continent of Europe. That *the first-born of Egypt* may signify the Gypsies will not be disputed: that *Greek* may mean the Romany tongue, and that *ducdame* may be a word or words in that language, will be admitted as possible. But to cause such meanings to appear *probable,* it must be shown that the use of a Romany expression, and references to Gypsies, come quite naturally from the mouth of *Jaques* at this particular point in the play. If I can show this, it will be admitted that the "Gypsy hypothesis" is at least worthy of consideration, it being most unlikely that all the evidence in its favour can be the result of chance.

Amiens' song was in praise of an outdoor, *Gypsy-like* life: —

'Who doth ambition shun
And loves to live i' the sun,
Seeking the food he eats
And pleased with what he gets."

Could there be a better summary of the Gypsy ideal? One is tempted to believe that Messrs. Crofton and and Smart were thinking of these lines when they wrote the Introduction to their *Dialect of the English Gypsies,* in Which the following passage occurs:—

"In these days of material progress and much false refinement, they present the singular spectacle of a race in our midst who regard philosophic indifference the much-prized comforts of modern civilization, and object to forego their simple life in close contact with Nature in order to engage in the struggle after wealth and personal aggrandisement."

The verse added by *Jaques* gives a cynic's view of the same life. He has been forced into it by circumstances, but he thinks that any one who takes to it by choice must be a fool: — the Gajo's criticism of the Rom. He has been put in mind of Gypsies by *Amiens'* song, but (characteristically, I think) does not trouble to reveal his train of thought to his companions. He, in character of the Gypsy in spite of himself, mystifies them with *duc-dàme*: his explanation of the word satisfies them without displaying his full meaning. He has railed at the "amateur Gypsy" in his satirical song: he will now try and sleep if sleep be possible on the kind of couch which this life in the woods offers to one used to the "comforts of modern civilization." If he cannot sleep, he will lie awake and rail at "all the first-born of Egypt" — at all those Gypsies who were born to the life and are ridiculous enough to like it.

According to the "Gypsy hypothesis," therefore, these obscurities are not so many isolated puzzles, but are all parts of a train of thought in the mind of *Jaques.* To accept this hypothesis as the true clue does not involve any absurdities or improbabilities. I leave it to the tender mercies of Shakspeare critics and Romany scholars. — *Charles Strachey*

SHAV   A Gypsy term that denotes a young unmarried Gypsy youth.
When a *shav* got married, he was a *Romoro,* a little *Rom,* that is, a little man.

SHEEP STEALING   In the eighteenth century in Scotland, sheep-stealing was a capital offense. A dramatic incident occurred in Berwickshire in this connection. A farmer, who had been missing sheep, lay in wait one night for the depredators. He caught Tam Gordon, captain of the Spittal Gypsies and Ananias Faa, his son-in-law, in the very act of stealing the sheep. Convicted, the two Gypsies were condemned to death. But, to the surprise of everyone, they were pardoned. It was generally understood that they were indebted to a lady bearing their own name, the Duchess of Gordon. The suspicion spread that the Duchess herself was of Gypsy blood: otherwise her interest in the Gypsies would not have been aroused.

SHELLS Among the Hungarian Gypsies the virtue or magical power of a sea-shell is regarded as a potent agent for luck. In Gypsy lore, voices are believed to issue from the large conch shells which are used as amulets.
Knives too are regarded as favorable amulets.

SHELTA This is the language used by itinerant Gypsy tinkers in Britain. Shelta reputedly stems from Celtic sources.
It was first discovered by Charles Godfrey Leland, the gypsiologist and anthropologist. He published an account of Shelta in 1882.
A brief vocabulary follows:

> scri — to write
> biyeg — to steal
> stall — to go, to travel
> durra — bread

SHERENGRO A Gypsy term denoting a leader of a tribe. A synonym for *voivode,* the common Central European expression to designate a tribal chief.

SHOE-STRING Gypsies in England regarded a shoe-string as a kind of amulet or protection. Other periapts and charms intended to bring luck or avert misfortune were sea-shells, knives, Maria Theresa silver dollars, a child's caul filled with garlic and four-leaved clover.

SIBERIA In the eighteenth century Polish Gypsies crossed. into Russian territory. They marched Eastward and ultimately reached Tobolsk, the Siberian capital.

SIGISMUND In the fourteenth century King Sigismund of Hungary allowed the Gypsies to select a magistrate from their own tribes.
He was on specially friendly terms with Ladislas, voivode or leader of the Gypsies.

SIGYNNES An Oriental people that inhabited Iran. Some gypsiologists have identified them with the Gypsies.
The Gypsies have also been identified with the Ethiopians, the natives of Bohemia, the Portuguese, even the lost continent of Atlantis.

SILVER BUTTONS The Gypsies like gold and silver ornaments, and have a particular fondness for silver buttons on their jackets. For a set of such adornments they would sometimes give as much as fifteen pounds. The women too spend a great deal on weighty gold rings for their fingers. In one case, three massive rings were soldered together, with a half sovereign on the top, which served in place of a stone.

SIMON SIMEONIS A Franciscan monk who mentions the appearance of the Gypsies in Crete for the year 1322.
It is claimed by gypsiologists that the Gypsies remained in Greece and absorbed many elements of the Greek language over a more prolonged period than in any other country of Europe.

SINGERS The Gypsies have been renowned as musicians and also as singers. In the Balkans they sang in inns and at local festivals. In Seville, when a café chantant was opened, most of the performers were Gypsies.

SINGING   When Charles Leland, the gypsiologist, visited Russia in the late 1880's, he heard the singing of the Russian Gypsies:

> the strangest, wildest, and sweetest singing I ever had heard — the singing of Lurleis, of sirens, of witches. First, one damsel, with an exquisitely clear, firm voice began to sing a verse of a love-ballad, and as it approached the chorus stole in, softly and unperceived, but with exquisite skill, until, in a few seconds, the summer breeze, murmuring melody over a rippling lake, seemed changed to a midnight tempest, roaring over a stormy sea, in which the *basso* of the black captain of the Gypsies pealed like thunder. Just as it died away a second girl took up the melody, very sweetly, but with a little more excitement, — it was like a gleam of moonlight on the still agitated waters, a strange contralto witch-gleam, and then again the chorus and the storm; and then another solo yet sweeter, sadder, and stranger, — the movement continually increasing, until all was fast, and wild and mad — a locomotive quickstep, and then a sudden silence — sunlight — the storm had blown away.

SINTES   An Oriental people whom some gypsiologists have identified as the Gypsies.
Most convincingly, they have been identified as the descendants of Hindus of Northwest India.

SISTERON   Early in the fifteenth century at the French town of Sisteron on the river Durance a party appeared calling themselves Saracens. They were received hospitably and permitted to encamp.
They were the first Gypsies in France.

SITTING POSTURE   Gypsies regularly take their meals while sitting on their heels. Turkish Gypsies likewise converse in this position. Among the peasantry of India it is also a common posture.

SKELTON, JOHN (c. 1460-1529)   English poet. The expression *Egyptians,* denoting the Gypsies, appears in his poem *The Tunning of Eleanor Rumming.* In the *Crown of Laurel,* published in 1526, the term Gypsy appears for the first time.

SKETCH OF BORROW   Charles Leland the gypsiologist knew George Borrow, author of *The Bible in Spain* and other noted works on gypsiology. Leland wrote thus:

> Apropos of Mr. George Borrow, I knew him, and a grand old fellow he was, — a fresh and hardy giant holding his six foot two or three inches as uprightly at eighty as he ever had at eighteen. I believe that was his age, but I may be wrong. Borrow was like one of the old Norse heroes, whom he so much admired, or an old-fashioned Gypsy bruiser, full of craft and merry tricks. One of these he played on me, and I bear him no malice for it. The manner of the joke was this: I had written a book on the English Gypsies and their language; but before I announced it, I wrote a letter to Father George, telling him that I proposed to print it, and asking his permission to dedicate it to him. He did not answer the letter, but 'worked the tip' promptly enough, for he immediately announced in the newspapers on the following Monday his 'Word-Book of the Romany Language,' 'with many pieces in Gypsy, illustrative of the way of speaking and thinking of the English Gypsies, with specimens of their poetry, and an account of various things relating to Gypsy life in England.' This was exactly what I had told him

that my book would contain; for I intended originally to publish a vocabulary. Father George covered the track by not answering my letter; but I subsequently ascertained that it had been faithfully delivered to him by a gentleman from whom I obtained the information.

I have since heard that a part of Mr. Borrow's 'Romano-Lavo-Lil' had been in manuscript for thirty years, and that it might never have been published but for my own work. I hope that this is true; for I am sincerely proud to think that I may have been in any way, directly or indirectly, the cause of his giving it to the world. I would gladly enough have burnt my own book, as I said, with a hearty laugh, when I saw the announcement of the 'Lavo-Lil', if it would have pleased the old Romany Rye, and I never spoke a truer word.

SLAVERY Although the Gypsies are characteristically a freedom-loving people, they have often been subjected to slavery. In the fourteenth century a Serbian prince presented a monastery in the Carpathian Mountains with Gypsy families as slaves. Even as late as the nineteenth century, in the Balkans, they still experienced serfdom under the lord of the manor.

In Spain, a similar situation prevailed in the sixteenth century. In Hugo de Celso's *Las Leyes de todos los Reynos de Castilla,* a kind of legal dictionary published in Vallalodid in 1531, references to the status of the Gypsies is made as follows:

Egyptians (that is, Gypsies) are not to move about these kingdoms and those that may be there are to leave them or take trades, or live with their overlord under penalty of one hundred lashes for the first time, and for the second time, that their ears be cut off, and that they be chained for sixty days, and for the third time that they remain captive for ever to those who take them. Decree of their Highnesses given in Madrid in the year 1499 and Law Number 104 in the Decrees. In Moldo — Wallachia — the Gypsies were forced into slavery in the seventeenth century.

SLAVERY IN RUMANIA Rumania was the last European country to liberate the Gypsies from slavery. Beginning with the year 1837, the Gypsies were emancipated by the Salem, then by the clergy under royal decree, and finally by the landowners, the 'lords of the manor.'

SLAVERY IN WALLACHIA An account was published, in 1839, relating in part to the Gypsies of Wallachia:

They are almost all slaves, bought and sold at pleasure. One was lately sold for 200 piastres, but the general price is 100. Perhaps three pounds sterling is average price, and the female Gypsies are sold much cheaper. The sale is generally carried on by private bargain. The men are the best mechanics in the country; so that smiths and masons are taken from this class. The women are considered the best cooks, and therefore almost every wealthy family has a Gypsy cook, Their appearance is similiar to that of the Gypsies in other countries; being all dark, with fine black eyes, and long black hair. They have a language peculiar to themselves, and though they seem to have no system of religion, yet are very superstitious in observing lucky and unlucky days. They are all fond of music, both vocal and instrumental, and excel in it. There is a class of them called the Turkish Gypsies, who have purchased their freedom from government; but these are few in number, and all from Turkey. Of these latter, there are twelve families in Galatz. The men are employed as horse-dealers, and the women in making bags, sacks, and such articles. In winter, they live in town, almost underground; but in summer they pitch their tents in the open air, for, though still within the bounds of the town, they would not live in their winter houses during summer.

SLAVIC ORIGIN According to some gypsiologists the Gypsies originated in Serbia. In one region in Spain the Gypsies are known as *Gitanos Serbos,* Serbian Gypsies.
Other gypsiologists claim that the original home of the Gypsies was Bohemia, or Portugal, or Persia, or Ethiopia.

SLAVIC WITCHES In Slavic Gypsy folklore witches assemble at intervals, always by full moonlight, at a crossroad. It is hazardous for a wayfarer to pass at such a time, as they can betwitch him and sink him into a profound sleep.

SLOVAKIA Slovakia, like other Central European countries, has long been the home of the Gypsies. They have settled in hamlets and townships, in mountain regions, and particularly in the capital city of Bratislava. Many of them have migrated to this central city from other areas, from Hungary, Bulgaria, and Rumania.
Some Gypsies, on the other hand, have moved from Slovakia to Macedonia, once, in the Middle Ages, the early home of the migrants.

SMITH, ADAM (1723-1790) Famous Scottish economist. Author of *Inquiry into the Nature and Causes of the Wealth of Nations.* As a child, he was carried off by the Gypsies and remained with them for some hours until he was recovered.

SMOKING Pipe-smoking is an inveterate custom among the

Gypsies, even among the older women. On occasion, women smoke cigars as well.

SNAKE Among the Gypsies, the snake was an object of awe or fear. There is a tradition that they may have been serpent-worshippers, as was the case in ancient cults. The Gypsies spent many years in Greece, absorbing into their language many Greek elements and also Greek customs. The ancient Greeks had a domestic snake cult, which continued into modern times.

SNAKE DAY In some Gypsy tribes there is a Snake Day, when the Gypsies try to find and kill a snake, to ensure good luck for the following year.

SNAKE-MEN In London, Charles Leland the gypsiologist had a strange encounter:

> The last snake-masters whom I came across were two sailors at the Oriental Seamen's Home in London. And strangely enough, on the day of my visit they had obtained in London, of all places, a very large and profitable job; for they had been employed to draw the teeth of all the poisonous serpents in the Zoological Garden. Whether these practitioners ever applied for or received positions as members of the Dental College I do not know, any more than if they were entitled to practice as surgeons without licenses. Like all the Hindu *sappa-wallahs,* or snake-men, they are what in Europe would be called Gypsies.

SOCIETY MARRIAGE In Scotland, in the eighteenth century, a Gypsy girl of the name of Fall was married to a Scotsman, Sir John Anstruther of Elie, baronet. The Gypsy wife was not held in any great esteem, for the

neighborhood knew of her Gypsy origin. They called
her Jenny Fall, her maiden name.

When her husband stood for election as a Member of
Parliament, his opponents howled through the streets
the song of the *Gypsy Laddie*.

SONGS A Gypsy song that belongs in medieval Spain runs
as follows:

> En los sastos de yesque plai me diquélo,
> Doscusañas de sonacai terélo, —
> Corojai diquélo abillar,
> Y ne asislo chapescar, chapescar.
> On the top of a mountain I stand,
> With a crown of red gold in my hand, —
> Wild Moors came trooping o'er the lea,
> O how from their fury shall I flee, flee, flee?
> O how from their fury shall I flee?

Appended is a specimen of a song in the vulgar or
broken Romany spoken by English Gypsies:

> As I was a jawing to the gav yeck divvus,
>   I met on the dron miro Romany chi:
> I puch'd yoi whether she com sat mande;
>   And she penn'd: tu si wafo Romany.
> And I penn'd, I shall ker tu miro tacho Romany,
>   Fornigh tute but dui chavé:
> Methinks I'll cam tute for miro merripen,
>   If tu but pen, thou wilt commo sar mande.
> One day as I was going to the village,
>   I met on the road my Romany lass:
> I ask'd her whether she would come with me,
>   And she said thou hast another wife.
> I said, I will make thee my lawful wife,
>   Because thou hast but two children;

416

Methinks I will love thee until my death,
If thou but say thou wilt come with me.

SONS OF CAIN   The Gypsies were at one time regarded as
the descendants of Cain. They were a cursed people,
workers in metals, skilled in music. The term Cain is
itself a Semitic word signifying a worker in metals.

SORROWFUL YEARS

The wit and the skill
Of the Father of ill,
Who's clever indeed,
If they would hope
With their foes to cope
The Romany need.
Our horses they take,
Our wagons they break,
And us they fling
Into horrid cells,
Where hunger dwells,
And vermin sting.
When the dead swallow
The fly shall follow
Across the river,
O we'll forget
The wrongs we've met,
But till then O never:
Brother, of that be certain.

SOURCE OF GYPSY MAGIC   There are many good reasons
for believing that the greatest part of Gypsy magic was
brought by the Romany from India. It is also interesting
to observe that among the Gypsies there is still extant,
on a very extended scale, a Shamanism which seems to
have come from the same Tartar-Altaic source which

was anciently found among the Accadian-Babylonians, Etruscan races, and Indian hill-tribes.

SOUTH AMERICA   The Spanish Gypsies who refused to establish a fixed settlement and engage in regular occupations, were sent in the eighteenth century to perform military service in South America. In South America they were known as Chinganeros.

SOUTHAMPTON COMMITTEE   Under the sponsorship of the Rev. James Crabb, who was well acquainted with Gypsy life, a committee was formed in Southampton, in 1827, whose object was the improvement in the spiritual and economic life of the English Gypsies.

SOUTHWELL, ROBERT (1560-1595)   Poet and Jesuit martyr It was said that, as a child, he was stolen by the Gypsies.
Traditionally, the Gypsies have consistently been accused, in most of the countries of their sojourn, of kidnapping non-Gypsy children. According to gypsiologists, the evidence for such acts has been slight and largely inconclusive.

SPAIN   Early in the nineteenth century, asserted a gypsiologist, Spain was overrun by roving troops of Gypsies who attacked wayfarers in remote spots and were a danger to the inhabitants.

SPAIN   Gypsies appear in Spain in the latter half of the fifteenth century. Although the term Gitano is commonly used as synonymous with Gypsy, it appears that in language and customs Gitanos and Gypsies have distinct and essential differences.
For centuries the Gypsies in Spain experienced ruthless treatment from the civic authorities and from the govern-

mental agencies. At the end of the fifteenth century they were banished. In the sixteenth century again banishment was in force. Some time later Philip II urged them to settle in villages and townships, in small communities. But in the seventeenth century persecution was again revived. The Gypsies, as in other countries of their sojourns, were identified with robbers, rogues, imposters, fortune-tellers. Late in the seventeenth century they were prohibited from pursuing their customary occupations as smiths. They were, in short, regarded officially as public bandits.

Charles III, however, in 1783, granted them a degree of emancipation, and designated them as Neo-Castilians.

SPANIARD AND GITANO Writing of the relationship between the native Spaniard and the Spanish Gypsy, George Borrow the gypsiologist declared:

> The position which the Gitanos hold in society in Spain is the lowest, as might be expected. They are considered at best as thievish chalans, and the women as half sorceresses, and in every respect thieves. There is not a wretch, however vile, the outcast of the prison and the presidio, who calls himself a Spaniard, but would feel insulted by being termed Gitano, and would thank God that he is not. And yet, strange to say, there are numbers, and those of the higher classes, who seek their company, and endeavor to imitate their manners and way of speaking. The connections which they form with the Spaniards are not many; occasionally some wealthy Gitano marries a Spanish female, but to find a Gitana united to a Spaniard is a thing of the rarest occurrence, if it ever takes place. It is, of course, by intermarriage alone that the two races will ever commingle, and before that event is brought about, much modification must take place among the

Gitanos, in their manners, in their habits, in their affections, and their dislikes, and, perhaps, even in their physical peculiarities; much must be forgotten on both sides, and everything is forgotten in the course of time.

SPANISH ANTAGONISM Perhaps, wrote the gypsiologist George Borrow, there is no country in which more laws have been framed, having in view the extinction and suppression of the Gypsy name, race, and manner of life, than Spain.

SPANISH DECREE Under Ferdinand and Isabella of Spain, in the late fifteenth century, Gypsies were required to leave the country on pain of harsh penalties, unless they established themselves in a definite location and stopped their roaming ways.

SPANISH DICTIONARY In the eighteenth century Dictionary of the Spanish Academy, the term *Gitanos* was explained as referring to a people who were self-styled Egyptians and whose lives were conditioned by their nomadic habits.

SPANISH GYPSY SONG

I stole a plump and bonny fowl,
　But ere I well had dined,
The master came with scowl and growl,
　And me would captive bind.
My hat and mantle off I threw,
　And scour'd across the lea,
Then cried the beng with loud halloo,
Where does the Gypsy flee?

SPANISH EDICT In 1492 King Ferdinand of Spain decreed the extermination of the Gypsies. They disappeared, however, in hiding, and returned in as great numbers as before.

SPANISH GYPSY TERMS Among the Spanish Gypsies the tribal chief is known as Manus. His wife, who is the matriarch, is the Manuza.

In the Balkans the Gypsy tribal leader was known by the indigenous name of voivode.

SPANISH IMAGE OF GYPSIES Literary Spain, in the sixteenth and seventeenth centuries, took cognizance of the phenomenon of Gypsies in their midst. For instance, Vicente Espinel (c. 1551-1624), Spanish writer and musician, is noted for his picaresque novel, partly autobiographical, *Vida del Escudero Marcos de Obregón,* which was published in 1618. It contains a scene in the forest of Ronda, depicting Gypsy caravan life.

Miguel de Saavedra Cervantes (1547-1616), famous for his novel *Don Quixote,* also produced a series of twelve stories under the title of *Novelas Ejemplares.* One of them *La Gitanilla,* The Little Gypsy, has the theme of a child stolen by the Gypsies: a motif that became increasingly popular in later centuries. Gypsies also appear in Cervantes' comedy *Pedro de Urdemalas.*

In *Lazarillo de Tormes,* a picaresque novel of unknown authorship, Gypsies appear. Lope de Vega, the dramatic poet and founder of the Spanish national drama, uses the Gypsy motif in *La Estrella de Sevilla.*

Jeronimo de Alcala and Francisco Lopez de Ubada likewise use Gypsy themes, with caravan life, horse-dealers and all.

In the seventeenth century Antonio de Solis' comedy appeared, The Little Spanish Girl of Madrid. In all the instances listed, it is evident that the Gypsies had, in whatever way, impressed their mark on the Spanish scene.

SPANISH MOORS   Many hypotheses have been entertained by various gypsiologists regarding the original home of the Gypsies. One such hypothesis was that they were descendants of the Moors of Andalusia, in Spain.

SPANISH NAMES   The Spanish Gypsies have been in Spain for so many centuries that in the course of time they have acquired Spanish national names, such as Vargas, Fernández, Heredia.

SPANISH PROHIBITIONS   In the law passed by Charles III of Spain in 1783 against the Spanish Gypsies, several articles specify both the injunctions and the penalties with respect to the conduct of these Gypsies.

Article II forbids, under penalties, the Gypsies 'using their language, dress, or vagrant kind of life, which they had hitherto followed.'

Article XI prohibits Gypsies from 'wandering about the roads and uninhabited places, even with the pretext of visiting markets and fairs.'

Article XII: 'Those who have abandoned the dress, name, language or jargon, associations and manner of Gitanos, and shall have, moreover, chosen and established a domicile, but shall not have devoted themselves to any office or employment though it be only that of day-laborer, shall be proceeded against as common vagrants.'

Article XX: dooms to death, without remission, Gypsies who, for the second time, relapse into their old habits.

SPANISH PROVINCES   Some Spanish provinces, on account of the meagreness of the crops and the poverty of the inhabitants, did not appeal to the Gypsies. These provinces included Galicia and the Asturias. More attractive to the Gypsies were Valencia and Murcia, La Mancha, Castile, Estramadura, Andalusia. In these provinces the soil was fertile, the inhabitants were wealthier, the prospects of plunder greater. Here too were horses and mules that they could handle.

Hence, in companies of thirties and sixties, they made their way particularly in Andalusia, where through the centuries the largest number of Gypsies settled, in villages and towns and notably in Seville.

SPANISH WRITER ON GYPSIES: Don Juan de Quiñones published a slim book in 1632, in which he described the Spanish Gypsies:

> They roam about, divided into families and troops, each of which has its head or Count; and to fill this office they choose the most valiant and courageous individual amongst them, and the one endowed with the greatest strength. He must at the same time be crafty and sagacious, and adapted in every respect to govern them. It is he who settles their differences and disputes, even when they are aware that there is one habitual drunkard here. A deep and dark spirit of revenge seems to be the worst trait in their characters; and at their merry-makings or carousals, which are now however of rare occurrence, this revengeful spirit is most apt to exhibit itself. Most or all of the Gypsy parents have been married: the greater number, however, in an irregular manner. The majority of the children have been baptized. They almost invariably intermarry in their own tribes. The interior of their houses is usually dirty, and the furniture of a very mean description. You rarely find them, except when very poor, destitute of a blazing fire. Most residing in a place where there is a regular justice. He heads them at night when they go out to plunder the flocks, or to rob travelers on the highway; and whatever they steal or plunder they divide amongst them, always the captain a third part of the

whole of the tribe can read. The parents generally express themselves as extremely desirous that their children should be instructed, and they speak of education as the only legacy which a poor man has to leave his children.

SPIES   In the Middle Ages, and in later centuries, Gypsies were frequently regarded as foreign agents, spies sent by hostile powers to probe into the economy and the military possibilities of the land they had chosen. Martin Del Rio, a Spanish demonographer and priest who belongs in the sixteenth century, says: What is the purpose of their inquisitive searching into the towns?
Should not these vagabonds be restrained, even if they are only innocent foreigners?

SPIRITS   In Gypsy mythology the Zracne vile are evil spirits of the air.
Pçuvushi are beneficent earth spirits.
Nivashi are water spirits that have vindictive tendencies.
The good spirits are known as *davanni*: the evil spirits are the *more*.
This dual principle is closely akin to the ancient concept of the Mithraic cult. Ahura Mazda is the spirit of beneficence, while Ahriman is the spirit of evil. Between them there is an unending cosmic conflict.

SPIRITS OF THE DEAD   There is a belief that the spirit of a dead Gypsy may revisit the earth as a demon or a vampire. As a protection against such an occurrence, a thorn-bush is placed on the grave.

SPIRITUAL BELIEFS   In his travels throughout Spain George Borrow came into close contact with many types of

Gypsies and was able to study their mentality. Of their spiritual life he says:

> Religion they have none. They never attend mass, nor did I ever hear them employ the names of God, Christ, the Virgin, but in execration and blasphemy. From what I could learn, it appeared that their fathers had entertained some belief in metempsychosis. But they themselves laughed at the idea, and were of the opinion that the soul perished when the body ceased to breathe. And the argument which they used was rational enough, as far as it impugned metempsychosis: "We have been wicked and miserable enough in this life," they said, "why should we live again?"

SPOKEN ENGLISH The English Gypsies in the nineteenth century had difficulty with the pronunciation of certain English words, as the following examples indicate:

Dictionary was pronounced .... dixen
Gentleman was pronounced .... gemmen
Increase was pronounced .... increach
Equally was pronounced .... ealfully

SPORT In England, particularly in the nineteenth century, the Gypsies were often attendants at race-courses. They were also fond of the prize-ring, both as spectators and participants. In his *The Zincali,* George Borrow describes a fight between two gangs of Gypsies in an English meadow.

STAFFORDSHIRE In 1539, in Staffordshire, England, two Gypsies were condemned to death for their lawless existence. They were, however, acquitted on payment of a huge fine.

STAND AND SIT There are many peculiarities in Gypsy syntax and vocabulary. There are also many common ideas that are difficult if not impossible to express in the Romany tongue. For instance, in no dialect of the Gypsy language, from the Indus to the Severn, is there any word for 'stand', though there is a word for 'sit', which is *besh*.

STANLEY AND LOVELL These two names, which two tribes of English Gypsies use as their own names, probably stemmed from the fact that on their arrival in England the Gypsies were attached to the two aristocratic families of Stanley and Lovell and that they adopted the names as their tribal designation.

STARKIE, WALTER (1894-1970) Professor of Spanish at Dublin University. He also held at various times high governmental and academic positions. A gifted linguist, he was passionately interested in the Gypsies, in their legends and particularly their music. He lived with the Gypsies in Spain and Hungary and other regions in the Balkans. As he wandered with the Gypsies he learned their music and their languages and dialects, and he often entertained his hosts with his own renderings on his violin. He is the author of a fascinating series of books on his Gypsy experiences. Among them are: *Scholars and Gypsies, Raggle-Taggle, Spanish Raggle-Taggle, In Sara's Tents.*
Starkie was at one time President of the Gypsy Lore Society.

STATE OF RUSSIAN GYPSIES In most of the provincial towns of Russia, in the nineteenth century, the Gypsies, said a traveler, were to be found in a state of half-civilization, supporting themselves by trafficking in horses, or by curing the disorders incidental to these animals. They did not appear in the Government of St. Peterburg, from which they had been banished.

STATE OF THE GYPSIES A nineteenth century Scottish gypsiologist introduced his subject by inquiring:

> How does it happen that in Europe there exists, and and has for four hundred years existed, a pretty numerous body of men distinct in their feelings from the general population, and some of them in a state of barbarism nearly as great as when they made their appearance amongst us?
>
> Such a thing would appear to us in no way remarkable in the stationary condition so long prevalent in Asia. But in a country that is generally looked upon as the stronghold of European civilization, how does it happen that we find a people, resembling in their nature, though not in the degree, the all but fabulous tribe that was lately to be found in the Wastes of Newfoundland? Or like the wild men of the jungle, who, under the influence of the missionary, are now raising crops, building dwellings, erecting school-houses?
>
> But some of the Gypsies with us may be said to do few of these things. They live among us, yet are not of us. They come in daily contact with us, yet keep such distance from the community as a wild fowl. They cling like bats to ruined houses, caves, and old lime-kilns; and pitch their tents in dry water-courses, quarry-holes, or other sequestered places, by the wayside, or on the open moor.

STATE RECORD A contemporary Frankfurt chronicle recorded: 24th. December, 1782: Not long ago it was published that forty-five of the man-eaters had been executed in Hungary. Her majesty (Maria Theresa) not thinking it possible that the Gypsies in confinement could have been guilty of such crimes, sent a commissar to examine minutely into the affair.

On his return it was confirmed that they were really man-eaters and that there are actually among them sons who have killed and eaten their own fathers.

STATUTE UNDER HENRY VIII According to Statute 22 in the reign of Henry VIII of England, it appears that the Gypsies at that time, must have been in England some years, and must have increased in numbers and in crime.

STEVENSON, ROBERT LOUIS (1850-1894) The Scottish novelist and poet, himself an adventurous wanderer, felt that no one could resist the romantic lure of a Gypsy encampment.

ST. JOHN'S EVE Certain traditional ceremonies and rites are associated with a Gypsy marriage. In the Balkans the bride burns flowers that she has gathered on St. John's Eve. This ritual is a defense against sickness.

For *bacht,* to ensure good luck, she hangs up in her house a bunch of garlic, which absorbs all evil into itself. After the marriage ceremony water is thrown over the wedded couple and they are rubbed with a little bag filled with thorn-apple seeds: an apotropaic means of averting the Evil Eye.

ST. PETERSBURG Although the Gypsies were to be found in all parts of Russia, they were banished from the Government of St. Peterburg in the nineteenth century.

STRABO (63 B.C.-21 A.D.) This noted Greek geographer and historian mentions a tribe called Sigynnes. They have been identified with the Zyghes, a Gypsy group that, in their early wandering, settled on the banks of the Danube.

STUDY OF GYPSIES In The Zincali, George Borrow asserts that the Gypsies can be best studied, as he did, from personal observation and acquaintance both with tribal ways and with the language.

STYLES IN FORTUNE-TELLING The Gypsy practice of fortune-telling is much the same everywhere, in Hungary or Spain or England. The Gypsy, when she *dukkers* the *vast,* that is, reads the hand, has three possible styles: the lofty, the familiar, and the homely, according to the status of her client. An old Spanish ballad, translated into English, illustrates the lofty style. A few stanzas run as follows:

> Late rather one morning
>> In summer's sweet tide,
> Goes forth to the Prado
>> Jacinta the bride:
>
> There meets her a Gypsy
>> So fluent of talk,
> And jauntily dressed,
>> On the principal walk.
>
> "O welcome, thrice welcome,
>> Of beauty thou flower!
> Believe me, believe me,
>> Thou com'st in good hour."

Surprised was Jacinta;
    She fain would have fled;
But the Gypsy to cheer her
    Such honeyed words said:

"O cheek like the rose-leaf!
    O lady high-born!
Turn thy eyes on thy servant,
    But ah, not in scorn.

"O pride of the Prado!
    O joy of our clime!
Thou twice shalt be married,
    And happily each time.

"Of two noble sons
    Thou shalt be the glad mother,
One a Lord Judge,
    A Field-Marshal the other."

SUDRAS An Oriental people, driven eastward by Tamerlane. They have been equated by some gypsiologists with the Gypsies.
Although it is now definitively determined that the original home of the Gypsies was India, the Gypsies have been hypothetically regarded as natives of Portugal, Ethiopia, Bohemia, Egypt.

SUMPTUARY LAWS In the reign of Henry VIII sumptuary laws directed against the Gypsies restricted their mode of dress. In addition they were forbidden to wear jewelry of any kind, even a silver button or ornament except as a badge of service.

SUPERIOR GYPSY George Borrow, the nineteenth gypsiologist who studied the Gypsies in Spain, quotes a description of a superior Spanish Gypsy from the memoirs of a Spaniard. The setting is in the year 1584:

430

At this time, they had a count, a fellow who spoke the Castillian idiom, with as much purity as if he had been a native of Toledo. He was acquainted with all the ports of Spain, and all the difficult and broken ground of the provinces. He knew the exact strength of every city, and who were the principal people in each, and the exact amount of their property. There was nothing relative to the state, however secret, that he was not acquainted with. Nor did he make a mystery of his knowledge, but publicly boasted of it.

SUPERSTITIONS Like all persons whose knowledge is extremely limited, the Gypsies are very superstitious. They believe in apparitions and witchcraft, and in the existence of invisible beings, capable of doing them an injury. They have also a belief in omens. They hold it to be very ominous of evil, before commencing a journey, to meet with certain animals early in the morning, or with persons possessing certain features or deformities, and on such occasions they will unload their carts or asses, and wait a more auspicious season for their journey.

SUPPRESSION In the Middle Ages, in Spain, the Gitanos were forbidden to live in certain sections of a town, or to hold meetings, or to intermarry. Yet these restrictions were never accepted by the Gypsies.

SUPPRESSIVE EDICTS Philip the Fourth of Spain promulgated in 1633 an edict containing the following articles regarding the Spanish Gypsies:
Article I: Under the same penalties, the aforesaid people shall within two months leave the quarters where they now live with the denomination of Gitanos, and shall separate from each other, and mingle with the other inhabitants, and shall hold no more meetings, neither

in public nor in secret; that the ministers of justice are to observe, with particular diligence, how they fulfill these commands, and whether they hold communication with each other, or marry among themselves; and how they fulfill the obligations of Christians by assisting at sacred worship in the churches; upon which latter point they are to procure information with all possible secrecy from the curates and clergy of the parishes where the Gitanos reside.

Article II: And in order to extirpate, in every way, the name of Gitanos, we ordain that they be not called so, and that no one venture to call them so, and that such shall be esteemed a very heavy injury, and shall be punished as such, if proved, and that nought pertaining to the Gypsies, their name, dress, or actions, be represented, either in dances or in any other performance under the penalty of two years' banishment, and a mulct of fifty thousand maravedis to whomsoever shall offend for the first time, and double punishment for the second.

SURNAMES   The surnames of English Gypsy families include: Glover, James, White, Pidgley, Saunders, Ayres, Willett, Carew, Churen.

SURVIVAL   Despite the long and dolorous chronicle of their rejection in virtually every country they reached, the Gypsies have a resilience that confirms their continuity. Cervantes himself wrote of them:

> Having learnt early to suffer, we
> suffer not at all.

SURVIVAL UNDER HOSTILITY   The Gypsies never flourished so in Europe as during the days when every man's hand was against them. It is said that they raided and plundered about Scotland for fifty years before they were definitely discovered to be mere marauders, for the Scots themselves were so much given up to similar pursuits that the Gypsies passed unnoticed.

SUSTENANCE The sustenance of the Gypsies and their normal livelihood are based to some extent on begging. But they also engage in a variety of employments, some temporary, others of much longer duration, at the discretion of the Gypsy himself. Skilled work includes leather craftsmanship, repairing metal utensils. More to their liking are singing dancing and playing the violin in cafés and other public places. Fortune-telling and circus performance engage others. There is, also poaching, stealing poultry, even horses. Traditionally, too, the Gypsies are coppersmiths and blacksmiths, and are adept in gold and silver. They are bear-trainers and acrobats. Boys shine shoes, sell newspapers, pilfer. In South-Eastern Europe the Rudari Gypsies make spoons and bowls, toys. In many regions, in England and in the Balkans, basket-weaving is a common occupation. In dealing with horses they can transform a moribund nag into a strong and healthy animal.

SWATURA A Gypsy expression signifying fanciful tales that included realistic elements. The contents dealt usually with supernatural and occult episodes, sorcery and witchcraft and all the apparatus of the invisible and mysterious malefic agents.

SWEDISH GYPSIES A few family groups migrated to Sweden at the turn of the country. These families, founders of Swedish settlement, were: Bolotjogoni, Jelleschti, Govaneschti, Tjurconi, Bombeschti, Hack, Jantjeschti, Fynfyrojeschti. For the men, their personal and nicknames were: Pika, Bango, Krischka, Steyo, Savka, Soner, Euri,

Franny. For the women: Buch, Bolka, Saliska, Nina, Sinfai, Fenella, Dosha, Zillah, Mona, Fezenta.

SWEETENING MARRIAGE Description of a Spanish Gypsy marriage ceremonial, by the gypsiologist George Borrow:

> The most singular part of the festival was reserved for the dark night. Nearly a ton weight of sweetmeats had been prepared, at an enormous expense, not for the gratification of the palate, but for a purpose purely. These sweetmeats of all kinds, and of all forms, but principally yémas, or yolks of eggs prepared with a crust of sugar (a delicious bonne-bouche), were strewn on the floor of a large room, at least to the depth of three inches. Into this room, at a given signal, tripped the bride and bridegroom dancing *romalis,* followed amain by all the Gitanos and Gitanas, dancing *romális.* To convey a slight idea of the scene is almost beyond the power of words. In a few minutes the sweetmeats were reduced to a powder, or rather to a mud, the dancers were soiled to the knees with sugar, fruits, and yolks of eggs. Still more terrific became the lunatic merriment. The men sprang high into the air, neighed, brayed, and crowed; while the Gitanas snapped their fingers in their own fashion, louder than castanets, distorting their forms into all kinds of obscene attitudes, and uttering words to repeat which were an abomination. In a corner of the apartment capered the while Sebastianillo, a convict Gypsy from Melilla, strumming the guitar most furiously, and producing demoniacal sounds.

SWINBURNE, HENRY Author of *Travels through Spain in the years 1775-6.* Writing of the Andalusian dance called the manguinday, performed by the Gypsies, Swinburne declared that this dance had negro elements brought from Havannah.

434

Swinburne declared that the Spanish Gypsies accepted the Christian faith formally, but that they were commonly regarded as unbelievers.

SWISS CHRONICLE In their outspreading marches through Europe the Gypsies usually had their movements and actions recorded in chronicles, official documents, decrees and edicts. Thus in the Baltic area the towns of Hamburg and Lübeck as well as towns in Germany and Switzerland and Provence marked the appearances of the Gypsies in their midst.

A Swiss chronicler, Justinger, recorded in the fifteenth century that a band of some two hundred Gypsies had appeared in certain towns in Switzerland. They were believed to have come from Egypt and presented Letters of Protection from King Sigismund of Hungary. Their leaders, who were well dressed and mounted on horseback, called themselves earls and dukes, while their followers looked wretched and poorly clad. They were permitted to encamp outside the towns, at night: but their conduct was far from exemplary.

SWITZERLAND Tarot cards, used generally by Gypsies in their practice of fortune-telling, were introduced into Switzerland in 1377 A.D.

SYLVAN MYTHOLOGY To the Gypsies the fields and forests, the streams and hedges, are haunted by invisible spirits and demons who harass human beings and must be placated by means of chants and invocations, amulets and spells and incantations.

In deep pools of water, for example, lurks the dreadful Waterman, the *Wodna Muz*, who lies in wait for victims. In every forest lives the forest mother, the *Weshni dye*, who is believed to be benevolent to human beings, especially toward children who have lost their way in the wood. The Panusch, however, is an amorous spirit who haunts the silent woodland shades and lies in wait for for helpless maidens.

In deep forests and lonely mountain ranges there wanders about a wild huntsman of superhuman size. Once he met a peasant who had shot ninety-nine bears, and warned him never to attempt to kill another one. But the peasant disregarded his advice and, missing his aim, was torn to pieces by the bear.

SYMPATHETIC CHARM An English Gypsy technique, intended to cause harm to one's enemy, is to stick pins into a red cloth rag and then to burn the rag.

In primitive society and in pagan cults and medieval sorcery this type of sympathetic magic was a prevalent procedure.

SYMPATHY WITH THE GYPSIES Sympathy with the Gypsies, declared the American gypsicologist Charles Leland, implias sympathy with Nature:

The Gypsies are human, but in their lives they are between man as he lives in houses and the bee and bird and fox, and I cannot help believing that those who have no sympathy with them have none for the forest and road, and cannot be rightly familiar with the witchery of wood and wold. . . . Only in Ruysdael and Salvator Rosa and the great unconscious arts lurks the spell in whcih to express their sense of nature and its charm, *fresco* life, and he who does not recognize it in them, but they have this sense, and there are very, very few who, acquiring culture, retain it. . . . Gypsies are the human types of this vanishing, direct love of nature, of this mute sense of rural romance, and of the *al fresco,* life, and he who does not recognize it in them, despite their rags and dishonesty, need npt pretend

436

to appreciate anything more in Callot's etching than the skillful management of the needle and the acids.

SYNTHESIS Gypsy music combines Oriental rhythms with the folk melodies they have encountered in their wanderings. The result is a subtle blending of the two elements into a purely Gypsy form that remains idiosyncratic to the Gypsies.

SYRIA In Syria the Gypsies often maintain themselves by snake-charming, as their remote ancestors did in their primal home in India.

Generally, however, the Gypsies engaged in metal work as tinsmiths, coppersmiths, iron workers, tinkers. The women, on the other hand, consistently adhered to their traditional practice of fortune-telling.

T

TABLE MANNERS Gypsies, at a meal, usually place a wooden board on the ground, and set a communal pot of stew or similar dish on it. The members of the family use this pot in common. There are no forks. Fingers take their place, as in Elizabethan days in England. Wild berries, mushrooms, herbs are all grist to the menu. A staple diet in Eastern Europe is maize pudding. Another staple and popular dish, when it is available, is the hedgehog. Also, at times, the Gypsies will eat carrion meat. Pig is relished, especially when fattened. The pig is extolled as Homer extolled the fat oxen at a sacrificial feast. To eat with a knife and fork is no part of a Gypsy's politeness. Nor is a table or plate thought necessary. Even a dish is frequently dispensed with. The whole kitchen and table apparatus consists of an earthen pot, an iron pan, which is also used as a dish, a knife, and a spoon. When the meal is ready, all the family sit around the pot or pan. Then the boiled or roast meat is divided into pieces and distributed to the members. Teeth and fingers serve for knives and forks, and the ground serves for table and plates.

The above details describe a meal early in the nineteenth century, in Central Europe.

TABORA A Gypsy term that denotes a tribal community. The expression is used particularly in Eastern Europe.

Kumpania is another expression that denotes a group of Gypsies consisting of several family units, independent of other units of the same type.

TABU There are many tabus that condition the deportment, food habits, talk, gestures, postures of men and women and children among the Gypsies. One almost general tabu, recognized among the tribes throughout Europe, was that a woman must never pass in front of a man, even her husband, when he is seated.

No Gypsy will allow a dog to eat from a dish intended for human beings. If the dog does so, the dish must be destroyed.

Among tabus honored by the Gypsies of Europe is the tabu concerning the vessels touched by women in recent childbirth. Such vessels are regarded as unclean.

TAIARI A Gypsy term applied to Gypsies who are locksmiths.

Among the Gypsies, each occupational group has its own descriptive designation. For instance, the bear-trainers are called *oursari*: ursus, in Latin, means a *bear*.

TAIKONI A Gypsy tribe that inhabits Sweden. The Gypsies were in Sweden in 1727, when they were ordered to be banished. But they persisted and remained in the country.

TAMERLANE According to philological investigation into the linguistic elements in the Gypsy tongue — which is an amalgam of many languages and dialects — the Gypsies came originally from India. They were, however, it is said, driven out Westward by Tamerlane toward the close of the fourteenth century.

TAN   This is the Gypsy term for a tent. The tent takes the place of a more permanent dwelling.

The caravan, horse-drawn, was until recent times a more self-contained habitation. The caravan is still in use, but motorized.

TANGIER   The city of Tangier has a Gypsy settlement called the *mahala.*
Many Gypsies, in earlier centuries, were persecuted and banished from Spain. Some crossed over to the North African littoral, settling in Tangier and elsewhere.

TAROT   The pack of cards known as the Tarot was regarded in the nineteenth century by the noted gypsiologist J. A. Vailliant as related to the astronomical and astrological cosmic system.
In the eighteenth century there was a contention that the Tarot was of Eastern origin and constituted the Book of the Ancient Egyptians, expounding the Royal Path of Life.
The Tarot is assumed to have been brought by the Gypsies during their migrations from India. It is used by them as the apparatus for divination.
The cards are arranged according to the Egyptian Tarot or the Marseilles Tarot with occidental symbols.
The usual pack contains 78 cards: of which 22 are called the tarots. The tarots correspond to the 22 letters of the Hebrew alphabet.
There are four suits: wands, sceptres or clubs: cups, chalices, or goblets: swords: money, circles, or pentacles.

On the twenty-two cards there are emblematic figures which have occult significance. Among these figures are:

440

The Pope, Justice, The Wheel of Fortune, Osiris Triumph-
ant, Death, The Devil, The Universe.

J. A. Vaillant was the first to propose that the Gypsies
brought the Tarot into Europe.

TARTAR COUNT In Germany in the fifteenth century the
tribal leader of a band of Gypsies was known as a Count
of the Tartars of Little Egypt. Other honorific titles
assigned to the leaders by themselves were: Duke, Prince,
Marquis, Lord, King. As Little Egypt was a *terra in-
cognita* in the Middle Ages such titles were accepted at
their assumed value.

TATTOOING Tattooing, usually on the face, is commonly
practiced among the Gypsies, both male and female.
It is designed for apotropaic purposes, as a defense
against the Evil Eye.

TCHOVEKHANO A Gypsy term that denotes a ghost or
spectre. The expression is in use among the Turkish
Gypsies.

Gypsy folklore is filled with tales of malefic spirits, ghouls,
vampires, demons that prey on the living.

TEA In their migrations through the country, the English
Gypsies acquired some of the habits of the people. For
instance, the frequent drinking of tea. But when times
were hard with them they used English herbs, of which
they generally carried a stock, such as agrimony, wild
mint, and the root of an herb called spice-herb.

TEACHING THE GYPSIES Unless they are taught better
principles, warned a Gypsy *aficionado* over a century
ago, than they possess at present, and unless those on
whom they impose use their understanding, it is to be

feared that swindling will long continue among them, as they are so ingenious in avoiding detection. When they are likely to be discovered, a total change of dress enables them to remove with safety to any distance.

TEMESKI KRIS TE ROMENGO JINAPEN   This is the Romany name for the National Council for Gypsy Education, with headquarters in London.

Since the end of World War II many European countries have soberly surveyed the situation and the status of the Gypsies, their economic standing, their civic, national, legal position, and the prospective possibilities regarding the education of the Gypsy children. In a number of cases steps have already been taken to ameliorat the general condition of the Gypsies and to bring them into a participating and accepted national context.

TERMS FOR GYPSY   In all, with reference to the countries through which the Gypsies have passed, the Gypsies have been designated by some fifty appellations of varying degrees of offensiveness. For to the natives they have always been the unwanted intruders. The most general term to identify them has been Gypsy.

TETUAN   In Tetuan, Spanish Morocco, there is a Gypsy quarter for Gypsies who have migrated from Spain.

Many large cities throughout Europe have special quarters assigned to the Gypsies, or chosen by them: in Seville, Budapest, London, New York.

TEUTONIC FRENZY   From the fifteenth century on into the eighteenth, the Gypsies in Germany were exposed officially to restrictive measures. Their undesirability reached a climax when they were banished from German territory or hanged publicly.

THACKERAY, WILLIAM M. (1811-1863)   The English novelist, in his monumental novel *Vanity Fair,* uses the term *Bohemian,* normally applied as an appellation to Gypsies, to designate one who is free and unconcerned about life.

THANKS   Thanks are offered in Romany by the expression: Nais tuki — Thank you!
The use of the expression indicates that, despite their rough and unconventional ways, the Gypsies have an innate sense of gratitude.

THE ARTS   The Gypsies in the last century have made a notable contribution to the arts. Tikno Adjam (1875-1948) produced a body of Romany poetry. Among painters were Torino Zigler and Jacob Richard. Luis Heredia Maya, a Spanish Gypsy, is a sculptor.

THE BIBLE AS AMULET   George Borrow the gypsiologist published the Gospel of St. Luke in Madrid, in 1838:
The women were particularly anxious to obtain copies,

THE CAPTAIN AND THE GYPSY   An anecdote involving the intricacies of Gypsy fortune-telling:
A British naval captain expected to be promoted to admiral. He also hoped to be married soon. Informed of a Gypsy who was notorious as a fortune-teller, he sent for her. Before going to his residence, the Gypsy collected information about him. When she was invited in, she ordered a large glass of spring water, into which she poured the white of a new-laid egg. As the sun shone on the glass, she worked so successfully on the captain's imagination that he declared to the lady whom he was to marry that the Gypsy had shown him, in the egg and water, the ship in which he would hoist the admiral's flag, the church in which he was to be married, and his bride on the way to church.

The Gypsy imposed upon the captain so flatteringly that he gave her three sovereigns and asked her to come on the following Monday. But the Gypsy did not appear again.

THE CRESCENT Many ornaments worn by Gypsy women are of crescent form and are regarded as lucky amulets. Among other charms that the Gypsies favor are seashells and knives.

THE DEAD At a Gypsy feast or similar celebration the dead are remembered in silence. In addition, some drops of wine or liquor are spilt on the ground, as a kind of libation to the spirits of the dead.

THE DOG'S COLLOQUY This is the title of a story by Cervantes. The dog is the spokesman and interpreter in depicting the actual life of the Gypsies in Spain.

THE FIRST DAY Genesis I.I-4 rendered in Romany:
Drey the sherripen Midibble kair'd the temoprey a the puv;
Tá the puv was chungalo, tá chichi was adrey lis;
Tá temnopen was oprey the mui of the boro put.
Tá Midibble's bavol- engri besh'd oprey the panior
Tá Midibble penn'd: Mook there be dute! tá there was dute.
Tá Midibble dick'd that the doot was koosho-koshko
Tá Midibble chinn'd enrey the dute tá the temnopen

THE GITANA The dress of the Gitanas is very varied. The young girls, or those who are in tolerably easy circumstances, generally wear a black bodice laced up with a string, and adjusted to their figures, and contrasting with the scarlet-colored saya, which only covers a par of the leg. Their shoes are cut very low, and are adorned with little buckles of silver. The breast, and the upper part of the bodice, are covered either with a white handkerchief, or one of some vivid color. And on the head is worn another handkerchief, tied beneath the chin, one of the ends of which falls on the shoulders, in the manner of a hood. When the cold or the heat permits, the Gitana removes the hood, without untying the knots, and exhibits her long and shining tresses restrained by a comb. The old women, and the very poor, dress in the same manner, except that their clothing is more coarse and the colors less in harmony.

THE GYPSIES OF KIRK YETHOLM There was a large colony of Gypsies at Kirk Yetholm, in Roxburghshire, Scotland. A letter written by one who observed the conditions of the Gypsies reads:

I do not think that the Gypsies of Kirk Yetholm are much addicted to drunkenness. There are particular seasons and occasions when they drink to excess, and at such times may be guilty of dreadful extravagances, but I am not aware that there is one habitual drunkard here. A deep and dark spirit of revenge seems to be the worst trait in their characters; and at their merry-makings or carousals, which are now however of rare occurrence, this revengeful spirit is most apt to exhibit itself. Most or all of the Gypsy parents have been married: the greater number, however, in an irregular manner. The majority of the children have been baptized. They almost invariably intermarry in their own tribes. The interior of their houses is usually dirty, and the furniture of a very mean description. You rarely find them, except when very poor, destitute of a blazing fire. Most of the tribe can read. The parents generally express themselves as extremely desirous that their children should be instructed, and they speak of education as the only legacy which a poor man has to leave his children.

THE BIBLE IN SPAIN This book by George Borrow was published in 1842. It is a vivid and comprehensive narrative describing the author's experiences, as an agent of the Bible Society, in Spain and Portugal. In Spain Borrow translated the Testaments into a Spanish Gypsy version. He on one occasion found himself in jail, and underwent a varied series of personal encounters. Virtually his was a pilgrimage, during which he made many discoveries about the Gypsies. He also formed friendship with unique Gypsy characters and came upon strange sights and scenes.

Perpetually on the move, adrift in Spain, he was a man of action, but also a man of meditation, a remarkable observer. He was thus able to imprint his observations in vital, dynamic prose.

Among the Gypsies who stand out prominently in his account are: the Antonios, the Manchegan prophetess, the Gypsy hag of Merida, and Balthasar.

THE BOHEMIAN A poem which is expressive of the Gypsy-Slavic nature, by Charles Leland:

And now I'll wrap my blanket o'er me
 And on the tavern floor I'll lie,
A double spirit flask before me,
 And watch my pipe clouds melting, die.
They melt and die, but ever darken
 As night comes on and hides the day,
'Till all is black: then, brothers, hearken,
 And if ye can write down my lay.
In yon long loaf my knife is gleaming,
 Like one black sail above the boat;
As once at Pesth I saw it beaming,

446

Half through a dark Croatian throat.
Now faster, faster, whirls the ceiling,
    And wilder, wilder, turns my brain;
And still I'll drink, till, past all feeling,
    My soul leaps forth to light again.
Whence come these white girls wreathing round me?
    Barushka! — long I thought thee dead;
Katchenka! — when those arms last bound thee
    Thou laid'st by Rajrad, cold as lead.
And faster, faster, whirls the ceiling,
    And wilder, wilder, turns my brain;
And from afar a star comes stealing
    Straight at me o'er the death-black plain.
Alas! I sink. My spirits miss me.
    I swim, I shoot from shore to shore!
Klara! thou golden sister — kiss me!
    I rise — I'm safe — I'm strong once more.
And faster, faster, whirls the ceiling,
    And wilder, wilder, whirls my brain;
The star! — It strikes my soul, revealing
    All life and light to me again.

THE GYPSIES OF MODON AND THE 'WYNE OF ROME-NEY' The wine called Rumney was not of native Venetian growth: it came from Modon in the Peloponnese, a seaport then under the suzerainty of Venice. Niccolo Frescobaldi, who visited the town on the 19th of September 1384, describes it as 'a fair fortress and well walled in the land of Romania,' and mentions the vintage which he calls in the plural *le Romanie,* the point which struck him most being that there was no old wine to be had. The wine was, he explains, so rich that when making it the casks had to be smeared inside with resin to prevent in from going mouldy. 'At the Venetian town of Modon in Greece grows the Romenye,' says Porner:

William Wey, one of the earliest of the English pilgrims, bears his testimony to 'a wine called Rumney,' and Sir Richard Guildford to 'moche Romney and Malvesey.' In the anonymous *Information for Pilgrims,* published about 1498 by Wynkyn de Worde, we read that Modon 'is a grete yle & plenteuo'. It is .III. C. myles from Corphu. And there growyth wyne of Romeney': and a similar German work lays stress on the size of the grapes which grew there, though it does not mention the wine by name. But it was not for its wine alone that Modon was famous. As Hopf and Wiener have shown, it was the headquarters of the Greek Gypsies in the fourteenth and fifteenth centuries. Frescobaldi mentions a number of *Romiti* outside the walls of the city, whom he thought to be penitents doing penance for their sins; but the testimony of subsequent travellers proves that they were Gypsies and that, though their sins were plenty, their penitence was but small. Experience had taught the later visitors wisdom, since the band of Gypsy 'penitents' who visited western Europe in 1417 had opened people's eyes to the meaning of their pilgrim guise. But Frescobaldi lived before that invasion, and it is interesting to find that they conveyed to his mind the impression which they took much pains to force on the rest of Europe later. Perhaps it was their acquaintance with pilgrims at such places as Modon which led them to adopt that guise.

Pilgrims were not the only persons with whom they were confused. One German travel-book writes of them as fugitive Albanese; though the author identifies them with the wanderers who 'come to Germany and are called Egyptians'. Like others he condemns them as beggars who gain a livelihood by betraying Christians to Turks. Modon he describes as 'one of the chief towns of Romania'; and he mentions the 'Romenie which grows hard by." Even here, however, they are identified with the Gypsies; and other travellers are unanimous in the identification. Indeed Harff's description, which will be quoted later, is sufficient alone to settle their identity. We are therefore very fortunate in having not only several descriptions, but at least one picture of the colony. Bernhard von Breyden-bach journeyed to Jerusalem in 1483, and found outside Modon 'the Gippenn who are called Gypsies,' whom he condemns as 'nothing but spies and thieves, who claim to come from Egypt when they are in Germany; but it is all a lie, as you yourselves well know.... At Modon grows the genuine Romanie and nowhere else in the world.' But Breydenbach did not travel alone; he took with him Eberhard Reüwich as his draughtsman, to il-lustrate the book in which he described his travels, and it is to the latter's pencil that we owe a large plate of Modon with the Gypsy quarter behind it. Such pictures are of course always suspicious, as the artist may have drawn them from memory; but if the huge fivefoot picture of Venice, the only one which I can judge from personal observation, can be taken as a criterion for the accuracy of the rest, the Modon plate ought to be a tolerably good likeness. In it we see a fortified town with a long jetty running out so as to form one side of a harbour; and behind the town a hill, which is doubtless Frescobaldi's *Poggio della Sapienza*, and the Mount Gyppe of other ac-counts. At the foot of the hill, just outside the town walls, are a number of huts of various shapes and sizes. Some of them might be intended for tents, but probably they are all huts, as Harff speaks only of 'reed-covered huts', and Breydenbach in his *Peregrinatio* calls them *tuguria*. He there gives the number at 'about three hundred in which dwell certain poor folk like Ethiopians, black and unshapely,' adding the information that they were called Saracens in Germany, and claimed falsely to come from Egypt. In reality they were natives of Gyppe, near Modon,

449

and spies and traitors. He does not state explicitly that the mountain behind Modon was called Gyppe, but many other travellers do. Alexander Pfalzgraf bei Rhein (1495), for instance, after rather strangely expressing surprise at the number of Greeks and Jews he saw in the Greek town Modon, continues: 'Near Modon lies a hill called Gype, and there are about two hundred little houses of huts inhabited by the Egyptians called Heathen. Some people call this hill and its appurtenances Little Egypt.' Much doubt has been thrown on the names Gyppe and Little Egypt and the latter, from which some of the early fifteenth-century invaders of western Europe claimed to some, has been sought far and wide. But there seems no reasonable doubt that the pilgrims are correct in their account, and that the two names were temporarily applied to the camping-place of the colony of Gypsies behind Modon. The name Little Egypt is sufficiently paralleled by the 'Little Jewry' of some English towns; and the mistake of those who have sought for it elsewhere has lain in supposing that it contained the clue to the legend of Egyptian origin, whereas the name was merely derived from that legend.

Certainly, even if Modon is Little Egypt, that is no reason for asserting with Grünemberg that all Gypsies had 'their origin thence, and their home there.' He visited Modon in 1486, and not only bears witness to the Gypsies, but like Breydenbach gives a picture of Modon. The illustration in the MS. of his travels at Gotha is stated by Röhricht and Meisner to show the Gypsy quarter consisting of about three hundred 'Häuser aus Rohr'; but, unfortunately, information kindly supplied me by the librarian, Dr. Ehwald, proves that it is only too like Breydenbach's plate, being in fact nothing more than a copy of it. The plate in the other surviving MS. of Grünemberg, now at Karlsruhe, shows the town from another side, and is useless for our purposes, since it excludes the Gypsy quarter. Grünemberg also mentions the Romany wine, stating that it was so strong that it had to be mixed with twice its volume of water before it could be drunk. And considering the mass of evidence accumulated for the existence both of the Romany wine and the Romanichels at Modon, it is very tempting to connect the two, especially when one finds that the same wine existed at Nauplion where, as Hopf has proved there was a Gypsy colony at least as early as the middle of the fourteenth century, and in Crete, where Philipp van Hagen in his *Hodoporika* (1528) states 'many Jews and Gypsies dwell among the Christians'. Peter Fassbender, whose pilgrimage was undertaken in 1492, bears witness to the existence of the wine both at Modon and in Crete, though he elects to call it Malvasia Romany.

He adds that it is a cheap wine, but, as we learned also from Frescobaldi, will not keep for more than a year. Now Johann Graf zu Solms (1483) states that the only wine of Modon is Malvasia: and several other pilgrims mention Malvasia in Crete, but none, so far as I can find except Fassbender, mention Rumney; so that apparently the two names were occasionally confused. In any case the wines were probably closely alike, as one originated in and took its name from Napoli di Malvasia or Monembasia, and the other from Napoli di Romania, the modern Naplion, both in the Peloponnese. Napoli di Romania was so called because it was situated in the land which at that time bore the name Romania, a name which once embraced the whole Byzantine Empire, but had come to be confined roughly to modern Greece. Whether the Gypsies too took their name from the old Byzantine designation or not is a moot point; but though the Gypsies of Corfu early became agriculturists, their presence in the special wine-growing districts can only be regarded as a

451

coincidence. Perhaps, indeed, the existence of the wine drew them thither; but on the evidence of the travellers who mention them, there is nothing to connect them with the production or the sale of it; which indeed was quite as well. They are thirsty souls that dwell in tents, and not over energetic. Had they had a hand in its making, there would probably have been little to export; whereas there must have been a considerable export trade in "Romeney' and 'Malvesey' are mentioned together in an English document of 1418, 'rumney and malmesyne' in the *Squire of Low Degree* (circ. 1457), and in 1531-2 Henry VIII. passed a law regarding the price of 'malmeseis Romaneis sackes' and 'other sweter wynes.' The name attained such celebrity that there was even a "vinum hispanense romenye'. Possibly it is through the latter that two of the rarest of Burgundies bear the names Romanée St. Vivant and Romanée Conti.

Whether the use of Romanie in the sense of 'brandy' or 'rum' among the Tinklers is in any way connected with its use as a word for Greek wine, or whether it is rather derived from the old cant term 'rum booze' for any good drink, it would be idle to discuss. But what this large colony of Gypsies did at Modon, if they were not connected with what was apparently its chief industry, is more worth consideration. The simplest explanation would be that they were drawn thither by the knowledge of the frequent visits of pilgrims, on whose credulity they hoped to impose. Where the carcase is, there will the birds be gathered together; and the Gpysies are very carrion-crows for scenting out an opening for their many arts, as visitors to the sands of Blackpool have good reason to know. But, if it was so, the pilgrims carefully conceal the fact. Fassbender says that 'they live in great poverty, and practise nothing but smithcraft, which they perform in a strange manner of their own, and the only two pilgrims who give a description of the colony at any length speak of them too as mainly smiths. Their description of the Gypsies' method of working is worth quoting for comparison with Lencheraud's notes on the Gypsy smiths of Zante, which has been cited by Wiener. Harff's account, which refers to the years 1496-9, is the fullest: *'Item'* we went out to the outskirts, where dwell many poor, black, naked people called Euyginer in little huts covered with reeds, about a hundred house-holds, whom, when they travel in these lands, we call heathen from Egypt. This people practise there all kinds of trades, such as shoemaking and cobbling, and also smithcraft, which was very strange to see, as the worker's anvil stood on the ground and he sat by it like a tailor in this country. By him sat his wife also on the ground and span. Between the two lay the fire. By it were placed two small leather sacks like bagpipes, which were half buried in the earth by the fire, so that the woman, as she sat and span, now and again lifted one sack from the ground and then put it down again. That gave the fire air through the ground so that he could work. *Item* this people is from a land called Gyppe which lies about forty miles from the city of Modon. This district was taken by the Turkish king within the last sixty years, and some of the gentry and counts would not submit to the king and fled do out country, to Rome to our Holy Father the Pope seeking consolation and assistance from him. Wherefore he gave them introductory letters to the Roman Emperor and all princes of the realm, asking them to further them on their way and assist them, since they were expelled for Christ's sake. They showed the letters to all princes, and none would assist them. So they perished in misery leaving the letters to their servants and children, who still to this day abide in these lands and claim to be from Little Egypt. But this is false, since their elders were natives of the land

453

of Gyppe, called Suginien, which lies not half way from here at Kolu to Egypt. Wherefore these wanderers are knaves and spyers-out of the land. . . . *Item* in this country grows no other wine but Romennije, which is very strong and good.'

Dietrich von Schachten, who visited Modon in 1491, writes:—

Item at Modon outside the city on the hill by the wall there are many miserable little huts, where the Gypsies, so-called in Germany, dwell, very poor people and generally all smiths. They sit down on the ground for their work and have a pit made in the earth in which they keep the fire and if the man or woman has a pair of bellows in his hand, they are quite contented, and blow with the bellows, a miserably poor thing that is beyond description: and make a great number of nails and very well.

The pilgrims' evidence then proves nothing except that they were smiths, cobblers, and spies, and, though it is unsatisfactory in supplying no reason for their choice of Modon as a place of settlement, it is at least good evidence that we have real Gypsies to deal with. Smithcraft is universal among them; and according to the Montenegrian legend they have dealt in nails since the crucifixion, cobbling the Gypsies of Kronstadt still practise seated in the market-place: and spies they have always been held to be. Indeed, their habits and trades, their vices and virtues, their appearance and nature, are immutable so far back as we can trace them; and we may be sure that the Modon colony could no more resist the temptation of *dukkering* the pilgrims than any modern *dai*. It is therefore probable that the pilgrims were a little unwilling to confess their follies, and that it was their presence and the chance of turning an honest, semi-honest, or frankly dishonest penny out of them, which mainly attracted the

454

Gypsies to Modon. For it was not only at Modon that they were found, but at several other important pilgrim stations as well. At Nauplion the Venetian governor renewed their privileges in 1494, in Crete Symon Simeonis found them as early as the fourteenth century; and there is evidence of their presence at Jaffa. Herzog Heinrich von Sachsen and his fellow-pilgrims were imprisoned in a khan and only freed by liberal bribery, and the Gypsies were credited with having betrayed the duke, who was travelling incognito, to the Turks. Thirty years earlier Graf Eberhard von Würtemberg had a similar experience, from which he did not escape so easily. But whether his took place at Jaffa is not certain; it may have been further inland, since Steffan von Gumpenberg (1449-50) claims to have met Gypsies by the Sea of Galilee: 'When we had ridden about eight miles we came to a deserted inn, lying on a flowing stream; and there came a whole host of Gypsies, carrying their houses on camels, and having all their cattle with them; and the oxen and cows carried their goods and children.' If this is really a description of a band of Eyrian Gypsies, then they must in the fifteenth century have been in very comfortable circumstances, as they owned camels and cattle. But it is possible that he confused Gypsies with Arabs, like Felix Schmid (1433) in his *Evagatorium*. There he tells us in one passage that the desert of Syria and Arabia is peopled by Zigari, and in another that these Zigari are identical with the Zigineri 'who in our day have traversed Europe with their wives and children, and are not permitted to enter towns since they are expert thieves.' He adds that he had questioned one who admitted that he was a Chaldaean and spoke Chaldee, which he quotes as proof positive of the falsity of their claim to Egyptian origin. Yet in the first passage he admits that some held the dwellers in the desert, and among them presumably the

455

Zigari, to be genuinely of Egyptian origin, being the descendants of the Egyptian thieves expelled according to Diodorus Siculus by King AEtisanes from Egypt.

But in defence of those particular Gypsies it may be noted that Steffan von Gumpenberg had previously made acquaintance with wild Arabs in Bethlehem, and did not call them Gypsies but Heathen: 'On Thursday, while we were hearing mass by the manger, there came heathen into the churches with their wives and children; they were black, bearded, and shaggy, and looked like the Devil. And they behaved so abominably towards us that the brethren thought they would never see us again. They were some of the wild heathen and wanted to return to the desert.' It would seem as though there must have been some difference in the appearance of the two bands to account for the difference of denomination, since *Heiden* is clearly not used here as synonymous with Gypsies.

Schmid's, or rather Foresti's, assertion that the Gypsies are Chaldaeans is directly at variance with the views of the other pilgrims who, as we have seen, in most cases regard them as natives of the Peloponnese. The *Niederheinische Pilgerschrit's* confusion of them with the Albanese, supported by the mention of the two together at Modon by Hans Werli, is that the Gypsies emigrated from Wallachia and Rumania to Greece with the fugitive Albanese about the middle of the fourteenth century. But, though the theory is attractive, there are several weak points in it. By Hopf's own showing there were *homines Vageniti*, who after his careful investigation can hardly be denied to be Gypsies, in Epirus before 1346, since in that year Catherine of Valois extended the privilege of adopting new Gypsy vassals to the feudal lords in Corfu. And Symon Simeonis' Cretan Gypsies, who in spite of Hopf's doubts may be reasonably claimed as such, must in all probability have passed through Greece. Besides, his theory leaves little time for the adoption of the many Greek loan-words in the Gypsy language, seeing that the great movement into western Europe began in 1417; though that difficulty may be got over, if we accept Sinclair's theory that the Gypsies learned their Greek not in Greece, but in Asia Minor. Certainly Hopf would seem to be wrong in arguing that it was those who remained behind in Wallachia who sent out the 1417 band, since one of their leaders was Andrew, count of Little Egypt, which was in all probability Modon itself.

Hopf's argument, like most of the theories about the comings and goings of the Gypsies, is based on the supposition that their movements are influenced by external historical events. But surely such a supposition is quite unnecessary and indeed erroneous as a general rule, though instances may be found to support it. For example, it seems as though the conquest of Modon by the Turks in 1500 caused most of the Gypsies there to desert their quarters, since Tschudi in 1519 found only thirty houses left. Probably the decrease in trade owing to the cessation of pligrim-traffic largely accounted for their departure. But even before the actual advent of the Turks, there must have been a considerable migration, since the colony had decreased from three hundred huts to one hundred between the visit of Breydenbach in 1483 and that of Harff in 1496-9. That such large numbers could pass unmentioned shows that the chroniclers' and historians' notices of Gypsy migrations did not by any means embrace all the large movements which took place. The adventures of these particular nomads are quite unrecorded; but it is not perhaps too rash to recognise our Modon friends in the 'Bohemians and fools styled Bohemians, Greeks, and Egyptians' of the Constitution of Catalonia (A.D. 1512), and the Greek-speaking Spanish Gypsies who were seen in 1540. If they were mere descendants of the 1417 band they would hardly have kept up their Greek for a hundred years. Most probably the early invaders of Spain were a mixed band, consisting partly of descendants of the 1417 band, reinforced by later arrivals from Modon, since some of those spoken to in 1540 knew Greek and other did not. Again no great historical event heralded the extensive movement of Gypsies which took place all over western Europe in 1907; and this certainly suggests a doubt as to whether any catacysm need have preceded their arrival in Greece, or anywhere else. And surely one would not expect it. Gorgio politics, save when aimed directly at himself, have little or nothing to do with the Gypsy; and to changes of dynasty he is as impervious as the Vicar of Bray. But to the Wanderlust he bows his head; and the Wanderlust is irresponsible. The man who would sit calmly through an earthquake will shoulder his pack in feverish haste and stride out towards the blue hills, when.

'He must go—go—go—away from here
On the other side the world he's overdue:
'Send your road is clear before you when the old
   Spring fret comes o'er you
And the Red Gods call for you!"

E. O. Winsted

THE GYPSY FORTUNE-TELLER

Where have you been, my darling,
   That you come so late at night?

And where have you been, my own love,
   That your purse has grown so light?
I have been in the forest, darling,
   I have heard the wood birds sing,
Where the squirrel picked nuts for the winter
   And the fairies had made a ring.

458

A Gypsy came through the forest.
  She was wrinkled, brown and old;
And she looked in my hand, and I listened
  To the fortune that she told.

She told me I soon should marry
  A lady with yellow hair —
A lady with yellow hair, blue eyes, love,
  And cheeks like the wild rose fair.

My hair is yellow as sunshine,
  My eyes are violet blue;
And wasn't it worth the money
  To hear that I'll marry you?

Janet Tuckey

THE GYPSY SNAKE-CHARMER   The Gypsiest-looking Gypsy in Cairo, with whom I became sonewhat familiar, was a boy of sixteen, a snake-charmer; a dark and even handsome youth, but with eyes of such wild wickedness that no one who had ever seen him excited could hope that he would ever become as other human beings. I believe that he had come, as do all of ancestors, and that he had taken in from them the serpent nature. They had gone snaking, generation after generation, from the days of the serpent worship of old, it may be back to the old Serpent himself; and this tawny, sinuous, active thing of evil, this boy, without the least sense of sympathy for any pain, who devoured a cobra alive with as much indifference as he had just shown in petting it, was the result.

THE HOUSE-DWELLER   The following poem demonstrates the Gypsy dislike for a permanent home:

  You passed me by this werry way,
  And 'sarishan' you said to me.
  I've often wondered, since that day,

459

What sort of person you might be.

Says I: 'Them's Gypsy words he spoke
And where could he ha' learnt, and how?'
I don't see much o' Romany folk,
I'm livin' in a house, sir, now.

I hate this sort of life, I do!
I'm Romany, and want to roam. —
Just fancy 'sarishan' from you,
And only English talk at home!

E. H. Palmer

In Romany, 'sarishan' means 'How do you do?'

THE HUKNI   An English Gypsy term that means a ruse. The Spanish Gypsies call the same practice *hokkano baro,* the Great Trick. George Borrow gives an instance of the *Hukni*:

The Gypsy makes some poor simpleton of a lady believe that if the latter puts her gold into her hands, and she makes it up into a parcel, and puts it between the leady's feather-bed and mattress, it will at the end of a month be multiplied a hundredfold, provided the lasy does not look at it during all that time. On receiving the monet she makes it up into · a brown paper parcel, which she seals with wax, turns herself repeatedly round, squints, and spits, and then puts between the feather-bed and mattress — not the parcel of gold, but one exactly like it, which she has prepared beforehand, containing old halfpence, farthings, and the like; then, after cautioning the lady by no means to undo the parcel before the stated time, she takes her departure singing to herself:—

O dear me! O dear me!
What dinnelies these gorgies be!

THE KING AND THE GYPSY A king of England, who loved his people and his God better than kings in general are wont to do, occasionally went hunting. One day the the chase lay through the shrubs of the forest. The stag had been hard run, and to escape the dogs had crossed the river at a deep stop. As the dogs could not be induced to follow, it was necessary to make a detour along the banks of the river, through some thick undergrowth. The roughness of the ground, the long grass and frequent thickets, obliged the sportsmen to separate. Before they had reached the end of the forest, the king's horse showed signs of fatigue and uneasiness. The king therefore, in his compassion for his mount, turned down the first avenue in the firest and determined to ride gently to the oaks, to wait for his attendants.

The king had only proceeded a few yards when, instead of the cry of the hounds, he fancied he heard the cry of human distress. As he rode forward, he heard it more distinctly.

"Oh, my mother! God pity and bless my poor mother!" The curiosity and kindness of the sovereign led him instantly to the spot. It was a little green plot on one side of the forest, where there was, spread on the grass, under a branching oak, a little pallet, half covered with a kind of tent: and a basket or two, with some packs, lay on the ground a few paces from the tent.

Near the root of the tree he observed a little swarthy girl, about eight years of age, on her knees, praying, while her black eyes ran with tears.

The compassionate king inquired:

"What, my child, is the cause of your weeping?"

The little creature at first started, then rose from her knees, and pointing to the tent, said:

"Oh, sir! My dying mother!"

"What", cried the king, dismounting and fastening his

horse up to the branches of the oak, "what, my child? Tell me all about it."

The little girl now led the king to the tent. There lay, partly covered, a middle-aged Gypsy woman, in the last stages of a decline, and in the last moments of life. She turned her dying eyes expressively to the royal visitor, but not a word did she utter.

The little girl then wept aloud, and stooping down wiped the dying sweat from her mother's face.

The king, greatly affected, asked the child her name and about her family, and how long her mother had been ill.

At that moment another Gypsy girl, much older, came out of breath to the spot. She had been to town and had brought some medicine for her dying mother. Observing a stranger, she modestly curtsied and hastening to her mother knelt down by her side, kissed her pallid lips, and burst into tears.

"What, my dear child," said the king, "can be done for you?"

"Oh, sir" she replied, "my dying mother wanted a religious person to teach her and to pray with her before she died."

The king instantly tried to comfort the distressed daughter.

"I am a minister, and I can comfort and instruct your mother."

He then sat down on a pack, took the dying Gypsy's hand, and talked of redemption. She looked up and smiled, but it was the last smile.

At this moment some of the king's attendants rode up and found him comforting the Gypsy girl.

He now rose up, put some gold into the girls' hands, and promised them his protection.

He then mounted his horse while his attendants stood in silent admiration.

THE MEDICINE-SELLER The patter of a Gypsy medicine-seller, as transcribed by the gypsiologist Charles Leland: We Gypsies are, as you know, a remakable race, and possessed of certain race secrets, which have all been formulated concentrated, dictated, and plenipotentia-rated into this idealized Elixir. If I were a mountebank or a charlatan I would claim that it cures a hundred diseases. Charlatan is a French word for a quack. I speak French, gentlemen. I speak nine languages, and can tell you the Hebrew for an old umbrella. The Gypsy's Elixir cures colds, gout, all nervous affections, with such cutaneous disorders as are diseases of the skin, debility, sterility, hostility, and all the illities that flesh is heir to except what it can't, such as small-pox and cholera. It has cured cholera, but it don't claim to do it. Others claim to cure, but can't. I am not a charlatan, but an Ann-Eliza. That is the difference between me and a lady, as the pig said when he astonished his missus by blushing at her remarks to the postman. Better have another bottle, sir. Haven't you the change? Never mind, you can owe me fifty cents. I know a gentleman when I see one. I was recently down east in Maine, where they are so patriotic, they all put the stars and tripes into their beds for sheets, have the Fourth of July three hundred and sixty-five times in the year, and eat the Declaration of Independence for breakfast. And they wouldn't buy a bottle of my Gypsy's Elixir till they heard it was good for the Constitution, whereupon they immediately purchased my entire stock. Don't lose time in securing this invaluable blessing to those who feel occasional

463

pains in the lungs. This is not taradiddle. I am engaged to lecture this afternoon before the Medical Association of Germantown, as on Wednesday before the University of Baltimore; for though I sell medicine here in the streets, it is only, upon my word of honor, that the poor may benefit, and the lowly as well as the learned know how to prize the philanthropic and eccentric Gypsy.

THE NOBLE ART OF MENDICITY Among Gypsy women skill in begging implies the possession of every talent which they most esteem, such as artfulness, cool effrontery, and the power of moving pity or provoking generosity by pique or humor. It is something worth hearing when several Gypsies sit together and devise dodges, and tell anecdotes illustrating the noble art of mendicity, and how it should be properly practiced.

THE NUTS OR NATS The Nuts or Nats are Indian wanderers who correspond to the European Gypsy tribes and were in their origin probably identical with the Luri, the Gypsies who came from India to Persia. They are musicians, dancers, conjurers, acrobats, fortune-tellers, blacksmiths, robbers, and dwellers in tents. They eat everything except garlic.

THE OLD RELIGION Throughout the Middle Ages, particularly in the sixteenth and seventeenth centuries, the Gypsies in Europe were hounded with violent hostilities. They were regarded as allies of Satanic forces, as the surviving remnants of the Old Religion, the pagan mysteries, the sinister and secret cults that, with the advent and the influence of Christianity, had become a menace and a danger to organized Christian society and to the established religious system.

464

THEORIES ON THE GYPSIES In his study of *The Zincali,* George Borrow says that no race in the world affords, in many points, a more extensive field for theory and conjecture than the Gypsies.

THE ROMANTIC GYPSY In a theatrical sense, the Gypsy has been typified as a care-free, roving, personality wholly absorbed in music, dancing, romance — all set against colorful village greens, lush woodlands, or distant hills. That, to some extent, was the image of the Gypsy represented in Renaissance Italy in the social and entertainment field. In more recent times, the image has been repeated in the operetta entitled *Gypsy Love,* composed by the Hungarian Franz Lehar in 1910. Konrad Bercovici, in his fiction, followed somewhat the same lines in his romantic Gypsy tales.

THE ROMANY GIRL This is the title of a poem by Ralph Waldo Emerson (1803-1882), the American essayist and poet. Emerson took a deep interest in Gypsies and Gypsy lore.

THE SCAPEGOAT Among Hungarian Gypsies there is a curious trace of the concept of the scapegoat. On Easter Monday they make a wooden box or receptacle which is called the *bicápen,* pronounced like the English Gypsy word *bitchapen* and meaning the same, that is — a sending, a thing sent or a gift. In this, at the bottom, are two sticks across, "as in a cradle," and on these are laid herbs and other fetish stuff which every one touches with the finger; then the whole is enveloped in a winding of white and red wool, and carried by the oldest person of the tribe from tent to tent. After which it is borne to the next running stream and left there, after every one has spat upon it. By doing this they think that all the diseases and disorders which would have befallen them during the coming year are conjured into the box. But woe to him who shall find the box and open it, instead of throwing it at once into the stream. All the diseases exercised by the Gypsy band will fall upon him and his in full measure.

THESIS ON EGYPT As late as the nineteenth century, the belief persisted that the Gypsies were originally natives of Egypt. In the middle of the seventeenth century a certain German scholar, Thomasius, published in Latin a *Dissertatio philosophica de Cingaris,* a philosophical dissertation on the Zingari or Gypsies. His thesis was that they indubitably originated in Egypt.

THE THREE GYPSIES This poem by Nikolaus Lenau, the Hungarian epic poet (1802-1850), was translated into English by the gypsiologist Charles Leland:

I saw three Gypsy men, one day,
　Camped in a field together
As my wagon went its weary way
　All over the sand and heather.

And one of the three whom I saw there
　Had his fiddle just before him,
And played for himself a stormy air,
　While the evening-red shone o'er him.

And the second puffed his pipe again
　Serenely and undaunted,
As if he at least of earthly men
　Had all the luck that he wanted.

In sleep and comfort the last was laid,
　In a tree his cymbal lying,

Over the strings the breezes played,
O'er his heart a dream went flying.

Ragged enough were all the three,
Their garments in holes and tatters;
But they seemed to defy right sturdily
The world and all worldly matters.

Thrice to the soul they seemed to say,
When earthly trouble rites it,
How to fiddle, sleep it, and smoke it away,
And so in three ways despise it.

And ever anon I look around,
As my wagon onward presses,
At the Gypsy faces darkly browned,
And the long black flying tresses.

THE TRAVELING GYPSY Although the spacious migrations of the Gypsies are past, as they swept Eastward through the centuries from India to Persia, from Turkey to Greece, and through the countries of Europe, the inherent racial wanderlust of the Romany still persists. The English Gypsy, for instance, still travels in his caravan — or car — along the highways and lanes of rural England. He still seeks encampments in secluded spots. He still plies his old trade as tinker or smith or horse-dealer or basket-weaver.

THE TWO HUSSARS This is the title of a story by the famous Russian novelist Leo Tolstoi. It involves a gay evening spent by some officers and others in a Gypsy setting.

THE UBIQUITOUS GYPSY There is scarcely a part of the habitable world said a gypsiologist, where the Gypsies are not to be found. Their tents are alike pitched on the heaths of Brazil and the ridges of the Himalayan Hills, and their language is heard at Moscow and Madrid, in the streets of London and Stamboul.

THE VANISHING GYPSY Charles Leland the gypsiologist expressed the same view of the vanishing Gypsy. Yet the Gypsy still persists into the twentieth century.

THRACIAN ORIGIN Among many fanciful conjectures relating to the original home of the Gypsies, one assumption was that they came from Zigere, formerly a city of Thrace.

THREE KINDS OF GYPSIES In the Danubian region there were, in the 1880's, three kinds of Gypsies: one very dark and barbarous, another light brown and more intelligent, and the third, or *élite,* of yellow-pine complexion.

THREE KINGS In medieval Europe there was a legend that three Kings, the Magi of the Bible, were Gypsies. In the miracle dramas that were popular in those times the Gypsies were represented as professing fortune-telling ability, which they demonstrated on the Holy Family. Charles G. Leland, the folklorist and gypsiologist, clarified the tradition of the three Gypsy Magi. The Magi came from the East, and the Gypsies similarly came from the East. Hence the popular though illogical conclusion was the identification of the Magi with the Gypsies.

THRICE   It is said that the Gypsies enter a church three times in a lifetime: at baptism, at marriage, and at death.' In many cases, of course, the Gypsies have no formal Christian attachments.

THUGS   The *patrins,* the signs and ideographs that guide Gypsy tribes along the countrysides, are known to the Gypsies of many countries: England, Germany, Norway. The patrins were also known to the Thugs of India. And India has been established, by long philological and linguistic investigation, as the original home of the Gypsies.

THYME   The Gypsies know a bank where the wild thyme grows. It is used as a remedy for coughs. Boiled, it is taken cold, in the open air. If the thyme concoction is brought inside a caravan or tent, it is regarded as an unlucky omen.

TINGAR   In Rumania a Gypsy was called Tingar, which denotes a worker in tin. Hence the term tinker used in England and Scotland of itinerant Gypsy tinsmiths.

TINKERS   This term, denoting an itinerant worker in tin, is often applied to Gypsies in England and Scotland. But the actual identification of tinkers with Gypsies is not conclusive.

TITLES   The English Gypsies, states a gypsiologist, were formerly accustomed to denominate an aged woman in the tribe as the Queen. The term, however, had no political or extra-tribal distinction.
Similarly the tribal chief is frequently called the King. In the Middle Ages the leaders of large bands of Gypsies

traveling from one country to another assumed the honorifics of Lord or Earl, Marquis or Duke, with the added terminal descriptive phrase: of Little Egypt.

TOLERABLE TREATMENT For nearly a century and a half after the death of Elizabeth I, the English Gypsies seem to have been left tolerably to themselves, for the laws are almost silent respecting them.

TOLSTOI The nineteenth century Russian novelist had an intimate knowledge of the Gypsies who wandered through Russia in his days.
Gypsies appear in his story *The Two Hussars*.
Other literary figures took an interest in the Gypsies and their ways. Among them were Matthew Arnold, George Eliot, John Ruskin, Thomas Carlyle, Ralph Waldo Emerson.

TORERO Bullfighting has attracted quite a number of Spanish Gypsies. Among those who have made a name for themselves are the toreros Joselito and Rafael El Gallo.

TORREBLANCA This Spanish writer, author of a treatise on magic published in 1678, describes the chiromantic practices of the Gypsies as follows:
A practice turned to profit by the wives of that rabble of abandoned miscreants whom the Italians call Cingari, the Latins Egyptians, and we Gitanos, who, notwithstanding that they are sent by the Turks into Spain for the purpose of acting as spies upon the Christian religion, pretend that they are wandering over the world in fulfilment of a penance enjoined

470

upon them, part of which penance seems to be living by fraud and imposition.

TOOLS The Gypsies were skilled in working in metals. But their tools were usually inferior or primitive. Their common method of proceeding was to collect some pieces of rusty iron, old nails, broken horse-shoes, which they fused and shaped to their purpose. The anvil was a stone. The other implements were a pair of hand-bellows, a pair of pincers, a hammer, a vice, and a file. These were the tools that a nomadic Gypsy carried with him in his travels. Whenever he was disposed to work he was at no loss for fuel. On his arrival at a particular spot where he decided to remain a few days, or perhaps weeks, he took his beast, loaded it with wood, built a small kiln, and prepared his own coals. In favorable weather his work is carried on in the open air. When it is stormy, or the sun is too powerful, he retires under his tent. He does not stand, but sits down on the ground, cross-legged, to his work. This position is rendered necessary, not only by custom, but by the quality of his tools. The wife sits by to work the bellows, in which operation she is sometimes relieved by the elder children. The little ones sit, naked, round the fire.

TOUCHING IRON This superstition, which is intended to have the apotropaic purpose of averting malefic spirits, is current among many races. It was introduced by the Gypsies who settled in the province of Andalusia in Spain.

TOWN OR COUNTRY During the nineteenth century it was debated by the local authorities in England whether, if the Gypsies were driven from their haunts in the countrysides, they would not be forced into the town. But, it was argued, there would be no advantage for the Gypsies. They would change their condition only if they were given employment in the towns. But from the prejudice that existed against them, this was not probable. The severe treatment experienced, it was said, only led them to commit greater depredations.

In the area of Southampton, went on the argument, the lanes and commons were cleared of the Gypsy families. Their horses and donkeys were driven off, and a fine was levied on the Gypsies. They could not be reclaimed by continued prosecutions and fines. More humane measures should be adopted. And a hope was extended that there would be no more unjust prosecutions, that involved the rights, liberties, and lives of the Gypsies.

TRADITIONAL MUSIC   Although many Gypsies in the Balkans have studied music formally in conservatories, they are most addicted to their own traditional Gypsy melodies that have been transmitted from one generation to the next.

TRAITORS   The Gypsies, throughout the long centuries of their persecution in the European countries, were invariably held to be spies of hostile nations, vagabonds, thieves, idlers. In 1498 the German Reichstag decreed the expulsion of all Gypsies on the charge that they were traitors to all Christian countries.

TRANSCAUCASIAN GYPSIES   During the last century many travelers, English, German, and others, encountered in the area of the Euphrates, in Armenia and Persia, various tribes of Gypsies who Asiatic dialects contained elements of Persian and Arabic. These tribal groups were known under the names of Kabuli, Suzmani, Karaci. They all professed Islam. Most of the men were sieve-makers, while the women were described as excellent dancers and musicians.

TRANSMIGRATION OF SOULS Many Gypsies believe in metempsychosis or the transmigration of the soul after death.
There is also a belief that the spirits of the dead can work injury on the living.

TRANSMISSION OF WITCHCRAFT In the course of their wanderings for at least one thousand years, the Gypsies have practiced and promoted the occult arts in their long trek from India through Afghanistan and Persia. Then, continuing Westward, to Egypt, Greece, the Balkans and Western Europe.

TRANSPORTATION Early in the nineteenth century, under orders from Napoleon, Gypsies in the Basque country were rounded up, for the purpose of transportation to the French colonies.
Gypsies were also formerly deported from England to the American colonies.

TRANSYLVANIAN RIVERS The Gypsies who were employed or licensed by the state as goldwashers found that the Transylvanian rivers yielded the most gold.

TRANSYLVANIAN SUPERSTITION When a Gypsy is on the point of dying, a white dog licks his limbs to facilitates ease in dying. Gypsies are prone to believe in old traditional superstitions and practices that are implicated in their lives.

TRAVELING Formerly, English Gypsies employed ponies for traveling about the country: before the use of caravans, they regularly encamped in rod-tents.

TREASURE TROVE A Gypsy woman persuaded a stable groom to deposit with her all that he had. In return, she promised that she could put him in possession of a itate ease in dying. Gypsies are prone to believe in old his watch, and from two of his friends he borrowed ten more pounds.

The Gypsy engaged to meet him at midnight a mile from where he lived. She then told him to dig up out of the ground a silver pot, full of gold, covered with a clean napkin. He went with his pick-axe and shovel, at the appointed time, to the specified spot. But he met no Gypsy. She had gone off with the property she had obtained. But the groom waited until, startled by a hare, he ran off to his masters house to tell his tale.

TREATMENT IN THE NETHERLANDS In the eighteenth century, if Gypsies were found in the Netherlands, they were strangled, then decapitated.

Similar treatment was meted out to the Gypsies in other European countries during the Middle Ages.

TREATMENT OF ANIMALS The Spanish Gypsies used to administer privately an efficacious remedy for a sick animal but pretended to cure the animals not by medicine but by charms, which consisted of small variegated beans dropped into the mangers. By this means they fostered the idea, already prevalent, that they were people possessed of supernatural gifts and powers, who could remove diseases without having recourse to medicine.

By means of drao, they likewise procured food: poisoning swine, as their brethren in England did, and then feasting on the flesh, which was abandoned by the farmer as worthless: witness one of their own songs:

By Gypsy drow the Porker died.

I saw him stiff at evening tide.

But I saw him not when morning shone,
For the Gypsies ate him flesh and bone.

TRIALS   An English statute annulled all protection purchased
by the Egyptians or Gypsies. Two years later, in 1611,
the first Gypsies that were brought to trial on the statute
were four persons of the name of Faa, who were sen-
tenced to death.
The next trial, in 1616, involved three more Gypsies,
two named Faa and one named Baillie. They too were
condemned to die.
In 1624 eight men were doomed to death.
In January 1624, two Gypsy women, Helen Faa and
Lucretia Faa, and other women to the number of eleven,
were condemned to be drowned. Their sentence, however, was commuted to banishment, under penalty of
death,f or them and all their race.

TRIANA   The faubourg of Triana, in Seville, has from time
immemorial been noted as a favorite residence of the
Gitanos. And here, at the present day, they are to be
found in greater number than in any other town in Spain.
This fabourg is chiefly inhabited by desperate characters,
as, besides the Gitanos, the principal part of the robber
population of Seville is here congregated. Perhaps there
is no part even of Naples where crime so much abounds,
and the law is so little respected, as at Triana, the
character of whose inmates was so graphically deli-
neated two centuries and a half back by Cervantes, in
one of the most amusing of his tales, *Rinconete and
Cortadillo.*

George Borrow.

TRIBAL BANISHMENT   Among the Gypsies, there are rigid
cnoventions with regards to the status of women. If a

woman becomes an outcast from the tribe, her plaited hair is shorn off.

TRIBAL CHIEFS In Hungary four tribal chiefs or voivodes were assigned by the government. They had jurisdiction over their own tribes and clans in four different locations: in Leva, Kashau, Raab, Szatmar. Each Gypsy member of the tribe was required to pay a toll-tax of one florin annually. This tax was later abolished when a new voivode, a certain Peter Vallon, was appointed by Prince George Rakoczy of Transylvania (1591-1648).

TRIBAL MIGRATIONS In the first half of hte fifteenth century large Gypsy tribal groups, sweeping forward from the Ottoman Empire, penetrated into Austria, Bavaria, Bohemia. One party was led by a 'King'. Another tribal chief, fortified with papal bulls, letters of safe-conduct from princes and civic authorities was known as Duke Paul of Little Egypt.

TRIBAL NAMES In England, in the nineteenth century, the principal Gypsy tribes were the Stanleys, associated with the New Forest; the Lovells, attached to the London area; the Coopers settled around Windsor Castle; the Hernes, in the North Country, particularly Yorkshire; the Smiths, in East Anglia.
In Romany, the Stanleys are known as Bar-engres — signifying stony-hearts. The Coopers are Wardo-engres — wheelwrights. The Lovells are Camo-mescres — amorous fellows. The Hernes are Balors — hairy men. The Smiths are Petulengres — horseshoe men, blascksmiths.
The Gypsy suffix gro or geiro or, in Spanish, guero, stems from the Sanskrit kar. This Sanskrit root occurs in the final syllable of English words such as ironmonger, fishmonger, costermonger.

A Gypsy tribe often takes its name from the name of its leader. For example, the tribal leader of the Yonesti is Yono. On occasion the tribal name is taken from the name of the occupation of the tribal members. The Oursari, for instance, are bear-trainers. Other tribal designations include the Trinkilesi, the Zeregoui, the Boumboulesti.

TRISULA The Sanskrit name of Siva's blood-stained trident. This term is used by the Gypsies for the Cross. Throughout the centuries the Gypsies have alternately professed Christianity or Islam, but usually only in a nominal and expedient sense.

TROGLODYTES Gypsies have at times lived in natural cave-dwellings, as the only areas permitted to them by local or national authority. There are still such Gypsy troglodytes in the Balkans and the Carpathians. A very large Gypsy colony consists of a cave village near Granada, in the suburbs of Albaicín, in Spain.

TRUE GYPSY To express their intense identity to Gypsy ways and their adherence to their traditions, the Gypsies themselves have a saying: More Gypsy than the ribs of God.

TRUTH Socrates perceived the elusive nature of truth. Similarly Francis Bacon asked: What is truth?, in reference to Pontius Pilate. To the Gypsies, the concept of truth is more definitive. The Gypsy proverb runs: Tshatshimo Romani — the truth is asserted in Romany.

TRUTH ABOUT THE GYPSIES In his *The Gypsies in Spain* George Borrow acknowledges the help given him in Spain by the Gypsies in the distribution of the Gospels. But, he continues:

> Whatever they did for the Gospel in Spain was done in the hope that he whom they conceived to be their brother had some purpose in view which was to contribute to the profits of the Calés, or Gypsies, and to terminate in the confusion and plunder of the Busné, or Gentiles.

Borrow concludes:

> The author is anxious to direct the attention of the public toward the Gypsies: but he hopes to be able to do so without any romantic appeals in their behalf, by concealing the truth, or by warping the truth until it becomes falsehood. In the following pages he has depicted the Gypsies as he has found them, neither aggravating their crimes nor gilding them with imaginary virtues. He has not expatiated on 'their gratitude toward good people, who treat them kindly and take an interest in their welfare.' For he believes that of all beings in the world they are the least susceptible of such a feeling. Nor has he ever done them injustice by attributing to them licentious habits, from which they are, perhaps, more free than any race in the creation.

TSOCHANO This Gypsy term means a vampire, a Gypsy who has sucked human blood. A dead tsochano is mutilated so that the spirit can do no more harm to the living. Gypsy folklore is pervaded by imaginative tales dealing with phantoms and werewolves, vampires and demons that haunt the woodlands and rivers, the fields and the underground.

TUNISIA In Tunisia the Gypsies are reputed to be adepts in black magic. They interpret dreams, and are skilled in concocting erotic philtres and supplying the native population with all kinds of apotropaic charms and periapts.

TURKEY The Gypsies in Turkey, in the nineteenth century, were distinguishable by indelible personal marks, dark eyes, brown complexion, and black hair; and by unalterable moral qualities — an aversion to labor and a propensity to petty thefts.

TURKISH GYPSIES Alexandre Paspati, a Greek gypsiologist who in 1870 published a study of the Gypsies in the Ottoman Empire, wrote:

> Some Turkish Gypsies have settled in Constantinople. And they have become brutalized by their association with foreigners: false Christians and false Moslems, they are as poor and wretched as their nomad brethren and infinitely more addicted to theft and trickery in their business with the natives of the country.

TWO CLASSIFICATIONS In Hungary, for at least two centuries, the Gypsies were classified into two groups. The sedentary settled Gypsies were the *gletecore.* The nomadic Gypsies were termed the *kortorar.* These two groups had their own distinctive linguistic and social differences.

The nomadic Gypsies were the repositories of the old traditional tribal organization: the *maliya* or tribes, and the *gakkiya,* the clans. These tribal groups were under the leadership of the chief, the *voivode,* while the clans had chiefs termed *saybidzo.* The sedentary Gypsies and the nomadic Gypsies were mutually hostile. Intermarriage between the two classes was tabu. In more recent years the demarcation between the two groups has become less determined. Now there are, in a linguistic sense, two Gypsy Hungarian groups: the *romungro,* the Hungarian Gypsies: and the Wallachian Gypsies, the *vlasiko rom.*

TYPES OF PUNISHMENT   In many European countries, from the sixteenth to the eighteenth century, the Gypsies were subjected, apart from hanging and decapitation, to a variety of punishments. Their hair was cut off. They were scourged. One ear was cut off, sometimes both. Gypsies were deported to colonies. They were sent to galleys. They were occasionally put in prison.

TWO MIGRATIONS   It was the conviction of John Sampson, the renowned gypsiologist, that the Gypsies in Persia divided into two groups. One group, the Ben Gypsies, moved into the Middle East — Syria, Egypt, and Transcaucasia. The other group, the Phen Gypsies, migrated westward into Greece.

TWO KINGS   When the German Gypsies first arrived in the U.S.A., in Pennsylvania, in 1750, they had two kings as their tribal leaders. Among the Gypsies, the term *king* and the corresponding term *queen* are mere tribal honorifics.

TYPES OF TENTS   Gypsies use three types of tents. The tent with a pointed top is used by the constantly migratory Gypsies, as it is easy to set up and to dismantle. Other tents are low hung or semi-circular. They are used by the bear-trainers, the *oursari,* and the smiths, as they require more lateral room.

TZIGANIAS   In the larger towns of Hungary the districts in-

480

habited by the Gypsies were called Tziganias. In Spain, Transylvania, Tunsia there are similar quarters inhabited almost exclusively by Gypsies.

U

UHLIK, RADE Uhlik of Yugoslavia was one of the most eminent contemporary gypsiologists. He has produced a large number of books and studies on the Gypsies, their origin, and particularly their* language.

UN-BAPTISM Once a year, by night, as Charles Leland the gypsiologist relates, the Gypsies of Scandinavia assemble for the purpose of un-baptizing all of their children whom they have, during the year, suffered to be baptized, for the sake of gifts, by the gorgios, the non-Gypsies. On this occasion, amid wild orgies, they worship a small idol, which is preserved until the next meeting with the greatest secrecy and care by their tribal leader.

UNCHANGING WAYS Two reasons have been assigned to the fact that throughout the centuries the Gypsies have remained essentially a separate people, retaining their own hieratic and traditional ways in the face of constant change all around them. One reason is the fact of their origin in India and their consequent way of thinking. The other explanation lies in the circumstance of their social organization, close-knit as it always way, completely resistant to outside impacts. The Gypsies always lived with themselves, without reference to their fellow-men, their neighbors, without being affected by upheavals, social and political and military. They remained themselves, a remote oasis in the midst of flux and impermanence.

UNDERSTANDING GYPSIES All who lie on the earth, which is the grave and cradle of nature, and who live *al fresco,* understand Gypsies as well as my lady Britannia Lee. Nay, when some natures take to the Romany they become like the Norman knights of the Pale, who were more Paddyfied than the Paddies themselves. These become leaders among the Gypsies, who recognize the fact that one renegade is more zealous than ten Turks. As for the 'mystery' of the history of the Gypsies, it is time that it were ended. When we know that there is today, in India, a sect and set of Vauriens, who are there considered Gypsissimae, and who call themselves, with their wives and language and being, Rom, Romni, and Romnipana, even as they do in England; and when we know, moreover, that their faces proclaim them to be Indian, and that they have been a wandering caste since the dawn of Hindu history, we have, I believe, little more to seek.

UNDESERVED ODIUM It has been the lot of Gypsies in all countries to be despised, persecuted, hated, and have the vilest things said of them. In many cases they have only too well merited the odium which they have experienced in continental Europe. But certainly they are not deserving of universal contempt and hatred in England. The dislike they have to rule and order has led many of them to maim themselves by cutting off a finger, that they might not serve in either the army or the navy. And, I believe, there is one instance known of some Gypsies murdering a witness who was to appear against some of their people for horse-stealing. But these circumstances do not stamp their race, without exception, as infamous monsters of wickedness. Not many years since several of their men were hanged in different places, for stealing fourteen horses near Bristol.

There is not a family among them that has not to mourn over the loss of some relative for the commission of this crime. But, even in this respect, their guilt has been much overrated. For in many cases it is to be feared they have suffered innocently. There was formerly a reward of forty pounds offered to those who gave information of offenders, on their being capitally convicted. Those of the lower orders, therefore, who were destitute of principle, had a great temptation before them to swear falsely in reference to Gypsies. And it is known they sometimes availed themselves of this, knowing that few would befriend the Gypsies. For the sake of the above sum, justly called blood-money, they perjured themselves. But the Gypsies were thought to be universally depraved, and no one thought it his duty to investigate their innocence.

This is the view of the Rev. James Crabb, who worked among the English Gypsies, in the nineteenth century.

UNFORTUNATE PORKER The Gypsies, by means of a poison called drao or drab often poison an animal and, when it is dead, ask the farmer for the carcass, on which they feast. They celebrate the occasion with a song:

> By Gypsy drow the Porker died.
> I saw him stiff at eventide.
> But I saw him not when morning shone,
> For the Gypsies ate him flesh and bone.

UNGAROS   These are primitive wandering tribes found in Spain. They are regarded as Gypsies who had migrated from Transylvania.

UNIFORMITY OF GYPSY WAYS   A gypsiologist of the nineteenth century asserts:

> In whatever country we find the Gypsies, their manners, habits, and cast of features are uniformly the same. Their occupations are in every respect the same. They were, on the continent, horse-dealers, inn-keepers, workers in iron, musicians, astrologers, jugglers, and fortune-tellers by palmistry. They are also accused of cheating, lying, and witchcraft, and, in general, charged with being thieves and robbers. They roam up and down the country, without any fixed habitations, living in tents, and hawking small trifles of merchandise for the use of the people among whom they travel. The whole were generally frequenters of fairs. They seldom formed matrimonial alliances out of their own tribe. The language of the continental Gypsies is the same as that of those in Scotland, England, and Ireland. As to the religious opinions of the continental Gypsies, they appear to have had none at all.

UNIQUENESS OF GYPSIES   Almost two hundred years ago it was observed by a noted Gypsiologist that the Romany people were a singular phenomenon in Europe. Contemplation of their dwellings, attendance at their meals in their domesitc surroundings, consideration of their physiognomical characteristics all resulted in the fact that they always appeared a particular people, extraordinary in their uniqueness, strangely and sharply different from all other ethnic groups or families.

485

UNITED STATES Gypsies are said to have first appeared in the United States toward the end of the eighteenth century. They had been banished from England. When they reached America they were absorbed among the American Indians.

UNITY OF GYPSIES Racially, the Gypsies have retained their ethnic identity for more than one thousand years. Even at the present time they maintain their ancient nomadic ways and their tribal customs. Thus they have always lived on the fringe of civilized society or of civilizing circumstances without merging with non-Gypsy elements.

UNIVERSAL VIRGIN With regard to the Virgin of Christianity, the Gypsies conceive her as multiple, and even a Black Virgin, like Sara La Bohémienne, the patron saint of the Gypsies.

UNREGENERATE GYPSY A young female Gypsy, remarkable for the beauty of her person, was much noticed by a lady of rank. She was made to sit many times for her portrait, was introduced into the drawing-room, and became of consequence as one of the family. She might have done well, had she not given up all her prospects by running away with a Gypsy youth, for whom she had an attachment and with whom she has ever since lived in great misery. If less attention had been paid to her beauty and more to the cultivation of right principles, she might now have been reformed.

UNTOUCHABLES The term *Atsinganoi* used in the Middle Ages to designate the Gypsies who settled in Greece, means *Untouchables* or *Pariahs*. The expression was originally applied to a heretical Byzantine sect.

UPSALA   In 1560 the Archbishop of Upsala, in Sweden, published a decree, sanctioned by the king, forbidding priests to associate with Gypsies under any circumstances.

USELESS HEADGEAR   The Gypsies considered a covering for the head as useless. A rough cap was sufficient. The entire dress of a man might consist of only a pair of breeches and a torn shirt. Yet the Gypsy had a fondness for fine clothes. He would somehow procure a fine coat and wear it with torn or patched breeches. A notice in an early nineteenth century Gazette comments relevantly:

Notwithstanding these people are so wretched that they have nothing but rags to cover them, which do not at all fit and are scarcely sufficient to hide their nakedness, yet they betray their foolish taste and vain ostentation whenever they have an opportunity.

V

VAGRANCY ACT The Vagrancy Act, promulgated in England in 1824, forbade the telling of fortunes and erecting horoscopes under severe penalties. This act affected in particular the Gypsies who were settled in England.

VAILLANT, J. A. French gypsiologist who belongs in the nineteenth century. Author of *L'Historie vraie des vrais Bohémiens.* He concluded that the Gypsies stemmed through the Greeks to the Phoenicians.

VALENCIA In Valencia, Spain, a Gypsy camp lies near the city. There is, too a Street of the Gypsies. In many cities in Europe — in Seville, in Budapest — certain quarters are reserved for the Gypsies.

VAMPIRES In Hungary the Gypsies hesitated to walk out at dusk, on account of vampires who came out of their graves at sunset.
Gypsy folklore is permeated by tales of werewolves, woodland monsters, malefic spirits, ghosts and demoniac

creatures that haunt the fields and rivers and the underground.

VAMPIRE WOMEN The Gypsies have a belief in vampire women, who lure men encountered at the fairs and entertainment places. The victims are taken to the caves and isolated spots haunted by these women.

VARDO This Gypsy term denotes the wagon or caravan that is virtually the Gypsies' home. It holds all their domestic needs, their furniture, their personal belongings. The caravan used to be horse-drawn, but as the horse has largely disappeared, the caravans are now motorized vehicles, less picturesque than their predecessors, but more in line with contemporary conditions.

VARIANT BENG In Gypsy belief, Beng is the Devil. But for apotropaic purposes he is often called by indirect or descriptive names. He is the Evil One, or That One, or The Other One. Similarly, in other contexts, Satan is called Le Malin, or The Old Gentleman, or Old Nick, or Old Harry. Possibly to appease him and to avoid his malefic assaults by a euphemism.

VARIANT NAMES The Spanish Gypsies, in addition to being called Gitanos, were also known as New Castilians, Germans, and Flemings. The Gypsies themselves hated and rejected the term Gitano.
In the reign of Philip IV, however, a law forbade the terms New Castilians and Gitanos to be applied to Gypsies.
The term Germans was used of the Gypsies on the assumption that they passed through Germany on their way south. Flemings were, among the ignorant Spaniards, confused with Germans.

To the Gypsies, during their long history, there have been assigned various names relating to their presumed origin, their complexion, or their nomadism.

Tsigane is one of the most widespread terms used for Gypsies, with local or national variations. André de Ratisbonne, a priest, left a chronicle of events and under the year 1424 he refers to a certain people of Cingars, commonly called Cigawner: that is, Zigeuner, Tsiganes, Gypsies. Again, on account of the uncertainty of their origin, their customs and their wandering ways, the Gypsies have been variously designated as Pagans, Wanderers, Assyrians, Ethiopians.

VARIANT TERMS   Among the Gypsies the variant names for God are: O Del, Devel, Baro Devel. The Adversary, the Devil, is called Beng, or Bengi, or Bengui.

VEGETABLE POISONS   Formerly the Romanes were versed in vegetable poisons, which they could prepare for specific purposes, generally in the case of cattle. This practice, however, as a writer declared some fifty years ago, seems to have lapsed.

VENICE   Ottaviano Bruno, the Venetian governor of Nauplion at the close of the fourteenth century, permitted the Gypsies to settle in the Peloponnesus on payment of certain dues.

VERBAL FLEXIBILITY   In Romany, any word can become a verb: e.g., angil — forward
   m'angilov — I go forward
   angidyr — more forward
   m'angild'om — I go more forward

There is here an affinity with Japanese, where an adjectival form becomes verbal.

490

VERBAL IMPURITY Gypsy girls and women are unrestrained in speech and use lascivious and lewd expressions without any personal involvement. Their personal life remains unsullied. The Roman epigrammatist Martial similarly declared that his pages might be obscene, but his own life was unstained.

VICTORIAN INTEREST In the nineteenth century in England a deep literary interest in Gypsies became evident. George Eliot, for instance, wrote *The Spanish Gypsy*. Matthew Arnold, too, produced a poetic Gypsy theme entitled *The Scholar Gypsy*.

VIDOCQ Eugene Francois Vidocq (1775-1857) was a noted member of the French secret police. Of the Gypsies from Hungary who were moving into western Europe, he wrote:

> Raising my eyes toward a crowd in front of a menagerie, I perceived one the *false jockeys* taking the purse of a fat glazier, whom we saw the next moment seeking for it in his pocket. The *Bohemian* then entered a jeweler's shop, where were already two of the *pretented Zealand peasants,* and my companion assured me that he would not come out until he had pilfered some of the jewels that were shown to him. In every part of the fair where there was a crowd, I met some of the lodgers of the Duchess (the inn kept by a Gypsy woman in which Vidocq had spent the previous night).

VIGNETTE OF SPANISH FORTUNE-TELLER She comes not alone; a swarthy two-year-old bantling clasps her neck with one arm, its naked body half extant from the coarse blanket which, drawn round her shoulders, is secured at her bosom by a skewer. Though tender of age, it looks wicked and sly, like a veritable imp of Roma.

Huge rings of false gold dangle from wide slits in the the lobes of her ears. Her nether garments are rags, and her feet are cased in hempen 'sandals. Such is the wandering Gitana, such is the witch-wife of Multan, who has come to spae the fortune of the Sevillian countess and her daughters.

VIOLIN   The Gypsies, who are so passionately attached to violin music, have a legend regarding the origin of the instrument. At the instance of a Gypsy girl, the Devil fashioned a violin and bow from the bodies of her parents and her four brothers whom she sold to Satan. It is worthy of note that the eighteenth century Italian violinist, Giuseppe Tartini, has a composition entitle *The Devil's Sonata,* inspired, as he relates, by the Fiend himself in a dream.

VILA   A Gypsy term for a witch. In Gypsy folklore there are certain men, born the seventh or twelfth child in a family, who can gain the love of a vila.
Witches, vampires, ghosts and spirits, fairies and demons constitute, to a large extent, the substance of Gypsy folklore.

VIRGINIA   In 1715 nine Gypsies were transported from Scotland to Virginia. They were possibly the first Gypsies to to reach America.

VIRGIN OF HOPE   At the shrine of the Virgin of Hope, in Cadiz, Gypsy bullfighters appear, bent on supplicating the Virgin, praying for professional success. In the Macarena Quarter in Seville the Virgin of Hope is called La Macarena, because she is so closely associated with the Gypsies.

VIRILITY   To ensure virility in a boy, Gypsies concoct a brew consisting of cow's blood and beans. Hair taken from the boy's parents are burned to a powder and mixed with the concoction.

In the case of a girl, pumpkin or sunflower seeds replace beans.

VISIT WITH GEORGE BORROW   Charles Leland the gypsiologist describes a meeting with George Borrow the gypsiologist:

> I well remember the first time I met George Borrow. It was in the British Museum, and I was introduced to him by Mrs. Estelle Lewis, — now dead, — the well-known friend of Edgar A. Poe. He was seated at a table, and had a large old German folio open before him. We talked about Gypsies, and I told him that I had unquestionably found the word for 'green,' *shelno*, in use among the English Romany. He assented, and said that he knew it. I mention this as a proof of the manner in which the 'Romano Lavo-Lil' must have been hurried, because he declares in it that there is no English Gypsy word for 'green.' In this work he asserts that the English Gypsy speech does not probably amount to fourteen hundred words. It is a weakness with the Romany Rye fraternity to believe that there are no words in Gypsy which they do not know. I am sure that my own collection contains nearly four thousand Anglo-Romany terms, many of which I feared were doubtful, but which I am constantly verifying.

VOIVODE   This term is in common use in speech and in historical records in the Balkans and also in Greece.

It signifies a leader or chief of a tribe of Gypsies. King Sigismund of Hungary gave Letters of Safety in 1493 to Ladislas, Voivode of the Gypsies.

In opposition to the voivodes was the Russian or Slavic boyar, the 'lord of the manor.' Until well into the nineteenth century, he held the Gypsies in the Balkans in feudal serfdom.

VOLTAIRE   Voltaire devotes a chapter in his *Essai sur les moeurs* to the Egyptians. He considered these Egyptians to be survivors of the ancient priests and priestesses of Isis and the Syrian goddess.

Other gypsiologists who accepted Voltaire's view of an Egyptian origin include: Court de Gébelin, late in the eighteenth century and Robert Samuel, in the mid-nineteenth century.

VURZITORI   A Gypsy term meaning *goddesses of destiny.* The concept of dominant fate is similar to the notion of the three goddesses of fate in classical antiquity: Clotho, Lachesis, and Atropos.

W

WALES The Gypsies who settled in Wales were particularly strong adherents to their traditions and their language. and their language.

John Sampson the gypsiologist published in 1926 a study of the Welsh Gypsy language under the title of The Dialect of the Gypsies of Wales.

WANDERING MUSICIANS In Hungary and Transylvania, at Koloszvar and in other areas, during the harvesting and crushing of the grape vintage, Gypsy musicians would roam through the wine-garden and entertain the grape pickers with Gypsy melodies.

WARM WELCOME FOR BORROW On arriving in Moscow the gypsiologist found that the favorite place of resort of the Gypsies, in the summer time, was Marina Rotze, a species of sylvan garden about two versts from Moscow, and:

> thither, tempted by curiosity, I drove one fine evening. On my arrival the Zigánas came flocking out from their little tents, and from the tractir or inn which has been erected for the accommodation of the public. I addressed them in a loud voice in the English dialect of the Romany, of which I have some knowledge. A shrill scream of wonder was instantly raised, and welcomes and blessings were poured forth in floods of musical Romany, above all of which predominated the cry of *Kak camenna tute prala* — How we love

you, brother! — for at first they mistook me for one of their wandering brethren from the distant lands, over the great ocean to visit them.

WARNING   In the museum on the Free City of Nordlingen there are extant warning posters that illustrate the treatment of the Gypsies in German territory and equally throughout Europe, in former centuries. The posters depict floggings of Gypsies, both men and women, under the shadow of the gallows.

WATER   Apart from the requirements of cooking, Gypsies have an aversion to water as a cleansing agent. On the other hand, in Gypsy folklore, a water spirit or fairy plays a prominent part in the imaginative life of the people.

It is not quite a general maxim that the Gypsies shun water for washing. On the road they utilize the streams and rivers. In place of soap they often use plants and leaves that perform the same function.

WATERMAN   In the folklore of the Rumanian Gypsies there is an evil Wodna muz — a waterman who lurks in deep pools.

Gypsy folklore abounds in tales of evil spirits, water-fairies, vampire women, ghosts and demons that plague human beings and that dwell in the forests and the fields and the underground.

WATTUL   In some parts of Northern Asia the Gypsies call themselves Wattul, which seems to be the same as Petul in the generic name Petulengro. Petulengro is a common, almost generic name among the Gypsies. It denotes a smith who works in tin, or copper, or iron. Investigations by gypsiologists have determined that in their original home in Northern India the Gypsies were similarly engaged in metal work.

WEAPONS In medieval documents and other historical records the Gypsies are represented as bearing all kinds of weapons in their march through the European countries. They carried daggers and swords, sabres, the arquebus, pistols, pikes, muskets.

Thus armed, they traveled through Germany, France, even Finland until the eighteenth century. Their purpose was usually to defend themselves against attack, or sometimes to strike terror among the inhabitants.

WEDDING DATES The usual time for a Gypsy wedding is at Whitsun or in the autumn. No official ceremony takes place. The tribal chief himself acts as a priest, a *rasai*. The married pair step over a broom. The wedding contract is now completed.

WEDDING FESTIVAL Among the Spanish Gypsies in the nineteenth century, a wedding festival would involve the following features.

On a long pole a white handkerchief is tied, fluttering in the air. It is an emblem of the bride's *lácha* or purity. There is a tremendous din throughout the ceremony, with the tribal crowd in full voice. After the actual ceremony, there is singing and dancing and drinking.

At night, an enormous mass of sugary sweetmeats is strewn on the floor of a large room. The married couple enters the chamber and dance the *romalís,* followed by the other Gypsies. The entire ceremony is accompanied with shouts and jumping and guitar melodies. The festival lasts three days.

WELSH GYPSIES The most notable authority on the Gypsies of Wales, particularly their language, is John Sampson, author of a monumental work, *The Dialect of the Gypsies of Wales,* published in 1926. The Welsh Gypsies lay claim to a progenitor named Abram Wood, King of the Gypsies, who flourished in the seventeenth century. The Welsh Gypsy dialect has remained virtually unchanged since that time, especially in the Cambrian Mountains.

WELSH NAMES In the various countries where they have settled, the Gypsies have adopted local names. In Spain they have Spanish surnames. In Russia their names have Russian terminations. In Wales they are usually called Roberts, Woods, Williams, Jones.

WHEN GYPSY MEETS GYPSY A battle was raging between the French and the Spaniards in the Peninsular War. In the midst of a desperate encounter, a French soldier singled out one of the enemy, and, after a severe personal contest, got his knee on his breast, and was about to run his bayonet through him. His cap at this moment fell off, when his intended victim, catching his eye, cried: *Zincali, Zincali!,* at which the other shuddered, relaxed his grasp, smote his forehead, and wept. He produced his flask, and poured wine into his brother Gypsy's mouth; and they both sat down on a knoll, while all were fighting around. "Let the dogs fight, and tear each other's throats, till they are all destroyed. What matters it to us? They are not of our blood, and shall that be shed for them?"
This incident recalls a similar incident in Homer's *Iliad,* Book 6, involving Diomedes and Glaucus.

WILLOW-KNOTS To the Gypsies the forests and fields, the hedges and streams are peopled by spirits and malefic creatures that must constantly be placated by means of charms, incantations, spells, and other similar techniques.

To win a girl's love, on the other hand, is inocuous, but it requires certain traditional rituals. A Gypsy youth searches for willow twigs that have grown together into a knot. He cuts one of the twigs. Then he puts the twig into his mouth and repeats:

I eat thy luck.
I drink thy luck.
Give me that luck of thine,
Then thou shalt be mine.

WINTER COLONY In the nineteenth century a colony of Gypsies had their encampments at Kirk Yetholm, in the county of Roxburgh, in Scotland.

In other countries the Gypsies, abandoning for the moment their tents or caravans, sought shelter against the winter in huts, vacated houses, or caves, as in Granada and Seville.

WITCHCRAFT AND SORCERY Gypsy legends are full of accounts of demons and evil spirits that assail the living. Ghosts and vampires too are traditionally active in Gypsy lore. Gypsies have also retained a sinister reputation for sorcery and similar occult practices.

Gypsies are credited with casting spells, destroying crops and cattle by incantations and obscure drugs and potions, and with contriving the death of an enemy. They can bewitch or cast the Evil Eye, or use image magic. All the apparatus and magic rituals that were the common property of the medieval carcist are put under contribution. They have their weasels and toads and snakes associated with their furtive performances.

In the fifteenth century in France, Gypsies, as a foreign element in the French context, were associated with occult activities. They were accused of possessing the power of casting the Evil Eye, and as fortune-tellers they were equally suspect. Their knowledge of animals — bears and horses and performing dogs — led to the popular conclusion that these creatures were the familiars of the Gypsies, diabolic agents, collaborating in black magic.

The attitude of the people was strengthened by the Gypsy profession of reading the palm, casting horoscopes. In a more beneficent sense Gypsies were credited with a traditional knowledge of herbs and their healing properties. They were thus often consulted by the sick for recipes and concoctions and other remedial agents.

WITCH-DRUM Among Hungarian Gypsies a witch-drum is used in divination. This drum is a kind of tambourine covered with an animal skin and marked with stripes. On the drum are placed from nine to twenty-one seeds of the thorn-apple. The side of the drum is then struck with a small hammer, and the recovery or death of a person is estimated from the position of the seeds.

WITCHES AND GYPSIES An old couplet links the traditional belief in magic and witchcraft with the Gypsies:
Ki shan i Romani
Adoi san'i chov'hani
Wherever Gypsies go,
There the witches are, we know.

WITCH HAUNTS Gypsy folklore is permeated by sorcery and witchcraft, by spirits and demons that harass human beings. Among the Slavic Gypsies the witches haunt the deep woods and ravines, also places where ashes and refuse are thrown, or among dense bushes. As soon as the sun sets they assemble in orchards of plum

500

trees, or among ancient ruins. On summer nights they hold their revels in barns, old hollow trees, by dark hedges or in subterranean caverns.

WITCH-HUNTING In the seventeenth century, particularly in France but no less so in Spain, Gypsies were, in the popular view, thieves, pagans, and immoral. They were associated with Satanic agencies. They practiced the black arts. In this frenzied atmosphere thousands of Gypsies suffered death by burning at the stake.

WITCH-WIVES In Hungary, Gypsy women who were the seventh daughter in a family were known as *cohalyi,* wise woman, or *gule romni,* charming women. These women were trained from infancy by their mothers in medicine and magic.

WLISLOCKI, DR. HEINRICH VON A German scholar of Polish descent, who made intensive studies of Gypsy life while living with a Hungarian Gypsy tribe. His books were the result of personal experience and keen observation, and he made important contributions to gypsiology.

WOJT This Polish term was used to denote a Gypsy tribal chief. The word corresponded to the more common Eastern European expression: *voivode.*

WOMEN MUST WORK As is the case in many tribal communities, the Gypsies make their women support the family. The women generally do so by fortune-telling With their baskets containing small household wares, they introduce themselves to the servants in private houses, and often to the mistresses themselves. The Gypsies would claim that their divinatory powers come from heaven, to enable them to get bread for their families.

501

Often the Gypsies would be invited into gay and fashionable circles. Well paid, they were thus encouraged in their ways. One writer said it was astonishing how many people were deceived by the artful flattery of the Gypsies. For the Gypsy fortune-teller often made herself acquainted with the business and prospects of their clients. Generally, the Gypsy would prophesy a good future. To a girl. a desirable husband. To a youth, a prospective bride. Thus, suiting their deluding talk to the age, circumstance. anticipations and prospects of their clients, they rarely failed to please human vanity.

WOOD, ABRAHAM A Gypsy tribal leader or King who was reputed to have been the first Gypsy to have settled in Wales in the eighteenth century.

WORLD AN OYSTER To the Gypsies, the entire world is their home, with no frontiers, no confinements, no territorial breaks in their dedicated freedom. Their fitting epitaph is Robert Louis Stevenson's *Requiem*:
> Under the wide and starry sky,
> Dig the grave and let me lie.
> Glad did I live and gladly die,
> And I laid me down with a will.

WORLD GYPSY Although the Gypsies have no political structure, no organized body that represents the interests of the Gypsies as a whole, all Gypsies, in whatever circumstances and wherever they may be located, recognize the Gypsy ethnic relationship, despite the subdivisions into clans and more or less independent communities, and despite variations in dialect and in occupation. That is the essence of their unified identity, for within the range of Asiatic and European history they were never subject to political contexts.

WORLD MIGRANTS Apart from the countries of Europe and South America, the migratory Gypsies may be found in Egypt, in East Africa, or settled in small bands in New Zealand.

WORLD WAR II In World War II, when enemy forces occupied French territory, many Gypsies were able to help victims in concentration camps to escape into neutral zones. The Gypsies were under the leadership of a priest from Poitiers, the Rev. Father Fleury, S. J. At the end of the war, for his services, he was appointed Chaplain-General for all the Gypsies and nomads in France. Father Fleury also conceived the idea of transforming motor coaches into traveling schools for the Gypsy youth.

WORSHIP OF MOUNTAINS AMONG THE GYPSIES Old Gypsies of some tribes in North Hungary collect in a small bag earth from all the lucky mountains that they know of, in the hope that one of these may prove perhaps to be also a "mighty" one. This earth, placed in the grave of one deceased, lightens his journey to the "land of the dead" (*them mulengro*), of which we shall say more hereafter. And many nomadic Gypsies, at least once in their life, swallow in the same hope a morsel of earth from each "lucky" mountain known to them. If this earth chances to come from one of the seven "mighty" mountains, then he who has swallowed it can see all hidden treasures.

Not only the seven "mighty" mountains, but all "lucky" mountains generally, are hollow, like an inverted bowl. Within them dwell mortals changed into snakes or doves, and guard incalculable treasures. For having once in their life violated the sanctity (*usipen,* purity) of one of the lucky mountains, they were changed by the Sun-King into snakes if men, and doves if women. They can be released only by maidens or youths respectively, who must choose them for spouses. Alternately in the one and the other "lucky" mountain dwells also the four-eyed bitch, whom one often hears bark in the mountain. Her favourite abode is the mountain in Transylvania, between Homorod and Almás, where one can very often hear her bark at a great distance. One can sometimes see this bitch at a river quenching her thirst. As often as she drinks, incessant rain sets on. Perhaps she corresponds to the bitch Sarama, of Indian mythology, who is mentioned in the 180th Hymn of the tenth, and also in the 62nd of the first book of the Rigveda. So far as this bitch, who discovers hiding-places, breaks through the darkness of night (through forest or mountain), she seems to be the moon; so far as she breaks through the clouds (river), she seems to be the thunderbolt. This bitch drops her dung in front of the house or hut of men who are beloved by an "Urme" (fate-fairy). Such droppings are indistinguishable from those of an ordinary dog; therefore any one who, on issuing at early dawn from his tent or hut, finds dog's dung before it, should rub his left foot therein. If it proceeds from the four-eyed bitch, then his foot will lead him to great treasures. Of a man who is lucky in his undertakings or grows rich, even the settled Gypsies of Hungary say, "The bitch has dropped for him" (iukli leske cindyas). She often puts one of her whelps among those of an ordinary bitch. Such whelps are snow-white, with black rings round their eyes. Dogs thus marked are highly treasured by the Gypsies, for they are said to bring much luck to their possessors. In such dogs, too, a great swindle is carried on. In the spring of 1891, at Zombor (South Hungary), the tent Gypsy Milivoj Supancic paid me a visit, and begged for a present. He had been expelled from his tribe for disorderly conduct, and now must wander alone until he had made mnoey enough to purchase his readmission to the tribe. He asked me for a good black colour. I gave him

Indian ink, with which he cleverly painted black rings round the eyes of a young white dog he had with him. Some days after he visited me again, and told me he was on his way home (*kere*) to his tribe. He had got four gulden from a Bosnian Gypsy for his white "lucky" dog. Not only in prayers, uttered by the witch-wives and woiwodes, or by the oldest member of a family (*saibidyo*) on festalo ccasions, is mention made of the "seven mighty mountains" and the "lucky mountains," but also in magic formulas and conjurations, in wishes and curses. Most of these prayers show a wonderful blending of Christian elements, for they open with "Lord in Heaven, thou dear, sweet God in heaven, on Thy golden throne, by the seven golden trees, on the seven golden mountains sitting, look down on us poor folk. May Thy golden eye look down from the seven lucky mountains, and guard us poor folk," etc. Even settled Gypsies of central Europe make use of such curses as "May you never see a lucky mountain" (*Nikana tu the dikhes yek bactale bar*). "The devil slay me on the lucky mountain" (*O beng the marel man upro bactale bar*). "May the dogs eat thine heart on the lucky mountain" (*Jukla the can tire vodyi upro bactale bar*). "May you soon see a mighty mountain and be blinded" (*The dikhes tu sik yek bare bar the akor tu the koraves*). "The four-eyed bitch shall drive thee to to the lucky mountain" (*Staryakengre iukli tut andro bactale bar tradel*).

Mountains generally, and especially the "lucky" mountains, are places where one should utter a wish. This belief is especially prevalent amongst the Transylvanian, Roumanian, and Servo-Bulgarian tent-Gypsies. For trifling occasions one should not ascend a "lucky" mountain, and utter a wish. The Sun-King might change the mortal uttering it into a snake or a dove. But he who has a proper and important wish must for three whole days eat and drink nothing but mare's milk, and during these three days have no intercourse with his fellows. On their expiry he goes before sunrise to the "lucky" mountain, taking a piece of meat, two eggs of a white hen, two apples, and some blood of an animal in a new bowl. (*cf.* Andrian, p. 153). At sunrise he eats the food, drinks the blood, and utters his wish. The eggshells and the new bowl he buries in the earth shortly before descending the moun-tain, in order that the witches may not be able to frustrate his work (*holyipa leskre mangipneske paguba na the keren*).

If great misfortune befalls a wandering Gypsy family of South Hungary or an entire tribe, such as frequent deaths, infectious sicknesses, imprisonment of several members, etc., then the appointed member of the tribe ascends to the top of a "lucky" mountain, and pours ass's and sow's milk on it, and buries as many pieces of meat in the earth as there are members of the family or tribe on the mountain. Then a small fire is kindled, in which every one of those members must spit thrice. Some of the ashes left over must be taken away and preserved; they are said to guard buildings, tents, etc., from lightning. Not only in misfortune and trouble, but also in unlooked-for prosperity, the nomadic Gypsies of Turkey and Servia make an offering on "lucky" mountains. In the latter case it is made to the guardian spirit (*Butyakengo*). He to whom a great pieces of luck has happened unexpec-tedly hangs a pieces of meat to the bough of a tree that grows on a "lucky" mountain. If the meat is still there the next day, then the gift was too small, then he must hang another piece to the bough, and go on doing so every day until it disappears. The Sun-King is said to rejoice to see the *Butyakengo* eating these presents, and only to help such mortals to prosper as never forget their *Butyakengo*, but give him good victuals.

When on occasion of such offerings one of the above-mentioned "lightning-stones" is found, it is regarded as an oracular talisman, and is passed on from generation to generation as an heirloom. In doubtful emergencies, where to do or not to do is the question, the nomadic Gypsies of Servia and Bulgaria take this stone (*bicibakro bar*) into counsel. The evening before one smears this "tongue stone" with animal fat, covers it over span-high with grass and earth, makes water on this "hill"; next day one digs it up, and if it still feels greasy, that means the undertaking will succeed; but if it feels rough, and retains no trace of the fat, then one will not bring one's plans to an issue. If reddish marks come out on the stone, then the undertaking will be attended with great danger; but if much earth and grass adhere to the stone, this betokens much good luck, whether one does or does not accomplish the attempt, according as the stone shows or does not show traces of fat. The belief prevails that through the stone the Sun-King, who sees everything on earth, gives counsel to the inquirer.

Only so far as there is here mention of the Sun and the Sun-King can one speak of a sun-worship, to my thinking at least, such as Graf Rud. *v.* Wratislav. Mibrovic and A. Vaillant speak of in their works.

We come now to the mountains of the second rank, the so-called "Moon-Mountains" (*bar coneskro,* or sometimes only *coneya*). These are mountains of a middling height, which form the transition to the lofty mountains, and are called moon-mountains, because in popular belief the Moon-King, as he flew aloft, plucked them up, the portions of the robe of his mother, the Earth. These mountains, as a rule, have no special name in Gypsy folk-lore; but with the nomadic Gypsies of Turkey, so Dr. Svetosar Jakobcic tells me, they are also called mountains of the evil ones, *i.e.* the demons, because their summits are the demons' favourite dwelling-place. Formerly the demons could also abide on the lucky mountains, but once on a time Mother Earth grew angry with her son, the Moon-King, and forbade him ever to look on her by day, and at the same time assigned "the Moon-Mountains to the demons for a dwelling. A legend of the Transylvanian Gypsies runs as follows:

"Many thousand years ago the Sun-King wedded a wondrously fair maiden, with golden locks. When his brother, the Moon-King, heard of it, he thought within himself, 'You also must have a golden-haired maiden for bride.' So he set out, and traversed the whole great world, but a golden-haired maid found he not. Then he wedded a maiden who had silver hair. Both brothers in course of time had children innumerable, so that they did not know what to do with them. So once on a time the Sun-King said to his brother, 'Look here, let us eat up our children, the stars, and so make room for their successors.' The Moon-King agreed. When the Sun-King had devoured his children, his wife died of horror at his cruelty. Then the Moon-King thought, 'No, you must not eat your children, else your wife might die too.' When the Sun-King heard that his brother would not eat up his children, the stars, he wrathfully pursued the Moon-King and his children, the countless stars, and from that day forth till now has always been trying to catch them and devour them. He had eaten all his own children, all but the three fairest daughters, who still live, and are the loveliest women in the world. His children, too, appeared as stars in the heaven, but now he has only these three daughters, who sometimes in bright daylight fly high up in the air, and cast down black hot stones (meteorites) on the mortals beneath. Mother Earth was vexed at the quarrel between her two sons, and forbade the Moon-King ever to see her by day. Therefore the Moon only sometimes takes stolen glances at his mother by day. But as he is always having

508

more and more children, and has no room for them in in his dwelling, he often in his anger throws down a child on the earth (shooting-star)."

As the Moon is known to Gypsies as a friend of children, both he and his mountains play an important part in the spells for ensuring fruitfulness in women. A plant that shines far in the night grows on his mountains, and a woman may conceive from the mere smell of it. "She has smelt the moon's flower" (*Yoy luludyi coneskro sungadyas*) is said of unmarried women who conceive. Women who would fain have children, and have tried every means in vain, make offerings to the moon when it is full, burying on a mountain certain portions of two male and female birds, and two male and female four-footed beasts, and making libations thereon, or else they brew a certain broth on a mountain, and cast the pot with the broth to the full moon, saying, "I give you to eat, do you give me that to which I must give my blood to eat" (*Me day tutc the cal, de tu mange adoles, kaske mes mushinav the del mire rat.*)

On these mountains one sometimes finds in bright moon-light nights a glittering stone (the so-called "cat's silver"), whose possession ensures a magical attractive influence. Only women may pick it up, and carry it about with them, in which case they are beset by a whole multitude of lovers. Among the nomadic Gypsies of Servia the girls wear pierced stones of this nature plaited up in their hair. With affections of a certain kind one powders up these stones into brandy and drinks it.

The witches of every province hold their Sabbaths of a Friday night, on a moon-mountain, and similarly they renew their covenant with the devil every seventh year on one of them, for seven whole years collecting their blood, and giving it him to drink on such a mountain. Sometimes one finds stones on these mountains which, if one sprinkles them with water, become bloody, because the devil has spilt some of the blood on them Men, in the same way, who conclude a paction with the devil, must every seventh year give him blood from of a Friday night; but if one has to do so, one should never look backwards, not even though one be called by name, else the witches will spit in one's face, and then one dies. Rukuy Loko, one of the Hukuya tribe, went one Friday night on a mountain in Transylvania, and was found by us next day lying dead on a pathway. He really died of alcoholic apoplexy, but his kinsfolk, pointing to the dark-blue spots on his face, declared he had been spat upon by the witches, and had died of it. Neither should one kindle a fire on these mountains, for the demons and witches collect the coals and ashes left over, and when one sleeps, sprinkle one's body therewith, thereby covering it with boils.

The highest mountains belong to the Wind-King, and in the midst of them is the so-called "cats' mountain" (*bar mackengre*). In the belief of the tent-Gypsies of Transylvania, the souls of such dead folk as have sinned much are often changed into black cats, and as such must live many years before they can find release, and gain admission into the kingdom of the dead (*them mulengre*). Such cats live often in men's houses, whence they sometimes vanish after many years. They appear in a house without one knowing whence they came. Sometimes they lay a sparkling stone, which remains on earth only as long as one can count seven, then it vanishes into the earth. This stone is only to be found in the cats' mountain, where it is not so easy to come, for it is girt by a wall of fire. Only on St. John's Eve can one do so, for then the fire goes out for some hours. The Transylvanian tent-Gypsies regard the Fogarascher Mountain as such a "cats' mountain," and many of them there every year seek this sparkling stone on St. John's Eve. By means of this stone one can open up a locked-up room, and turn all metals into gold by merely touching them with it. Servian and Bosnian Gypsies, every time they pass a mountain supposed to be in the vicinity of a "cats' mountain," fling some pebbles into a bush, saying, "St. Elias, drive out the evil one, *i.e.* the demons of sickness, and bring the moon" (*Svate Ilya trada misecen telana cones*). They believe that the great God has made St. Elias the judge over these accursed cats, and accordingly invite him to drive the demons away from these spots, and to keep on eating a bit of the moon as it waxes.

Every Gypsy tribe of Central Europe places the kingdom of the dead in the mountain of the Wind-King. There the dead dwell, and thence they often descend into the happy valleys to live, *i.e.* to enjoy themselves like living mortals. The Istrian and South-Hungarian Gypsies, on the death of their parents, select two mountains of their province and call one "Father," and the other "Mother." Such mountains often pass by inheritance in a family from one generation to another, and if they are speaking of this or that mountain they say, "There where the father of so-and-so begins." "There where the mother of such an one rises," etc. Every Gypsy must once every year eat, fast, and drink on his father's and mother's mountain, and leave what remains over there and a pair of old shoes. As often as he passes these mountains he must bare his head in greeting, and spit once or twice, "that the deceased may not straightway fetch him to themselves." If father or mother appears often to him in a dream, he must go as soon as possible to the mountain of father or mother, and make an offering there, by burying the remains of a meal. On Whitsunday every one who has lost father and mother must cut two wooden little crosses, burn them, and scatter the ashes on the nearest mountain. With the tent-Gypsies of southern Transylvania every one on Whitsun morning goes alone to a tree or rock on an eminence, and there takes the shell off as many eggs as he can remember deaths in family.

Such is the extent of my knowledge of Gypsy folk-lore regarding the mountains. How much in it is the result of borrowing and transmission, I must leave to comparactive mythologists to determine. —

Heinrich von Wlislocki

WRITING FROM KNOWLEDGE It is utterly useless, says a gypsiologist, to write about the habits of the Gypsies, especially of the wandering tribes, unless you have lived long and continually with them. But up to the present time, continues George Borrow the gypsiologist, all the books which have been written concerning them have been written by those who have introduced themselves into their society for a few hours.

WRONGFUL IMPRISONMENT Not long ago, wrote a nineteenth century gypsiologist, a Gypsy was suspected of having stolen some lead from a gentleman's house. His cart was searched, but no lead being found in his possession, he was imprisoned for three months, for living under the hedges as a vagrant; and his horse, which was worth thirteen pounds, was sold to meet the demands of the constables.

Another Gypsy, who had two horses in his possession, was suspected of having stolen them, but he proved that they were his property by purchase. He was committed for three months as a vagrant, and one of his horses was sold to defray the expenses of his apprehension and examination.

512

WRONGFUL IMPUTATION It has been too much the custom, said a gypsiologist, to impute to the Gypsies a great number of crimes of which they either never were guilty or which could only be committed by an inconsiderable part of their race. They have often suffered the penalty of the law when they have not in the least deserved it. They have been talked of by the public, and prosecuted by the authorities, as the perpetrators of every vice and wickedness alike shocking to civil and savage life.

Y

YAKORI BENGESKRO A Gypsy expression meaning the Devil's Eye. This applies to the berries of the elder tree. This tree is regularly associated with the operations of sorcery.

The occult arts, in various aspects, play an important part in Gypsy tradition and in their lives as well.

YATES, DORA E. For many years she was the Hon. Secretary of the Gypsy Lore Society. For more than half a century she was associated with Gypsy life, particularly but not exclusively, in England and Wales. She knew the noted gypsiologists Dr. John Sampson and Walter Starkie. In addition, she was versed in Gypsy dialects. Her contacts embraced English Gypsies, and German, Rumanian, Greek, Hungarian Romanys.

Some of her experiences and adventures she described in her book *My Gypsy Days.*

YOGA There is a legend that, in the march westward from India, the Gypsies practiced Yoga and also taught it. In their original home in India they had long been familiar with the system.

YOUTH TRAINING The nineteenth century Scottish Gypsies trained their youth, as a chronicler declares, to follow their own footsteps:

The Gypsy youth, trained from infancy to plunder were formed into companies or bands, with a captain

514

at their head. These captains were generally the grown-up sons of the old chieftains, who, having been themselves leaders, in their youth, endeavored in their old age to support outwardly a pretty fair character, although under considerable suspicion. The captains were generally well dressed, and could not be taken for Gypsies. The youths varied in age from ten to thirty years. They traveled to fairs singly, or at least never above two together, while their captain almost always rode on horseback, but never in company with any of their men. Some of the chiefs, handsomely dressed, pretended to be busily employed in buying and selling horses, but were always ready to attend to the operations of their tribe, employed in plundering in the market. The children who were most expert in abstracting the money in this manner were rewarded with applause and presents; while, on the other hand, those who proved awkward were severely chastised. After the children were considered perfect in this branch of their profession, a pure, or other small object, was laid down in an exposed part of the tent or camp, in view of all the family. While the ordinary business of the Gypsies was going forward, the children again commenced their operations, by exerting their ingenuity and exercising their patience, in trying to carry off the pursue without being perceived by any one present. If they were detected, they were again beaten; but if they succeeded unnoticed, they were caressed and liberally rewarded.

Z

ZAPORI   These are the Moslem Gypsies of the Balkans. They have persistently continued their restless existence despite efforts to encourage permanent settlements.

ZIGANA   South of Trebizond, in Central Asia, are the Zigana Mountains, which have been putatively linked with the possible home of the Tsiganes, the Gypsies. Among gypsiologists, during the last century, there has been much debate regarding the original home of the Gypsies. They have been assigned to Egypt, Rumania, the Middle East, and even pre-historically to some remote region in the Eastern Mediterranean.

ZINCALI   A Spanish term used in the nineteenth century as a synonym for Gitanos. *The Zincali* is the title of one of George Borrow's studies of Spain.
On account of their migrations, through Asia and Europe, the Gypsies have acquired variant names stemming from the country of their sojourn.

ZINCAR   A Gypsy term meaning a worker in tin. The common designation of Tzigane is a corrupt form of Zincar. The Gypsies have occupational names associated with their trade or skill: for instance, the bear-trainers of the Balkans are known as *oursari.*

ZINGARI Zingari, that is, Tziganes or Gypsies, are said to have appeared in the Greek island of Cyprus in the fourteenth century.
It has been determined that the Gypsies, advancing from India toward Europe, settled for the longest time in Greek territory. Evidence of this fact is the large Greek vocabulary that has been absorbed into the Gypsy language.

ZINGARI PORTRAIT A nineteenth century portrait of a Zingari:
Among the Zingari are not a few who deal in precious stones, and some who vend poisons; and the most remarkable individual whom it has been my fortune to encounter amongst the Gypsies, whether of the Eastern or Western world, was a person who dealt in both these articles. He was a native of Constantinople, and in the pursuit of his trade had visited the most remote and remarkable portions of the world. He had traveled alone and on foot the greatest part of India. He spoke several dialects of the Malay, and understood the original language of Java, that isle more fertile in poisons than even "far Iolchos and Spain." From what I could learn from him, it appeared that his jewels were in less request than his drugs, though he assured me that there was scarcely a Bey or Satrap in Persia or Turkey whom he had not supplied with both. I have seen this individual in more countries than one, for he flits over the world like the shadow of a cloud; the last time at Granada in Spain, whither he had come after paying a visit to his Gitano brethren in the presidio of Ceuta.

ZOROASTER   In Gypsy legend, when the Gypsies advanced westward from their original home in India, they learned something of the Zoroastrian cult in Persia.

ZUTT   On account of their incessant wanderings, the Gypsies have been designated by many names. Among the Arabs they are known as Zutt: a term which relates the Gypsies to an Indian origin.